	Fourth Issue		Fifth Issue	
ntrollable vernment	Concentration of Power	Dispersion of Powers	Sm	
	Persian Monarchy		Greek	
ian Democ-				

DATE DUE

JUL 2 2 1997				
AUG 1 2002				Macedonian Empire
NOV 1 2002				Roman Empire, Jus Gentium
NOV 2 2 2006				
				Charlemagne, Holy Roman Empire
				Christian Universalism, Islam: Crusades

itution of Roman blic

-Saxon mblies

Carta

h Parliaments

ar Movement eform Papacy

Quakers, ish Civil War

macy of ish Parliament; e

eau

itution of the ed States

ples of French lution

				Sea-Power, Age of Discoveries
				Grotius: Growth of International Law
				Colonies
				Kant
GAYLORD			PRINTED IN U.S.A.	Imperialism
				Napoleonic Empire

m of British ament	Cabinet Government	Presidential System	Independence of Latin-America	Unification of Italy, Germany
			Weakening of Turkish, Austrian Empires	International Arbitrations
tions of resentative ocracy	Unicameralism	Bicameralism		Hague Conferences
Periodic tions	Centralization: Conditional Grants in Aid	Federal Unions: Switzerland, Canada, Australia	World War I National Self-Determination	League of Nations, I.L.O., World Court World Economic Depression
Expression of ion	One-Party Dictatorships	Commonwealth of Nations	Economic Nationalism	Air Age, Atomic Power Space Power
or Multi-Party ems	Imperialism	Local Autonomy	World War II Anti-Colonialism	United Nations NATO, Warsaw Pact European Community OECD

RESERVE ROOM

The Great Issues
of Politics

DISCARDED

35.00

Eighth Edition

THE GREAT ISSUES OF POLITICS

An Introduction to Political Science

Leslie Lipson
University of California, Berkeley

JA
66
L55
1989

PRENTICE HALL, Englewood Cliffs, New Jersey 07632

EL CAMINO COLLEGE LIBRARY

LIBRARY OF CONGRESS
Library of Congress Cataloging-in-Publication Data

Lipson, Leslie
    The great issues of politics : an introduction to political
science / Leslie Lipson. -- 8th ed.
        p.   cm.
    Bibliography: p.
    Includes index.
    ISBN 0-13-363920-7
    1. Political science.   I. Title.
JA66.L55 1989
320--dc19   88-15599
                                                          CIP

*Editorial/production supervision and
interior design: Joan L. Stone
Cover design: 20/20 Services, Inc.
Manufacturing buyer: Peter Havens*

© 1989, 1985, 1981, 1976, 1970, 1965, 1960, 1954 by Prentice-Hall, Inc.
A Division of Simon & Schuster
Englewood Cliffs, New Jersey 07632

All rights reserved. No part of this book may be
reproduced, in any form or by any means,
without permission in writing from the publisher.

Printed in the United States of America

10 9 8 7 6 5 4 3 2 1

ISBN   0-13-363920-7   01

PRENTICE-HALL INTERNATIONAL (UK) LIMITED, *London*
PRENTICE-HALL OF AUSTRALIA PTY. LIMITED, *Sydney*
PRENTICE-HALL CANADA INC., *Toronto*
PRENTICE-HALL HISPANOAMERICANA, S.A., *Mexico*
PRENTICE-HALL OF INDIA PRIVATE LIMITED, *New Delhi*
PRENTICE-HALL OF JAPAN, INC., *Tokyo*
SIMON & SCHUSTER ASIA PTE. LTD., *Singapore*
EDITORA PRENTICE-HALL DO BRASIL, LTDA., *Rio de Janeiro*

to David

Contents

Second Issue—Part 1

6
The State and Society, 133

Second Issue—Part 2

7
Politics and Economics, 156

Fourth Issue—Part 1

10

Concentration of Power vs. Dispersion of Powers, 255

Fourth Issue—Part 2

11

Localism, Centralism, and Federalism, 282

Fifth Issue—Part 1

12
The Size of States and the Relations between Them, 310

Fifth Issue—Part 2

13
Nation-States vs. International Order, 336

14
The Dynamics of Political Change, 363

Preface

A book should capture and, as far as possible, reproduce the spirit of its subject matter. It is the theme of this book that politics consists of certain fundamental issues. These are constants which do not change. They form the unbroken threads unifying the experiences of all countries and centuries. But each of these issues permits alternative solutions. As a former French premier said: "To govern is to choose." Politics has a dynamic quality because we are forever seeking new and better solutions. Debate over ideal values and the means to put them into practice is the heart of the process.

In this book I have tried to elucidate these issues and to explain their meaning in the context of their history and philosophy. Although plenty of factual material is contained in these pages, it is not my intention to cram the reader's mind with masses of descriptive data concerning the structure of government and the operations of the state. Such data become intelligible only when they are selected and arranged in terms of their significance. They must then be evaluated qualitatively—or they are so much dead lumber.

I have interpreted the alternative solutions to the various issues by examples chosen from different times and places, by comparing governments of contrasted types, and by the array of opposite philosophies. Each issue is discussed, however, in the manner most appropriate for its understanding, rather than in accordance with a single stereotyped pattern. Some chapters, therefore, are primarily analytical; others have more of a developmental theme. In some, the philosophy predominates; in others, the history. The preparation and the publication of this eighth edition took place in a period (1987–1989) distinguished by the bicentennials of two major events in political history—the drafting of the United States Constitution and the outbreak of the French Revolution. Both of those decisive deeds provided solutions, for their day and age, to several of the issues discussed in these pages.

Like our forebears two hundred years ago, we too confront a turning point in history. Fundamental choices are now presenting themselves in world politics, of which some are already urgent, while others will have become so as we arrive at the start of a new millennium. It is appropriate, therefore, if we hope to create the future we desire, that we should carefully analyze the present in terms of the great issues of politics, among whose various solutions we must forever choose.

What is this turning point we now face? In part, it revolves around the changes effected by technological innovations, many of which profoundly disrupt our established patterns of behavior and, in contradictory fashion, both enlarge and restrict our opportunities for action, individually and in groups. To select among these opportunities and to organize them is the very stuff of politics, as interpreted here. Yet another aspect of this turning point consists in a long-term shift in the geopolitical balance from the north Atlantic area to the Pacific basin. The European continent—for four centuries the dynamo of global development—has declined, as a result of its own internecine warfare, into a theater where events now take place whose source is generated from without. The outlines of the twenty-first century will be shaped in the Pacific, that vast region where civilizations as different as those of China, Japan, the Soviet Union, and the United States converge.

In the successive editions, I have felt an obligation to test the validity of my general treatment by applying it to the interpretation of major contemporary events and newly salient social trends. This edition continues the themes and mode of analysis of its predecessors, but is augmented with ideas and material drawn from the events of the past ten years. The comparative range has been extended. Not only do the Soviet Union, China, and Brazil receive a fuller treatment, but the recent experiences of India, Poland, Nicaragua, and the Philippines are incorporated into the discussion. At the same time, contemporary controversies over the role of the state in the economy, the decentralization of government, the buildup of armaments, and the quest for a lasting peace are considered in the light of the great enduring issues.

In the task of revision I have incurred several debts, which I gratefully acknowledge. First, my warm thanks are due once again to the people at Prentice Hall, who have accorded this book their continuing support. Sheila Saxby has succeeded for a third time in converting the untidy scrawl she received into something both legible and aesthetic. And most importantly, Helen has provided me at home that indispensable atmosphere of gentle good humor which nourishes a writer's creativity.

Acknowledgments

Quotations from the works of other writers have been reprinted in this book with the consent of the following publishers whose kind permission is herewith acknowledged:

Jonathan Cape, Ltd., London; Doubleday & Company, Inc., New York; and the Trustees of the T. E. Lawrence Estate, for the excerpt from *The Seven Pillars of Wisdom* by T. E. Lawrence.

J. M. Dent & Sons, Ltd., London, and E. P. Dutton & Co., Inc., New York, for passages from the *Republic* by Plato, translated by A. D. Lindsay; *Leviathan* by Hobbes; *Discourse on Political Economy* by Rousseau, translated by G. D. H. Cole; all printed in Everyman's Library.

Houghton Mifflin Company, Boston, and Reynal & Hitchcock, New York, for excepts from the English translation of *Mein Kampf* by Adolf Hitler.

Mrs. George Bambridge, Doubleday & Company, Inc., New York; Macmillan Company of Canada; and Methuen & Co., Ltd., London, for the quotation from *The Seven Seas* by Rudyard Kipling.

Set justice aside, then, and what are kingdoms but great robberies?

AUGUSTINE

As I was born a citizen of a free State and a member of the Sovereign, I feel that, however feeble the influence my voice can have on public affairs, the right of voting on them makes it my duty to study them.

ROUSSEAU

But howsoever, an argument from the Practise of men, that have not sifted to the bottom, and with exact reason weighed the causes, and nature of Commonwealths, and suffer daily those miseries, that proceed from the ignorance thereof, is invalid. For though in all places of the world, men should lay the foundation of their houses on the sand, it could not thence be inferred that so it ought to be. The skill of making, and maintaining Commonwealths, consists in certain Rules, as doth Arithmetique and Geometry; not (as Tennis-play) on Practise only: which Rules, neither poor men have the leisure, nor men that have had the leisure, have hitherto had the curiosity, or the method to find out.

HOBBES

In so complicated a science as political economy no one axiom can be laid down as wise and expedient for all times and circumstances and for their contraries.

JEFFERSON

The Great Issues
of Politics

1

Introduction to the Study of Politics

The Freedom of the Individual

Understanding is the beginning of freedom. To be free is to control one's own life. There are two sides to freedom: the negative, which is freedom from restraint; and the positive, which is freedom to act. We enjoy the former whenever we are not subject to another person's compulsion. Only then can we exercise positive freedom. The latter is the opportunity to choose between alternatives and to act on our choice. Through this freedom we develop our potentialities, and therewith our individuality.

Wisdom is not the whole means to this end, but it is the most important. Our feelings—such as hope or fear or courage—enter into our decisions, as does strength or weakness of character. But motivations, as the word implies, are the driving forces, supplying power so that we propel ourselves to act.[1] Understanding is different, because it is an intellectual process. It is like the driver who decides where to go and selects the route. To choose the good, we must form some idea of what it is.

Freedom or coercion are concepts which apply to an individual or to a

[1] "Thought by *itself* moves nothing." My italics. Aristotle, *Nicomachean Ethics*, VI.2. 1139a.

1

group. The criteria for judging freedom are the same for both. But an individual differs from a group in the capacity to exercise a choice and in the influences that lead to a decision. It is these contrasts, this mix of similarities and differences, that make the study of human society and its politics so extraordinarily complex. As we try to understand what freedoms we have or could have, great issues arise.

These statements already imply certain assumptions—and they are assumptions about human nature. Since politics is produced by human action, political inquiry always implies an image of human nature. The image which I consider valid will permeate the following discussion and color my conclusions. Hence, I shall be explicit at the outset, so that the reader will discern how the argument is constructed and where it leads.

The notion of freedom presupposes a special view of what it means to be human. It implies, first, that we can and do make choices which are not necessarily predetermined or predictable; and second, that having freedom of choice is good, so that the freer we are the better. Both assumptions are rejected by some thinkers. The former, they say, is an illusion; the latter, spurious.

Those who argue that freedom is illusory are determinists or, in the form some moderns have given this doctrine, behaviorists. In their view, everything we do is settled without our consciously willing it by stimuli that shape us, whether we like it or not. Freud, Pavlov, Watson, and Skinner have been leading exponents of this doctrine—which must mean that their own formulations of it, if it be true, were predetermined for them.

Both those who theorize about the psychology of the individual and those who speculate on the sociology of the community often reach the same conclusion that authoritarianism is inevitable. Freud envisaged the individual as driven by forces deeply embedded in the unconscious, which leave their permanent imprint on the embryo in the womb and the infant in the cradle. Behaviorists from J. B. Watson to B. F. Skinner have held that all of a person's attitudes and actions are patterned from birth onward by external stimuli and can therefore be determined if the environment is sufficiently controlled. Marx argues that broad classes of people, which in different periods he defines as free men and slaves, lords and serfs, or bourgeoisie and proletariat, behave as they do because of compulsions arising from their positions within the "relations of production." Similarly many sociologists since the time of Auguste Comte, along with today's systems analysts, regard individuals as puppets going through the motions and performing the roles prescribed by the social order.

Although the textures of these doctrines vary, they are of one design. They explain how we behave in terms of the influences exerted upon us, emphasizing what the environment does to us and minimizing what we can do to it. Above all, they deny that we could choose to act otherwise than we do. How we behave is how we must.

Others take a different tack. They concede that freedom may be possible, but they consider its value dubious at best or bogus at worst. What matters, they insist, is how freedom is used. If you are ignorant, foolish, or malicious, your freedom to act can harm others besides yourself. Many people, they go on to say, are deficient in moral maturity or intellectual capacity. For them, the wisest course is to submit to those who know better how to guide them in the right direction. The outcome of such reasoning is plain. The bias being elitist, the conclusion is antidemocratic.

Everybody who seeks to understand politics must face the implications of such beliefs. If that image of humanity is correct, our conception of politics and of the art of government can only be authoritarian. But if such beliefs are false, politics—and social action generally—will be conceived in the opposite manner. It makes all the difference, therefore, whether we see ourselves as the creatures of our institutions or as their creators, as flotsam adrift upon the stream of events or as regulators able to direct their flow.

Where the Determinists Go Wrong

My view is the reverse of determinism. That psychology has exaggerated its elements of truth out of all proportion. In consequence, its image of human nature is distorted. Not only do determinists make false assumptions, but they fail to account for certain facts which are clear beyond doubt.

To begin with, the concept of determinism is a fuzzy one. It hovers ambiguously between causation and necessity. Perhaps this explains why so many are confused about its meaning and accept it uncritically.[2] One could plausibly argue that every human action has a cause (in the sense that action Y is the consequence of circumstance X). But it does not follow that every action is necessitated (in the sense that, because of X, only Y could ensue, and not W or Z). Causation admits of alternatives; necessity does not. What produces a human personality is a complex interaction between nature and nurture, between genetic and environmental factors. But the mystery that confounds the determinists and behaviorists is that the influences of the two sets of factors cannot be wholly known. Nor, *a fortiori,* can their intermixture. Hence, if the amount of each factor and its strength can never be measured exactly, it follows that no programming can guarantee its results.

The portion of our nature that we inherit is not derived solely from our parents or other immediate progenitors. In fact, the genetic pool,

---

[2]For an example of this confusion, see Thomas Hobbes's *Leviathan,* chapter 21, "Of the Liberty of Subjects": "because every act of man's will, and every desire, and inclination proceedeth from some cause, and that from another cause, in a continuall chaine . . . they proceed from *necessity.*" Italics in original.

which supplies the building components of the individual, includes the contributions from remote ancestors whom we never knew but whose traits can surface in some generation centuries afterward. No computer can correlate all this because the information fed into it will always be incomplete. Nor can any amount of selective breeding wholly eradicate the latent genes of which we are unaware.

What holds true of genetics applies equally to the environment, which can never be so completely controlled as to yield whatever behavior a planner desires. In the Soviet Union, a totalitarian regime has tried systematically for over seven decades to indoctrinate its citizens with approved opinions and prevent their exposure to contrary ideas. Two generations have been born since the Communist Revolution of 1917. Yet nowadays, there are leading Russian intellectuals—artists, writers, scientists, and other scholars—who dissent from the controls that envelop them. Similarly, one can think of persons who were trained and indoctrinated in carefully controlled environments where the pressures to conform are very strong (for example, the priesthood or the military), but who later rebel and reject what was forced upon them. We see children of the same parents, brought up in the same household, who differ markedly in abilities and personality. This can even be the case with twins. Abraham Lincoln, born to a family of no known distinction and raised in the backwoods of Kentucky and southern Illinois, developed utterly differently from others in his neighborhood exposed to similar influences.

Can one avoid the conclusion that those behaviorists who think that human action can be predetermined are chasing fantasies? Environment alone is never the whole explanation of how a person develops. Surely there is an irreducible, unfathomable, and unpredictable core of human free will which the methods of science, whether biological or social, are incapable of explaining. Indeed, if anyone can have insight into these matters, it is likely to be the poets and the artists. They come closer to the hidden springs of human conduct through intuitions that leap beyond empirical data and rational calculus.

This discussion of freedom in the individual carries implications for social conduct and, thereby, for politics. Here, too, the determinists claim to detect the operation of vast impersonal forces, or so-called laws of the historical process, to which necessarily, albeit unknowingly, our individual actions conform. On that view, freedom is twisted inside out; it becomes a species of compulsion and degenerates into bowing to necessity, exactly as Hobbes conceived it. Political scientists who teach along that line—and just now they are the majority—compose textbooks which are commentaries on power, on the conflicts between those who compete for it, and on the necessity of our submitting to those who win it.

This book is founded on other assumptions. I reject the behaviorists' approach because I believe in the capacity and desirability of human beings for independent action, singly and collectively. Politics is a branch of social conduct, where nothing is predetermined beyond our power to change. Nothing that we have inherited or are now doing is exempt from our capacity to keep or alter. All social actions, social organization, and social institutions are the product of human activities, past and present. Being made wholly by human beings, they are not necessitated for us by external forces or impersonal laws. Rather they are molded through causes that originate in ourselves and therefore can be changed by human will. Whatever blessings we enjoy in civilization are the fruits of our own work. By the same logic, so too are many of the curses. Poverty, ignorance, unemployment, despotism, and war—the worst scourges that afflict humanity—generally wreak more disaster than do hurricanes, earthquakes, or volcanoes. But, whereas the latter are not of our making, the causes of the former lie within humanity's power when our own doings become our undoing. *A fortiori*, therefore, where the causes spring, resides the cure. Human beings can change what human beings have made.[3]

All this implies that society can be made intelligible and that politics is a sphere of purposeful behavior through which we could live better than we do now. Treated as a subject of study, the events of politics can be clarified by rational analysis. Conducted as a practical art, the substance of politics may be improved by the values we choose to apply. When the results of understanding enlarge our powers, the use of reason can bring self-liberation. Before there can be action, however, there must be decision; before decision, a choice among alternative values; before choice, deliberation; before deliberation, knowledge. The mind must analyze before the will decides.

The Ant's-Eye View of Society

But this is a picture of politics as it ought to be, not as it normally is. Indeed there are times when we seem, not masters of our social fate, but slaves of circumstance; when the paths of rationality and freedom are blocked by obstacles; when politics, far from yielding inspiration and betterment,

---

[3]It is a basic human trait that we apply intelligence to reorder our environment with a purpose. That this was characteristic of primitive men has recently been stressed by an archaeologist in his introduction to a monumental comparative survey of the earliest known societies: "All these assaults by man upon his surroundings, every exploitation of his fellow-animals or of the familiar plants around him, each intrusion of human will into the natural order of things, mark the emergence of man as an animal differentiated from the rest of his kind by the deliberate intention behind his acts, rather than a blind response to instinct. Civilization, however defined, is something essentially artificial and man-made, and to that extent self-conscious. A human community is one deliberately organised, and not the outcome of such a pattern of reflexes as produced the ant-heap or the bee-hive." Stuart Piggott in *The Dawn of Civilization* (London: Thames and Hudson, 1962), p. 12.

bears all the stigmata of corruption or chaos. For various reasons we are less successful than we might be in treating the maladies of a disordered world. First, a mass inertia arises from widespread passivity. Because many fear the disturbances that accompany innovation and doubt their ability to control its course, they acquiesce in known evils rather than risk the unpredictable chances of change. Second, we are all, to some extent, creatures of habit and imitators of the past; and though it is to the past that we also owe whatever freedoms we enjoy, the sanction of age has the effect of prolonging many practices that restrict the opportunity to invent and improve. Most adults are conservative much of the time. When the philosopher Diderot proposed his ideas for governmental reform, the Empress Catherine of Russia responded: "Ah, my dear friend, you write upon paper, the smooth surface of which presents no obstacle to your pen. But I, poor Empress that I am, must write on the skins of my subjects which are sensitive and ticklish to an extraordinary degree."[4]

Nor is the paralysis of the will that stems from habit or timidity the only impediment to progress. Action can also be inhibited by paralysis of the intellect. Before we act, most of us want to be reasonably sure about what we are doing or whither we hope to move. Not only do we disagree about our objectives and the means of realizing them, but we cannot always be sure about our diagnosis of current ills and their causes. We may be dedicated to ideals that we call democracy, freedom, justice, welfare. But we dispute their definition because each can mean different things to different people, and the applicability of an abstract notion to particular circumstances is always arguable.[5] We dislike depressions. We condemn injustice. We hate wars. We want to prevent them from starting; or, when they begin, we want to end them. But do we know what their causes are? Can we confidently prescribe how to avoid them in the future? Considering that so much is at stake in the policies that governments choose, how high is the probability that our answers will be correct?

Many of the puzzles that confront us when we face the problems of our social system and seek to remedy them have a common source in this fact: human society is composed of millions of persons, and social processes are the sum-product of numberless individual actions. In order to decipher this confusing network of contacts among people, we study the past; we note contemporary events; we look at our fellow creatures and at ourselves. But seeing is not the same as having insight. Sometimes we feel as bewildered as if we gazed, uncomprehending, at an ant heap and saw a swarm of movements whose meaning we could not fathom. It is hard to

---

[4]Quoted in R. M. Murray, *Studies in English Social and Political Thinkers of the Nineteenth Century* (Cambridge: Heffer and Sons, 1929), 1:157.

[5]See my article, "The Philosophy of Democracy—Can Its Contradictions Be Reconciled?" *Journal of International Affairs*, vol. 38, no. 2 (Winter 1985), pp. 151–60.

obtain an overall view of a complex society, to detect the significant details and relate together those that are causally connected. It is even hard for individuals to recognize what quota they contribute, however infinitesimal, to a general social mosaic which all have helped to piece together but none has planned. When the economy undergoes inflation, the majority seek to protect themselves by boosting prices, pressing for higher wages, charging bigger fees. Yet, if too many behave alike, the net effect is that nobody benefits. The same can happen in an armaments race, where governments that distrust one another pursue security severally by methods that yield collective insecurity. Rather than act blindly, we search for a rationale, a principle of cause and effect, a set of laws perhaps that will make the relationships plain. Failing that, the behavior of a mass of people often reenacts the tragedy of Hamlet. For our doubts bring indecision and lead to postponement and delay.

> And thus the native hue of resolution
> Is sicklied o'er with the pale cast of thought,
> And enterprises of great pith and moment
> With this regard their currents turn awry
> And lose the name of action.

The World Prospect

Never was it more urgent than now to look at politics afresh, to reassess the government and misgovernment of humanity, and take stock, worldwide, of the direction in which we are drifting or being led. Without doubt, we live in a revolutionary age. Before the year 2000, the human race must confront a number of related problems that together contain higher risks of global catastrophe than ever in the past; paradoxically, we also have greater opportunity than heretofore to improve our lives as individuals and communities.

The clear and present dangers we confront consist of both new and ancient ills. The rate of population growth is a new threat. For hundreds of thousands of years, the human population of our planet increased very slowly. In fact, we did not reach one billion until about 1830. The second billion, however, was added within one century (1830–1930), and the third in only three decades (1930–1960). In 1986, we passed the figure of five billion. Hereafter, unless deliberate measures are adopted to restrict the number of births, our numbers will double every 20 years or so. When one contemplates the implications of these figures—the certainty of overcrowding and of struggles for ever scarcer resources, the likelihood of mass poverty, famine, and war—can one avoid the conclusion that those governments and churches which oppose birth control are sinning against humanity?

A related trend which aggravates these dangers is that we are so rapidly using up, and even willfully destroying, the irreplaceable resources of our planet.[6] Everywhere we are poisoning the soil and polluting the air and water on which our lives depend. The rate of deterioration and destruction is most rapid, of course, in the vicinity of the huge urban and industrial concentrations that increasingly dominate our modern society. There are two major reasons, in addition to population growth, why this is taking place. One is the psychology which urges us constantly to acquire new possessions and to consume ever more material goods. This attitude is encouraged by business people, who make a profit from what they sell; by advertisers, who stimulate demand with a mix of truth, half-truth, and untruth; and by economists, who engage in growth worship and measure a people's achievement on the graph of the gross national product.[7] The second, and connected, reason is the technological development which feeds the desire to accumulate and is nourished by it. Today's technology is both a blessing and a curse. Infinitely resourceful and ingenious, and drastically revolutionary in the changes it offers, it transforms the physical environment and reshapes human relations without sufficient foresight or concern for consequences. For each problem it "solves," technology generates new ones. Its innovations spawn a network of systems, ever more complex; and this occurs so rapidly that we have scant occasion to adapt. In its application, too much of our technology is ruled by this reckless attitude: If it's feasible and profitable, we'll do it!

The disregard of science and technology for human values is at its worst in the proliferation of military weapons. The contemporary arms race—to which we and the Russians are the worst contributors, with the French, British, and Chinese following in our wake—has led to a situation where the means of offense have completely outstripped the means of defense. Such is the accumulation of nuclear bombs in the Soviet Union and the United States, and such the capacity to deliver them with rockets, that not only could each of these two governments destroy the other's population several times over, but together they could exterminate all human life on this planet. Power of that kind ought not to be lodged in human hands. What is more, the bigger producers give or sell their armaments to smaller governments—many of them unstable and unsavory— thus providing the means to begin local conflicts that could easily spread. And, if we ask why this has come about, the answer is: because the pursuit of scientific knowledge and technical innovation has too often been directed by aggressive politics and economic greed.

[6]See Donella Meadows et al., *The Limits to Growth* (Washington, D.C.: Potomac Associates, 1972).

[7]The GNP is a strictly quantitative measure. It estimates a price tag for the whole volume of goods and services a community produces. It does not assess their quality or usefulness or the fairness of their distribution. For a critique of GNP-worship, see E. F. Schumacher, *Small Is Beautiful* (New York: Harper & Row Torchbooks, 1973).

Serious as these dangers are, they are further compounded by evils inherited from the past. Society has been based traditionally on a double standard. The commonest form of government has been some species of oligarchy, wherein a small number of privileged persons lord it over the rest.[8] The same pattern has generally prevailed throughout the social system. Wealth has always been distributed unequally, with a handful living in luxury while the masses exist in poverty. This situation persists today in most parts of the world and is intensified by the disparities between the more developed economies and the underdeveloped. In fact, the gap between richer and poorer is growing. Meanwhile, other established forms of discrimination continue to perpetuate inequality and provoke a sense of injustice. Scarcely anywhere in the world do people of different races consort together in the same community under equal conditions. Religious prejudice, reinforced by differences of culture, foments dislike and even hatred—witness the conflicts in Ulster and Cyprus, between Arabs and Israelis, between Indians and Pakistanis, between Tamils and Sinhalese. And most pervasive of all—because it has lasted the longest and is the most widespread—the male half of the human race kept the female half in a position of legal, economic, and social dependency amounting in some places to actual servitude.

Whether these conditions will continue depends wholly on our awareness and our attitudes. Such situations will remain unchanged or will worsen if we do not care about them. If we care enough, they could all be altered. There are, in fact, some signs that give modest, but genuine, grounds for hope. In the last two decades a rising chorus of voices has been protesting these new dangers and ancient degradations, bringing them to the forefront of consciousness and thereby awakening our consciences. The underprivileged have made some definite gains—small in comparison with what is needed, but large in relation to the past. Since the late sixties, public opinion has been aroused by the threats to our environment—threats we daily see, hear, taste, and smell—and television has literally brought home the atrocities of war to millions who formerly were oblivious to its effects. The future does not have to be what power-seeking governments or profit-seeking corporations would decree. The future could be humanized and become humane. Or it could be the reverse. However we act or fail to act, the moral responsibility will be ours.

Information and Understanding

If "the proper study of mankind is man," as Pope said, our primary duty as citizens is to learn about the state. This is something that we owe to ourselves because government touches everybody, and consequently all of us

[8]See chapter 4, section on "A Classification of Elites."

have a common interest in its actions. The price we pay for not understanding politics is servitude to others or to circumstance. Several thousand years ago a revolutionary change occurred when law was first committed to writing, instead of being deposited in the memory of a few and passed on from mouth to mouth. Once written, it could more easily be known and studied, its interpretation debated, and officials punished for not adhering to the text. The significance of that change is shown by the example of contemporary states where the decisions of government continue to be shrouded in mystery and ordinary people are in the grip of tyranny. There is no way of knowing how much stupidity, how many mistakes, what evil acts, are regularly concealed in the various dictatorships that continue to dominate the majority of the human race. Nor have the modern democracies been immune from this disease. During the period when the United States was conducting undeclared war in southeast Asia, three presidents (Kennedy, Johnson, and Nixon) deliberately covered up activities they had ordered, then publicly lied about them—as did a succession of secretaries of state and defense and presidential advisors.[9] Secrecy and falsification are part of the regular stock-in-trade of modern governments.[10] Understandably, former Senator Fulbright, when asked for his reflections on the Vietnam experience, responded: "The biggest lesson I learned from Vietnam is not to trust government statements."[11] His point is underscored by the evidence, made public in 1987, of untruths by President Reagan and various high officials in his administration. Their deception was designed to conceal the secret sales of weapons to Iran and the subsequent diversion of the proceeds, in defiance of congressional legislation, so as to finance military operations against the leftist government of Nicaragua. What Alexander Solzhenitsyn said of the Soviet Union applies to countless regimes, both past and contemporary, both democratic and dictatorial: "In our country the lie has become not just a moral category, but a pillar of the state."[12]

Even in states which make a virtue of publicity and expect their cit-

[9] A former government official, who challenged the system in those years and became the central figure in a *cause celebre*, told me that he reached his decision early one morning saying to himself: "I will not be ordered to lie."

[10] "The United States now possesses more than 20 million documents that are hidden from public scrutiny by the censor's stamp. . . . Men familiar with this hoard insist that only 10 to 30 percent of the papers have any genuine bearing on national security." *The Anderson Papers*, by Jack Anderson and George Clifford (New York: Random House, 1973). During 1973 and 1974 President Nixon used every device and stratagem to avoid handing over to the federal courts and congressional committees the records and taped discussions they needed for investigating the charges against himself and his aides. When *The White House Transcripts* were finally published, crucial passages had been deleted or altered. The incontrovertible evidence of Nixon's complicity and guilt in obstructing justice became public only after a unanimous Supreme Court ordered him to surrender some further tapes.

[11] J. William Fulbright was chairman of the U.S. Senate's Committee on Foreign Relations at the time of the Vietnam War. He investigated many of the secret activities and public lies of President Johnson and members of his administration.

[12] In a written statement to foreign journalists in Moscow, 21 January 1974.

izens to participate in politics, the difficulties in the path of understanding, and thus controlling, a modern government are truly formidable. Not only are its operations obscured by their vastness and complexity, but the information about it is now so detailed and voluminous as well-nigh to baffle an inquiring intellect. Anybody who wants visual proof of this fact has only to observe the size of the catalog at the Library of Congress or visit the collections of public archives or scan the corridors of records in the filing division of a big department. The single episode of General MacArthur's dismissal by President Truman in 1951 occasioned a Congressional inquiry whose hearings and testimony filled over 8000 pages of print. The assassination of President Kennedy was exhaustively investigated for 10 months by a commission that set forth its findings in a report of 300,000 words and in 26 bulky volumes of testimony. The reelection of President Nixon in 1972 was accompanied by so many illegal acts and unethical practices that in 1974 he resigned in disgrace. This occurred after hearings before a Senate committee and the House Judiciary Committee, which extended to many thousands of pages of testimony and questioning, as well as grand jury indictments and trials in the courts of law whose proceedings fill yet more thousands. All the paperwork of the federal government was estimated by the General Accounting Office in 1973 to occupy nearly 30 million cubic feet of space.[13] The footage of federal files alone would stretch from Washington to Cairo, from the Oval Office in the White House to the tombs of the Pharaohs. Year by year, the task of digesting these enormous amounts of material—all the statutes and statistics, debates and directives, opinions and orders—becomes increasingly difficult. Our civilization sinks neck-deep in paper, and those who would think about its problems risk being crushed by the weight of documentation.

In the field of technology, necessity has been called the mother of invention. In politics, necessity is the mother of absolutism. Rousseau's political classic *The Social Contract* opens with the words: "Man is born free, yet everywhere he is in irons." He would have been nearer the truth had he written: "People are born helpless, but everywhere they have the capacity to become free." Also, one should add, they have the capacity to conduct their lives better than they do now. In politics, everything can be found that is contained within the individual. Love, will, passion, and hatred play their parts, along with memory, knowledge, and logical thought. Kindness and mercy are present, but so are cruelty and evil. The differences between the various political systems are attributable in large degree to the relative influence which each of these exerts.

Up to a point, our understanding of politics can be susceptible to

[13]Reported by Associated Press, *San Francisco Chronicle*, 8 September 1973. On the same general topic, the *Economist* has written: "In the past few decades, presidents have produced on average about 20m pieces of paper during their terms of office. Mr. Ford, although he was only two years in the White House, produced over 16m pages and needed nine trucks to take them away." 19 February 1977, p. 47.

rational analysis. But reason alone does not encompass everything, nor does it possess a monopoly of truth. The deeper insights in this branch of learning, as in all others, do not derive from the collection and classification of empirical data, necessary though these are. They come from feats of imagination, from the audacity that takes a leap in the dark. Our ultimate assumptions about humanity, especially about our potential for creative growth and ethical advance, will always be a blend of reason and intuition.[14]

Since the state is wholly constructed of, by, and for human beings, its study is a form of self-analysis. Hence, complete detachment is impossible. To understand politics is somewhat like being both spectator and critic of a play when one is also acting in the cast. This means, of course, that all political inquiry includes a subjective element. There is no way to get around this and no need to explain it away. Quite the contrary. If we are aware of how we respond as individuals to war, taxes, elections, the flag, and so on, and if we are honest in recognizing our own attitudes, this is to our advantage. Such awareness can help us interpret the responses of others and see meanings in what otherwise would appear a chaos.

Without interpretation, the factual data of politics are devoid of significance. An event in the history of art may help us understand this point. In 1501 the government of Florence invited sculptors to submit their designs for using a 17-foot block of Carrara marble that had lain in the cathedral courtyard for 70 years. An earlier sculptor had begun working on it, but had given up. Subsequent artists had judged the marble to have been gouged so deeply as to be ruined. The winning design was Michelangelo's. He carved for three years; the result was the statue of *David*. Asked how he found the solution for the problem of the "ruined" marble, Michelangelo said simply that he had seen the figure imprisoned and set it free.

My point is that, where others only looked with sight, Michelangelo looked with insight. Can this suggest something to a student of politics? Meanings and interpretations are not taken from thin air or pulled out of a hat like the conjuror's rabbit. When we, as critic-spectators, judge the drama in which we also play a role, our judgment is based on certain principles or criteria. Which ones are appropriate? From what angle of vision do we view the action? How do we disentangle the plot?

Permanent Problems, Changing Solutions

Philosophical inquiry always asks two basic questions: What is reality, and how do we know it? In studying politics the same questions arise. We must know what politics consists of and how we can best understand it. Since

---

[14]See Elizabeth Monroe Drews, *Learning Together* (Englewood Cliffs, N.J.: Prentice-Hall, 1972) for a treatment of this theme by a humanistic psychologist.

intelligent choices are impossible unless we discover what the alternatives are, where can we find them? Two sources suggest themselves—historical experience and imaginative speculation. In order to understand before acting, we need the equivalents of a map and compass. We should know the terrain and topography, the main routes and distances. Without these, we cannot compare early practices with modern, or detect the similarities and differences in the present, or decide our preferences for the future.

The purpose of this book is to provide such a map and compass, without which we would have no idea what routes are open and where they take us. This is a book about politics—and its accompanying institutions, the state and government—because, if we are to plan our course, we need to be clear about the values we prefer and the organizations most likely to put them into effect. Politics is central to this process because it is essentially a choice between values. States and governments are involved because these are the structures through which we work toward the values we have chosen.

The fact that alternatives exist suggests a way to analyze the state and understand its politics. This book expresses the belief that political history and contemporary government exhibit certain patterns which render them meaningful. When the patterns are clear, events that otherwise appear chaotic can be seen in significant relationships. Because our lives are spent amid flux, we are acutely aware of a continual need to adjust, individually and collectively, to technological invention, social innovation, rapidity of movement, economic instability, threats of war, and doubts concerning long-held ethical values. While recognizing the urgent compulsions of change, we need—in order to adapt intelligently—to discover any relevant parallels between our times and the past in terms of factors which do not change.

The analysis offered here attempts to fill these two requirements. It interprets politics in terms of fundamentals which remain constant and reveals the rhythms in their variations and mutations. To put it briefly, all governments face certain basic issues which they must somehow settle. These issues form the substance of politics. They are permanent. They cannot be evaded. However, they permit alternative solutions that leave mankind with the possibility of choosing or of substituting one preference for another. Because changes occur in the context within which these problems are tackled, change itself is as constant a factor as the issues. Conditions, techniques, methods, and institutions are highly variable. Political systems resemble one another—or differ—according to their respective preferences for solving each issue singly and for combining the solutions. In this way we can distinguish intelligibly between the political characteristics of broad historical periods, such as classical antiquity, the Middle Ages, the modern nation-state; and of contrasted systems, such as dictatorship or democracy, class rule or equalitarianism, nationalism or international organization.

The Great Issues

The core of politics consists of five basic issues. The first of these arises from the fact that, because we are associated within the state, we must have some relation to one another. What form is that to take? Should all of us be placed on an equal footing? Or are some to be superior to the rest? The same point may be phrased differently: Is citizenship exclusive or all-inclusive? If the former, then the people who make up a state are divided into two groups, one having rights of full citizenship and the other treated as inferiors or subjects. If citizenship is all-inclusive, however, then everybody will have the same basic status without discrimination or limitation. The governing principle is a regime of privilege in one case, of equality in the other.

A second issue arises from controversy over the functions which a state performs for its members. Originating for mutual protection,[15] the state has traditionally widened its sphere of action. Thus, the inevitable questions are presented: Is there a limit to what the state is justified in undertaking? Are there some things it cannot do well? If a limit is necessary, where should it be set? On this point schools of philosophy, as well as the practices of politics, have been opposed from times ancient to the present. Some have held that no social activity and no group can, or should, be exempt from the jurisdiction of the state. Others maintain that somewhere a boundary line must be set within which the state may move freely, but outside of which it is trespassing.

The third and fourth issues revolve around the authority which enables the state to perform its functions, but they are occupied with separate aspects of it. One problem is to determine the source from which authority is derived. This question has become acute because, in order to provide services to its citizens, the state needs to acquire and exercise power. Since its powers are funneled into the hands of the government, and since the officials who staff the latter are far fewer than the rest of the community, the relation of government to governed becomes a debatable issue. Those who govern, besides claiming authority, seek to justify using it; the governed, however, may try to retain the ultimate control over political power. If the distribution of power within the state is visualized as a pyramid,[16] the government can be likened to the apex, and the remainder of the people to the base. Authority can then be imagined either to stem from the base and travel up to the apex or to originate in the apex and flow down to the base. Under the first view, the government is controlled by, and is responsible to,

[15]This point is developed in chapter 3, section on "The Universal Drive for Protection."

[16]As Robert M. MacIver suggests in *The Web of Government* (New York: The Free Press, 1965), chapter 5.

the people. Under the second, the people are subjects to those who govern and are obliged to obey their commands.

Nor is the query about its source the only fundamental issue raised by the existence and establishment of authority. Irrespective of whether it originates from the base of the pyramid or its apex, another issue concerns the manner in which that authority is subsequently organized. One possibility is for power to be concentrated at a single focal point. Alternatively, it can be subdivided into powers that are then diffused. These can be parceled out among separate branches of the government and distributed among different levels. Checks and balances may be either introduced or removed. Whichever happens, the machinery of government will vary accordingly.

The fifth basic issue is that of magnitude—both of the area the state covers and the population it contains—and the connected problem of relations between separate states. How large should the unit of government be? Is there an optimum size for a state? Are there limits to its dimensions? How are independent states related? Must their relations be hostile? Can they be peaceful? These are vexing questions in the cogitations of political theorists and the calculations of statecraft. Since the Western world has already experimented with units as diverse as the city-state, nation-state, and empire-state and continues to experiment with new forms of international organization, much can be learned from comparing governments of small, middle, large, and mammoth scale and tracing the patterns of interstate politics.

Analysis of the Great Issues

These five issues can be summarized as follows:

1. The coverage of citizenship: Should it be exclusive or all-inclusive?
2. The functions of the state: Should its sphere of activity be limited or unlimited?
3. The source of authority: Should it originate in the people or the government?
4. The structure of authority: Should power be concentrated or dispersed?
5. The magnitude of the state and its external relations: What unit of government is preferable? What interstate order is desirable?

Logically, each of these topics is distinct from the rest. Each, moreover, can be analyzed alone because it pivots on a unique problem. The first issue deals with the reciprocal rights and duties of members of the state; the second, with the scope of governmental functions; the third, with the birthplace and legitimizing of authority; the fourth, with the institutionalizing of power; and the last, with the size of territory and population.

All these issues present an opportunity to choose between at least two possibilities. This is self-evident in a sense, because the factor of choice marks the essence of the problem. If there were no room to choose, there could be no issue.

The breadth of the choice presented under the various issues can be envisaged in this series of contrasts:

> The first issue is the choice between equality and inequality.
> The second issue is the choice between a pluralist and a monistic state.
> The third issue is the choice between freedom and dictatorship.
> The fourth issue is the choice between a dispersion of powers and their unification.
> The fifth issue is the choice between a multitude of states and a universal state.

Thus described, the choice in every case appears to lie between two alternatives. In actuality, however, more than two possibilities present themselves, because every issue may be resolved at intermediate stages between the opposite poles. Thus, the functions undertaken by government can be more or less limited. Powers can be more or less dispersed. There may be more or less freedom, and so on. Theory conceives of absolutes; practice is always a matter of degree.

Here then is a way to make the political process intelligible. The key is that five basic issues are involved, and that all admit a choice. The types of government and the consequent character of the state vary with the respective decisions. Since there are so many issues, and at least two solutions for each, numerous permutations and combinations of political patterns are possible. This variety constitutes the fascination and the challenge both to those who practice the art of politics and to those who systematize its study into a body of organized knowledge. No people can establish a government without confronting these five issues, nor can they avoid including some decision about each in the pattern of whatever state they choose. Every state institutionalizes its answer to the basic problems with which the five issues are concerned. A student of politics cannot find any governmental system of nonnomadic peoples in any place or period that does not contain its solution of these issues. Wherever the great issues are present, there is politics. Wherever politics is found, there are these issues. Such an analysis, moreover, interprets the political process in dynamic terms, for no solution can ever be fixed or final. All government has a touch of the temporary and the tentative.[17] We change our preferences. We oscillate from one pole

---

[17]"While principles may be eternal, interests are in all cases subject to change." Jacob Burckhardt, *Reflections on History*, from the chapter on "Religion determined by the State." Printed in *Force and Freedom* (New York: Pantheon Books, 1943), p. 236.

to another. Ceaselessly, we alter the edifice of government, remodeling its floor plan and façade.

Synthesis of the Great Issues

Such changes are conditioned, however, by another fact. It was suggested above that each issue is unique and can be distinctly analyzed. That is true only in logic. Reality never corresponds perfectly to logic; neither, therefore, can our analysis. To elucidate the nature of politics, one could take a cue from the comment of Marc Chagall on the painting he executed for the ceiling of the Paris Opera: "There is nothing precise in it. One cannot be precise and still be true." In political practice, the issues are not entirely separate. Rather, they are connected and interact. Nobody can say precisely where one stops and another begins. Their edges are ragged, not sharp. Analysis of political complexities into five issues, each having its varying solutions, is an aid in simplification. Yet it would be oversimplification, and hence distortion, if politics were finally presented as an amalgam of five mutually exclusive categories, somehow glued together.

The analogy of a watch may help to explain this. We divide the dial arbitrarily into 12 hours and 60 minutes. Such intervals show us the time at the moment we are looking. But time itself is a continuum. It is a ceaseless, unbroken flow. And so it is with politics. When the analyses are done, the need remains for resynthesis. As governments operate in reality, the five issues act upon and interact with each other, just as the minute hand moves simultaneously with the hour hand. Indeed, whatever choice is adopted in politics under the heading of any issue can scarcely fail to have some effect on the decisions concerning all or some of the others. Thus a change anywhere tends to promote accompanying changes elsewhere. The history of politics, briefly stated, consists of trying alternative solutions for the basic issues in new combinations.

The Method and Its Implications

This approach to the subject involves both a picture of the content of politics and a method of studying it. As between matter and method, the relative priority is not in doubt. In any field of learning the substance to be understood must control the methodology. That order should not be reversed, nor should a commitment to a particular method dictate one's view of the subject. In this particular case, the characterization of politics as an arena of debatable choices in five substantive topics invites an appropriate method.

To begin with, if we are to comprehend the nature of politics, we should not confine our attention to the contemporary period or to events of recent memory. One cannot properly grasp the meaning of the present—still less, chart a course of action for the future—without delving into the past. There is a valid point in the response of General de Gaulle to a historian who suggested that the problems of contemporary France dated back to 1936. "Why not to 1513," said de Gaulle, "or, if you prefer, to 1425?" In more general terms, the relation between the study of politics and history was thus expressed by a British historian, J. R. Seeley, who helped to develop the discipline of political science late in the nineteenth century:

> History without political science has no fruit;
> Political science without history has no root.[18]

Such an approach to politics supplies a corrective to an undue concentration on the more pressing problems of the moment. Otherwise we tend to forget that what may seem a major problem to us (for example, the relation of the state to the economy) was not always so, and that controversies over which our ancestors shed blood (such as the relations of church and state) do not move all peoples to acts of violence today. To understand politics, it is necessary to step, as it were, outside our immediate context in space and time, to see our world as a whole and, in Spinoza's phrase, "under the guise of eternity." Many persons usually take for granted the prevailing ideas, the dominant institutions, of their period and place; and, if on the whole these serve our needs, we judge them good. But does this mean that what we are familiar with and accept is right and good only for ourselves, and only here and now? Are our practices and principles equally appropriate for contemporary peoples elsewhere? How does our particular system of government resemble those of the past? Does it exhibit any features that are distinctive or unique? In either case, how do we explain both the continuation of the old and the invention of the new?

The logic contained in these questions also suggests the wisdom of using comparisons to find the answer. If it is unwise to restrict our scrutiny to our own century, so would we be at fault in failing to look beyond our own country. To learn about the government of a single state at a particular phase of its history is not the same as analyzing the political process. For politics is a seamless web, woven continuously from past to present and retracing its design from state to state. The fundamental issues which form its content must therefore be observed from the perspective of space as well as time. This requires that governments be studied by a comparative method. The politics of a particular country may sometimes be best understood by comparisons with its own politics in earlier periods; sometimes, howev-

---

[18]*Introduction to Political Science* (London: Macmillan & Co., 1919), p. 4.

er, by comparisons with the governments of other peoples, past or present. This helps us to distinguish between what is accidental or transitory and what is fundamental or permanent. In this way, too, the causes of political phenomena may be more accurately divined than if no such comparisons were attempted. For example, anyone who wishes to know why the United States is a federal union may obtain clues from the United States alone. But, since Switzerland, Canada, India, and Australia are also federal unions, a study of the reasons why they are similarly governed will be likely to lead to valid generalizations about the causes of federalism; and these will be more securely founded by resting on a broader base.[19] Hence, the comparative method is employed throughout this book, and the nature of politics is illustrated by examples drawn from any era or area whose experience is relevant to the issue. We can learn about government not only by observing modern America or Britain or Russia or Japan but also by studying the lessons of the birth of the nation-state, the medieval experiment in church-state dualism, the growth and collapse of the Roman Empire or that of the Incas, and the legacy of ancient Athens.

But that is not all. The reference to earlier periods and the use of comparisons contribute to a more intelligent understanding by means of classification and clarification. Since the core of politics consists of choice, the orderly analysis of data forms the prelude to an act of judgment. In politics we are perennially arguing pro and con, debating the merits and demerits of alternative policies, disputing the wisdom of ultimate goals, and weighing the efficacy of possible means. In short, we are engaged in a search for values. The political process—not only as discussed in philosophical treatises but also as actually conducted in daily life—abounds with invocations of ideals. People dedicate their governments to life, liberty, and the pursuit of happiness; to equality, justice, peace and good order, to the eradication of class divisions, and similar noble purposes. But how are these defined? How is democracy itself to be interpreted so that we shall know when we have it? What happens, moreover, if one ideal appears to conflict with a second? Life is sometimes sacrificed for liberty. Liberties can be lessened for the sake of equality. The public safety may clash with the rights of the individual. At one stage of their history, people are embattled for private enterprise; at another, for the general welfare. At one time they prize their freedom from the state; at another, their security through the state. It may be their wider union that they hold most dear, or states' rights and local autonomy. Concepts and abstractions have their place in politics because human beings identify their particular interests with these broad symbols; then, since beliefs influence conduct, the choice of the symbol and its definition and future application affect the course of history.

[19]As is the theme of Kenneth C. Wheare's *Federal Government,* 4th ed. (New York: Oxford University Press, 1964).

Theorizing about values, itself a speculative activity, is not independent of reality. Quite the contrary! The idealizations of philosophy have a habit of becoming the currency of the marketplace. Conversely, ideas grow out of experience; and when they are developed into a coherent whole—which is what philosophy aims at—they are signposts to further experience. Thus Rousseau, repelled by French society in Paris and Versailles in the mid-eighteenth century, wrote a doctrine of protest to which some of the architects of the French Revolution appealed for their justification. The men who framed the Constitution of the United States two centuries ago retained many principles from the English tradition of constitutionalism and the structure of colonial government. But they went further and hammered out the new design of a federal union, containing governments of limited jurisdiction, which has provided the model for extensive imitation and further experiment. Political doctrines do not hover weightless in a sealed chamber removed from the everyday world. They are a working part of the living reality of society and its governance. Consequently, they help us understand the state and render it intelligible. Theory serves, in part, as a form of mental shorthand, compressing innumerable facts into a few short symbols; in part, it is an aspiration for a future that we should like to see realized. "The beginning of all practicality in politics," wrote Hubert Humphrey, "is a vision of things as they ought to be."[20]

Politics and Ethics

The formulation of political ideals is thus central to the conduct of politics, and the study of the subject embraces the concepts of political philosophy. As Bismarck defined it, politics is "the art of the possible." As here conceived, however, politics is the art of selecting the most worthwhile among whatever policies are possible. The essence of politics is choice, which involves a deliberate preference for one set of values over another.[21] The values themselves are not taken for granted, nor are they somehow determined apart from the political process. Politics is a search for ends as well as means. Through practical politics, values are disputed, their relevance is tried, and their validity is tested. Likewise, the striving for values injects into politics a purpose and a rationale. That indeed is the significance of the issues which this book presents. For these are the focal points in the controversies between rival values whose adoption or rejection, fulfillment or failure, make up the core of politics.

But if the issues present a choice between opposing values, and if

[20]From a message he sent to a convention of World Federalists. Quoted by Norman Cousins in *Saturday Review*, 4 March 1978, p. 12.

[21]"To govern is to choose," said Pierre Mendes-France, a former prime minister of France, who knew whereof he spoke.

every value aspires to an ideal, how does the ideal relate to the actual? What kind of alternatives do these issues present? Do they enlighten us about what actually occurs, or do they guide us toward what ideally should occur? Or can they help in both respects?

Though many aspects of these questions are perplexing, some points are clear. Starting with what is, the five issues reach out to what ought to be. We can think of them as yardsticks which measure the gap between what we have and should have, or as signposts that point the direction and tell the mileage from where we are to where we should like to be. This does not mean, however, that the world of reality ever can or will conform exactly to dreams of the ideal. The laws of logic are not the laws of politics or ethics. In pure thought, ideas can be developed beyond the point that practice can attain.[22] Moreover, one ideal is sure to come into conflict with another at some point. An example is the contrast between liberty and order, either of which, if fully developed, would destroy the other. Practical considerations require that the two be mixed in limited amounts.

The formulation of ideals nevertheless serves an indispensable purpose. Such Euclidean definitions as a point having position but no magnitude, or a line having length but no breadth, are concepts which no actual line or point can match. Yet it is the ideal that sets the standard whereby we test and judge the real. The same could be said about the markings on a compass. In reality, the captain of a ship or airplane very rarely sets a course due south or due north. But by such points on the compass, one can fix other directions. The great issues occupy a similar role in politics. They constitute direction-points or ultimate goals that are ideally conceivable. They serve, therefore, as a measuring stick for testing reality. Thus we may judge how closely we approximate the ideal or, conversely, how far we are falling short. Pure and perfect equality or liberty cannot be realized in practice. But to envisage such concepts gives policy and action their meaning. By contemplating what should be, we illuminate what is.

Humanism and Politics

During its long history as a field of intellectual inquiry, the study of politics has fluctuated between two tendencies which may be inferred from the preceding discussion. In the first systematic political theory written in Europe, the Greek philosopher Plato expressed the contrast through his two protagonists in the *Republic*—Socrates and Thrasymachus—and the debate has continued ever since. It has proceeded with vigor and plausibility, because each position contains its element of truth.

[22]As Ralph Barton Perry has written: "It is of the essence of ideals that they should be unattainable. They define not what men possess but what they seek." *The Humanity of Man* (New York: George Braziller, 1956), p. 99.

Some have thought that the political process derives its character from permanent traits in human nature. Faced with similar situations, people are supposed to react similarly. If enough instances are observed, they can be gathered into generalizations enabling us to describe how people ordinarily behave and thus predict their future behavior with reasonable probability. Such generalizations are the laws of politics. To formulate them is political science; to apply them is the art of government. On this view, both the content of politics and the categories of analysis are rooted in the actual, and speculation about them confines itself to the possible or the probable. So conceived and so practiced, politics is independent of morals. Ethics, therefore, is irrelevant to the inquiry. As Machiavelli put it: "For how we live is so far removed from how we ought to live, that he who abandons what is done for what ought to be done, will rather learn to bring about his own ruin than his preservation."[23]

Others, by contrast, affirm the union of politics with ethics. They argue that politics is the intentional pursuit of human betterment by organized public means, just as ethics seeks the same end by private means. It is true that in politics we see individuals struggling for power, groups mobilized to press for special interests, systems at times tyrannically managed, and institutions deflected from their proper purposes. Nobody would gainsay these facts. But is it any less true that politics also involves the judgment on them? People observe and then evaluate in terms of right and wrong. The Watergate affair is a case in point. The underworld of *realpolitik* comes eventually before the higher court of moral judgment. Ethical values are central to actual political behavior. Moreover, can one deny that there is more to politics than its seamy side? Altruism and benevolence, self-sacrifice, dedication to the public good, a solicitude for human welfare—these too are manifest in political history as well as the pathology which is the stock-in-trade of self-styled realistic writers. Hence, if ethical elements are part of the substance of politics, how can ethical appraisal be excluded from its understanding?

Students of politics have sometimes pursued their disagreements over methodology with a vehemence similar to the controversies about politics itself. Conflicts between opposing political systems and their supporting philosophies were hotly conducted in the wake of the major revolutions of the last 300 years—the English, American, French, Russian, and Chinese. People have justified the existing order or have risen in revolt, they have defended their privileges or argued for reform, generalizing their points of view in terms of an array of doctrines—conservatism or liberalism, capitalism or socialism, racism or integration. These rivalries continue in the present-day competition between democratic and communist systems, as well as between different types of democracy and different brands of com-

[23]*The Prince,* chapter 15.

munism, and similarly between the Chinese and Indian methods of engrafting Western innovations upon Asian traditions. It is as true now as in the past that politics forms the arena where people choose the values for organizing their societies. Hence the nature of the subject indicates the method of its study. If politics is the search of a society for public ethics, the study of politics is a research into the results, ethically judged.

The Values in Politics

It follows that the word *science* in the title *political science* should not be taken too literally. The study of politics can be considered "scientific" to the extent that, in the search for truth, we seek to ascertain facts with accuracy and to relate causes to consequences. Beyond that, the methods conventionally attributed to the physical sciences—i.e., forming generalizations inductively from empirical observations or from experiments conducted under controlled conditions—have only limited use in social inquiry. For that matter, their sometime paramountcy is now questioned in the physical sciences themselves. In the history of science, many of the revolutionary discoveries and revealing insights did not result from using the method as postulated from the seventeenth century to the nineteenth. On the contrary, they were the products of a leap in the dark, of audacious guesswork, of creative imagination.[24] Experimentation normally comes into use afterward to test the validity of the original intuition. This has been convincingly argued by Karl Popper in his seminal work on the scientific method[25] and is attested by scientists who recognize that a restrictive method, too slavishly followed, will not lead to truth. Nor are the conclusions of the physical scientists endowed with that degree of certainty to which the determinists of psychology and sociology so irrationally aspire. Such, for example, is the element of uncertainty in the measurable behavior of wave and particle, that the physicist Heisenberg formulated an "indeterminacy principle" to admit a range of related variations that elude precision.

A fortiori, what is true for physical science is truer still when the subject of study is humanity or the works of human creativity. With the aid of modern instruments, a student of art can learn many facts about a painting by Rembrandt or Michelangelo. One can test the pigment, photograph the brush technique, and conduct microscopic analyses of the materials and their use. But what does this add up to? Such data do not reach the core of the painting. They cannot explain the sensibilities and intuition of the artist

---

[24]Einstein was asked: "How is it that you arrived at your theory?" "In vision," was the reply. Dimitri Marianoff, *Einstein* (New York: Doubleday & Co., 1944), p. 68.

[25]*The Logic of Scientific Discovery* (London: Hutchinson, 1959). This was the first English translation of *Logik der Forschung,* published in Vienna in 1934. See Bryan Magee, *Popper* (London: Fontana/Collins, 1972).

or tell us why a canvas covered by an old wrinkled face or a scene such as *The Creation of Adam* stirs our emotions.

And it is the same with politics. The measurements and models, systems and statistics, games and other gimmicks, so much in vogue in contemporary "scientific" research, yield some information and suggest some clues. But do they touch the heart of the subject? There is more to politics than can be reduced to a linear flow from the id to the IBM. All the complexities of human nature, with its many-sidedness, its good and evil, attractiveness and repulsiveness, are present in actual politics. Of this, the techniques of science can explain only so much. The rest—in fact, the most important part of the subject—consists of human interpretation which necessarily contains a subjective element. Thus in any political study we must employ many categories, not only true or false, but also good or bad, right or wrong, wise or foolish. Our chief preoccupation is with choices, priorities, values, and issues—to which institutions, procedures, and power, though important, are secondary.[26] Politics, so viewed, is a continuing adventure in the quest for civilization, and its study a perennial inquiry into human backwardness or betterment.

[26]See the discussion in chapter 3, section on "The Ethics of Power."

2

Individuals, Groups, and Society

When we study ourselves as social creatures, all the relations between human beings are relevant. The name we give to the entirety of these relations is society. Politics is one such relationship, and that fact has two implications. First, politics can only be fully understood within its complete social context. Second, any facet of our social life may at one time or another acquire a political relevance. To understand politics, therefore, we must start with a picture of society as a whole, and then observe the genesis of politics within the social matrix. These are the topics of this chapter and the next. Here, I shall discuss the conditions which give rise to society and its component groupings. Chapter 3 will explore the emergence of a political function and, with it, the birth of the state and its government.

We know that our political attitudes are so closely connected to the rest of our social life that even the most exact analyses cannot completely disentangle one from the other. The outlook we display on political issues and the judgments we express on governmental actions are shaped by the whole social amalgam, any one of whose aspects may assume a temporary prominence. All of us are influenced, for example, by the manner in which we earn a livelihood and by the monetary return that this brings. Teachers, farmers, trade unionists, business people, and civil servants cannot be expected to hold identical views on economic matters. They produce differently, render different services, respond to different social demands, are vulnerable to different risks, and are differently rewarded. Thus one can understand why in Denmark the pluralism of economic life is reflected in the politics of a multiparty system. There is or has been a party for industrial wage earners, another for urban business people, a third for small farmers, and a fourth for large farmers. Elsewhere, the principal bond of social cohesion is religious belief and the organization that sustains it. In this case, Protestants may group together because they are Protestants, and Catholics because they are Catholics, a fact directly relevant to politics in Switzerland and the Netherlands. Religious division may even provoke animosities which lead to political separation, as occurred in Ireland, India, and Palestine. Differences of language, too, create communities of speech and culture that complicate a wider union; witness the problems of Canada, Spain, and Belgium. Likewise, where the population contains more than one race, politics will develop in their relationships. Miscegenation may be accepted, as in Hawaii or Brazil; or some type of coexistence may be worked out with a tendency toward mutual tolerance; or official policy may segregate and discriminate, as in South Africa.

These examples could be multiplied manyfold. But they suffice to show that politics is deeply embedded in the fundamentals of the social order and draws content from its characteristics. Any of these factors may explain why people are liberals or conservatives; why they vote for a certain candidate, if indeed they vote at all; why they advocate a foreign policy of toughness or conciliation. Hence the analysis of politics should begin where society itself begins—that is, with the formation of groups. Society is a cluster of groups, and these are the breeding ground for politics.

Since all human beings live in groups and the state is one organized grouping among many, some initial questions arise whose answers throw light on the issues of politics. For what purposes do groups exist? How do their members relate to one another and to the whole group? What unites the various groupings?

The Social Character of Human Beings

A virtually universal truth—such as the fact that ours is a social species—must stem from circumstances deeply rooted in human nature. Indeed, the rare exceptions (those who lead a hermit existence) serve to prove the rule. Their psychology and mode of living have been described by the literary imagination, as in *Timon of Athens* or *Robinson Crusoe*, and by philosophers, presenting various pictures of how we would behave if there were no bonds uniting us. Perhaps the grimmest picture is the one drawn by a seventeenth-century Englishman, Thomas Hobbes. Having sought security in France while civil war between Royalists and Parliamentarians was ravaging his native land, he proceeded, during the 1640s, to write his celebrated *Leviathan*. In somber hues he sketches the outline of a presocial stage. Hobbesian creatures are driven by their "naturall passions," of which fear is uppermost, to preserve themselves against attack. Because of their all-pervading suspicions and distrust, they are unable to combine. They search for security in isolation or by getting their blow in first. Thence ensues "a warre of every man against every man. . . . In such condition," he writes, "there is no place for industry; because the fruit thereof is uncertain: and consequently no culture of the Earth, no navigation, nor use of the commodities that may be imported by sea . . . no arts; no letters; no society; and which is worst of all, continuall feare, and danger of violent death; and the life of man, solitary, poore, nasty, brutish, and short." Hobbes concedes that such a state of affairs "was never generally so, over all the world," but he asserts "that there are many places, where they live so now." As evidence he mentions "the savage people in many places of America," who "except the government of small families . . . have no government at all"—an erroneous view of the nature of Indian tribal structure, but one that was widespread in the seventeenth and eighteenth centuries. Hobbes claims to see other analogies in the dissolution of authority through civil war and in the international relations of independent states, though in such cases he confuses the absence or breakdown of the state with the absence or breakdown of society.[1] No doubt, Hobbes's intellect is carried away by his imagination, but he underlines the truth that we all require association with our fellows. Human life is accurately described as life in groups.

The reasons for this are elemental. In early years we depend on parents and other adults for life, sustenance, and upbringing; as we mature, we act with others in order to accomplish what we cannot do alone. Because our needs compel us to be interdependent, groups are rooted in human nature, and in this sense they are natural. The history of our species is a continuing evolution from bare subsistence to broadening choices. This ceaseless quest for improvement results in civilization.

The needs we satisfy by cooperation with our fellow creatures are not only the necessities of food, shelter, and clothing, but also the widening demands that mark a progressive civilization. There are large areas of the world—the periphery of the Sahara, for example—where it is still idle to speak of achieving the good life, since life itself is precarious and hazardous. However, in communities where people have eliminated the perils of death from hunger or exposure, the social order is directed to many objects not necessary for subsistence, but which may contribute to a better or at least a more comfortable life. As society evolves from a preoccupation with necessities to the satisfaction of a vast range of desires, people under-

---

[1]For this distinction, see chapter 6, section on "The Reconstruction of Unity." The quotations are from the *Leviathan*, part 1, chaps. 13 and 17.

go a profound psychological as well as material change. This is expressed in the enlargement of their field of choice and the exercise of critical judgment. A necessity is both predetermined and inescapable. In order to stay alive, for instance, we must have food. Within limits, we can choose what to eat and when; where to find our food, or how. But the goal is fixed without our willing it, since eat we must.

With wants in the broader sense, however, the area of selection extends both to the means and to the formulation of ends that can be altered, expanded, and ranked in order of priority. The structure that was adequate to provide a rough shelter from wind and rain later evolves into a house with an architectural style. Those who dwell in it develop the institution of the family, and, living together, infuse into a building the emotional attachments of a home. Food and drink acquire the sophisticated and selective character of dining or diet. Clothing is designed for comfort or fashion. In a culture where people can decide how much to raise in taxes and where to spend their money, they can choose between having more policemen on patrol or a job-training program for the unemployed, improving the schools or the sewage-disposal, encouraging high-rise buildings or beautifying the parks.

A preoccupation with bare existence belongs to a level of thought and discussion less complex than a concern about a standard of living, for a standard involves comparisons and consequent valuations. A modern community relearns this basic truth whenever it undergoes the experience of a major war. Its concern immediately switches from bettering its living standards to preserving life itself. Those whose wants have reached the stage of inquiry about a standard of living are making intellectual comparisons and ethical choices. When we select a pattern of life from the available alternatives, our preferences are transmuted into terms of good and bad, of right and wrong—in a word, of values.[2]

This is the distinguishing mark of our species, for what makes us preeminently human is that we are value-selecting animals.[3] On the foundation of necessities, we build an elaborate structure of choices which stamp us as rational and moral beings. And whatever values we choose to adopt, we incorporate into our lives by group action. In large measure this evolving process through which we formulate and attain our wants is social in character. "The gains of commonwealths," as Charles E. Merriam has written, "are essentially mass gains."[4] Without associating in groups, we would never have become humanized, nor could we long remain so. Cooperation is truly the source of civilization.

[2]In the Biblical myth, it was after Adam and Eve tasted the fruit of the tree of knowledge of good and evil that they became specifically human.

[3]For a presentation of this view, see Elizabeth M. Drews and Leslie Lipson, *Values and Humanity* (New York: St. Martin's Press, 1971).

[4]*The New Democracy and the New Despotism* (New York: McGraw-Hill Book Co., Whittlesey House publication, 1939), p. 37.

Self-Development and Selfishness

But there are other relationships between human beings beside the cooperative. We are not all altruists; we do not always cooperate. To be more accurate, some persons behave selfishly most of the time; the rest of us— except for a few saintly individuals—are selfish on occasion. What consequences follow from actions whose primary focus of interest is the self? Some can be good. Each person is a unique creation. The use of our capacities, the development of our individuality, is a worthwhile goal that everyone has the right to seek and society has the duty to encourage. Humanistic psychologists, such as Abraham Maslow, refer to self-actualization as the process through which our humanness finds expression. But self-development changes its character when it impinges on others, at which point the results become socially relevant. The consequences of an action may be intended or unforeseen. In either case, they spread out, like the ripples from a stone flung into water. Anybody who is affected by someone else's acts has an interest in what he or she does. If the results are beneficial, no one is likely to object. This optimistic possibility was the basic assumption of Adam Smith, the Scottish founder of laissez-faire economics, who had been a professor of moral philosophy.[5] He thought that, while pursuing our own self-interest, we may, without knowing or intending it, be "led by an invisible hand" to promote simultaneously the interest of society. How these good effects are produced or whose is the invisible hand, he did not explain.

But what if the results are harmful? An individual can harm others in thousands of ways. When too many persons are smoking in a crowded room, the air becomes filthy for everybody—nonsmokers included. When we drive our automobiles, we pollute the air and contribute to smog. However well meaning we are individually, when too many do the same thing at the same time in the same place we can produce a collective disaster. In the common interest, therefore, we must protect ourselves, which is possible only when we regulate or prohibit certain types of behavior. Thus, as John Stuart Mill and John Dewey agree, some restraints on individual liberty become justifiable and necessary.[6]

The need for restraint is even greater when individuals act competitively and aggressively. This happens when two or more persons wish

---

[5]Adam Smith, *The Wealth of Nations*, vol. 4, chap. 2. For a discussion of laissez faire, see chapter 7, section on "Laissez-Faire—The Economists' Declaration of Independence."

[6]John Stuart Mill, the British exponent of mid-nineteenth century liberalism, draws a distinction between actions that affect only oneself and those that also involve others [*Essay on Liberty*, Everyman's Library (New York: E. P. Dutton & Co.), pp. 72–75, 136–37]. It is very doubtful, however, whether such a distinction is tenable. For are there any actions whose effects are confined solely to the self? Mill recognized and raised this difficulty in the *Essay*, but his answer is not to the point. See also the discussion in John Dewey, *The Public and Its Problems* (New York: Holt, Rinehart & Winston, 1927), p. 12.

to possess the same object or enjoy some limited resource whose use is then denied to others. Competition occurs when the interests of the self dominate over one's concern for other people. This is the situation when each seeks to gain an advantage over any rivals who stand in the way. Inherently, competition sets individuals and groups against each other in a hostile relationship. It is, therefore, destructive—and, if carried to its ultimate conclusion, self-destructive. For the aim of competition is to eliminate the opponent, in which case competition ceases. Wherever it is unrestrained, competition tends in the direction of monopoly until it eventually destroys the conditions of its own existence. When competition is utterly cutthroat, the throat that gets cut is its own.

What is a society to do about the results of competition? Three possibilities suggest themselves. The competitors may be left to battle it out. Or people may organize into groups and determine by an agreed procedure what settlement is just for all parties concerned. Third, as an intermediate course, the group may refuse to decide the outcome, but, like a referee, may prescribe the rules of conducting the contest. The first of these possibilities is merely Hobbes's "warre of every man against every man" all over again. Its results are so destructive that people generally prefer a more orderly solution. The two latter methods (though one is confined to the regulation of means and the other regulates both means and ends) are alike in employing group authority to mitigate the destructive results of unrestrained competition.

The Alternatives of Cooperation or Competition

Paradoxically, although human society presupposes cooperation, many persons behave in the opposite manner and believe that competition is superior. In fact, the literature of social thought abounds with instances of this contradiction between the two principles. Some examples will illustrate how philosophies and their ethical conclusions differ, according to where the priority is placed.

In ethical theory, many doctrines emphasize the cooperative side of human relations and prescribe a course of conduct based on our need for one another. Witness the injunction of the Gospels to "love they neighbor as thyself," or the Golden Rule to "do unto others as you would have others do unto you." In similar vein are these eloquent words of John Donne: "No man is an *iland*, intire of it selfe; every man is a piece of the *continent*, a part of the *maine*; if a clod be washed away by the sea, *Europe* is the lesse, as well as if a *promontorie* were, as well as if a *mannor* of thy *friends* or of thine owne were; any man's *death* diminishes *me*, because I am involved in *Mankinde;* and therefore never send to know for whom the *bell* tolls; it tolls for *thee*."[7]

Some readers may consider such statements to be noble precepts, but impractical. We pay lip service to ideals of this kind, but nobody really lives by them. If that is your feeling, it would be well to remember some saintly persons who demonstrated in recent practice that such principles are possible—think of Eleanor Roosevelt, Pope John XXIII, Martin Luther King, Mahatma Gandhi, Albert Schweitzer. All these were inspired by a common faith in a universal human family. All tried to change the world around them and to reform its governing institutions. All encountered opposition, of course, and two were assassinated—one in India, the other in the United States. As Emerson wrote: "The power of love, as the basis of a State, has never been tried."[8]

Opposed to universal benevolence are dogmas of universal selfishness. In one passage, Niccolò Machiavelli thus summarized his view of humanity: "For it may be said of men in general that they are ungrateful, voluble, dissemblers, anxious to avoid danger, and covetous of gain; so long as you benefit them they are entirely yours; they offer you their blood, their goods, their life, and their children, as I have before said, when the necessity is remote; but when it approaches, they revolt."[9] No less self-centered was the characterization offered by Hobbes, who considered that "of the voluntary acts of every man, the object is some *good to himselfe*."[10] He even goes to the length of arguing that pity "ariseth from the imagination that the like calamity (of another) may befall himselfe,"[11] which is as clear a case as may be found of twisting the truth to save a theory.

In economic thought and the policies based thereon, some further instances of the same tendency occur. During the nineteenth century the economic theory prevailing in Britain and the United States assumed that the principle of competition constituted the strongest stimulus to work, and even that it produced the greatest good for society as a whole and for its members severally. Adam Smith, who initiated this doctrine, believed the most potent motivation to be "the natural effort of every individual to better his own condition, when suffered to exert itself with freedom and security."[12] When this belief is harnessed to the principle of the division of

---

[7]*Devotions*, no. 17. Italics in the original.

[8]In his essay on *Politics*.

[9]*The Prince*, chapter 17. Elsewhere in *The Prince*, and in other works, Machiavelli speaks more charitably of his fellow creatures.

[10]Thomas Hobbes, *Leviathan*, part 1, chap. 14. Italics in the original.

[11]Ibid., chap. 6. This definition of pity was refuted by Bishop Butler, Sermon 5, no. 1, note *a*, and by Rousseau in the "Discourse on the Origin of Inequality," in *The Social Contract and Discourses*, trans. G. D. H. Cole (Everyman's Library), pp. 196–200.

[12]Smith, *Wealth of Nations*, vol. 4, chap. 5.

labor, which forms the opening theme of the *Wealth of Nations,* there arises that peculiar linkage, the economic relation, in which each pursues and satisfies a particular interest and yet simultaneously satisfies some interest of others. Smith recognized that "man has almost constant occasion for the help of his brethren." But he goes on to say that it is in vain for a man to expect that others will help him "from their benevolence only. . . . He will be more likely to prevail," runs the argument, "if he can interest their self-love in his favor, and shew them that it is for their own advantage to do for him what he requires of them. Whoever offers to another a bargain of any kind, proposes to do this: Give me that which I want, and you shall have this which you want."[13] That is selfishness developed to a high degree, but tempered by some qualifications. For Smith concedes that even self-lovers must cooperate. This he is bound to admit, since, once the division of labor is chosen as a starting point, it follows that specialists are interdependent.

The State of Nature and the Nature of Society

The gratuitous assumption of the classical theorists was that universal egoism determines economic behavior and permeates our social relations. This was aided in the nineteenth century by inferences drawn from biology. The concept of evolution envisaged human beings as linked with other animals in a continuous chain of being. The nature of other species thus seemed to suggest analogies for understanding ourselves on the assumption that the basic requirements of "nature" may be modified within society but cannot be wholly eradicated or permanently transformed. The question then arose: What was the nature of "nature"? What lessons did it teach? As is often the case, people looked at the same phenomena, selected different data, and arrived at opposite conclusions.

One line of argument consisted of variations on the theme of the Greek philosopher Heraclitus, who pronounced that "strife is the parent of all things." The world was seen as a jungle, and the jungle as a battleground. Nature's law was to use your claw. It was the lot of the weak to be dominated or exterminated by the strong or the cunning. Such doctrines were applied by Herbert Spencer to social theory in combination with the other "natural laws" of Smith's economics. The outcome was simple: Let dog eat dog. Which side then did morality take? Ethics followed nature, siding with the eater, not the eaten.

On this point let Spencer speak for himself:

> Pervading all nature we may see at work a stern discipline, which is a little cruel that it may be very kind. That state of universal warfare maintained

---

[13]Ibid., vol. 1, chap. 2. For a critique of the nature of economic exchange see A. D. Lindsay, *The Modern Democratic State* (New York: Oxford University Press, 1947), pp. 103–5.

throughout the lower creation, to the great perplexity of many worthy people, is at bottom the most merciful provision which the circumstances admit of. It is much better that the ruminant animal, when deprived by age of the vigor which made its existence a pleasure, should be killed by some beast of prey, than that it should linger out a life made painful by infirmities, and eventually die of starvation. . . . Meanwhile the well-being of existing humanity, and the unfolding of it into this ultimate perfection, are both secured by the same beneficent, though severe discipline, to which the animate creation at large is subject. . . . The poverty of the incapable, the distresses that come upon the imprudent, the starvation of the idle, and those shoulderings aside of the weak by the strong, which leaves so many "in shallows and in miseries," are the decrees of a large, far-seeing benevolence. . . . Nevertheless, when regarded not separately, but in connection with the interests of universal humanity, these harsh fatalities are seen to be full of the highest beneficence . . . which brings to early graves the children of diseased parents, and singles out the low-spirited, the intemperate, and the debilitated as the victims of an epidemic.[14]

Such ideas were reinforced when Charles Darwin, nine years after the *Social Statics* had appeared, published his epochal *Origin of Species.* If humans and monkeys were descended from a common ancestor, whatever conditions promoted the survival of the latter must also be relevant to the former. Darwin, moreover, offered clues to such analogies in his hypotheses of "the struggle for existence" and "the survival of the fittest." Biological species had evolved by success in combat and by adaptation to environment. Mankind must, therefore, subdue or be subdued, destroy or be destroyed.

Opposite inferences, however, were drawn by the Russian anarchist, Prince Kropotkin. Serving for five years in Siberia as a young cavalry officer, he used his opportunity to study the behavior of wild animals in their natural habitats. Observation led him to conclude that the Darwinians were misrepresenting the facts. A murderous struggle for existence was not what he discovered among the higher animals, even among the carnivorous. Insufficient attention had been given, in his view, to the evidence of cooperation which exists on all rungs of the ladder of evolution, and increases among the more advanced species. What he had read in zoology and anthropology, along with what he had observed, brought him to the following conclusion:

> "Don't compete!—competition is always injurious to the species, and you have plenty of reasons to avoid it!" That is the tendency of nature, not always realized in full, but always present. That is the watchword which comes to us from the bush, the forest, the river, the ocean. "Therefore combine—practice mutual aid! That is the surest means for giving to each and all the greatest safety, the best guarantee of existence and progress, bodily, intellectual, and

---

[14]Herbert Spencer, *Social Statics,* part 3, chap. 25, sec. 6 (London: Chapman and Hall, 1850), p. 322.

moral." That is what nature teaches us; and that is what all those animals which have attained the highest position in their respective classes have done. That is also what man—the most primitive man—has been doing; and that is why man has reached the position upon which we stand now. . . .[15]

The contrast is indeed vivid. There could hardly be a sharper antithesis than that between Kropotkin's ideas and Spencer's. And the lives of certain individuals bear this out. Could any two human beings be more unlike than, say, Hitler and Pope John? Or could the impact of two lives on humanity in general be more dissimilar? The questions, then, to consider are these: What are the implications for society of competition and cooperation? Since their results differ so, which is better? Can we have a community in which people are able both to compete and to cooperate?[16] If not, which of the two should we practice ourselves and encourage in others?

When we look around, we find that our social system contains institutions grounded in contrary ideals and manifesting opposite tendencies. Cooperation is generally at its highest in the family, even though rivalry and tension divide some families, and some marriages terminate in desertion or divorce. The business world, on the other hand, generally functions with a high degree of competition. As for government, contrast domestic with international politics. In countries where most people feel a common identity and purpose, domestic policy is marked by a substantial amount of cooperation (or consensus, as it is also called). The opposite is true for relations between states. There it is competition that predominates and power in the pursuit of self-interests,[17] not justice, that prevails—so much so that humanity still wrestles with the problem of how to restrain national policies that hurt others and promote active cooperation in matters of mutual interest. Thus in the family, and within the nation, the emphasis is on cooperation; in business and in international relations, it is on competition.

These differences demand evaluation by moral standards. Are the relations between the members of a family normally superior in ethical terms to those of business? Is there normally less destructive hostility in domestic politics than in the international arena? The answers are self-

[15]Peter Kropotkin, *Mutual Aid: A Factor of Evolution* (New York: Alfred A. Knopf, 1925). The quotation is from the concluding paragraph of chapter 2.

[16]The same point underlies Schopenhauer's parable of the procupines, which Freud cites in *Group Psychology and the Analysis of the Ego*, chapter 6. "A company of porcupines crowded themselves very close together one cold winter's day so as to profit by one another's warmth and so save themselves from being frozen to death. But soon they felt one another's quills, which induced them to separate again. And now, when the need for warmth brought them nearer together again, the second evil arose once more. So that they were driven backwards and forwards from one trouble to the other, until they had discovered a mean distance at which they could most tolerably exist." The original can be found in Schopenhauer's *Parerga and Paralipomena* (1851) under the heading of "Parables."

[17]"This country has no eternal friends or eternal enemies. It has eternal interests." Lord Palmerston, British Foreign Secretary and Prime Minister.

evident, and I take them as further proof that cooperation is superior to competition, both for the individuals who practice it and for society at large.

This is necessarily the case because competition divides, whereas cooperation unites; competition is destructive, cooperation is constructive. Competition develops the self in rivalry with others, whereas cooperation develops the self in harmony with others. It would be possible for a society to function solely through cooperation, without any competition; the reverse is impossible. In fact, even groups which are constituted around the intention to attack others have a measure of internal cooperation.[18] Thus, the requirements of competition lead to some cooperation, but the latter never brings people into competition. So, for society and its politics, the paramount need is to act cooperatively.

Relations among People in a Group

Reality is always influenced by our thoughts of what it ought to be. If people think that cooperation has beneficial results, then their conduct will follow accordingly, as will the pattern of their social relationships. When we emphasize cooperation, we are giving priority to matters of common interest, to whatever binds us together. It is the reverse, of course, when we stress competition. In that case, each person is preoccupied with the self; we focus on differences and uniqueness.

Can we understand such opposites? Which picture of our relationships with our fellow creatures is valid? Can they be equally true? There are various ways of asking this fundamental question: What is a group and what are the relations among the people who comprise it? The answers to this question are many and varied because the situation is complex.

When we try to understand something as intricate as human society, we seek to make the problem intelligible by dividing it into parts and observing how they are connected. The question then arises: Which is to be regarded as the whole, and which are the parts? What, in other words, is the unit whose unity has significance? One may approach the group from the standpoint of the individuals who comprise it, or the individuals from the standpoint of the group to which they belong. In the latter case, we refer to human beings as associated in a group. In the former, a group is said to consist of its members. Which is the reality to be explained, the group or the individual? And, whichever of these we take as the primary unit, how do we explain the other?

---

[18]Plato pointed out that even a band of outlaws, which seeks to plunder the rest of society, must cohere around its own principle of justice. Witness the old phrase: "Honor among thieves."

As might be expected, both possibilities have found support. Some argue that the unit is the group and that we individuals are its vulgar fractions. Others say that the unit is the single human being. Each view has been defended by analogies that supposedly illustrate the nature of a social group by comparisons with other associations. For those who hold that the group is the unit, a favorite parallel is the biological organism. The members of a social body are then thought to resemble the members of an animal body, wherein all parts are functionally related and none can exist in separation from the rest. On this theory, just as the body has a natural unity, so has a social group. It then becomes a false abstraction to conceive of the individual as a person divorced from relationships with others. An arm lives only as part of an organic whole. Amputated from the body, it dies. An opposite conception results when the individual is believed to be the unit. It is then the single human being who is viewed as a natural unity and the group that appears artificial. Society is considered an aggregate, not an organism. A human group is thought to resemble a heap of stones. They are associated, yet separable. A stone may be removed from the heap, but it remains a stone.

The first comment to be made on these contrasts is that their opposition itself needs explaining. If opinions so contrary have been formulated, each may contain some elements of truth and correspond to certain facts. Plainly there is a sense in which every human being is unique and has a distinct existence, physically and psychically. When the bell tolls for John Jones, John Donne may say that it tolls for me also. But at that moment I can hear it and John Jones cannot—and that is no small difference! Moreover, although a characteristic is attributed to a group, a group as such does not exist, or feel and move, or act and suffer. It is what its members are. It does only what they do. In speaking about it in the singular, one is generalizing about them in the plural. Yet in another sense, a group is an intelligible and describable fact and has a kind of meaning that single human beings do not. John Jones may have died, but the group of which he was a member continues to exist with virtually the same characteristics it possessed in his lifetime. People are united by an intricate network of connections. They do not all move in one direction, like traffic on a one-way street. At countless crossroads they react and interact. They cannot separate themselves from the relationships that arise from their cooperation or their competition, their needs and their deeds. Each such relation is a projection from one's personality, and, like a shadow, belongs both to the person who casts it and to the place where it falls. Unless the projections are included, their source cannot be properly understood.

To explain the character of this relationship between individuals in a group is a perennial question of social thought. Being subtle, the essence of the relationship has eluded precise description. Consequently, from Plato to the present, theorists have resorted to analogies. Groups have been variously depicted as if they were the same as an organism, a contract, a system, the physical universe, and so on. All such comparisons are helpful up to a point; but beyond that the facts cease to correspond. When pressed too far, analogies become misleading.

A clear inference may be drawn from all these attempts. Let us comprehend a human grouping as it is, and not as if it were something else. The truth is that a group of human beings is unique. It forms a class by itself, and the best way to understand it is to see it in its own true colors. The unique quality that all human associations possess can be thus described: A group is composed of individual members who must become parts of a whole since, unless associated, they are unable to develop themselves. Yet it is the parts, and only these, that possess a consciousness both of the self and of the whole, and are thereby capable of contributing to the whole its purpose and organization. In a paradoxical manner, human beings exist separately but are inseparably united.

The Variety of Groups

That statement, however, does not complete the analysis of groups, for there are further facts to note. One reason why it is difficult to fathom the nature of a group is that we are tempted to regard it as existing by itself, and to consider the relations among its members as circumscribed within its borders. But that is not the case. In truth, we belong to many groups. So varied are the relationships created by human needs that the same persons, like the pieces in a kaleidoscope, form and reform, combine and recombine, into numerous associations with myriad patterns. Groups are as prolific as the causes of cooperation; many groups coexist because our needs vary so much.

The best way to describe and classify groups is by the purpose they seek to fulfill. Many associations, for example, are created in response to material necessities and wants. Such "economic" groups correspond to the innumerable phases of the process of production, distribution, and consumption. To lift a weight takes the strength of two; to repair a fence between two farms, the neighbors work together. These instances may seem a far cry from the intricate structures of a modern economy. But just as the symphonies of Beethoven presuppose the simpler harmonics of a birdcall or tom-tom, so do underlying similarities of principle persist through the evolution of social organization, from rudimentary to complex. A business firm is an organization of persons engaged in supplying some commodity or service on terms profitable to themselves. The joint stock company, the corporation, a banking or insurance system, and a cooperative store are familiar instruments by which people pool their resources and accomplish on a larger scale results otherwise unattainable.

The trade union, once treated as a criminal conspiracy, became a recognized and generally a conservative part of the established order. Nowadays, like the medieval guild, it seeks to promote the security of its members both by providing a standard of skill and by eliminating mutually ruinous undercutting in the competition for jobs.

As a need like the economic, which is common to all mankind, has produced our economic associations, so other universal or widespread needs have evoked their counterparts. All of us are curious about ourselves and our environment. We learn, we teach; we wonder and ponder; we wish to know and to understand. As a reasoning animal, whose mind communicates its thoughts through the faculty of speech, the human being has a need for education which can be satisfied only by a cooperative endeavor. Our store of knowledge was transmitted through the generations and is bequeathed to the human race as our common intellectual heritage. To encompass its vast dimensions requires the meeting of many minds in a fellowship of learning. Hence a network of institutions provides an organized response to our desire to know. Similarly, but without laboring the point, we may cite other familiar instances where a felt need stimulates association. Belief in a Supreme Being and the wish to worship have produced the world's religions. The family group gives companionship to adults and an upbringing to children. The cultural interests of like-minded people find a medium in operas, theaters, art galleries, libraries, symphony orchestras, the ballet, and so on, just as fondness for recreation and physical exercise results in sporting and athletic clubs.

Components of Groups

These comparisons permit us to subdivide a group into its components and then, as in table 1, to analyze the features it shares with others and those specific to each kind. Of what elements is a group composed? The first is necessarily the membership, since without this there would be no group. Members are variously named and related according to the nature of their association. In a church, they are the congregation or, in terms of the belief they profess, the faithful. In a family, they are parents, children, uncles, cousins—or, all inclusively, relatives. In a business firm, they are owners, managers, employees. A state has citizens or subjects, rulers and officials. How is membership acquired in the group? Sometimes by the voluntary choice of the person who seeks admission and of the existing members who decide to admit. Thus a person may undergo conversion and then be initiated into a religious faith, or may apply and be accepted at a school or university. One may be appointed to a job in a business firm, be naturalized as a citizen, marry and start a family. Sometimes the act of joining a group is involuntary, as when an infant is born into a family, is baptized into a

TABLE 1. The Components of Groups

ELEMENTS COMMON TO ALL GROUPS	ELEMENTS OF RELIGIOUS GROUPS	ELEMENTS OF EDUCATIONAL GROUPS	ELEMENTS OF FAMILY GROUPS	ELEMENTS OF BUSINESS FIRMS*	ELEMENTS OF THE STATE
1. Members	Congregation The Faithful	Teachers Students	Parents Children	Owners, Managers, Employees	Citizens, Subjects, Officials
a. How they join	Initiation Baptism Conversion	Appointment Admission	Marriage Birth Adoption	Purchase of shares Hiring for job	Birth Naturalization Residence
b. How they leave	Nonattendance Excommunication	Retirement Resignation Graduation Expulsion	Desertion Death Divorce	Sale of shares Resignation Dismissal	Renunciation Deportation Deprivation of citizenship
2. Functions†	Worship	Teaching Learning	Cohabitation Propagation	Manufacturing Sales	Protection, Justice, Welfare
3. Institutions	Church, Temple, Mosque, Synagogue	School, College, University	The Home	Firm Corporation	The State
4. Rules	Canon law, Ritual, Mosaic law, Koran	Regulations Classroom discipline	Marriage Fidelity	Articles of incorporation Shop rules, etc.	Law Custom
5. Governing authority	Congregation Clergy	Teachers Administrators	Parents	Management Foreman	Government Officials
6. Revenue	Donations Tithes	Grants Fees	Income	Profits	Taxes, Loans, etc.
7. Ideas	Theology Creed	Pedagogy Curriculum	Monogamy Polygamy Polyandry	Property, Private ownership, Contract, Competition	Political theory

*The business firm is selected as an example of one type of economic grouping.
†The functions listed in the table are not intended to be complete and exhaustive. Those stated in each case are the central and primary ones, not those that are secondary and derivative. All groups tend to acquire additional functions.

39

church, and automatically receives the citizenship of the country of its birth. Similarly, membership in the group may be terminated by voluntary act of the individual or under compulsion from the group. You may sever your link with an organized religion by nonattendance, or it may excommunicate you. You may graduate from school or college, or drop out or be expelled; resign your job or be fired; renounce your allegiance or be stripped of citizenship.

If the members constitute the original element in any group, its functions form the second. Members associate to fulfill a purpose by carrying on a function. The chief function of the family is to propagate and live together; that of the religious group, to worship; of the firm, to conduct a business; of the state, to protect. Functions such as these cannot be performed without organization, structure, and system. In other words, every organization that maintains its identity and retains its continuity begets a progeny of institutions. Though variously named, the latter are fundamentally alike in the role they perform. Education is institutionalized through schools, colleges, and universities. Religion is organized by temples, mosques, synagogues, or churches. Business is carried on by the firm or corporation. The family clusters round the home. Likewise the state acts through government and its specialized agencies—the legislature, law court, administrative department, and civil service.

When an institution is organized, three further elements appear: a body of rules, a governing authority, and revenue. Every association produces rules that define the relations of its members, allot their rights and responsibilities, and prescribe its operating procedures. In a church, this takes the form of canon law and ritual. In the family, the law of marital relations reinforces the moral code of fidelity. A business firm not only has internal regulations but also conforms to general trade practices and operates inside the framework of laws of contract, property, corporations, and so on. The state is both creator of law and creature of custom. To enforce its rules and give general guidance to the group is the task of its governing authority. This appears under different guises, depending on the nature of the association—as the management, clergy, parents, teachers, or government. Similarly, in every group an essential ingredient is its revenue—if that term is understood to comprise the physical and material resources by which the group accomplishes its purposes. Thus a school or university is maintained by public funds or private fees and endowments; a business, by its profits; the state, by taxes and fees; the family, by its property and income.

Finally, there is one more component. Every group is both producer and product of the ideas concerning it which exist in its members' minds. These ideas are an integral part of the life of the group since they embody the hopes and aspirations of its members, expressing their conception of the group's purpose and their understanding of its processes. The ideas that sustain the group are not always explicitly formulated. In certain cases they are inarticulate, and are divined rather than defined. Even if expressed, they may not always be systematized into a coherent philosophy. For example, family systems are numerous and various, as are the types of political systems. But while political theories are many, theories of the family are few. This does not mean, however, that the family group lacks its ideology. Nor, for that matter, can religion fulfill its purposes without a theological creed; a university, without an educational philosophy; or a business firm, without a theory of economic behavior.

The Unity of Society

This analysis shows that human groups are many in number and different in purpose. It also reveals how complex is the sum total of associations, i.e., society, comprising all relationships and organized groups. But just as society consists of many groups, every human being also has numerous memberships. By nature, we are joiners. Each person belongs to a collection of groups, no one of which can embrace every interest. Not only is society a pluralistic union of groups, but the ways in which individuals associate are also plural.

The numerous groupings into which all people enter bring them sometimes into relations with the same persons, but more usually with different ones. Thus, as a partner in a business firm, A may be associated with B, C, D, and E; as a university alumnus, with C, D, L, and M; as a worshipper in a church, with W, X, Y, and Z; and so on. As the purposes for combination vary, so all of us find ourselves associated with different samples of our fellow creatures. Neither in function nor in membership are the groups identical.

These obvious facts produce most controversial implications. In the first place, the use of the singular term *society* to describe the sum total of relationships and groups involves a major assumption. One should raise, rather than beg, these fundamental questions: Is society truly a unity? Is there anything that embraces the plurality of groups? If so, what makes it a whole? Does this oneness occur only subjectively in our minds and attitudes, or does it also manifest itself in some external structure and organization? A second difficulty arises from the first. It can be readily seen that the processes of cooperation create social relations, and that these relations receive an orderly character through the formation of groups. But once the groups have been formed, what regulates the relations between groups themselves? How is the grouping of groups arranged? Human needs and interests cannot be so demarcated as to prevent all contact or overlap. When one speaks of the economic need, the educational need, or the cultural need, these are not a string of airtight compartments but rather the many facets of a community that functions as a whole. Human needs interlock; we pursue objectives that conflict. So it is with the resulting groups, as some examples will indicate.

Divided Loyalties of the Individual

Business practices, backed by economic theory, sanction the lending of capital for interest. But religion may condemn this as the sin of usury. Painters interpret the world as they see it and insist that they pursue their art for its own sake. Yet a critic may charge that they offend the moral susceptibilities of others, and assert the subordination of art to ethics. Parents wish their children to be educated so that their opportunities may be broadened. But the poverty of the home makes it necessary to increase the family earnings by sending children into early employment. A man and a woman wish to marry. But the church to which one of them belongs forbids the union on the grounds that the other party belongs to a different church or has been divorced. An industrial firm wants to erect a factory that will employ many workers on a desirable piece of land in a city of expanding population. The same area is sought by educational authorities for a school and playground, by a building contractor for a housing project, by a movie exhibitor for a theater. How are such conflicts resolved? Who arbitrates the merits of the contending claims? On what principles is a just decision based?

Such cases are not imaginary. They are scenes from actual life. If they possess drama, it is because any situation of conflict is inherently dramatic. Nor is this conflict one that exists solely between groups. It goes deeper, since within each human being and inside each group a struggle develops between contrary sentiments, attitudes, habits and ideas. All of us belong to a number of systems that correspond with our respective interests and needs. But these interests overlap, the needs crisscross, the systems clash. A father of a family has an obligation to his wife and children which may be at variance with his financial circumstances. The adherents of a religious faith accept dogmas, which, as participants in an educational program, they may be expected to question. An artist may seek to portray a person or a situation truthfully as these appear. But to do so may be running counter to the conventions of the social order. Each of these systems—the economic, religious, cultural, and familial—lays claim to the loyalty of its members. Since each system, however, covers only a segment of our total needs and interests, the allegiance that each can exact must itself be partial. How then can a person come to a decision when faced with antagonistic demands? Amid so many claims, how is one to know which to respect?

The Search for Social Harmony

Two answers to these questions are possible. The competition of loyalties could be resolved by compromise. Strictly understood, this means that neither of the rival claims is completely satisfied. Instead, an agreement is reached at some intermediate position. Each side succeeds on some points, and concedes on others. But if this is done, one naturally inquires: Who acts as intermediary? Who negotiates the compromise? On what principles is it based? How are these determined? Even these queries, however, do not apply to conflicts whose nature permits no compromise whatsoever. Take, for example, the demand of Roman emperors that they and their deified predecessors be worshiped as divinities by inhabitants of their empire. Between this demand and the religious beliefs of their Christian subjects, no compromise was possible. Or consider the implications of the most divisive domestic issue that has erupted in the United States since the achievement of independence: the institution of slavery. There was no midway point for settlement between one who upheld the principle that human beings may be bought, owned, and sold as the legal property of other human beings, and one who asserted that they may not. The two views could not be reconciled or harmonized. As the judgment of Solomon indicated when two women claimed the same child, the price of compromise was to kill the baby. The outcome of the slavery question was in fact left to the arbitrament of war; and arms decided not which view was better, but which in practice would prevail.

As a second possibility of resolving conflict between groups, when compromise is impracticable or inadmissible, the loyalty to one group must bow before the loyalty to another. But how is this achieved? Who decides which group shall predominate and by what means it shall triumph? One method is to use force, with the consequent suppression or overpowering of the unsuccessful side. A second is the voluntary submission of one side after peaceful persuasion. A third is to appeal to some larger association which will choose between opposing claims in the light of a still wider union. Thus the difficulty of harmonizing cooperation with competition, of groups with individuals, is viewed in broader focus when it is treated not simply as a matter of relations between persons within a single group but as a complex of interrelations between numerous groups whose members are associated and reassociated in diverse ways.

Consequently it is necessary to reframe the earlier question, of how to describe the relation of the group to the individual. This can now be more accurately expressed as the problem of organizing many multimembered groups of human beings into one multigroup society. Can the principles of social theory and the practices of social organization devise a rationale for uniting the various groups with their many members and the various members with their many groupings? The search for this union can end only with the discovery of an interest sufficiently broad to absorb all partial, lesser interests and of an association wide enough to embrace the lesser, limited associations. It is time, therefore, to turn to the origins of the state and the contribution of government.

3

The Origins of the State

Politics, State, and Government

Of the numerous organized groups that constitute society, the state is the special concern of the student of politics. As with all human associations, the state emerges and exists within society. The taproots of government reach down into the same soil that nurtures the family and the church, the corporation and the trade union, the school and the club. But what is it that stimulates the state to grow in its own particular manner? What are the seeds of the political process? Why the need for government and where does it originate? These are some of the questions that this chapter will explore.

Their phrasing, however, reveals a problem which confronts every analysis of this subject. The difficulty is partly conceptual and partly verbal. Our topic involves three basic terms: *politics, state,* and *government.* Frequently, these are used as synonyms, and many definitions employ them interchangeably. But the facts we have to explain, and the ideas they incorporate, imply some genuine distinctions, for which we need different words if the meaning is to be clear. Hence, this discussion will differentiate between politics, state, and government so as to clarify the facts. Society was defined earlier as the broadest possible concept, embracing all human rela-

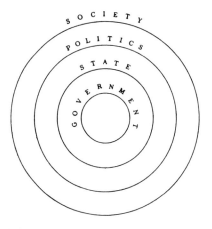

FIGURE 1

tionships and groups. If we proceed from the broad to the narrow, the concept that comes next is politics. By *politics* I mean a process of active search for the best solutions to the five issues outlined in chapter 1, which will be analyzed in chapters 4–13.

More limited than politics is the concept of the state. This is the institution through which the dynamics of politics are organized and formalized. The state consists of citizens with their rights and duties, institutions and jurisdictions, principles and powers. It is a network of structured relationships. The point that politics is broader than the state can be easily demonstrated. Wherever the state exists, there is also politics. But the converse is not true—that wherever politics exist, so does the state. We can speak of international politics, but as yet there is no supranational state. We can talk of politics within churches or corporations or trade unions, although none of those is a state. The state, however, comprises another and narrower concept—that of government. Every state has its government, and the latter signifies those specific persons who hold official positions and wield authority on behalf of the state. Governments in this sense will change while the same state continues. Government, therefore, implies a distinction within the state between rulers and ruled. We can visualize this series of concepts as concentric circles, where society is the outermost and government, the innermost (see figure 1).

The Primary Function of the State

If all groups are organized in response to some social need, the state, being a universal institution, must correspond to needs that are universal. Hence, it should be possible to infer the need to which the state responds by studying the functions it undertakes. Anybody who surveys the vast complex of activities undertaken by the state in different periods and places must wonder why they are conducted by this particular association. We know that certain functions were conducted by the state long ago, while others were added more recently. There is wide agreement that some duties are appropriate for the state to undertake and controversy about the suitability of others. Consequently we begin to ask whether the functions of government can be classified into primary and secondary, original and derivative, essential and optional. To answer such questions, it would help to identify one function and say, "This without dispute is *the* function of the state." Or, approaching the same point from another direction, we should ask, "What is the minimum indispensable function the state must perform in order to be a state? Is there any activity of the state so vital that, were it performed by another association, the latter in effect would be or become a state?"

The Universal Drive for Protection

To these questions the facts of government disclose an answer. Among the common concerns of all human beings is the desire for security of life and limb. Everywhere people seek guarantees of protection from physical harm. But though the urge to ward off bodily threats is universal, different means of protection have been employed. It has not been uncommon, for example, for human beings to rely primarily on themselves. In most historical periods—and almost certainly in the prehistoric—weapons were kept in the home and were carried on journeys. The first line of defense against attack upon one's person or possessions was also, in a sense, the last. It lay in one's own strong arm, since the help of others, even if offered, might arrive too late. But under certain circumstances self-reliance would be inadequate. This was so when the likelihood of attack was constant; when the techniques available to an aggressor placed the defense at a disadvantage; and when the chief disturbance to one's peace came, not from within the group, but from the strength of another organized group outside. Security, therefore, to be effective, had to be collective. The protection that people could not obtain singly had to be found by cooperating as a group. But when a need, like this for protection, remains constant, the method by which the group satisfies it is to develop practices and procedures which must be continually repeated. At some stage, by virtue of repetition, these become accepted. They are then endowed with formal organization. In a word, they are institutionalized. What we call an "institution" is the outgrowth in structured form of the repetitive practices with which a group fulfills a common need. The nucleus of the state is formed when a group of persons have institutionalized their own protection.

So far, however, this analysis of the need for protection has consisted more of assertions than proof. Is there evidence to show that protection is the original function of the state? The answer can be drawn from various sources, including historical data and the analysis of present-day governmental functions. The historical evidence, though fragmentary, is sufficient to justify some highly probable conclusions. Since about 3000 B.C. enough is known to warrant the use of the term *history* by contrast with earlier *prehistory*. At the dawn of history, however, the institution of government already existed. It was born, therefore, in the prehistoric night before the dawn. Hence any assertion about the origins of the state must repose mainly on conjecture.[1]

Nevertheless there is testimony to show that an intimate connection has always existed between the organization a group adopts for its defense and for its government. When human beings lived as nomads, hunting or herding their food supply, their mobility necessitated a military organization since they transported their families and possessions with them. The able-bodied males on their mounts were a cavalry; the wagons of a caravan made a defensive post. The change from nomadism to a settled habitat, associated with the shift from hunting or tending animals to planting crops, altered the tactics of protection because the objects to be defended—the home and its source of food—were stationary, and a person who planted a seed had to remain there until the crop ripened. Consequently, though people who became agriculturists preferred the plains which were easier to sow and reap, they also required a defensible frontier on the rim of the plain and some fortress in the interior. Out of this need, and the institutions occasioned by it, the primary function of government was founded.

Cities began when people clustered together for social and economic reasons, and a government was needed to give organization and security. The world's oldest known city is Jericho, for it has been occupied continuously since about 7800 B.C. From early times, Jericho was strongly fortified with a watchtower and its famous walls.[2] Archaeological inquiries into the beginnings of civilization in Mesopotamia have explained the circumstances in which the state emerged. In the area watered by the Tigris and the Euphrates, urban centers evolved to control a river-borne commerce and an expanse of fertile fields. The social order of Akkad and Sumer and Babylon was a combination of temple officials, merchants, craftsmen, and

[1]See Melville M. Herskovits, *Man and His Works* (New York: Alfred A. Knopf, 1948), pp. 114 ff., and especially p. 120. Arnold J. Toynbee points out in his *Civilization on Trial* (New York: Oxford University Press, 1948, pp. 36–37) that the period of time about which we have some historical information is infinitesimally small in relation to the age of the earth and the evolution of humanity. Modern scientists estimate that the planet may have existed for some 2000 million years and life for perhaps 500 to 800 million years. The earliest known remains of humanlike creatures, the family of hominids, have been dated to over three million years ago. "In terms of evolutionary history," according to Dr. Louis Leakey, "man's separation from his closest cousins—the apes—is now carried back more than a million generations."

[2]See James Mellaart in *The Dawn of Civilization* (London: Thames and Hudson, 1962), pp. 41–58.

landowners, competing for influence. The scattered cities, all independent, struggled for control of the land and water. What happened under these conditions is thus described: "A new institution was needed to restrain these conflicts. By the beginning of historical times the State had emerged, but it was embodied in the single person of the *city-governor* or king, who may be just 'corn-king' and war-chief amalgamated and writ large."[3] The Greek *polis*, ancestor of the term *politics*, signified the strong point where scattered farmers and villagers could gather, where the women and children would be secure, and where the defense had military advantages.[4] The center of Athenian civic life, and the dominating feature of its topography, was its "high polis," or Acropolis. The city of Rome likewise commenced its history as the rallying point for scattered rural settlements in the Latin plain whose inhabitants could find protection on the seven hills beside the River Tiber.

Elsewhere in early times, not only has the duty of protecting the group devolved upon its able-bodied males, but often the privilege and responsibility of government have been entrusted to the same hands that bear or once bore the burden of defense. Under the Athenian constitution of the seventh century B.C. prior to Solon's reforms, the citizen body was divided into three classes, each having different rights. The classes were determined by property qualifications, but they were also distinguished by their military functions. A parallel to this Athenian example is provided by Rome, where one of the citizens' assemblies was known as the *Comitia Centuriata*. Its organization reproduced the "centuries," or "hundreds," which were the basic units in the formation of the Roman army.[5]

Similarly in the Teutonic world the same carry-over from war to government may be observed. The Roman historian Tacitus published in A.D. 97 the earliest known literary study of the Germans and says this of their tribal organization:

> On minor matters their chief men consult alone; on more important business they all meet. . . . Their love of liberty makes them independent to a fault: They do not assemble all at once or as though they were under orders: but two or three days are wasted by their delay in arriving. They take their seats as they come, all in full armour . . . if the opinion expressed displeases them, their murmurs reject it: if they approve they clash their spears.[6]

---

[3]V. Gordon Childe, *What Happened in History* (Baltimore, Md.: Penguin Books, 1954), pp. 99–100.

[4]See Ernest Barker's introduction to *The Politics of Aristotle* (New York: Oxford University Press, 1946), p. lxv.

[5]See E. A. Gardner and M. Cary in *Cambridge Ancient History*, vol. 3 (New York: The Macmillan Company, 1923–1939), p. 594, where they state, "Though the property classes were based on wealth, their original purpose certainly was not fiscal, but rather military, as was the purpose of the Roman *centuriae*."

[6]Tacitus, *Germania*, trans. W. Hamilton Fyfe (Oxford: The Clarendon Press, 1908), sec. 11.

On this point modern experience confirms ancient history. What happens in the twentieth century to a state which engages in a major war? When the safety and existence of the entire community are imperiled, everything is subordinated to the struggle for survival. The need to organize for defense and attack takes priority over all other activities. Centers of production are guarded and expanded. Huge military establishments are thrown together. The whole economy is diverted to the equipment and supply of the armed forces. Abruptly and compulsorily the rhythms and patterns of daily life are changed to a new design. The cells that make up the family group are plucked apart, and some are killed. The home itself may suffer destruction. Citizens respond to new stimuli. They dress in uniforms; they drive toward a goal which they call victory. And to accomplish this result, the state assumes the responsibility. Its functions are enlarged to embrace all aspects of society with military relevance—which in the total warfare of this century means practically everything. Not only was protection the *raison d'être* of the state in ancient times; but whenever a modern people is momentarily preoccupied with protecting itself and destroying an enemy, the state literally "takes over."[7] Furthermore, the defeated state falls under the control of the victors, as happened after World War II in the military occupation of Germany, Italy, and Japan. In other words, the government of the state, which cannot protect itself for the time being, ceases in effect to be a government.

It is not only from outside, however, that the security of the group can be menaced. One's safety may be disturbed by individuals who belong in the same group. Thus the outlaw or gangster is in the group, but places himself "out of its law." Furthermore it is possible for conflict between groups—between a corporation and a trade union, for instance—to be carried to lengths where other interests are prejudiced and where the unity of the society to which they belong may be jeopardized. Government must therefore guard against the internal aggressor as well as the external. As this is phrased in the preamble to the Constitution of the United States, while one governmental function is "to provide for the common defense," another is "to insure domestic tranquility." How does the state meet this need? What principles are implied in its solution? And what problems then arise?

The Nucleus of the State

For a starting point, consider this account by Herodotus of an actual event, the consolidation of the ancient kingdom of Media. According to "the Father of History," the Medes were living in anarchy and suffered from

---

[7]For statistical evidence on this point, expressed in budgetary terms, see chapter 11, section on "The Military Impact on Federalism."

insecurity. Their need presented an opportunity which a far-seeing individual was ready to grasp.

Among the Medes, there was a wise man named Deioces, the son of Phraortes. Deioces coveted absolute power and this was what he did. The Medes, at that time, were living in separate villages and there was much lawlessness throughout the whole land. Being already a person of repute in his own village, and knowing that the just is the enemy of the unjust, he became even more zealous to practice justice. His fellow-villagers, seeing how he behaved, used to choose him to judge their quarrels. In his ambition for power, he gave them just and straightforward decisions and this conduct brought him great praise from the citizenbody. Consequently when residents of other villages, who formerly had met with unfair judgments, learned that Deioces was the only man whose decisions conformed to justice, they gladly frequented his home so that they too could have him for their judge. Finally they would go to no one else. As more and more litigants kept on appearing when they learned that suits were always settled with fairness, Deioces knew that everything was falling into his lap. Whereupon he announced his unwillingness to hold sessions where he had done so previously, or to continue adjudicating. For, as he put it, it was not profitable to him to settle his neighbors' disputes day after day and neglect his own business. Then when looting and lawlessness broke out among the villages to an extent even greater than before, the Medes assembled and discussed what had taken place, most of the speakers, in my estimate, being friends of Deioces. "Since we cannot live in the country in its present state," they said, "come, let us constitute somebody as our king. Thus the land will be well governed and we shall conduct our affairs without being uprooted by lawlessness." By these arguments they persuaded themselves in favor of a monarchy; and as soon as they began proposing candidates for the kingship, Deioces was the one most proposed and praised by all. So they agreed upon him for their king.[8]

This passage is worth quoting—not for its historical truth, but for the insight into the fundamentals of organizing a state. When people conflict in their dealings, they need an orderly process to compose their differences, and a recognized tribunal to give decisions whose binding character they will accept. To promote cooperation and confine competition within limits that are not injurious, society erects protective ramparts. The duties of the mediator, arbitrator, judge, and ruler are like steps on an ascending ladder of government. But the ascent is only possible under two conditions. There must be a widespread understanding that the restraints imposed through law and order are less irksome than the disturbances that erupt in their absence. Further, the tribunal to which disputing parties resort must inspire confidence on the grounds that its procedures are fair and its decisions just. In the Herodotean story, Deioces fulfilled these requirements. He was therefore able to found a state and become its king.

A celebrated episode in the history of Switzerland also illustrates the role of the honest arbitrator in cementing the foundations of the state.

[8]Herodotus, *Histories*, i. chaps. 96–98 (my translation).

During the fifteenth century the Swiss Confederation was at the height of its military power, since its citizens were then the finest foot soldiers in Europe. The country was expanding through pressure on its neighbors, some of whom became its subjects, while others joined the confederation or were associated as allies. The change in Swiss power and the enlargement of the state provoked internal tensions between urban and rural centers. The original members were principally rural, while some of the new adherents contained strong cities with manufacturing and mercantile interests. In 1481 a controversy erupted about raising Solothurn and Fribourg from the status of allies to that of full confederates. The oppostion of the rural cantons was voiced so strongly that there was a risk of the confederation splitting apart. At this point during a meeting of the Diet at Stans, Nicholas von der Flüe, an eminent man who had retired from political life, suddenly intervened in the discussions and by sheer weight of argument, force of personality, and disinterested patriotism, composed the rivalries and achieved an acceptable settlement. Acting as arbitrator and conciliator he brought to both sides an awareness of their common interest in staying united and in making reasonable concessions to one another. The understandings thus reached strengthened the state, while enlarging its membership, and thereby saved Switzerland.[9]

More recent history confirms these observations. Whenever human beings are uprooted from their established ways and exposed to the hazards of a new environment, a social bond has to develop anew. Their prime political need is then to organize in common for protection and physical security. The settlement of the United States by European immigrants contains many incidents of this nature. The pioneers who peopled an unmapped continent were exposed to risks at one another's hands and to the hostility of the Indians whose lands they seized. Life on the frontier was not far removed from Hobbes's characterization of the state of nature—solitary, poor, nasty, and brutish. At times it was also short. A man who rode within sight of another on a backwoods trail did not know whether to trust the stranger; both had their guns ready for the draw. Wherever something essential was in short supply, such as water in the West, men fought for its control. Like medieval barons with retainers, ranchers armed their employees to protect boundary stakes and cattle from neighboring rustlers. The conflict between an agriculture based on slaves and one employing free labor brought violence and bloodshed, as in Kansas, and ultimately a civil war. An event like the discovery of gold in California attracted an inrush of adventurers, whose aggressive individualism raised the temperature of the economic order to a fever while that of the social order dropped to zero.

In newly settled territories, if people came to work and stay, rather

---

[9]On this subject, see William Martin, *Histoire de la Suisse* (Lausanne: Librarie Payot, 1943), pp. 74–75, and G. Soloveytchik, *Switzerland in Perspective* (London: Oxford University Press, 1954), p. 154.

than to loot and depart, they wanted that minimum stability and security without which progress is impossible. Hence they were forced simultaneously to construct a community out of a mosaic of individuals who previously had no connecting ties, and to found a state by establishing law and enforcing order. It was necessary for state and community to grow together, since, until and unless political institutions were created, the soft tissue of society lacking a skeleton was formless and flabby. A state was born in the West when scattered individuals banded together and established the sheriff's office. The state did not grow up, however, until his authority was generally obeyed. Only then was a framework of security organized within which other social institutions—such as economic, religious, educational—could proceed about their respective tasks.

This can also be seen happening in reverse whenever a settled and organized community breaks down into civil war. As the state disintegrates and rival parties seek to capture its machinery, ordinary people may be reduced to presocial and prepolitical savagery. The Russian author Boris Pasternak alluded to this in his account of the events that accompanied the Bolshevik Revolution and the subsequent civil war between Reds and Whites. "That period," he wrote, "confirmed the ancient proverb, 'Man is a wolf to man.' Traveller turned off the road at the sight of traveller, stranger meeting stranger killed for fear of being killed. There were isolated cases of cannibalism. The laws of human civilization were suspended. The jungle law was in force. Man dreamed the prehistoric dreams of the cave dweller."[10] A still grimmer example is the case of the Congo after the Belgians gave up their rule in the early 1960s. Rapidly, as tribe turned savagely against tribe, the edifice of central authority disintegrated. With anarchy substituted for order, nothing was secure and nobody was safe.

Yet more recently, the tragedy of disintegration has been reenacted in Lebanon. Only a few decades ago that small state was being compared to Switzerland—as an oasis of sanity and stability in a turbulent region. The Lebanese had emerged from World War II with an agreement among its major communities to share political power and coexist in peace. Thus a Christian served as president, a Sunni Muslim as prime minister, a Shiite Muslim as speaker of the parliament. This *modus vivendi* was challenged when the Muslims, perceiving that their numbers had increased faster than the Christians, began demanding a larger share in the legislative representation. Then from the outside, the apple of discord was hurled which drove the communities apart. The Palestine Liberation Organization, ejected from Jordan by King Hussein's army, sought refuge in Lebanon and there proceeded to construct a state within a state. Unable to absorb the intruder, the Lebanese turned on each other in civil war so violent that the Arab

---

[10]Boris Pasternak, *Doctor Zhivago*, trans. Max Hayward and Manya Harari (New York: Pantheon Books, 1958), p. 378.

League intervened. Before long the Syrians, who had continued to claim parts of Lebanon as theirs, had occupied much of the country. Subsequently the Israelis mounted an invasion from the south in order to destroy the bases from which the PLO were launching attacks upon their people. Since that time, Lebanon has plunged into anarchy. The numerous communities—Maronites, Sunnis, Shiites, Druzes, Palestinians, and others—have their own militias commanded by their own warlords, supported or opposed by Syria, Israel, or Iran. Beirut itself, the sometime capital of a nonfunctioning state, is divided by an internal frontier, the "green line" which demarcates the Muslim and the Christian sections. Kidnappings, assassinations, gunfire and warfare; treachery, intrigue, and broken agreements—these were the tragic spectacle which Lebanon presented to the world in the nineteen seventies and eighties. The "state," under such conditions, was a fiction; its "government," a tragic farce; its politics, a process of murder. No superstructure of law, justice, and basic services can hold together when its foundations have been swept away and violence stalks the land.

Protection, Order, and Justice

What are the implications of this analysis? First, it demonstrates that what began as protection broadened out. Human beings expect more than physical safety. To conduct their ordinary daily dealings with their fellow creatures, they require a minimum of stability which depends on mutual trust. Furthermore, people acquire relationships with material goods. Through their labors they accumulate possessions which they wish to preserve as property. Hence the function of safeguarding life and limb is expanded to throw a general framework of security around the relations of person to person and of persons to things. The best term to describe this is *order*. Order is only able to grow after protection is assured, and an orderly way of life is what government nurtures. This is what the traditional phrases signify that ascribe to government the provision of "law and order" or "peace and good order." In other words, if order is to give peace, it must rest upon law and upon agencies capable of enforcing it. Order is the product of common rules effectively applied through common institutions.[11]

But that is not all. There is order in a barracks as there is in a prison.

---

[11] This point is made with characteristic clarity by Jean Monnet, the French statesman who played the leading role in creating Western Europe's Coal and Steel Community and the Common Market (see chapter 13). These agencies were invented to overcome the anarchic nationalism, economic and political, of independent states. "To establish this new method of common action," wrote Monnet, "we adapted to our situation the methods which have allowed individuals to live together in society: common rules which each Member is committed to respect, and common institutions to watch over the application of these rules." Quoted in *The Common Market*, ed. Lawrence B. Krause (Englewood Cliffs, N.J.: Prentice-Hall, 1964), p. 44.

In fact, the most orderly place on earth is a cemetery. Yet a barracks, a prison, or a cemetery is not a state—even though the modern dictatorship with its police state has features that resemble all three. Something more than order is required for the fully developed state. Just as order grows out of protection, so a further goal grows out of order. A clue to its nature may be discovered in this passage by Augustine:

> Set justice aside, then, and what are kingdoms but great robberies? because what are robberies but little kingdoms? for in thefts, the hands of the underlings are directed by the commander, the confederacy of them is sworn together, and the pillage is shared by the law amongst them. And if those ragamuffins grow up but to be able enough to keep forts, build habitations, possess cities, and conquer adjoining nations, then their government is no more called thievish, but graced with the eminent name of a kingdom, given and gotten, not because they have left their practices, but because that now they must use them without danger of law.[12]

History indeed confirms the accusation that kingdoms are great robberies. Monarchs have traditionally used their opportunities for self-enrichment, like birds of prey feathering their own nests. Witness the wealth of the Hapsburgs, Bourbons, and Romanovs. Queen Elizabeth II of Great Britain is often described as "the world's wealthiest woman." How did her ancestors acquire so much? In Nicaragua, the Somozas are said to have accumulated assets worth between 400 and 500 million dollars in just over four decades.[13] In Iran, the Pahlavis reportedly amassed billions of dollars in only two generations. The speed record, however, in this disreputable history of personal enrichment from political power probably belongs to Ferdinand Marcos, the dictator of the Philippines until he was deposed in 1986. His ill-gotten gains from a decade of cronyism, corruption, and assassination of opponents have been estimated at several billions of dollars. Under these circumstances, may one inquire what happens to justice?

Society may arrive at the stage of order based on law. It may eliminate anarchy and be systematically organized. But merely to establish order is not enough. Order must embody what people consider just. A system organized to ensure protection, but where people are not persuaded that they are justly treated, may gain obedience, but never allegiance. Justice consists in both a method and a result. The method is fair dealing. The result is to recognize equally the basic interests of all individuals and groups and promote a harmony between them. People will feel that they have justice when their community accords them all an equal chance and safeguards their fundamental interests in a manner proportionate to the like interests of others. As Herodotus shows, a government can originate under two conditions. The understanding must be widespread that the restraints imposed through order and its law are less irksome than the disturbances

---

[12]*Concerning the City of God*, bk. iv, chap. 4, trans. John Healey (1610).
[13]*Christian Science Monitor*, 22 June 1979, p. 13.

which erupt in their absence. In addition, the tribunal to which disputants resort must inspire confidence in the fairness of its procedures and the justice of its decisions. Deioces fulfilled these requirements. He was therefore able to found a state and become its king. But, as Augustine reminds us, if you remove justice, what distinguishes a state from a band of robbers?

The Use and Monopoly of Force

The next questions are: By what methods and through what institutions are these results achieved? What happens when a community mobilizes to protect itself, then founds a system of order, and finally establishes justice? Every association must employ the methods that are indispensable, or best fitted, for performing its primary function. If the state originates in the need for protection, to it belong initially any techniques which insure attainment of that objective; and if the state is to progress toward broader goals, the techniques of government must evolve in the process. Granted that protection, order, and justice are successive ends to which the state aspires, what are the means for obtaining each?

Since an institution must possess the means appropriate to its function, it follows that, if it is to give protection, the state must have force[14] at its disposal. Protection against attacks from outside cannot be provided unless the group can repel force with force. Likewise, protection against attack from within calls for agencies—for example, police, militia, army, courts, and prisons—capable of applying coercion to the disorderly and the lawless. The tribunals that are supposed to settle disputes must be able to enforce their decisions. Otherwise none of us will have assurance that the rules we obey will be observed by others. It is therefore the special purpose for which the state originates, namely to afford protection, which imposes on the state the necessity of employing force. Many of the problems that distinguish the state from other associations flow from the simple yet fundamental fact that the state must use force or it cannot even begin to be a state.[15]

Let us consider what some of these problems are. First, because it must employ force, the state inevitably seeks to monopolize it. Any force not controlled by the state represents a potential source of resistance and a limit to what the state can do. In order to be unchallenged in performing its

---

[14]Here and elsewhere, unless the context states otherwise, "force" is used in a literal, not a metaphorical, sense. It means physical restraint or coercion, actual or threatened.

[15]This truth is recognized by those anarchists who condemn force and argue that acting voluntarily is morally superior to acting under compulsion. Knowing that the state cannot function without possessing its agencies of enforcement, they favor the total abolition of the state in order to accomplish their goal of eliminating the coercion of one human being by another.

protective function, the state seeks to be the sole possessor of coercive techniques. Conversely, whenever force is available for use by associations other than the state or by persons other than the government, there exist in embryo the potential makings of a substitute state and government. An incident which illustrates this fact is cited by Augustine in the sequel to the passage quoted earlier:

> For elegant and excellent was that pirate's answer to the great Macedonian Alexander, who had taken him: the king asking him how he durst molest the sea so, he replied with a free spirit, "How darest thou molest the whole world? But, because I do it with a little ship only, I am called a thief: thou, doing it with a great navy, art called an emperor."[16]

Alexander could not tolerate the pirate because the state, to maintain itself, must be a monopolist of force; the state then attempts to moralize this monopoly by serving the ideal of the public good. The little gang appears antisocial[17] because it preys upon the larger community and puts its special advantage before the general interest.

History exemplifies the danger that threatens the state when any force is organized within its midst to break its monopoly. During the sixth century B.C. Peisistratus usurped power in Athens and established a dictatorial regime. He accomplished a coup d'état by employing a bodyguard that had been assigned to him by his fellow citizens after he had feigned attacks upon his life.[18] The closing century of the Roman Republic from 133 B.C. to 31 B.C. witnessed a cumulative series of futile efforts by the Senate to control its armies in the field. At the end of victorious campaigns abroad, successive generals—such as Marius or Sulla, Pompey or Caesar, Antony or Augustus—were able to bend the government to their will or make themselves masters of the state. There were even periods when the Senate could not keep order in the streets of Rome and lay at the mercy of the vicissitudes of violence between rival gangs like those of Clodius and Milo. Then when the republic, which could not rule an empire, gave way to emperors who could, the latter, too, were at times made or unmade by the captains of the Praetorian Guard who garrisoned the capital city, or by army commanders in a distant province. In the Middle Ages when feudal regimes in Western Europe were highly localized,[19] the kings of England or France found it difficult to exercise authority over powerful nobles who were secure in their castles and could place in the field a body of retainers and vassals wearing their livery. If medieval monarchs could not control

---

[16]*Concerning the City of God*, bk. iv, chap. 4.

[17]Not always, however. Some robbers, or small gangs, became folk heroes (e.g., Robin Hood) when their purpose was to steal from the rich to help the poor.

[18]Aristotle describes this in his *Constitution of Athens*, sec. 14. See also Plato's *Republic*, viii, secs. 505–6, where the allusion is to Peisistratus and others of his kind.

[19]See chapter 10, section on "The Medieval Dispersion of Powers."

what the historian Fortescue called their "overmighty subjects," it was because the latter were backed by private armies.

Essentially the same has been true of the modern state. When would-be dictators emerge in the midst of weak regimes, they seek to subvert the armed forces and organize militias of their own. In Italy between 1920 and 1922, Mussolini overawed and paralyzed the government by mobilizing his Black Shirts and obtaining the passive connivance of the army. Hitler organized thugs to capture the city streets and ended up molesting the whole world. Elsewhere, it is by launching a military rebellion that a politically ambitious officer overturns the civilian authorities and installs himself in power. This is what Franco did in Spain in the 1930s; thereafter, for a third of a century his brutal regime relied on repression by the police and the army. Until mid-1974, the Greek army also put up a fair imitation of the Spanish. And there have been scores of such military dictators, long-lasting or short-lived, in recent decades. Many of the governments in the Middle East, southeast Asia, and Latin America now belong or have recently belonged in this category. The rule of the gunmen, in uniform or not, is indeed a phenomenon as widespread as it is depressing. Even the gangs that flourished in various cities of the United States during the Prohibition era form an aspect of the same story. When Capone dominated the Chicago underworld in the 1920s and conducted illegal rackets on a vast scale, was it not in his gunmen that a major portion of the city's power was located? Nor is it without significance that what the gangster offers to the victims of his blackmail he calls "protection." In the same category are the terrorists, or urban guerrillas, who have become so ubiquitous since the 1960s. These groups—as in Germany and Italy, in Argentina or throughout the Middle East—are unlike old-style brigands or gangs whose rationale was economic. Contemporary terrorists are politically motivated and devote themselves with fanaticism to some cause or mission. Their actions demonstrate how a mere handful, who are ready to die and utterly ruthless, can produce chaos in an orderly society. The lesson is obvious. The state must either monopolize the force of the community or risk surrender to whoever can muster counterforce for its overthrow. The logic of coercion dictates monopoly.

Officials and the Public

When one speaks, however, of force being monopolized by the state, what exactly is meant? The state is an abstraction. In practice, acts of government are done by a few on behalf of everybody. Those who act may be variously described as representatives, agents, deputies, officials, or, simply, the government. It is characteristic of the state to entrust its use of force to persons who are recognized by the whole community as acting on their behalf. In this sense a distinction can be drawn between public and private, official and unofficial, government and governed; and a different social significance attaches to the same action according to the persons who perform it and the methods they employ. Thus it is one thing for a mob to track down and lynch a suspect; another, for a sheriff to conduct an arrest. It is one thing to carry on a personal vendetta, and another to seek remedies for a wrong through a judicial process. When law reposes in the police rather than in a mob, when defense is secured by a standing army and not by guerrilla bands, the trained professional acting under public orders is substituted for the unauthorized acts of private individuals. Save under the extreme necessity of self-defense, citizens may no longer take the law into their own hands once it has been entrusted to officials. If they do, their actions lack the character of law and they then become "outlaws."

This latter truth was brought home to the American people in the period from 1963 to 1968 when four men of national prominence were assassinated by gunshot. These were President John F. Kennedy, his brother Senator Robert F. Kennedy, the Black Muslim leader Malcolm X, and the Reverend Martin Luther King, the campaigner for civil rights who was an apostle of nonviolence and had received the Nobel Peace Prize. Such well-known victims belong within the broader context of a people with an appallingly high rate of deaths from shooting.[20] Some 200 million firearms are estimated to be in private hands in this country—more than in the armed forces of the United States, the USSR, and the NATO countries combined. Is it any wonder that, with guns so easily accessible, too many are used and persons in public life become targets?

On the other hand, an emergency may arise whose dimensions lie beyond the ordinary resources of officialdom. In those cases, the principle that the official is the agent of the community is reinforced by invoking the aid of the citizens themselves. Under English common law if a policeman blows his whistle when he is attacked or is trying to make an arrest, any able-bodied citizen within earshot must go to his assistance. Similarly, the sheriff in western territories in an earlier day would call out the posse to help him track an outlaw. The theory is that the policeman is the agent of all the citizens. When the latter go to his aid, therefore, they are momentarily doing for themselves what he does ordinarily on their behalf. For similar reasons, under extraordinary conditions threatening the whole community, reinforcements may be mobilized by doctors fighting an epidemic, by firemen extinguishing a conflagration, or by engineers trying to contain a flood. Finally, in the ultimate case of total warfare, the profes-

---

[20]In 1983 homicides from handguns alone were: 10 in Australia, 6 in Canada, 8 in Great Britain, 35 in Japan, 7 in Sweden, 27 in Switzerland, 9014 in the United States. Data from *Handgun Control,* Inc. derived from official figures of the respective countries.

sional army is expanded through universal conscription, and all fit persons are enlisted.

Force and Consent

How then does the government come to exercise the coercive force of the whole? What is it that enables a few to wield the force of many? The answer can be found if one remembers that, though the functions of government begin with protection, they evolve beyond their starting point. Protection grows into order and order seeks to blossom into justice. Something similar happens with the techniques of government, since a method that was adequate at one stage of development ceases to be so at the next. Force may be sufficient for protection. But to create order, more is required. This extra is *power*. What is power? It is simply force with some consent added. How large a volume of consent is debatable. Indeed the quantity may vary, with consequential differences of great importance.

Let us examine more closely this relation between force and consent. All governments in the world use force, and even the most dictatorial is supported by some minimal measure of consent. People always want certain results from their government, and they are willing that their officials have the means of bringing those results to fruition. Therefore, they give their consent to the general body of law which prescribes the order they desire; and, along with law, they approve coercive enforcement against those who would infringe it. The nature of this relationship has been well stated by A. D. Lindsay:

> Many people think that the state's use of force gives the lie to the doctrine that government can rest on consent, yet it is also clear that without some sort of consent the government's force would not exist. These puzzles confound more people than should be so confounded. Men have been accustomed so much to think of the law as restraining other people than their respectable selves that they easily think of the state's force as necessary to enable some people to restrain others. . . . But a little consideration will show us that we need and desire the power of the state to restrain ourselves. Consider a simple example from traffic control. We most of us think there ought to be laws regulating traffic, compelling us to light our lamps at a certain time and so on. Such rules have our consent and approval. Yet most of us, if we are honest, know that we are likely to break those laws on occasion and that we are often restrained from breaking them by the sanctions of the law. Most laws are like that. They will work and can be enforced because most people want usually to keep them. The state can have and use organized force because most people usually want common rules and most people want those rules to be universally observed; there must be force because there are rules which have little value unless everyone keeps them, and force is needed to fill up the gap between most people usually and all people always obeying.[21]

[21]*The Modern Democratic State* (New York: Oxford University Press, 1947), p. 206.

Power and Authority

Power is an ability to achieve results through concerted action. It is the product of the mobilization of support and involves a relationship between a group and its agents. The latter may be described as delegates or representatives, in the sense that they follow the group; or as leaders, if the group follows them. The building of consent may depend on the capacity of a group to organize itself coherently, formulate its program, and instruct its representatives; or alternatively on the capacity of a leader to attract adherents and win a following.[22] The support elicited will thus be reciprocal. A group supports its agents, while they support the group. Franklin D. Roosevelt, in a critical period of domestic economic breakdown and aggressive international militarism, confidently offered programs that gave people new hope. Thus he was the first to be elected president four times.

But the evolution of governmental techniques does not terminate with power. As order, to be securely stabilized, attempts to gain acceptance as justice, so does power aspire toward a concept yet more advanced. If protection is sustained by force and order by power, justice requires authority. What does authority mean, and how is it distinguished from power? To understand the contrast, one must introduce a further refinement into the distinction between the government and the governed. In fact, the governed subdivide into two parts—the supporters of the government and its opponents. This means that the citizens who compose the state are actually made up of three groups:

1. Representatives (or leaders) and their official subordinates
2. Those who support the representatives
3. Those who dissent and oppose the representatives

Power consists in the fusion of items 1 and 2. It is able to include that ingredient of force which makes government ultimately effective, because of the support mobilized in its favor. But the claims of power to hold sway are, by definition, valid only for those who consent. Likewise, the rightness of its force is justified only in the eyes of those who render it support. The force that power may deploy will be resented, and may be resisted, by those who disagree. Opponents may have to submit to the decisions of power; but submission is different from acquiescence. The imperatives of power may secure compliance; but this is not the same as allegiance.

What demarcates authority from power is that the former is power

---

[22]A memorable witticism was pronounced during the French Revolution by a politician who saw a mob rush by in the street and dashed out of the house after them, saying, "I am their leader: so I must follow them."

recognized as rightful. Authority is a rule which all accept as valid. Its exercise is therefore sanctioned by those who approve the particular act or agent and is tolerated by those who disapprove. Confronted with power, the citizen has a choice: whether to support or oppose. Confronted with authority, it is one's duty to obey. Resistance to power is lawful; resistance to authority, unlawful. Power is naked; authority is power clothed in the garments of legitimacy.

How this transformation takes place can be illustrated in two episodes, one ancient and one modern. The first is the sequel, as Herodotus relates it, to the rise of Deioces to the kingship.

> Deioces ordered them to build him a palace worthy of a king and to guard it with spearmen. This the Medes did. They built him a large, strong palace on a site that he picked, and authorized him to select any of the Medes for his bodyguard. Once established in authority, he compelled the Medes to build a single capital city and equip and adorn it, devoting less care henceforth to other towns. In this, too, the Medes obeyed him, and thus he built the great strong fortress called Agbatana with its girdle of walls rising one above the other. . . . These fortifications Deioces built for himself—especially round his own palace—but the rest of the people he ordered to live outside the walls. When all was completed, Deioces instituted a ceremonial, the first of its kind. Nobody from outside could enter the royal quarters or see the king. All business was transacted by messengers. No one, moreover, could laugh or spit in the king's presence. The reason for surrounding himself with this solemn etiquette was to keep out of sight of his former companions who had been brought up with him, who belonged to equally good families, and who were as brave as he. For seeing him, they might resent his position and plot against him; but if he were unseen, they might think of him as being of more than common clay. With this protocol arranged and his absolutism established, he was a stern watchdog for justice. . . . If he learned of anyone waxing insolent, he would send for them and punish them according to their offense. For he kept his spies and informers up and down the country that he ruled.[23]

Much political science is compressed into this narrative. A number of human beings, suffering from anarchy, sought to improve their lot. They wished to resolve their disputes by a method that would be fair to the antagonists and by conditions that could be accepted as just. Voluntarily, they turned to one of their members, their need dovetailing with his capacity and ambitions. After repeated experience with him, they found the results they wanted. Continued acceptance of his verdicts created the strongest presumption that they were binding. In order to formalize its newfound security, the group became supporters of Deioces. By these steps the influence he had acquired was converted into power. The latter, once it was recognized and sanctioned, became authority. After this, he was entitled to enforce the law that he expounded. His decisions, compliance with

[23]Herodotus, *Histories*, i, chaps. 98–100 (my translation).

which was formerly optional, were thenceforth compulsory. Resistance or disobedience was visited with coercion.

A comparable modern case—the birth of a state and the erection of the authority to govern it—is described by one who saw it happen and contributed his share. In the *Seven Pillars of Wisdom*, T. E. Lawrence describes his experience during the first World War when he was attempting in conjunction with Feisal to instigate a revolt of the Arabs against the Turks. A major obstacle was to overcome the ancient tribal jealousies and feuds between the respective Arab chieftains and their followers. So that they would combine and not bicker at cross-purposes, they had to be persuaded to adjust their animosities, to merge themselves into a whole larger than the tribe, and accept a superior authority as binding. This was Feisal's occasion and his challenge. Lawrence thus relates it:

> Except that all its events were happy, this day was not essentially unlike Feisal's every day. . . . The roads to Wejh swarmed with envoys and volunteers and great sheikhs riding in to swear allegiance. . . . Feisal swore new adherents solemnly on the Koran between his hands "to wait while he waited, march when he marched, to yield obedience to no Turk, to deal kindly with all who spoke Arabic (whether Bagdadi, Aleppine, Syrian, or pure-blooded) and to put independence above life, family and goods." He also began to confront them at once, in his presence, with their tribal enemies, and to compose their feuds. An account of profit and loss would be struck between the parties, with Feisal modulating and interceding between them, and often paying the balance, or contributing towards it from his own funds, to hurry on the pact. During two years Feisal so laboured daily, putting together and arranging in their natural order the innumerable tiny pieces which made up Arabian society, and combining them into his one design of war against the Turks. There was no blood feud left active in any of the districts through which he had passed, and he was Court of Appeal, ultimate and unchallenged, for western Arabia. He showed himself worthy of this achievement. He never gave a partial decision, nor a decision so impracticably just that it must lead to disorder. No Arab ever impugned his judgments or questioned his wisdom and competence in tribal business. By patiently sifting out right and wrong, by his tact, his wonderful memory, he gained authority over the Nomads from Medina to Damascus and beyond. He was recognised as a force transcending tribe, superseding blood chiefs, greater than jealousies. The Arab movement became, in the best sense, national, since within it, all Arabs were at one, and for it, private interests must be set aside.[24]

There then is a picture of the growth of authority rendered possible because it was being founded on consent, with force at its disposal. Feisal met the need of the Arab tribes for a wider system of order, into which he infused his concepts of justice. Thereby his power became authority; and thereby he made history.

[24]*Seven Pillars of Wisdom* (New York: Garden City Publishing Co., 1938), chapter 30, pp. 175–76.

The Evolution of Political Ends and Governmental Means

What I am arguing is that both the ends of the state and the means of government undergo a progression. Because protection, though necessary, is not enough, human beings construct a system of order; and from order they strive for justice, because the most durable order is that which people deem just. A similar progression occurs with the techniques which government employs to fulfill these ends. The prerequisite for protection is force. But since the latter alone cannot sustain a system of order, power is generated by the admixture of force and consent. Finally, if order is to culminate in justice, power must be transmuted into authority.

Each stage, therefore, builds on, and develops beyond, the one preceding. Authority is a shell without a filling if it lacks power, and power may be flouted with impunity unless it can wield force. Justice enhances, yet depends upon, order, without which men could have no confidence or trust in each other; while order itself must be based on the protection that makes them secure. These relationships and sequences are expressed diagrammatically in figure 2.[25]

The foregoing account outlines the historical origins of government and sketches an ideal development which some states subsequently realize in practice. Manifestly it does not describe what all states are actually like or what they succeed in becoming. Many states never reach the level of justice. Some establish it for the majority only. In that case, what the majority regards as justice the minority views as a system of "law and order" imposed unjustly by majority power; the minority may then resort to force of its own, which by definition is illegal, to resist that power. Other states advance little beyond protection. Many governments are unable to convert power into authority. In others again, the blend that produces power consists of more force and less consent. How does this happen and what are the political consequences?

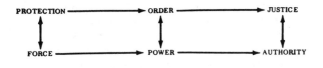

FIGURE 2

25It should be noted that even justice is not necessarily the final stage of this evolutionary development. Various modern states are striving for a further ideal that lies beyond justice. See sections of chapter 14, "From Protection to Perfection" and "Politics and the Good Life."

Abuse of Force

The ends of the state—protection, order, justice—are achieved by the means of government—force, power, or authority. It has been said that the end justifies the means. But this is untrue, because some means are so immoral that no end can justify them. The truth is rather the contrary. Because we pass moral judgments on methods and goals alike, the means can stultify the end. In the field of statecraft, especially, the implications of this are far-reaching. Perhaps more than any other institution, the state is peculiarly affected by the nature of the means it employs, and their abuse may fatally vitiate its ends. The possibility of this occurring arises from two facts already mentioned: the claim of the state to monopolize force, and the choice of representatives and officials to perform the functions of government. When these facts are combined, the result is to place this monopoly in the hands of officialdom. Thus the rest of the community may be at the mercy, or under the grip, of their own officials, since the latter have means of coercion at their fingertips. Because protection depends on the opposition of force to force, a group which has institutionalized its protection cannot avoid entrusting to officials the means of physical compulsion. But what guarantee is there that the force, which is intended to be used for the group, may not be used against it?

Plato expounded this problem in a memorable passage of the *Republic:*

> "Then we are quite clear as to what must be the bodily characteristics of our guardians?"
> "Yes."
> "And as to their mental qualities, we know they must be spirited."
> "Certainly."
> "Then, Glaucon," I said, "with such natures as these, how are they to be prevented from behaving savagely towards one another and the other citizens?"
> "By Zeus," he said, "that will not be easy."
> "Still, we must have them gentle to their fellows and fierce to their enemies. If we can't effect that, they will prevent the enemy from destroying the city by doing it first themselves."[26]

More pungently, the Roman satirist Juvenal inquired in words that have become proverbial: "But who will guard the guardians themselves?"[27] Force, like fire, can be a useful servant of mankind. But it is a dangerous master; and like fire, once out of control, it has vast potentialities for destruction. This perennial truth, had any doubted it, was proven once

---

[26]*Republic,* ii, sec. 375, p. 55, trans. A. D. Lindsay (Everyman's Library).
[27]*Sed quis custodiet ipsos custodes? Satires,* no. 6, lines 347–48.

again when mass protests and demonstrations were organized during the late 1960s. The same scenario was reenacted with horrifying similarity in Chicago and New York, Paris and Tokyo, Mexico City and Berlin. Once violence is unleashed—be this the revolutionary stratagem of dissident groups or the repressive force of established authority, or both—restraints vanish and brutality prevails. The resort to violence by private groups can never be justified, morally or politically, when it is directed against a system which offers a regular and effective constitutional procedure for encompassing change by peaceful means. But when the powers that be react by unleashing what one American report described as "a police riot," the result for the individual citizen is even worse. The police are there for the public's protection against private lawbreakers. Against police excesses, how shall we protect ourselves?

Many governments are so widely detested that they can stay in office only by policing the people under their control. This truth is borne out by the language we use in political discussion, since our words express concepts that summarize our experience. The term *police-state* signifies a regime in which coercive force predominates, where the government functions as a gendarmerie, and where it is no coincidence that the words *executive* and *executioner* stem from the same root. The regimes which fell in Teheran and Managua in 1979 had long seemed unassailable because the rulers could count on a loyal and well-equipped army. But when the power base of the Shah and Somoza crumbled, military force could not sustain them. Their opponents succeeded in massing such a counter-force, as power tilted to their side, that the Iranian Army and Nicaraguan National Guard disintegrated. Similarly when Marcos was overthrown in 1986, the climactic events which forced him to flee the country he had pillaged were the mass demonstrations in Manila by people supporting Corazon Aquino. But what finally enabled them to control the streets was the split in the army, both in the leadership and among the soldiery. Enough switched sides for a popular uprising to succeed.[28]

The Paradox of Power

Because power consists of force plus consent, the difficulties attending the use of naked force are still present when the latter is buttressed by consent to generate power. Those in power can abuse the force at their command by seeking to impose their order on the recalcitrant, and the means lie at their disposal when they are so minded. Hence the existence of force and the construction of power, which are the inescapable products of our need

---

[28]Other countries governed in the 1980s by similarly repressive regimes were—to mention only a few—Chile, Pakistan, and Poland. It will be interesting to see whether their dictatorial rulers go the way of Somoza, the Shah, and Marcos.

for protection and order, are the root-cause of government's perennial dilemma. Force and power there must be. Otherwise there can be no government; nor can some basic ends of the state be attained. But such means permit restraints upon the opponents of government, which can be extended to the point where freedom is endangered. Power is susceptible to abuse by those who possess it and is then convertible into tyranny. What originates as an instrument of service can culminate in a weapon of enslavement. Hence many of the controversies concerning the organization and functions of the state revolve around the problem of fixing limits within which power may usefully be employed and beyond which it cannot safely be increased.

As applied to power these considerations are more complex than as applied to force. That is because power includes that quota of consent which, by definition, is absent from force. If the state consisted only of a simple bisection into government and governed, its problems would at least be more clear-cut. In fact, however, all government is an eternal triangle, whose three angles are those in office, their supporters, and their opponents. Power flows from the supporters to the government, which then exercises it over both its supporters and the opposition. But what makes a vital difference in these relationships is the amount of consent that goes into power, as compared with the volume of dissent. Every government uses force and, initially at least, is supported by some consent. This is true of dictatorships as well as democracies. Lenin, Stalin, Hitler, Mussolini, and their brethren today could not have gained power or stayed on top without the support of like-minded persons who were content to do their bidding. There is an enormous difference, however, in the respective quantities of force and consent that combine into power, and in the relative importance of each. As a general rule, the broader and stronger the consent, the fewer the occasions to employ force. Conversely, wherever the apparatus of force bulks large in the machinery of government and is in constant use, it is reasonable to suppose that the supporters of government are not strong enough to control their opponents by other means. Every police state relies heavily on methods of coercion, because its rulers are not backed by enough consent and therefore have not sufficiently transformed their power into authority.

Nor should one overlook the effect on government of the lapse of time. Power, and even authority, may initially be built on a foundation of consent that is wide and deep. But as the years pass, these foundations can crack. A Deioces wins a kingdom with willing acclaim. Yet he himself in later years, or his successor, may lose support through tyrannical acts. The authority, which was once legitimate and just, can then be perverted into despotism. Temporarily, a ruler or ruling group may continue to wield power with waning consent. They succeed for a while because people at large are imbued with obedient habits, are paralyzed by inertia, and severally are inferior to the force mobilized by the ruler.[29] Once rooted, power is not easily shaken. But having consumed its initial capital of consent, it falls into the bankruptcy of despotism. Then, when the sustaining conditions of government are removed, when justice vanishes and order has to be imposed, people start inquiring into the purposes that justify the acts of government, at which point the insolvency of political pretensions is laid bare. For if the state requires force, or power, or authority to perform a service, it is the continuation of the service, and this alone, that warrants the continuation of the means.

Thus force enables a regime to outlive the consent with which it was formerly endowed. In erecting the force to serve them, people also create a technique for dominating over them. Mobilized because of their wish, that force may later be directed against their wish. This possibility reaches the extreme point when a government uses force, not to protect the governed, but to protect itself against them. In that case the rulers reveal the truth about their political situation in the architectural style of their governmental buildings. When a regime is on guard not only against external foes, but against some of its own people, it houses itself within a fortress for safety from its domestic opponents. Thus in medieval Italian cities, the ruling faction would shelter behind stout walls and equip itself with lofty watchtowers, at the same time prohibiting others from doing likewise. Observe the exterior of the famous Signoria in Florence, and what you see—allowing for the sculptural embellishment—is not a city hall but a citadel, and designed with that end in view. So have the despots of Russia and Germany dwelled in their Kremlins and their Berchtesgadens, as if in a constant state of seige. The perils of their position were understood and are described by Plato:

> "It seems to be that in our inquiry on this matter (a good and an evil life) we must get light from the following sources."
> "From which?"
> "By examining each of those rich individuals in cities who own a great number of slaves; for they have this point of similarity with tyrants, that they are rulers of many. No doubt the tyrant has the best of it in point of numbers?"
> "He has."

[29]Hence as an English philosopher pointed out in his justification of the ultimate right of a people to rebel, "People are not so easily got out of their old forms as some are apt to suggest. They are hardly to be prevailed with to amend the acknowledged faults in the frame they have been accustomed to. . . . Great mistakes in the ruling part, many wrong and inconvenient laws, and all the slips of human frailty will be borne by the people without mutiny or murmur. But if a long train of abuses, prevarications, and artifices, all tending the same way, make the design visible to the people, they cannot but feel what they lie under, and see whither they are going, it is not to be wondered that they should then rouse themselves, and endeavour to put the rule into such hands which may secure them the ends for which government was at first erected. . . ." John Locke, *Second Treatise of Civil Government*, sec. 223, 225, pp. 230–31 (Everyman's Library).

"You know, I suppose. that they live unconcernedly, and are not afraid of their servants?"

"Well, is there anything for them to fear?"

"Nothing," I said; "but do you see why that is?"

"Yes. The whole city gives assistance to each individual."

"Excellent," I said, "But suppósing one of the Gods were to take a man who possesses fifty slaves or even more and were to lift him and his wife and children out of the city and put him down with all his property and his slaves, in a desert place where there would be no free men to come to his assistance, do you not suppose that he would be in the most terrible fright in apprehension lest he and his children and his wife should be killed by their servants?"

"In the worst of frights," he answered.

"Would he not then be compelled to pay court to some of those his slaves, to make them many promises, and to set them free, quite against his desire, and stand revealed as his own servants' toady?"

"He would certainly have to do so or die," he said.[30]

Plato's insight should give us pause to reflect when we observe the spectacle of governments in the present day. We take it for granted that such conditions would prevail in Moscow, since secrecy, authoritarianism, and a conspiratorial atmosphere are ingrained in Russian tradition. But it has been a revelation and a shock to discover how far the federal government of the United States has moved in the same direction since the 1960s, a discovery made possible by investigations into the misdeeds of the Johnson, Nixon, and Reagan administrations both at home and abroad. Anybody elected President of the United States is walled off nowadays from ordinary contacts and is guarded in the White House and other encampments. One reason for this is the genuine possibility of assassination by psychotics or terrorists. Another is the psychological or political twist which happens to some incumbents so that they identify their personal survival with the national security and fortify their position by cultivating the mystique of the presidency among the public at large. At any rate, it is now known that under the Johnson and Nixon administrations the surveillance employed at home and abroad by the FBI and CIA against those whom they dubbed enemies was used domestically against political opponents, conscientious objectors, and intellectual dissenters. When those in office use such methods to stay there, democracy is being killed from within.

The Philosophy of Anarchism

The state's resort to force has often evoked an ethical revulsion that generates political consequences. Many persons of high moral ideals are so affronted by the raw brutality of the coercive apparatus of governments—of

[30]*Republic,* ix. secs. 578–79, p. 278.

the police, prisons, and army—that they veer around to a completely anti-thetical position. Any violence, they argue, used by one human being against another is not only morally wrong, but makes morality impossible. Ethical behavior has to flow freely and spontaneously; it cannot be externally imposed. Consequently, they say, an institution which insists it cannot perform its task without at times employing force is *ipso facto* immoral. The only thing to do with the state, therefore, is to abolish it along with its whole apparatus of coercion.

That, of course, is a summary of the philosophy of anarchism. It is a viewpoint that students of politics should note because it raises the question that logically comes first: Is government necessary? Anarchism, as the word signifies, is a philosophy that argues for a society without government. Its ethical values are of the highest. It prefers cooperation to competition, freedom to power, spontaneity to coercion. Assuming that human beings are naturally good, it asserts that we are driven into bad habits by our institutions and by the powerful who control them.

These doctrines commended themselves to some distinguished thinkers in the nineteenth century—for example, Godwin in Great Britain, Proudhon in France, and Thoreau in the United States. But it is significant that Russians paid the most attention to this theory and produced three of its best-known exponents: Bakunin, Tolstoi, and Kropotkin. These men had much in common. All were born of noble families; all served as young officers in the Czarist army. From this experience they emerged thoroughly alienated from their country's government.[31] It is indeed no accident that the most repressive regime in Europe should have produced such outspoken anarchists. Contrary to what the behaviorists assume, conditioning can provoke the opposite reaction.[32]

The anarchist philosophy is at its best in stressing the basic goodness of human nature and in advocating voluntary cooperation among free individuals. It is at its weakest, however, in deciding how much order such a society would require and how to treat those who break whatever rules it adopts. Communities based on anarchist principles have functioned in small groups whose members were highly motivated and idealistic and whose technology was fairly simple. Anarchism has yet to be tried in a large society with a complex technology and organization.

---

[31]Shortly after the Crimean war ended, Tolstoi expressed his feeling thus: "Human law—what a farce! The truth is that the State is a plot, designed not only to exploit but also to corrupt its citizens. For me, the laws laid down by politics are sordid lies—I shall never enter the service of any government anywhere." Tolstoi wrote this in a letter from Paris in 1857 immediately after witnessing a public execution by the guillotine. Quoted in Henri Troyat, *Tolstoi* (Garden City, N.Y.: Doubleday & Co., 1967), p. 167.

[32]As Gordon W. Allport sagely remarked: "The fire, that hardens the egg, melts the butter." The same alleged cause can produce opposite consequences.

Confusion of Politics with Power

Because force is brutal and power, once acquired, may be transformed by abuse, the essence of the state and the nature of the governmental process are often misunderstood. Every student of the state observes that it controls the organized force of the group, and we know that those who monopolize force misuse it at times and on occasion with success. These indisputable facts have led to conflicting interpretations. Because the state wields force in order to provide protection, and because force, to be effective, must be amassed as a monopoly, many regard this force not merely as the instrument by which the state operates, but as its principal characteristic. Seen from this viewpoint, the state is differentiated from other associations and is definable by virtue of its being the sole rightful monopolist of the force available within society. Max Weber, for example, wrote:

> Ultimately, one can define the modern state sociologically only in terms of the specific *means* peculiar to it, as to every political association, namely, the use of physical force. Of course, force is certainly not the normal or the only means of the state—nobody says that—but force is a means specific to the state. Today the relation between the state and violence is an especially intimate one.[33]

When so much stress is placed upon the state's exercise of force, this feature is no longer treated as a tool incidental to performing the function of protection. Instead, force is placed in the center of the analysis of the state, and the latter is then discussed in terms not of the needs it serves but of the specific method it employs. The emphasis is moved from ends to means with the result that they are reversed. What once was considered the instrument is now conceived to be the master. Instead of using force to carry out its protective function, the government is pictured as performing that function so as to maintain its capacity to coerce.

Next, the logic is extended from the narrow concept of force to the broader one of power. Because government is energized through power, the central problem of the state on this view is how to accumulate it. Politics is then considered the arena where the struggle for power is conducted; and power is no longer regarded as the tool through which other results may be accomplished, but as if it were itself the objective to be attained. Under those circumstances, the reversal of means and ends is complete. Arguments that once interpreted the state in terms of the functions it

---

[33]Max Weber, *From Max Weber: Essays in Sociology*, trans. and ed. by H. H. Gerth and C. Wright Mills (New York: Oxford University Press, 1958), pp. 77–78. Italics in original. It is a significant blind spot in the thinking of the sociologist that he could not observe any specific goal as peculiar to the state.

undertakes are twisted into justifications of the power it must employ. George Orwell has thus stated the point: "Power is not a means, it is an end. . . . The object of persecution is persecution. The object of torture is torture. The object of power is power."[34] The practices that follow from this attitude raise some crucial questions about the relation between power and ethics. If the political process is in truth a battle for might, what is its relevance to choices between right and wrong or evaluations of good and bad?

The Ethics of Power

Three views are possible, each of which has its exponents. First, power may be clothed with moral approval and upheld as good. When the accumulation of power is viewed as the goal of the state, the next step is to argue that what conduces to might is right and then to conclude that might is right. Second, power may be thought to be unconnected with moral choice. The sphere of the state and the processes of politics are deemed amoral, as having no concern with matters of right or wrong. The latter belong to a different order of inquiry, much as art is often held to exist for art's sake exempt from moral connotations. In this case it makes no sense to pass judgment on the state, except in terms of whether it succeeds in maintaining power. The third possibility is that power may be condemned as evil, on the ground that its control of force involves coercion which is morally wrong. If the state, then, is preeminently a power-wielding institution that employs force, condemnation of force leads to condemnation of the state as immoral. This value judgment is reinforced empirically by the knowledge that power is often abused and is employed in ways and for ends that affront a civilized conscience.

The three views lead to different deductions. The first results in glorifying power and the state that employs it. The second carves out spheres of interest, assigning politics to a separate compartment of life. The third seeks to combat the evils of power either by adopting the extreme position of the anarchist, who says that all coercion is morally wrong and that consequently the state must be abolished; or by upholding the less drastic view that the functions of the state had better be confined to a minimum, since the fewer they are, the less power will exist. Such divergent conclusions are made possible by the ambiguity in the concept of power. Since power combines some force with some consent, people's opinion of power will vary according to whether it is the force or the consent which appears uppermost in the compound. But divergent though they be, the various conclusions share a common origin and derive from the same

[34]*Nineteen Eighty-Four* (New York: Harcourt, Brace & World, 1949), pp. 266–67. From the speech of an Inner Party member.

premises. They spring from a preoccupation with the techniques which the state uses rather than the end it pursues, and they substitute the means for the ends as the essential criterion of the state.

Nothing has given rise to more misconceptions about the activities of government and the place of the state in society than this false emphasis with its gratuitous switching of priorities. Numerous political scientists sanction this distortion of the truth by equating politics with power and pretending that their picture of it is "value-free." Such a claim is pure fantasy since no inquiry into human society by a human being can ever eliminate the subjective element. Nevertheless, much of the research and writing by political scientists since 1950 has been dominated by categories drawn from behavioral psychologists and Weberian sociologists. Power and politics were treated as synonymous; the study of government was the analysis of "the decision-making process"; its human participants were portrayed in terms of a fictional model of a "Political Man" competing aggressively for larger amounts of power.[35] The result of this one-sided bias has been a caricature of the subject, exaggerating some of its features and omitting others. Power and politics are, of course, related, but the correct view of the relationship is this: Policy is what politics is about, and policy decisions always involve a choice among values. Power comes into politics, necessarily but secondarily, because without it no policy can take effect.[36]

To clarify the substance of politics and view it undistorted is the purpose of this book. Thus far, I have inquired into the why and wherefore of social groups and have traced the genesis and growth of the state and its government. Now begins the analysis of politics in terms of the five permanent issues which make it what it is. The next ten chapters, in pairs, will examine these issues and the would-be solutions, both classic and contemporary, which humanity has tried in the quest for civilization.

[35]Here are examples of this thinking from Harold D. Lasswell and Abraham Kaplan, *Power and Society* (Yale University Press, 1950). "Political science, as an empirical discipline, is the study of the shaping and sharing of power." p. xiv. "The *political man* (*homo politicus*) is one who demands the maximization of his power in relation to all his values, who expects power to determine power, and who identifies with others as a means of enhancing power position and potential." p. 78.

[36]Substantially the same point was made in the opening sentences of this leading editorial in the *Times* of London: "First what, then how. First look at the merits of the question, then work at the feasibility of the best solution. First study policy, then study politics. This is and always has been the basis of all good government, and bad government inevitably results from the opposite course of looking at the political pressures first and allowing them to shape the policy" (16 January 1968). In this phrasing, the concept of politics is virtually synonymous with that of power.

First Issue—Part 1

4

The Rule of Privilege

Politics is generated by relations between people. The first issue of politics, therefore, is to choose a principle to govern those relations. A state is its members. Some rule must determine whom to recognize as members and how to acquire that status. Because membership entails rights and responsibilities—or, opportunities to act in certain ways as well as duties toward others—states derive their character from the principles by which they are allotted. Inevitably, the division of society into government and governed raises questions about their mutual relations. Who, for instance, should compose the government? Are all persons qualified to serve? What rights do the governed possess? Should everybody have the same fundamental rights? Or is the community to be divided between first- and second-class citizens? Let us consider what is implied in these queries, for the answers will shape the character of the political system.

The Argument for Inequality

Broadly speaking, two answers may be distinguished. One argument assumes that governing is a specialized undertaking, which requires expert knowledge and demands more than ordinary qualities of character or mind. Government, so conceived, is not an activity appropriate to the common run. Its "secrets of empire," insofar as these may be revealed, are variously pictured. Those who consider ruling a skill which springs from intuitive imagination speak of it primarily in aesthetic terms. To them, governing is an art[1]—more or less fine. Others believe that politics should be conducted according to a body of rules which can be studied and learned. They place it under the purview of reason and label it science. Still others, interpreting life in relation to a Supreme Being or some superhuman forces, envelop their concept of politics with the aura of magic or theology. Government to them is a mystery, indeed a fragment of the greater mystery of existence. But whether art, science, or mystery, government is deemed the preserve of the chosen.

If these assumptions are accepted, certain conclusions follow. Once the process of government is viewed primarily from the standpoint of the expertise needed for its performance, only a minority of the population will be judged to meet the required standard. Otherwise, the standard set and the skill prescribed would have little meaning. Thus the chosen turn out to be few, and government becomes—in the literal Greek sense—an "oligarchy."[2]

The opposite view affirms that while the task of ruling, namely the actual choice of policies and exercise of authority, is not a job for every Tom, Dick, or Jane, they are at least competent to judge and, if necessary, to criticize what their "betters" do. Should this be conceded, the chosen few must somehow be answerable to the vulgar many. That being so, those who by definition are less wise and less worthy should nevertheless control their betters. In the long run this could imply the subordination of the few and their ultimate loss of caste. Those who shrink from such a conclusion resist inserting the wedge that cracks their logic. Not only do they argue that government must be conducted by experts, but they deny that the quality of their work can be appraised by anybody less skilled. Excluded from participation in ruling, the many cannot even be allowed to judge their rulers. The chosen few are not merely the practitioners of politics; they are also the sole judges of their own handiwork.

This argument assumes a variety of guises from crude to sophisticated. An earthy example is the remark of a Sudanese tribal chief to a British official at the time when the Sudan was administered by an Anglo-Egyptian condominium. The Britisher was explaining a new plan for holding an election among the people of his area. "Surely, this is great nonsense," said the old chief, "this talk of consulting the people and asking them to elect their representatives. If I have a valuable herd of cattle, I do

---

[1]See Jacob Burckhardt, *The Civilization of the Renaissance in Italy* (New York: Oxford University Press, 1945), where chapter 1 is entitled "The State as a Work of Art."

[2]*Oligarchy* means rule (*arche*) by the few (*oligoi*).

not ask them to elect a representative bull . . . I send a trained herdsman to watch over their welfare. Mind you, if I let them run wild, in course of time a bull will make himself the master, but only after much fighting, and in the meantime the herd will be ravaged by lions and hyenas."[3] The attitude expressed here has been common throughout history, although the statement of it is seldom as frank and ingenuous. People in the mass are seen as cattle who need a herdsman. His job is to keep them in order and protect them against predators. In any case, should there be no herdsman, the cattle will still have to submit to a master, who will inevitably be the strongest and toughest of their number.

Exactly the same thought was expressed by Thomas Carlyle:

> Aristocracy and Priesthood, a governing class and a teaching class: these two, sometimes separate, and endeavoring to harmonize themselves, sometimes conjoining as one, and the King a Pontiff King:—there did no society exist without these two vital elements, there will non exist. It lies in the very nature of man. You will visit no remotest village in the most republican country of the world, where virtually or actually you do not find these two powers at work. Man, little as he may suppose it, is necessitated to obey superiors. . . . He obeys those whom he esteems better than himself, wiser, braver; and will forever obey such; and even be ready and delighted to do it.[4]

Frederick the Great, as one might expect, proceeded from similar assumptions. "It is necessary to show the people," he said, "as one shows a sick child, what they must eat and drink." Next to this may be placed a statement of Hitler: "The parliamentary principle of decision by majority, by denying the authority of the person and placing in its stead the number of the crowd in question, sins against the aristocratic basic idea of nature."[5] Also in this category belong the doctrines of the modern Spanish philosopher José Ortega y Gasset, who asserted unequivocally that inequality is the law of social existence:

> Society is always a dynamic unity of two component factors: minorities and masses. The minorities are individuals or groups of individuals which are specially qualified. The mass is the assemblage of persons not specially qualified. . . . I uphold a radically aristocratic interpretation of history. Radically, because I have never said that human society *ought* to be aristocratic, but a great deal more than that. . . . Human society *is* always, whether it will or no, aristocratic by its very essence, to the extent that it is a society in the measure that it is aristocratic, and ceases to be such when it ceases to be aristocratic.[6]

[3]Quoted in "Cross Purposes in Egypt," *Round Table* XLIV (June 1954), p. 235.

[4]Thomas Carlyle, *Past and Present*, vol. 4, chapter 1, on "Aristocracies."

[5]*Mein Kampf* (New York: Reynal and Hitchcock, 1939), p. 103.

[6]*The Revolt of the Masses* (New York: W. W. Norton & Co., 1932), pp. 9 and 14. Italics in original.

Such statements portray a picture of human nature. The common meeting ground for all doctrines of the chosen few is that for political purposes humanity must be separated into two groups. These are distinguished by fundamental differences which are both qualitative (that is, superiors vis-à-vis inferiors) and quantitative (that is, the few vis-à-vis the many). Implied in this division is the belief that the differences among human beings include some so basic as to outweigh any resemblances. Inequality thus becomes the cardinal principle on which the relations between members of the state are patterned. Rights and duties are then apportioned, not uniformly, but according to differences in status and function. The chosen few, who constitute the ruling circle, refer to their system as an aristocracy.[7] Seen from the other side, the same appears a regime of privilege.

A Classification of Elites

Any theory of aristocracy, or advocacy of government by an elite, must face two related problems. It has first to justify the power which a few exercise over many and explain why these few are the worthier to govern. Second, it must devise a means of separating lions from lambs. This requires some criterion of inclusion in the elite and exclusion therefrom. The two problems are closely connected because the success of any justification depends largely on the nature of the criterion adopted. In practice, types of aristocracy have been numerous because so many criteria have been used. The principles invoked or used to select the chosen few and reject the inferior masses include: race, ancestry, age, sex, religion, military strength, culture, wealth, political power, and knowledge. This classification of types of elites is diagrammed in figure 3.

To avoid misunderstanding, two comments on the classification should be added. These ten criteria, though distinguishable, are not always mutually exclusive. Indeed, most elites known to history have combined two or more. For example, those of reputedly superior ancestry may also be the wealthiest; or a self-styled superior religion may be that of a conquering people who excel in military strength. Furthermore, while these criteria and their permutations differ, all have in common that they glorify inequality. To this principle all doctrines of aristocracy are inexorably committed. With those reminders, let us explore the ten criteria as postulated in theory and applied in practice.

[7]Literally, "rule by the best."

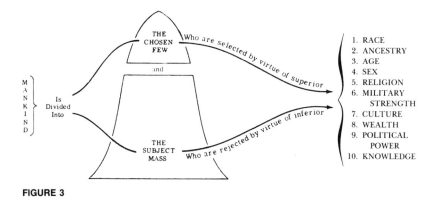

MANKIND Is Divided Into

THE CHOSEN FEW — Who are selected by virtue of superior
and
THE SUBJECT MASS — Who are rejected by virtue of inferior

1. RACE
2. ANCESTRY
3. AGE
4. SEX
5. RELIGION
6. MILITARY STRENGTH
7. CULTURE
8. WEALTH
9. POLITICAL POWER
10. KNOWLEDGE

FIGURE 3

The Myth of Racial Superiority

One way of distinguishing between human beings is to classify them into racial groups. For such distinctions to be valid, the term *race* should be defined with exactitude. Unfortunately it is often employed with a loose imprecision—sometimes innocent, sometimes deliberately misleading— which impairs its usefulness for discussion. In writing, as in daily speech, examples abound of references to "the human race," "the Negro race," "the British race," "the Jewish race," "the white race," "the Indian race," and so on. Evidently not all these usages are correct, since some include, contradict, or overlap with others. What sense can be made, for instance, of the term "British race"? If pigment be the test, then the British belong to a wider grouping of people with white skins. If the test be religion, then the British, who are overwhelmingly Christian and predominantly Protestant, can hardly be separated from other Protestant Christians. If it be language, the use of English in the British Isles (where there are many dialects and accents) does not mark off its inhabitants from the English-speaking people of the United States. If, however, the determinant be political, and "the British race" refers to a group that shares a common historical tradition and lives under the same government, the meaning becomes clearer—but then some other term, possibly *nation,* should be substituted.

Race can receive only one clear connotation, and it will be used here in that sense alone. An anthropologist has called it "a principal division of mankind, marked by physical characteristics which breed true. "In this sense," he points out, "the word race is a biological term, and is restricted to the bodily characteristics that distinguish one group of human beings from another."[8] Thus defined, one may apply the word to Caucasians,

[8]Melville J. Herskovits, *Man and His Works* (New York: Alfred A. Knopf, 1948), p. 133. A sociologist, however, points out that the anthropologists do not agree among themselves as

Mongolians, or Negroes, and to subdivisions of these main stocks; then one can discover and describe objectively the physical traits peculiar to each. When all such facts are collected and classified, what is revealed? That there are differences? Yes, but how should they be interpreted, and what is their social relevance? Admitting that differences exist, can anybody assert that one kind is the superior?

This is not possible except on one condition, namely that certain traits are demonstrably related to the better performance of certain functions. Take the human nose, for example. Since its function is to smell, if wider or longer nostrils are clearly correlated with a keener power of scent, then the superior nose is the one with greater length or breadth. But can this argument about the part be transferred to the whole? On the analogy of noses, this would be possible if human beings could be shown to have a function, in terms of humanity, which some races are better fitted to perform than others. In that case—and only then—would it be arguable that a particular race is superior or supreme, a doctrine that reaches its climax in the assertions that the inferiors are not really human but subhuman, or that the master race is made up of supermen (*Uebermenschen*).

This is exactly the reasoning that Aristotle employed to justify the institution of slavery. According to him, a person's goal or end (*telos*) is to maintain happiness by leading a life of virtue under the governance of reason. Since reason makes virtue possible, and virtue ensures happiness, anybody insufficiently endowed with reason can be neither virtuous nor happy unless placed under the control of someone who is so endowed. In this way, both masters and slaves benefit. The former, who need to own property in order to develop their potentialities, possess slaves as "animate tools."[9] The latter live the life best for them by obeying their superiors in wisdom.[10] Slavery is therefore a natural institution, because it conforms to physiological and psychological differences in human nature. The argument flows logically from premises to conclusion, if three major assumptions be accepted: that a human being, as human, has a definable function; that happiness, virtue, and reason are understood in the Aristotelian sense; and that differences between individuals, inherited at birth, are too great to be modified by learning afterward.

---

to precisely which physical criteria constitute a race. Conceding that race "is fundamentally a biological concept," he argues that, in terms of social relevance, a group may be thought to be a race even though, in scientific fact, it is not. "Thus," Professor Herbert Blumer suggests, "it would seem that a reasonably accurate, realistic and workable concept of race is that it is a class or group of human beings who are regarded and treated in social life as a distinctive biological group with a common ancestry." See his "Reflections on Theory of Race Relations" in *Race Relations in World Perspective*, ed. Andrew W. Lind (Honolulu: University of Hawaii Press, 1955), pp. 3 and 5.

[9]*Politics*, i, chapter 4, sec. 2.

[10]Ibid., chapter 5, sec. 9.

Apart from its interest as a theoretical exercise in logic, the argument's political importance lies in the efforts made to apply such principles in practice, or rather in the attempts of those who discriminate anyway to borrow from Aristotle the color of justification and respectability. While virtually every historical period, continent, and civilization yields its harvest of examples, some of the most significant may be gleaned from the nineteenth and twentieth centuries. The enslavement of human beings was permitted by law in the British Empire until 1833; in Russia, where it assumed the form of serfdom, until 1861; in the United States until 1863; in Brazil until 1888. In the decade or so before the American Civil War, the South's defense of its "peculiar institution" was often couched in Aristotelian terms which confidently asserted the permanent inferiority of one human group to another. At the close of the nineteenth and beginning of the twentieth centuries, when colored peoples stirred restlessly in resentment at the imposition of alien white rule, some European and American writers reaffirmed a belief in racial differences and their own preordained supremacy. Such was the spirit of Rudyard Kipling's ballad *The White Man's Burden,* or his *England's Answer* where he wrote:

> Truly ye come of The Blood; slower to bless than to ban;
> Little used to lie down at the bidding of any man. . . .
> Thus for the good of your people—thus for the Pride of the Race.[11]

A similar attitude inspired the Frenchman De Gobineau and two American writers, Madison Grant and Lothrop Stoddard.

But it is a twentieth-century German who has earned the fame of formulating the doctrine in its starkest manner and applying it the most thoroughly. Before seizing power, Adolf Hitler had written:

> Any crossing between two beings of not quite the same high standard produces a medium between the standards of the parents. . . . But such a mating contradicts Nature's will to breed life toward a higher level. The presumption for this does not lie in blending the superior with the inferior, but rather in a complete victory of the former. The stronger has to rule and he is not to amalgamate with the weaker one, that he may not sacrifice his own greatness. . . . Just as little as Nature desires a mating between weaker individuals and stronger ones, far less she desires the mixture of a higher race with a lower one, as in this case her entire work of higher breeding, which has perhaps taken hundreds of thousands of years, would tumble at one blow. . . . What we see before us of human culture today, the results of art, science and techniques, is almost exclusively the creative product of the Aryan. . . . For the formation of higher cultures, the existence of inferior men was one of the most essential presumptions because they alone were able to replace the lack of technical means without which a higher development is unthinkable. The

[11]From *The Seven Seas* by Rudyard Kipling. Reprinted by permission of Mrs. George Bambridge and Doubleday & Company.

first culture of mankind certainly depended less on the tamed animal, but rather on the use of inferior people.[12]

For more than a decade, while the National Socialists ruled Germany, these beliefs were promulgated as the official policy of the government of a major European state. In their name were enacted the so-called Nuremberg laws, prescribing the conditions of citizenship and proscribing all marriages between those of "superior" and "inferior" blood. In their name were committed atrocities against people of the Jewish religion which resulted in the mass extermination of six million Jews. In their name the German government prepared and unleashed a war for the domination of Europe, in which millions of Europeans and Americans perished.

Since the downfall of that regime, another country has emerged into notorious prominence because of a government that officially promotes the supremacy of one racial group over the rest. In the Republic of South Africa the dominant race is of European ancestry, but it counts for one-seventh of the country's population.[13] This group is itself subdivided into a majority (approximately three-fifths) who speak Afrikaans and a minority whose language is English. The former are the descendants of Protestants who emigrated from the Netherlands, France, and Germany in the second half of the seventeenth century. The forebears of the latter came to South Africa during the nineteenth century after Britain annexed the Cape at the end of the Napoleonic Wars. The past relations of Afrikaners and British were so bitter that they led to two wars, the second of which ended in 1902. Among the seeds of discord—besides differences in Protestantism, economic technology, and political outlook—was a contrast of attitudes toward the Africans, analogous in some ways to those of white Americans toward Negroes in North and South during the nineteenth century. Irreconcilable Afrikaner nationalists never forgave the British for emancipating their slaves and for conquering the two independent Republics to which they had "trekked" in the interior.[14]

The racial majority in South Africa, 73 percent of the whole, is composed of Africans. Of the indigenous peoples, the Bushmen and Hottentots have virtually disappeared, but the Zulus survive in strength in the province of Natal where they are concentrated. Elsewhere, the contemporary African population consists mainly of Bantu-speaking peoples, descendants of tribes which migrated to the southern part of the continent. In

---

[12]*Mein Kampf*, pp. 390, 392, 397, 404, 405.

[13]The population of South Africa in the late 1980s totaled some thirty-four millions. There were twenty-five million blacks, five million whites, three millions of mixed race, and one million Indians.

[14]The constitution of the South African Republic contained a clause that read: "The people desire to permit no equality between coloured people and the white inhabitants of the country, either in church or state." Quoted in Alexander Brady, *Democracy in the Dominions* (University of Toronto Press, 1947), p. 307.

addition, there are nowadays some three million persons of mixed race, designated officially as Colored and clustered in the Cape Province. Finally there are one million Indians whose forebears were brought to Natal by the British to labor on the sugar plantations.

In this divided country, only the Europeans enjoy full political rights. Since 1948 the Nationalist party, representing the majority of the Afrikaners, has won every election and has continuously controlled the government. Its major policy has been to organize society in terms of a policy of racial separation which was called *apartheid*. Based on assigning a racial classification to every human being, including those of mixed race, this policy proceeded to segregate the different races and assign to each its status in the political system, in the economy, and in social groupings. Some forms of segregation were horizontal, in the sense that the rights and opportunities allotted to certain groups made them inferior, while others were superior. The other forms were vertical, in the sense that physical distance was imposed through the requirements that only persons of a particular race could reside in designated areas. As it was carried out, *apartheid* in principle spelled white supremacy in practice, since the whites alone directed the separation and determined the lines of division. That supremacy was continued in the constitutional revision of 1983, which created a Parliament of three houses balanced by an independently selected and powerful president. The three chambers are reserved, respectively, for whites, coloreds, and Asians. There is none for Africans. And, to be doubly sure, the President is chosen by an electoral college, 50 of whose 88 members must be white. Increasingly, therefore, as the minority attempts to perpetuate its privileges, the South African government functions as a repressive police-state. Since the 1970s, the immorality of these policies and the murderous ferocity displayed in enforcing them have become an international issue, stirring the conscience of most of humanity. Impelled by the politics of fear, a small band of backward-looking bigots defies the movement of modern world history and prepares its own ultimate disaster.[15]

But the sin of racial arrogance is no monopoly of whites. Each race, it seems, fashions its idea of excellence after its own kind. Chinese and Japanese spokesmen have pronounced that yellow-skinned people are racially superior to others. Similar notions have not been lacking among the redskins. The Western poet[16] who wrote so condescendingly about "the poor Indian" and his "untutored mind" would have been astonished to learn that at least some Indians believed the reverse. Among the Cherokees, whose knowledge of mankind extended to Europeans and Negroes, this myth is related about the origin of races. The Great Spirit created human

---

[15]This critical account of South Africa's Nationalist regime was first written, with some of the same wording, in this book's second edition, published in 1960.

[16]Alexander Pope, in the *Essay on Man.*

beings out of dough, modeling three figures which he put in an oven. Overanxious to see the results, he opened the door and took out the first figure too soon. It was whitish, half-baked, unattractive. But the act was irrevocable, and a white race descended from the sorry specimen. Next he drew out his masterpiece, a figure perfectly cooked to a rich reddish-brown, which of course became the progenitor of the redskins. So proudly did he admire his handiwork that he forgot all about number three, until alas! he smelled something burning. Too late, he removed it from the oven, a blackened cinder—ancestor of the Negroes.[17]

The Aristotelian assertion that by nature some are masters and others are slaves lends itself too readily to the Nazi perversion: "All that is not race in this world is trash."[18]

The Cult of Ancestors

The doctrine which divides human beings into superiors and inferiors by virtue of inborn physical and psychological differences may take another form. The emphasis can be placed on a person's family, rather than on race. In other words, the line of division between human beings is still surveyed in terms of hereditary factors which are transmitted at birth and supposedly are not acquired or modified afterward; but a smaller group, the family, is substituted for the larger one of race. According to this thinking, it is a person's lineage or pedigree that counts. The merits of one's ancestors, rather than of one's own self, may secure a lofty position in the social order for a person without effort on his or her part; or they may assign a lowly status despite an individual's abilities.[19] The lions and lambs become the high-born and low-born, the aristocrats and masses.

When an elite is so constituted, one must distinguish its central feature from the attendant consequences. The central fact is the perpetuation of an aristocracy over successive generations by the hereditary principle. A group of families recognize each other, and are accepted by the rest, as members of a privileged circle. In any one generation the odds are heavily against the demotion of any of these families or the admission of a new one. At the outset, of course, and before its hereditary character becomes fixed,[20] such a system must originate in some alternative scheme of differ-

---

[17]The story, cited in Herskovits's *Man and His Works*, pp. 68–69, was reported by a Belgian anthropologist. The identical theme has also been found among the brown-skinned Malayans.

[18]*Mein Kampf*, p. 406.

[19]See chapter 5. The connection between the concepts of aristocracy and lineage is revealed in the Spanish word *hidalgo*, and the corresponding Portuguese *fidalgo*, meaning a "nobleman." The former is an abbreviation of *hijo de algo;* the latter of *filho de algo.* Both expressions mean "son of a Somebody."

[20]For the example of Venice, see the section in this chapter entitled "Money Power."

entiation. Those families which eventually emerge as superior may have succeeded earlier in accumulating greater wealth or conducting a conquest. Thereby they win an advantage which they pass on by inheritance. Furthermore the members of a family within the charmed circle can amass possessions through social influence, just as they may enhance their personal abilities because of their opportunities and experience. In judging the merits of a hereditary aristocracy, however, one is not primarily concerned with their wealth, their powers, their polish, or their knowledge of affairs. These factors are either the cause or the consequence of the point that is really in issue: the acceptance of kinship as the determinant of one's social status.

The basic assumption of such an aristocracy is the belief that planned, selective breeding among human beings can produce characteristics that parents will transmit to their offspring, so that a "higher" type may evolve. Whether this view be true or not only the specialist in genetics will venture to assert. The student of politics, however, can affirm that no actual aristocracy ever conformed to this ideal. Indeed, if experience warrants any hypothesis, it can as well support the contrary. The aristocracies that survived the longest were those like the Roman and British, who accepted periodic or continuous infusion of new stock, while once-famous lines, like the Hapsburgs or Bourbons, have run to seed from excessive inbreeding. But, apart from genetic difficulties, the hereditary principle involves social consequences that are open to major objections. One of these is its rigid application to highly variable circumstances. The principle ignores the fact that no one stratum of society has a monopoly of great ability and that its reproduction in successive generations cannot be guaranteed. A second obnoxious feature is its system of ancestor worship, which classifies the living, not for what they are, but for what their forefathers were. Too often has the luster of a noble house conferred an inflated valuation upon an ignoble scion. Too often have the talents of those less fortunately born been denied creative outlets. To base distinctions on heredity is to predetermine the lives of all by a criterion in no way related to personal effort or exertion. One's parentage cannot be chosen, altered, or escaped.

Be this as it may, examples of the hereditary elite may be found in all periods of history and all parts of the world. The Homeric poems, which mix fact and fiction in one of our earliest literary pictures of a European society, relate the deeds of a cluster of eminent families acknowledged in war and peace as the leaders of the Hellenic World. Their prerogatives come to them by right of birth, and, since their lineage is illustrious, they may be addressed by their own name (for example, Achilles, Agamemnon, Odysseus) or by the patronymic (Son of Peleus, Son of Atreus, Son of Laertes).[21] The same status that accords them rights also imposes duties.

---

[21] All of these are kings (*basileis*). But kingship has degrees, and some chiefs are kinglier than others (*basileuteroi*), and Agamemnon is kingliest of all (*basileutatos*).

Chieftains are under obligation to be champions of the army and fight in the front line. They receive the greater rewards of an exalted position, but run the greater risks. And what of the rank and file? They are the ever-present background, but nameless and nondescript. If individualized at all, they appear in the favorable role of the faithful and humble servant (for example, the swineherd Eumaeus, who stays loyal to his master Odysseus). Only once does Homer portray them in protest, and in that single instance he offers an unflattering characterization. Thersites, criticizing Agamemnon in the council of the chiefs, voices the first revolt of the underdog in western writing. For this the poet, who sang of and to the high-born, has him thrashed by Odysseus while the onlookers jeer.[22]

In subsequent centuries, for which more exact information is available, the same pattern recurs of a ruling aristocracy that faces an acquiescent or at times rebellious populace. Athens was controlled until the seventh century B.C. by an oligarchy of families known as the Eupatridae ("of good parentage"). Most of the other Greek city-states never evolved beyond this to the somewhat more equalitarian society and politics that appear in the Athens of the fifth and fourth centuries. In the Roman Republic the most momentous domestic controversy of the fifth, fourth, and third centuries B.C. was the Struggle of the Orders which has enshrined the names *patricians* and *plebeians* in our everyday vocabulary. The gulf between the two consisted of differences in social status, civil rights, religious ceremonial, and political power. The aim of the plebeians was to abolish privileges in which they did not share and to win equality. But, even when this was achieved, the grant to the plebeians of substantial equality with the patricians reformulated, rather than terminated, the domination of Rome by an aristocracy. Certain plebeian families were admitted to the clique of dominant clans, who monopolized for themselves and passed around among their own number the principal offices (*honores*) of the Roman Republic. Once anybody was elected to a major office, he and his family became ennobled (*nobilis*). Within the nobility so constituted, families were scaled in importance by the number of such officeholders they had produced; they were conventionally ranked as praetorian, consular, or censorian according to whether the highest office reached by one of their members was that of *praetor, consul,* or *censor.* Thus by the second century B.C. the odds were as strongly in favor of a Marcellus, Claudius, Julius, or Metellus to secure the office he desired, as they were against a "new man" (*novus homo*) from a family outside the *nobilitas.* Cicero, the orator without equal in Rome, relates with complacent pride that he was the first new man in a long time to break through the barriers and obtain a consulate.[23]

---

[22]Homer, *Iliad*, ii, lines 211 ff. Similarly unsympathetic portrayals of spokesmen for the underprivileged are the pictures of Cleon (the fifth-century Athenian) by Aristophanes and Thucydides, and that of Jack Cade in Shakespeare's *Henry VI.*

[23]He did so, however, as spokesman for the *Optimates,* the self-styled "best people."

Whatever variation there may be in detail, the common feature in this type of political organization is the division of the population into two classes. One is composed of relatively few members, the other contains the great majority, and the smaller group dominates the larger. Membership in each class is hereditary. Only rarely does movement occur upward into the preferred class or downward into the lower. Such a division of society into two levels is in many instances an oversimplification. A cross section of certain communities would show three strata and sometimes more. In fact, the entire community may be organized on the pattern that is common in a priesthood or the military, with a ladder of ranks on which people are assigned their places in a hierarchy. A familiar example of this is the system which evolved in western Europe after the strife and turmoil following the dissolution of the Roman Empire, namely, feudalism. Its essential feature was to erect a fabric of personal relationships on the basis of land ownership and tenure. The relations of men to land governed the relations of men to men. A man received land as a fief from another, to whom he swore an oath of fealty. The two thus became lord and vassal; and while it was the responsibility of the lord to protect his vassal, the latter's duty was to serve the former. This system of horizontal stratification was applied to both the spheres, temporal and ecclesiastical, into which medieval Christendom was vertically split. But though government was hierarchical in state and church alike, the ecclesiastical elite was saved from being hereditary by the rule of celibacy. A social order so built, and extended in principle to the universe, is eloquently sketched by Shakespeare in *Troilus and Cressida*.[24] The same notion is defended by the Victorian British philosopher A. C. Bradley, who wrote approvingly on the theme: "My Station and Its Duties."[25]

Submission to the Elders

Along with race and ancestry, two further methods for discriminating between human beings and assigning them a superior or inferior political status may be mentioned: namely, age and sex.

The idea that the right to govern is a prerogative of age has underlain the practice of many communities. It is associated with the belief that ruling is an art involving mature judgment; that this is largely acquired by experience; and that older persons necessarily possess an experience that is longer, riper, and therefore more trustworthy. In addition, a system which entrusts government to the aged because of their age is normally built upon a social base that attaches great importance to the family and, within

[24]*Troilus and Cressida* 1, 3, 75 pp.
[25]*Ethical Studies* (1876).

the family, stresses the authority of the father. The rule of the Elders is patriarchy writ large.

Examples are not lacking of political institutions whose *raison d'être* was to embody the authority of age. In a primitive community such a system is thus described by J. G. Frazer:

> Let us begin by looking at the lowest race of men as to whom we possess comparatively full and accurate information, the aborigines of Australia. These savages are ruled neither by chiefs nor kings. So far as their tribes can be said to have a political constitution, it is a democracy or rather an oligarchy of old and influential men, who meet in council and decide on all measures of importance to the practical exclusion of the younger men. Their deliberative assembly answers to the senate of later times: if we had to coin a word for such government of elders we might call it a *gerontocracy*. The elders who in aboriginal Australia thus meet and direct the affairs of their tribe appear to be for the most part the headmen of their respective totem clans.[26]

But the authority of age is by no means confined to the primitive. In the government of Sparta there was a powerful body called the *Gerousia,* or "Council of Old Men," membership in which commenced at the age of 60. More celebrated is the Roman Senate, a word that means the same as *Gerousia.* Composed of past and present holders of the higher offices in the Republic, for over four centuries this body was the nuclear force in the government of Rome. Likewise, the institutions of the Anglo-Saxon tribes distinguished between the Folkmoot, or meeting of male citizens, and the influential Witanagemot, or council of wise men who were the tribal elders. Modern Japan under its Meiji Constitution (adopted 1889) developed a similar council of elders, called the *Genro.* To it belonged the senior statesmen who had twice held the office or premier. The Genro acted informally as a consultative body to which the emperor might turn for advice about the formation of a new government or issues of high policy. Such indeed was the traditional Japanese respect for age that even the emperor was reluctant to give directions to an older man.[27] On this point, it is worth noting that the Constitution of the United States prescribes an age of 35 as the minimum for the presidential office. Political practice in the twentieth century, however, has added almost 20 years to that figure. Even allowing for John F. Kennedy, who was only 43 when inaugurated, the average age of the 16 presidents from McKinley to Reagan at the time of assuming office was 56. During the same period in the United Kingdom, 18 persons

---

[26]James G. Frazer, *The Golden Bough,* part I, vol. I, 3rd ed. (New York: The Macmillan Co., 1919–1935), p. 335. Italics in original. *Gerontocracy* means "government by the aged."

[27]"Baron Harada records that the emperor wished to speak to Prince Konoye, apparently to give him some advice, but was hesitant to do so directly. Remarked the emperor, 'After all, he is older than I, so I cannot very well order him specifically: "do this" or "do that"'" *Saionji Harada Memoirs,* 3 Sept. 1936, p. 1590. Quoted in Yale Maxon, *Control of Japanese Foreign Policy* (Berkeley: University of California Press, 1957), p. 4.

have served as premier from Salisbury to Thatcher; their average age when they first began their duties was also 56.

Only rarely in the past did an opportunity come to anybody under 35 to offer leadership in government. Exceptions were possible when the hereditary principle brought a younger person to the throne, or when a monarch deliberately selected somebody young as a first minister, or when a revolution catapulted new talents into the seats of power. Thus, Alexander the Great became king of Macedon at the age of 20. At his death, 13 years later, he was master of the entire region from Greece to what is nowadays Pakistan. Elizabeth I became queen of England and Wales when she was only 25 and quickly demonstrated her extraordinary capacity for statecraft. George III appointed the younger Pitt to be prime minister when he was 24, doubtless expecting he had found a pliant tool, but, as it turned out, misjudging his man. Thomas Jefferson was 33 years old when he wrote the Declaration of Independence, while Alexander Hamilton was 30 when he helped to draft the Constitution of the United States.

Since 1960, both the Kennedy phenomenon and the impact of the youth revolution have affected politics. One result is that some democracies have lowered the voting age. Another is the election to public office of persons considerably younger than used to be normal. The example of John F. Kennedy may have been of some help to Harold Wilson, who was 48 (well below the average) when first holding office as Prime Minister of Great Britain, and possibly to Pierre Trudeau, who became Canada's Prime Minister at the age of 49, and Olof Palme, Prime Minister of Sweden at 42. Likewise, at the municipal level, the number of men and women under 35 elected as city councillors or as mayors has markedly increased—although these still remain a small percentage of the total.

The Unfair Sex

More pervasive and more deeply rooted than distinctions based on age have been those derived from sex. Although anthropological research has established the existence of matriarchal societies, patriarchy has been the conventional mode of family organization. Politics, similarly, has normally been the function or monopoly of the menfolk. This was probably due to the primary connection between government and defense, which endows the able-bodied male with importance. But it is also to be explained in terms of the social specialization that assigned childrearing and domestic matters to the female and took the male out of the house as the hunter, farmer, or breadwinner. For over 3000 years the traditional forms of Western society excluded women from active participation in government, save when the operation of the hereditary principle conferred a crown upon one who reigned as queen in her own right. Not until the twentieth century did the fair sex begin effectively to challenge the monopoly of government by the unfair. Not until the second half of this century was it politically possible for a woman to become head of a government through a democratic process, as has now happened in Britain, India, Norway, Israel, and elsewhere.

Societies which discriminate on grounds of sex are open to the same objection as those based on heredity. They classify half the population as politically adequate or inadequate in an arbitrary manner since they assume a connection between fitness for government and factors which may not be relevant. Even if it were true that in most societies the men traditionally did most of the work outside the home and thus acquired an experience denied to women, it does not follow that any male is fit to govern or that all females are unfit. The belief that no woman has a talent for politics is a false presumption based on nothing better than male vanity or prejudice. Who could argue thus about Queen Elizabeth I or Catherine the Great, or for that matter, about Prime Minister Golda Meir? What makes for capacity in government is the talent of the individual, whether man or woman, as developed by the opportunities which society affords to gain experience. Indeed, the only appropriate criticism one could level against any of the queens and prime ministers just mentioned is not that they failed in exercising the arts of government, but that they imitated the techniques of power traditionally used by males and failed to raise politics to a higher level of values.

The principles examined thus far are race, ancestry, age, and sex. These factors have been discussed first because they differ from the remainder of the list in that they lie beyond our control. We cannot choose our race, ancestry, age, or sex; and though one's age changes during a lifetime, the process of growing old and the rate of change lie beyond our power. A community can decide whether it will distinguish politically between a few superior members and an inferior majority. If it does so, it can also decide whether to select one of these four principles as the criterion of division. But once such a choice is taken and one of these criteria is adopted, an individual has no say about the place to which he or she is assigned and no means of influencing the assignment. The application of the rule to particular cases cannot be modified, still less overruled, by the efforts of the person concerned or the discretion of others.

In the classification of elites presented earlier in this chapter, ten types were listed. Those yet to be considered are religion, military strength, culture, wealth, political power, and knowledge. These criteria differ from the preceding in that a community selecting its ruling elite by such methods makes it possible for individuals to join the charmed circle by their own volition and exertion.

Discrimination through Religion

Religion belongs in this discussion because, when institutionalized, it produces social consequences. Many are the instances where organized religion has sanctified a separation into upper and lower castes or classes. Sometimes theology appears to have been responsible for introducing a stratification and then solidifying the strata with divine cement. One such case is the effect upon Vedic India of the invasion of Aryans from the West who brought to a darker-skinned people the creed of Brahmanism and Hinduism.[28] Under its impact, Indian society was grouped into the four classes of Brahman, Kshatriya, Daishya, and Sudra—a hierarchy in descending order of priests, rulers, artisans, and slave-laborers. These became the hereditary castes which prescribed an individual's occupation and social status. The fourfold grading was based upon an authoritative text of the Hindu scriptures.[29]

At other times, religions whose creeds were fundamentally equalitarian have condoned and conformed to preexisting social cleavages which they helped to reinforce and justify. For example, the spirit of the Christian religion in its pure form emphasizes equality,[30] since affairs of the soul are held to be more important than those of the body, and all souls are deemed equally worthy in the eyes of God. But when the Emperor Constantine embraced Christianity as the official religion of the Roman Empire, the church accepted—for this world—the existence of a hierarchical society which included the institution of slavery. Similarly the medieval church tolerated serfdom. As R. H. Tawney has written:

> The canon law appears to have recognized and enforced serfdom. Few prominent ecclesiastics made any pronouncement against it. Aquinas explains it as the result of sin, but that does not prevent his justifying it on economic grounds. Almost all medieval writers appear to assume it or excuse it. Ecclesiastical landlords, though perhaps somewhat more conservative in their methods, seem as a whole to have been neither better nor worse than other landlords. . . . The disappearance of serfdom . . . was part of a general economic movement, with which the Church had little to do, and which churchmen, as property-owners, had sometimes resisted. It owed less to Christianity than to the humanitarian liberalism of the French Revolution.[31]

Correspondingly, the catechism of the Church of England in the eighteenth century gave its blessing to the division of society into classes;

[28]The word *Hindu* is not indigenously Indian. It came from Iran with the invaders, being a variant of the Iranian river name *Sindhu*.

[29]*Rigveda, x*, hymn 90, verse 12.

[30]See chapter 5, section on "The Classical Roots of the Doctrine of Equality."

[31]R. H. Tawney, *Religion and the Rise of Capitalism* (New York: Harcourt, Brace & World, 1926), chapter 1, "The Medieval Background," sec. 3, "The Ideal and the Reality."

serfdom was fully sanctioned by the Russian Orthodox church; slavery was defended by the southern branches of some American churches in the 1840s and 1850s, as it was also approved in South Africa by the Dutch Reformed church.

In the nineteenth century persons of liberal outlook who espoused the cause of equality found themselves in opposition to a trio of institutions which together defended their vested interest in privilege: the army, the nobility, and the church. In the Hapsburg Empire, for example, the leadership of the Catholic church was closely identified with the principles of legitimacy, autocracy, and monarchy, and the preservation of a stratified society. Likewise in France, the church, which had been a main pillar of the *ancien régime*, consistently resisted the Revolution and republicanism throughout the vicissitudes of constitutional change. Along with the king and the aristocratic landowners, it stood to lose its privileges whenever *liberté, égalité, et fraternité* should triumph. So too, in Spain, amid a social order of profound inequalities, the ecclesiastical hierarchy adhered to the old ways from which it had derived great power and profit. Dostoevsky chooses sixteenth-century Seville as the setting for his *exposé* of the power of the church, exercised at its most barbaric in the Inquisition. The Cardinal, who is Grand Inquisitor, states his contempt for ordinary humanity who willingly surrender their freedom to become the worshipful slaves of those who give them bread.[32] As aptly could the novelist have depicted the Orthodox church in his own Russia. Late in the Czarist regime, one of its highest officials, a procurator of the Holy Synod, penned his philosophy in a book that contains the frankest expression of an elitist outlook toward the mass of mankind.[33]

Religion may lend itself to the political stratification of humanity in other ways as well. Sometimes the group controlling the government is closely identified with an ecclesiastical organization which maintains that it alone has the true faith, and that nonbelievers cannot commune on terms of equality with the faithful. Those who profess an alternative faith may then find themselves relegated to a position of political inferiority and be denied equality of rights. In Britain the Protestant nonconformists who dissented from the Church of England were so treated from 1689 to 1828, as were Catholics until 1829. In other countries Catholics have meted out similar treatment to Protestants by imposing disabilities or inflicting persecution on those regarded as heretics. Jews, even when not subject to

---

[32]*The Brothers Karamazov*, part 2, book V, chapter 5.

[33]See K. P. Pobyedonostseff, *Reflections of a Russian Statesman*, trans. R. C. Long (London: Grant Richards, 1898), p. 44. "The prevalent doctrine of the perfection of Democracy and of democratic government, stands on the same delusive foundation. This doctrine presupposes the capacity of the people to understand subtleties of political science which have a clear and substantial existence in the minds of its apostles only. Precision of knowledge is attainable only by the few minds which constitute the aristocracy of intellect; the mass, always and everywhere, is *vulgus*, and its conceptions of necessity are vulgar."

pogroms and inquisitions, were normally denied equality of status in Christian countries until the nineteenth century. As for Islam—a word which means submission, to the will of Allah and the revelations of Muhammad—a sharp line is drawn between the true believer and infidel. Against the latter, holy war (*jihad*) must be waged.

Not without cause did the Roman poet Lucretius, after recounting the myth of Agamemnon's sacrifice of his own daughter to appease an angry Goddess, draw up the bitter indictment: "To so much evil could men be persuaded by religion."[34]

Control by Conquest

Government by physical might appears to be sharply contrasted with government by divine right. Yet for purposes of our present classification, the two belong to the same category, since both have the result of separating humanity into superiors and inferiors. Because of the intimate bond between the need for protection and the origin of government, prowess in war has frequently served as a basis for inclusion in the favored few.[35] A community in constant fear or suspicion of hostile neighbors in an area where terrain and topography offer no natural barriers for defense is likely to place a premium on fighting ability. Whoever excels in the military art will be accorded privileges and can exact obedience. No dividing line then exists between the military and civil sectors of government. Or rather, it is the military that absorbs and embraces the civil. Service in the armed forces becomes not merely a vocation or career, but a high road to social influence and political power.

But the dominance of the military can degenerate into the excesses of militarism. The history of Prussia yields a classic illustration of this danger. Living in an exposed position in the center of the north European plain, with no secure frontier to west or east, the Prussians traditionally thrust outward or were hemmed inward according to the relation of their striking power to that of their French and Slavic neighbors. By tight organization and by building an efficient army, the landowning Junkers contrived to be strong and secure. But the tool they had forged for safety became the instrument of their own disaster. The officers of the general staff and a succession of authoritarian rulers took the bit between their teeth. Fostering a spirit of militaristic expansion, they plunged through wars of aggression to their own and their people's destruction.

[34]*Tantum religio potuit suadere malorum. De Rerum Natura* (Of the Nature of Things), book 1, 1. 101.

[35]See the characterization of the Condottieri as state-builders in fifteenth-century Italy by Jacob Burckhardt, *The Civilization of the Renaissance in Italy*, chapter 1. Japanese history provides a similar case in point. The Shogunate was originally a military form of government; and the hereditary warriors, the *Samurai*, were a dominant influence in government from the eleventh to the fifteenth centuries.

Although it is the need for protection that brings a community to accept the authority of military experts, in yet another way the practice of warfare results in differentiation between human beings. The victors may follow up their conquest by imposing their rule upon the vanquished. Thus the weak are subordinated to the strong; and the latter, if they seek to maintain their rule, must preserve their military power.[36] A notorious example was the ancient Greek state of Sparta. The people whose discipline has become a byword were trained under the regimen, and lived in the manner, of an army barracks. Their fighting qualities, of legendary renown in the Greek world, were displayed at their finest in the heroism of Leonidas and the Four Hundred, holding the narrow pass at Thermopylae against the invading Persian multitude. But what is significant about the Spartans is that they employed in their domestic affairs the kind of organization appropriate to an army in the field. The reason was that they never lived entirely at peace, but always in a condition of suspended or expectant warfare. The Spartans migrated into Greece later than other Greeks and made their home in the Peloponnese when it was already occupied. They took their "living space" by force, and reduced the earlier inhabitants, Messenians by name, to the level of serfs, or *Helots.*[37] From that time, under the compulsion of their own policy and in fear of their subjects who outnumbered them, the Spartans militarized their mode of life and stayed permanently on guard against uprisings. The government maintained a secret organization (*Krupteia*), the equivalent of a Gestapo, whose duty it was to forestall revolt. On one occasion during the Peloponnesian War the *Krupteia* was responsible for the sudden rounding up and slaughtering at night of several hundred *Helots.* Such methods were incapable of doing more than prolonging a static despotism, where the master people eventually succumbed to internal dry rot. By contrast, the most successful empires of history are those like the Roman and the British, which, though founded in large part by force, subsequently developed the policy of elevating subjects to partners, and which, in the case of Britain, upheld at home the supremacy of civilians over the military.

The Claims of Cultural Leadership

Military conquest may be accomplished by one people at the expense of another who differ from them in culture as well as in fighting capacity. In this case the conquerors may assert their right to rule the conquered by virtue of their cultural, as distinct from their military, superiority. Used in this context the term *culture* requires explanation. It is perhaps best under-

---

[36]This is a further illustration of the point discussed in chapter 3, section on "Abuse of Force," that the force required for protection may be perverted by abuse. Internally, it takes the form of despotism; externally, of aggressive conquest.

[37]From a word meaning "captive."

stood in contrast to the term *race,* with which it is frequently, and erroneously, confused. Race,[38] properly defined, describes those human traits which are inborn and derive from heredity, while culture refers to other characteristics acquired by learning after birth and representing the influence of the environment on the individual. To anthropologists and sociologists, culture means the whole way of life of a person or group. To them it is the broadest of categories, embracing all aspects of social organization—political, economic, religious, and the rest. A political scientist, however, may be content with a less inclusive formula, one that excludes politics, economics, and religion, which are more conveniently treated as distinct categories. What remains is culture.

What is there in this remainder that is politically relevant? Among the social elements which constitute a culture are the family system, the principles and content of education, and the language which people speak and write. The relation that these bear to politics may be viewed from two angles. To the extent that people share the same family system and education and speak a common language, they belong to one community. The sense of social identity that flows from their awareness of this fact can contribute to political union. Probably the ingredient in culture closest to politics is language. Since language among literate peoples supplies the medium for transmitting and communicating the shared experiences of a group, a people's literature becomes a deposit of its history. Writers, therefore (no less than statesmen, soldiers, or prophets), can be venerated as heroes. Such is the position of Shakespeare among Englishmen, Dante among Italians, Cervantes among Spaniards, Goethe among Germans, and Pushkin among Russians.

Viewed internally, however, the features that unite a group into a community serve also to separate it from any other group that builds its families and education around different patterns and speaks another tongue. In this case, pride in one's culture may develop into the feeling that one's own is a better culture than some other from which it happens to differ. It has commonly resulted from such attitudes that an alien ruling group has based its right to govern upon the asserted superiority of its culture and that sometimes it seeks to suppress the culture which it considers inferior. Consider the treatment of Aztecs and Incas by the Spaniards, or that of Chinese by the Manchus. Prior to the 1918 the Austrians had similar attitudes toward the Slavs in their empire, as did the British rulers of India toward their Hindu and Muslim subjects. The French, who are notorious cultural imperialists, have always insisted on the supremacy of their language at the expense of others, both in metropolitan France and in

---

[38]See earlier sections in this chapter, "A Classification of Elites" and "The Myth of Racial Superiority."

their colonies overseas. Truly, the paths of empire-builders are strewn with the wrecks of a vaunted cultural preeminence.[39]

Money Power

Still another way to distinguish lions from lambs is through the possession of wealth. In this case the criterion by which human beings are differentiated is economic. People are classified as better or worse by reason of what they own and according to whatever index of riches happens to be in vogue in a given society. That index can be land, livestock, gold, precious stones, slaves, shares, or bonds—anything, in fact, that is conventionally accepted. Whoever succeeds in accumulating a large amount of these is assured of admission to the charmed circle. Whoever has too little to qualify, or owns nothing, is assigned an inferior status and is excluded from political participation. The name for this type of state is plutocracy, the Greek for "power of wealth."[40] On what theory is the ownership of riches regarded as justifying a right to rule? This question has been variously answered. Some argue that possessions constitute "a stake in the country," so that the more one owns, the greater one's stake. The wealthy not only have a large investment in the community, but stand to lose more if misgovernment occurs. Their concern to safeguard their fortunes makes them the more prudent custodians of the public interest. Or it may be said that, if government is to be conducted by "the best," then possessions can be taken as an objective yardstick of an individual's abilities and services to others. The wealthiest are to be adjudged the worthiest. Moreover, since an ample fortune emancipates its owner from the daily anxieties of earning a livelihood, this permits a fuller dedication to public affairs. Hence the well-to-do enjoy the leisure and detachment which make them a "natural" ruling class. Finally—and using different premises—those who call themselves realists may contend that, since wealth does in fact breed influence and power, to acknowledge the authority of the rich is merely to recognize the actual structure of power in society.

The doctrines that the distribution of political power will tend to correspond to the distribution of wealth, and that the difference between "haves" and "have-nots" creates political as well as economic cleavage are, of course, among the well-worn commonplaces of political thought. When Plato devised a ranking of states on a scale from perfect goodness to utter evil, he placed plutocracy in the middle of his five types.[41] He considered

---

[39]For a further discussion of the relation between culture and nationhood, see chapter 12, section on "Components of Nationality."

[40]The Japanese term *zaibatsu*, meaning "financial clique," is similar, though it does not include the notion of government.

[41]His ranking, from good to bad, was: (1) rule of philosopher-kings; (2) timocracy (government by soldiers conforming to a knightly code of chivalry); (3) plutocracy; (4) democracy; (5) tyranny. *Republic*, viii–ix.

its main defect the overaddiction to acquisitiveness and the amassing of riches. He explains it thus:

> "Then when in a city wealth and the wealthy are honoured, virtue and the good are slighted?"
> "Obviously."
> ". . . Then in process of time, from men who love victory and honour they become lovers of money-getting and of money; they give their praise and admiration to the rich man, and elect him to rule over them, but the poor man they slight?"
> "Certainly."
> "Then they lay down a law which is the distinguishing feature of an oligarchic constitution. They prescribe a sum of money varying in amount as the oligarchy is more or less extreme, and proclaim all disqualified for office whose means do not amount to the prescribed sum. . . . Such a city must of necessity be not one but two—the city of the rich and the city of the poor—rich and poor dwelling within the same walls, and always conspiring against one another."[42]

To similar effect is the judgment expressed by James Madison:

> The latent causes of faction are thus sown in the nature of man; and we see them everywhere brought into different degrees of activity, according to the different circumstances of civil society. . . . But the most common and durable source of factions has been the various and unequal distribution of property. Those who hold and those who are without property have ever formed distinct interests in society. Those who are creditors, and those who are debtors, fall under a like discrimination.[43]

However, although each was well aware that the economic distinction between rich and poor assumed a frankly political character, neither Plato nor Madison developed his analysis to the lengths that were reached by Karl Marx. For Marx and the Marxists went beyond their predecessors and the evidence in asserting that the economic factor determines other aspects of society, and in interpreting all history as a series of struggles between economic classes differentiated into exploiters (who own the means of production) and exploited (who toil on behalf of the exploiter). This doctrine, which claims to be a descriptive statement of fact, says both too much and too little. Too much, because it exaggerates the influence of the economic factor out of proportion to its actual size and significance, and because it claims to discover in all places and at all periods a polarization between hostile economic classes which has existed less generally than Marx imagines. Too little, because it fails to allow for the effect upon society as a whole of factors operating independently of economics, and further because it distorts or overlooks any actual situation which does not fit the doctrine.

[42]*Republic*, viii, sec. 551, pp. 246–47, trans. A. D. Lindsay (Everyman's Library).
[43]*The Federalist*, no. 10 (Everyman's Library), p. 43.

But though the Marxian theory may be too simplistic no one can deny the existence or the political relevance of economic divisions. Many states have proceeded from the assumption that the right to participate in government should be correlated with the ownership of property. Two examples will illustrate the point. The first is the government of a state which achieved splendor, power, and fame in the Middle Ages—the Republic of Venice. The Venetians owed their greatness to their skill in using the advantages of an unusual location. This cluster of islands, shoals, and mudbanks, belonging to land and water alike, had provided an early home for fishermen and a haven for the refugees who fled the invasion of the Huns. On the edge of the Italian peninsula, and at the head of the Adriatic, their seapower gave the Venetians security in defense and an avenue for commerce. Successfully combating their rivals—the Dalmatians and Genoese—they emerged as the major commercial power of the eastern Mediterranean, commanding the access to the Middle East and stretching a bridge of ships between Latins and Byzantines. The wealth that poured into Venice from the Levant enriched her merchants, and this plutocracy evolved into an aristocracy whose unequal status was derived from the profits of seaborne trade. As these merchant-princes, whose palaces fringed the Grand Canal, became a hereditary oligarchy, they changed the constitution of the Republic in order to entrench their privileges through political control. The original authorities had been the general assembly of the citizens (*concione*) and the annually elected *doge*. But by degrees, the wealthy families—fearing the power of many and envying that of one—weakened those two institutions by reducing their functions to ceremonial formalities. In their place, they concentrated the real government in a Grand Council (whose membership was restricted after 1296 by hereditary right), a Senate, and a secretive Council of Ten which supervised public safety and forestalled conspiracies. Such bodies effectively carried over to politics the socioeconomic realities of domination by a few great commercial houses.

A parallel, in the sense that it was designed to correlate political power with wealth, is the electoral organization adopted in Prussia and in force there until 1918. Representatives to the Prussian *Landtag* were chosen in districts, each of which returned one, two, or three members. These were elected, not directly by the voters, but indirectly by an electoral college. Every district was divided into subdistricts, to which was allotted one member of the electoral college for every 250 inhabitants. To choose the members of this college, the voters in the subdistrict were grouped in three classes, composed of those who paid direct taxes. The first class consisted of the wealthiest, who contributed one-third of the tax quota of the subdistrict; the second class, of those who paid another third; the third class, of the remaining taxpayers. Each class chose by absolute majority one-third of the electoral college membership of the subdistrict. Those so picked in all subdistricts, acting together as the electoral college of the district, voted for the representatives to go to the *Landtag.* The actual effect of these ingeniously complicated details can be seen in the figures for the year 1908, when the first class contained 293,000 voters (4 percent); the second class, 1,065,240 voters (14 percent); and the third class, 6,324,079 (82 percent).

Political Power

Of the various criteria for separating superiors from inferiors, those examined thus far result in political power as a by-product of something else. The right to rule, in other words, is vested in those who are distinguished by virtue of whatever factor happens to prevail or to be valued in their society. But there is one criterion for dominance, wherein political power is not the accompaniment of something else or its side effect. This is, in fact, political power—underived and self-generated. The superiors who control a community may consist of a governing group, differentiated from their subjects by the very fact that they have succeeded in monopolizing power. In modern times, the instrument for their supremacy is an organization designed especially for this purpose. It is the political party, conceived and structured to direct a movement which gives leadership to an otherwise amorphous mass. This phenomenon, though not without its forerunners, is primarily a twentieth-century innovation. Its climax is the one-party state, where, as the term implies, a single organization monopolizes power, takes charge of the machinery of government, then extends its controls throughout the social system.

Under these conditions, the members of the party constitute an elite, and those in the very top positions enjoy privileges and perquisites which set them over and apart from everybody else. Notorious examples have occurred in this century at the two extremes of the political spectrum. Despite sharp divergences in philosophy and program, the methods employed for enforcing their ascendancy by Germany's Nazis, Italy's Fascists, and Russia's Communists, have been markedly similar.[44] When a few individuals perch at the apex of a dictatorship and lord it over an entire country, everything is at their disposal—material goods, status, the granting of favors, unbridled self-indulgence. From the top down, privileges are meticulously rationed according to gradations of rank, so that those admitted to the charmed circle strive to keep what they have received and to move up the hierarchy.

In the contemporary Soviet Union, and in eastern Europe generally, the revolution which was launched against a social order divided into horizontal classes has ended with reintroducing a stratified pattern—the main

[44]See chapter 8, section on "Dictatorship in Modern Dress."

difference being that there is now a new set of beneficiaries. A Yugoslav Communist, Milovan Djilas, drew attention to this development in the mid-fifties, in a work entitled *The New Class.* "The party," he asserted, "is the core of that class, and its base. . . . The new class may be said to be made up of those who have special privileges and economic preference because of the administrative monopoly they hold." The result "is a class whose power over men is the most complete known to history."[45] The same theme was subsequently reaffirmed in various writings about the Soviet Union where the new class is now firmly entrenched as the boss of a regime originally intended to construct a classless society. "Power," says Hedrick Smith, "is the essential difference that marks off the political elite from all others."[46]

The Rule of the Wise

Of the types of oligarchy so far discussed, the three most likely to establish themselves in practice are government by warriors or wealth or political power, for these possess ample means of "persuasion" and are hard to resist. There remains one final type. It is the rarest and would be very difficult to establish. This is the government of the wisest. The argument in its favor consists of essentially simple points. It asserts that ruling—like the art of medicine or the science of engineering—calls for the professional knowledge of experts. It supposes that there is a body of knowledge concerning politics which can be discovered and learned. It then calls for an educational system to impart the "right" knowledge to the "right" people. There is no little irony in the fact that the earliest systematic treatise of political philosophy now surviving develops this hypothesis. The whole of Plato's *Republic* rests on two fundamental assumptions. One is the metaphysical doctrine that a distinction must be drawn between knowledge and opinion; that the subject matter of the former is reality, whereas that of the latter is appearance; and that the reality that is knowable includes the true forms or models of political ideals which must serve to guide the statesman. The second is the psychological assumption that human beings differ fundamentally in their intellectual endowment, and that only a small number are qualified and can be trained to reach the highest levels of philosophical inquiry and know the ideal. In Plato's view, it is these superior minds which truly comprehend the good and will therefore practice it; they alone deserve to be entrusted with political power.

[45]Milovan Djilas, *The New Class* (New York: Praeger, 1957), pp. 39, 69.

[46]Hedrick Smith, *The Russians* (New York: Quadrangle/The New York Times Book Co., 1976), p. 29. The same point is the central theme in a series of articles by David K. Willis in the *Christian Science Monitor,* 12–16 February 1979, and 14 January 1981.

Unless philosophers bear kingly rule in cities, or those who are now called kings and princes become genuine and adequate philosophers, and political power and philosophy are brought together, and unless the numerous natures who at present pursue either politics or philosophy, the one to the exclusion of the other, are forcibly debarred from this behaviour, there will be no respite from evil for cities, nor, I fancy, for humanity.[47]

To judge such a system of government is impossible because it has never been tried. If it ever were instituted, doubtless it would be authoritarian to the point of absolutism because those who are certain that they possess the truth can be quite intolerant of everybody else—witness Plato's own *Republic!* Moreover, as anyone who has served on the faculty of a large university can testify, those who have doctorates—a category not synonymous with the intellectuals, though it includes some—run their academic affairs in ways that fall short of an ideal model for government.[48]

Realistically seen, the history of politics consists in an elaborate documentation of the complaint voiced to his son by Oxenstierna, Sweden's famous chancellor in the second quarter of the seventeenth century: "My son, you don't realize how little wisdom is used in governing the world." True, there have been sporadic instances where individuals of superb intellectual and ethical standards have held the highest office in the state, but these are few enough to count on one's fingers. Witness Marcus Aurelius and Antoninus Pius in the Roman Empire; or, in modern times, Gladstone in Britain; Masaryk in Czechoslovakia; Jefferson and Wilson in the United States; Nehru in India. Civil services, too, when they have sought to recruit their officials according to the ability each displays in competition, have recognized the connection that should exist between powers of government and powers of mind. But nothing has ever been attempted in practice which comes anywhere near the rigorous and uncompromising logic of Plato's grandiose educational curriculum. The elite of the all-wise philosopher-ruler remains in the realm of fantasy. There let it remain!

Enough has now been said to illustrate the point that elites or oligarchies or aristocracies appear in many guises. All rest, however, on an assumption that the best government is one that the few best control. All take for granted the existence of superiority of a certain kind. All are dedicated to the principle of inequality, which is the law of their being. Nor are these aberrations, rarities, or deviations that have been considered in this chapter. On the contrary, most of the governments known to history have corresponded to one of the major types delineated here.

---

[47]*Republic*, v., sec. 473, p. 166.

[48]One professorial cynic has said: "The reason why campus politics are so dirty is that the stakes are so small."

5

"All Men Are Created Equal"

The Humanity That Unites Us All

"Human beings are divided into two groups: those who divide human beings into two groups, and those who don't. I prefer the latter." That remark satirizes the attitude discussed in the preceding chapter and keynotes the contents of this one. After a review of principles and practices that confine the right of governing to first-class citizens and demote the remainder to second-class status, let us study the alternative. This rejects the assumptions of elitists. It does not envisage the relation of government to governed as if it were analogous to that of doctor to patient, brain to body, potter to clay, shepherd to sheep, or any of the countless similes of this kind. Instead, it affirms that for political purposes the same basic rights must be accorded to all. If any are to be excluded from full participation, they should be the exceptions, not the rule. Not only should they be as few as possible, but their exclusion should require special justification (that is, those under a certain age, those committed to institutions for mental illness, those serving jail sentences for a criminal conviction, those who are citizens of another state, and so forth).

The purpose of this view is to affirm equality. This involves shifting the emphasis to the opposite of what attracted the elitists. They were preoc-

101

EL CAMINO COLLEGE LIBRARY.

cupied with singling out and emphasizing the features by which human beings may be distinguished and segregated. They accented differences and based their theories on dissimilarities. Anything might then be called upon to serve as an index for discrimination. The contrary doctrine stresses what we have in common. It accents likenesses, similarities, resemblances. It speaks in terms not of classes, but of humanity; not of ranks, but of equals. Within its categories there is no room for the concepts of subhuman or superman. All are placed on one level, encompassing the human race.

In describing these contrasts, let me be clear about what is at stake. Those who prefer the aristocratic doctrine do not deny that, even between superiors and inferiors, some overall similarities exist; and the advocates of all-inclusiveness concede that, side by side with the resemblances, there are also differences. The disagreement then resolves itself into a dispute over priorities. Granted that all people are alike in some respects and different in others, which factors should be considered more important? You will be an elitist if you think that the points on which people differ are the fundamental ones; an equalitarian, if you hold that the features wherein we resemble one another are primary. As the premises vary, so will the conclusions. The outcome of the former view is to emphasize whatever elements in human nature divide us; of the latter, those elements that unite.

Before the philosophy of equality is examined, a word should be said about its psychological significance. For the great majority of mankind the desire to be respected and treated as an equal presents a potent emotional appeal. It is all too true that most social and political systems have embodied the practice of privilege. Doubtless, this is the reason why equality, when evoked, has so explosive an effect. When the time comes for people to raise their heads and stand erect instead of bowing in deference, when they realize that they do not have to submit permanently to a second-class status, the feelings that result can lead to a tremendous rise in morale and energy. For the ideal of equal status human beings will undergo sacrifices and, in concert with their peers, will set great events in motion. Some of the most revolutionary movements in history have been sparked by a desire to achieve equality.[1] An example from the sphere of religion is the spread of Christianity in its first three centuries. Likewise, the great political revolutions of the seventeenth and eighteenth centuries—the English, American, and French—succeeded in large measure because the passion for equality was one of their driving forces. More recently, the Marxist philosophy and the Communist movement owe some of their earlier successes not so much to the content of the theory or the attractiveness of the party organization, but to the fact that they expressed an angry indignation against the in-

---

[1] This is recognized by such an advocate of inequality as Aristotle. Generalizing from Greek political experience, he correctly states that the prime object of many revolutions is a desire for equal treatment, *Politics*, v., chapters 1–2.

justices of inequality. Equality, even more than liberty, is the most revolutionary of political symbols. Whoever harnesses its power can shake and reshape the world.

The Case for Equalitarianism

However, the problem of the intellectual exposition of the equalitarian concept remains. Even when stress is laid upon unifying similarities, how is the right of everybody to participate in government explained? If the exponents of aristocracy conceive of ruling as a science, art, or mystery, what counterformulation is offered by their opponents? In a nutshell, what gives Thersites the right to talk back to Agamemnon? When we examine the foundations of the equalitarian view, we find that it rests on many pillars. Just as there are numerous species of oligarchy even though their central feature is identical, so do numerous roads lead to the unique goal of universal humanism.

For a start one could cite the old words: *Quod tangit omnes ab omnibus approbetur* ("Let all approve what touches all"). But to say this without proof is like asserting that the square on the hypotenuse of a right-angled triangle equals the sum of the squares on the other two sides, without detailing the logical steps that led Pythagoras to the conclusion. The foundations of equalitarianism can be outlined thus: All persons have the right to determine their own welfare. All have the right, therefore, to seek control over anything external to themselves that affects their welfare. The actions of government impinge on human welfare and leave nobody unaffected. Consequently all have the right to participate in controlling the state and contributing to its decisions.

The argument is impressive. By itself, however, it is insufficient to rebut the elitists. Their attack exposes a weak link in the chain of reasoning: the statement that "all have the right to seek control over anything external to themselves that affects their welfare." To affirm the right, they would say, is one thing; to exercise it, another. The right to control what touches your welfare depends first on knowing how to detect it; second, on being able to master it. Most people, the oligarch will argue, are not equipped intellectually to perform the first task and lack the power to carry out the second. Hence the assumed right is meaningless.

To this the equalitarian presents a countercharge. He asserts that the analogy between government and science or art can be misleading. To look only at the qualifications needed by rulers is to overlook the other side of the equation. If government consists of services provided by the rulers to the ruled, it is wrong to think only of those who produce the services and to ignore the consumers. Granted that I am not able to compose like Beethoven, write like Shakespeare, paint like Rembrandt, or invent like Edison, I can still appreciate their music, poetry, paintings, or inventions or even criticize a great master who sometimes falls short of the best. A person who could not design an automobile can nevertheless learn to drive one and can judge its performance. Government, in other words, is more than a matter of skilled technique applied by expert practitioners. It is above all else a problem of providing services to people who need them. In politics, as in economics, the start and finish of the process are human need and satisfaction. Traditionally, this truth is summed up in the everyday saying that "only the wearer knows where the shoe pinches."[2]

But the theory that embraces all persons as citizens has been placed on a higher plane. For the arguments of the equalitarians involve basic beliefs concerning the nature of humanity. As such, they cannot be divorced from larger issues of ethics and metaphysics. If this broadening of the scope of our inquiry occasions any surprise to the student of political science, let one reflect that there are many branches to the study of human society, that these are all related, and that no single specialization can boast the whole truth.

The Classical Roots of the Doctrine of Equality

1. The Stoics

In the history of Western political ideas the doctrine which emphasizes human equality is almost as old as its opposite. After Aristotle's death in 322 B.C., the most prominent star in the Greek philosophical firmament was Zeno of Citium, founder of the Stoic school. Against the background of turmoil following Alexander's conquests and early death, amid the breakdown of the once autonomous city-state and the overthrow of kingly dynasties, Zeno's theories were formulated to help individuals bear their trials with fortitude and lift their hopes toward new loyalties and wider horizons. The central theme of the Stoic philosophy is to equate rationality and deity. The divinity that shapes our ends is rational, and reason, conversely, is divine. The universe is the product of a divine purpose, manifesting itself throughout nature in a rational plan. Deity is not something external to the universe, inscrutably watching its creation and uncomprehended by its creatures. It is instead all-pervading, since where there is reason is God.

From these metaphysics the Stoic proceeded to draw conclusions with a social relevance. All human beings possess reason. True, the power to reason exists in each of us in different degrees. But wherever it is found, and whether it shines bright or dim, the light of reason is a spark of the divine fire. All of us, because we share in reason, share in the godhead. It is

---

[2]For an excellent discussion of this, see A. D. Lindsay, *The Modern Democratic State* (New York: Oxford University Press, 1947), pp. 269 ff.

less important that the reasoning ability of individuals is differently developed than that everyone alike possesses some ability to reason. Thereby the human species is united. On this account—and the point is fundamental to the Stoic—the concept of humanity (that is, the quality of being human) does not admit of degree. As human beings, all are equal. To assert that any individuals do not "belong," or to deny their equal title to consideration, is to exclude some fragments, however infinitesimal, of divinity.

2. Roman Law

With additions and popularizations, this philosophy competed successfully with the contemporary doctrines of Cynics and Epicureans and became the vogue among educated and professional people in the Mediterranean world. When Roman military and political power was absorbing Greece, and Greek culture and philosophy were humanizing Rome, Stoicism was imported to Rome under the influence of the Scipionic circle[3] and was imparted to Roman audiences by the philosopher Panaetius and the historian Polybius. What followed is an instructive episode in political and intellectual history. The century that marked the introduction of Stoicism coincided with the extension of Roman military power over the lands that fringe the Mediterranean. Newly conquered territories—Sicily, Greece, Spain, Gaul (France), Asia (Turkey), and the rest—were organized into provinces and absorbed into the empire of Rome. The inhabitants of these areas, so diverse in their cultural traditions and political maturity, their economic resources and religious doctrines, became the subjects of Rome, but not, at first, its citizens. To enforce the peace, Rome proceeded to safeguard the frontiers of its empire from external menace and to establish an internal system of order and trust. Contact and commerce between inhabitants of different provinces led to transactions involving trade, contracts, property, marriage, inheritance—transactions covering the whole gamut of social activities. A Gaul and a Spaniard, a Greek and a Sicilian might be involved in a dispute and seek to have their rights determined by litigation. But whose law would be applied in such cases? Not necessarily the law of Rome, for the civil law was applicable to citizens only. Confronted with a practical problem, the Romans responded in a practical manner. They established a new court to hear those cases where the rights of foreigners, *peregrini,* were involved. The presiding judge, *praetor peregrinus,* considered the legal principles in force in the territories of both parties to the dispute. If he could discover some common ground between them, he would adjudicate accordingly. If not, he would propose a solution based upon equity, that is, upon a conception of right and justice conform-

---

[3]The Scipionic circle was a group of political leaders, literary men, and philosophers assembling in the middle decades of the second century B.C., under the influence and patronage of the great soldier-statesman Scipio, the destroyer of Carthage.

ing to an abstract standard of fairness. The decisions rendered in particular cases and the principles they embodied were readopted annually in an edict which the judge issued to govern the proceedings of his court. Eventually, the accumulation of precedents hardened into a body of case law, which Roman jurists called the "law of the peoples" (*jus gentium*).

The stage was then set for a brilliant climax. Acting empirically, the Roman jurists developed from particular cases a coherent framework of general principles. In these were included the legal concepts that the various peoples of their empire were found to possess in common, as well as principles of equity that satisfied a sense of justice. Where the Romans had groped inductively from the particular to the general, the Stoic philosophers worked deductively. Arguing from metaphysical assumptions and moving from the universal to the particular, the Stoics concluded that all human beings are united through the common possession of reason. But the two systems—Stoic philosophy and Roman *jus gentium*—though they set out from opposite poles, drew close together and ultimately came within hailing distance. What was then easier than to suppose that the common concepts which the Romans discovered and applied by use of reason were the product of that same all-pervading reason which the Stoics divined as a law of the universe? It is true that the correlation was never exact. There were important points of divergence, as when the *jus gentium* condoned slavery which Stoic reason condemned. But in many areas the approximation was sufficiently close for jurist and philosopher alike to assume that their tracks were converging. Speculative metaphysics and pragmatic imperialism led jointly to the desired goal of the equality and unity of mankind.

Nor was the construction of the *jus gentium* the only way in which the Romans attempted to give effect to the principle that all are equal. No less momentous was the extension of their citizenship. This they proceeded to grant in stages both to individuals and entire communities, first among the Latins living nearby in the center of Italy, then to their allies in the rest of Italy, and afterward to inhabitants of the outlying provinces. The climax was reached in A.D. 212 when the edict of the Emperor Caracalla conferred the citizenship of Rome upon all free (nonslave) inhabitants of the empire. The nations of contemporary Europe are still far from possessing the common citizenship accomplished by Rome at the beginning of the third century. But idealistic as Caracalla's achievement sounds, it did not lack a materialistic side. The imperial treasury at that time was depleted and required new revenues. One lucrative source was the tax on the estates of the deceased, but this was levied by Rome only on its dead citizens. Enlarging the citizenry replenished the treasury.

2. The Gospel of Jesus

The trends initiated by Greek philosophers and Roman jurists were reinforced by the preachers of the Christian gospel. Jesus and the apostles, like many of their early believers, came mostly from humble origins. The appeal of the new religion was what could be expected of those who spread its message. Christianity spoke first to the underprivileged; to the lowly of this earth, not the mighty; to those who were rich only in hope and faith. Consequently its social teaching was inclined heavily toward equalitarianism. Human society in this life displayed the contrasts of luxury and poverty, power and weakness, eminence and lowliness. But the worth of the individual soul, which would outlive its bodily habitat, was to be judged not by a human being but by God, whose universal fatherhood made all people one family. Measured on the infinite scale of divine goodness, justice, and compassion, all human distinctions were trivial. As St. Paul said to the Galatians: "There is neither Jew nor Greek, there is neither bond nor free, there is neither male nor female, for ye are all one in Jesus Christ."[4] The philosophy here is Stoic. The legal doctrine—apparent to the apostle who affirmed "I am a Roman citizen"—is Roman. The religious aura is Christian. In that trinity the intellect, politics, and faith of antiquity found their culminating union.

It should not be forgotten, however, that the equality on which Christianity insisted was more pertinent to the next world than to this. It was in terms of their souls, which could be lost or saved, that all persons stood an equal chance. Indeed, it was the rich and the mighty who were handicapped in the race for salvation, since their earthly power exposed them to greater temptation and made them more liable to fall from grace. But this shift of the scene of equalitarianism to the hereafter made it possible for Christianity to acquiesce in, and either overlook or minimize, the inequalities existing here and now. Let us be content with our earthly lot, though it may be disagreeable, in expectation of glory in the life after death. Since "the powers that be are ordained by God," the Christian should submit to the wrongs inflicted by others with the certainty of being compensated by a divine justice.

The Modern Rebirth of Equality

In the history of the West there have been two periods in which humanity made notable advances in the direction of equality. The one just reviewed lasted 500 years from the rise of Stoicism to the Edict of Caracalla. The second, commencing in the mid-seventeenth century, has persisted through the twentieth and has not yet run its course. The circumstances that started and accelerated this modern movement are as noteworthy as the theories it has evoked. Chronologically these circumstances fall into three phases. The earliest dates from the middle of the seventeenth century to the end of the eighteenth. The next corresponds to the ten decades (1815–1914) between the defeat of Napoleon and the German invasion of

---

[4]Epistle to the Galatians, 3:28.

Belgium in World War I. The third phase has lasted from that time to the present. A survey of all three, by discovering whence we have come and where we now are, may help to understand better whither we may be bound.

The English, American, and French Revolutions

The first phase coincides with the revolutions in England from 1640 to 1688, in the United States from 1776 to 1791, and in France from 1789.[5] Each had somewhat similar objectives and therefore produced doctrines with many similarities. The aims of the revolutionaries, whether British, American, or French, included the overthrow of regimes not controllable by the governed. To justify rebellion against the legal order, it was necessary to show that right was on the side of those who rebelled. This could be done either by arguing that the state is founded upon a contract, and by asserting that the contract had been broken by the government; or by insisting that over the laws enacted by governing authorities there reigns some higher law, to which an individual may appeal. The rebellions, furthermore, were directed against an established ruling class basing its position on doctrines of legitimacy,[6] aristocracy, and hereditary right. To justify its replacement, one had to contend that the authority to govern did not belong exclusively to the monarch or the nobility, but was the common birthright of humanity which had been stolen from them.

These needs explain why the philosophies of Locke, Voltaire, Rousseau, Jefferson, and Paine place so much emphasis upon the hypotheses of a social contract and a law of nature, and on the vindication of individual rights to liberty and equality. The insertion of nature as a link in the chain of reasoning had a special purpose. Those who were dissatisfied with the existing order wanted a yardstick or standard of comparison. They found it helpful to suppose that a state of nature had preceded the organized civil state. This natural state was a blend of advantages and inconveniences, and governments were instituted in order to escape the latter—but not so as to lose the former. Of the advantages, the greatest appeared to be the relative equality of conditions existing among individuals and their consequential equality of rights. As Locke expressed it: "To understand political power aright, and derive it from its original, we must consider what estate all men are naturally in, and that is a state of perfect freedom to order their actions. . . . A state also of equality, wherein all the power and jurisdiction is

---

[5]For further discussion of these revolutions, see chapter 10. Because the French never completed their revolution, I have not ascribed it a terminal date.

[6]Legitimacy meant, in this context, a right to govern based upon ancestry.

reciprocal, no one having more than another."[7] If the actual conditions of organized society differed from this, if there were king and subjects, masters and slaves, luxury and penury, it was not from nature that the differences derived. Rather, they existed in contravention of nature, being the consequence of social institutions. Let mankind therefore reconstitute their governments so as to be guardians, not violators, of natural right. Such were the sentiments embodied in the great declarations of the American and French republics. The first of the truths that Thomas Jefferson pronounced self-evident in 1776 was "that all men are created equal." With similar effect the *Déclaration des Droits de l'Homme et du Citoyen*, adopted in 1793, proclaimed: "Governments are instituted to guarantee to men the enjoyment of their natural and imprescriptible rights. These rights are equality, liberty, security, and property. By nature and before the law, all men are equal."

Such statements were not only enunciated by individual thinkers but were affirmed officially by public bodies—by the Continental Congress of the United States and by the National Convention in France. No less impressive is the insistence on equality as a basic ideal, since this concept was truly revolutionary in relation to the social and political facts of that time. There were, however, two ambiguities in the concept and its phrasing. In the first place, all men were stated to be equal. It is unclear whether "men" signified males only or is used as a synonym for humanity. Also ambiguous is the appeal to nature as the basis and justification of the desired rights. People could dispute the circumstances of the assumed state of nature (whose details were derived from imagination rather than fact), and could also disagree about the law of nature which was supposed to prevail therein. Evidence and proof concerning natural law and natural rights were sought by reference to "reason," which was not always a sure guide to government if it gave different answers to different persons; or if not to reason, then the reference was to God, the Creator of nature and, therefore, of its rights and law. Once again, however, the interpretations were at variance, since not only did Christians disagree with non-Christians, but Protestants and Catholics themselves disputed the character of the divine dispensation. There were too many prophets who claimed to have heard the voice of God and tried to translate it into the vernacular. When a state contained among its citizens adherents of various faiths, which revelation should it accept?

Problems of this kind made it desirable, if equality and universality were to be upheld, to discover alternative doctrines as substitutes or supplements for natural law. At this point aid was forthcoming from moral philosophies, which, though disagreeing in other particulars, confirmed the

---

[7]John Locke, *Second Treatise of Civil Government*, chap. 1, sec. 4 (Everyman's Library), p. 118.

same central principle. This was the reassertion of the belief in the equal worth, fundamentally, of all human beings. In the mid-seventeenth century during the debates in Cromwell's army a Colonel Rainboro, one of the group known as the Levellers, declared: "Really I think the poorest he that is in England hath a life to live as the richest he." The same thought was echoed more than a century later by the German philosopher Immanuel Kant, who enunciated respect for human dignity in the somewhat cryptic command: "So act as to treat humanity, whether in thine own person or in that of any other, in every case as an end withal, never as means only."[8] With greater clarity, the founder of the English Utilitarians, Jeremy Bentham, remarked that each person should count for one, and nobody for more than one—perhaps the most succinct and least equivocal formula for equalitarianism ever compressed in a few words.

Gains for Equality in the Nineteenth Century

The relation of the Stoics, who formulated the abstract principles, to the Romans, who broadened outward from the particular to the general, is paralleled in both method and timing by the relation of the nineteenth century to its two predecessors. Whereas the seventeenth and eighteenth centuries hammered out the fundamental philosophies and the resultant declarations, the task of the nineteenth century was to bring actualities into closer approximation with those grand abstractions. When surveying events which are closer to our own time, we have the advantage not only of fuller historical records but also of more accurate statistical description. The concepts of an inclusive or exclusive citizenship can be measured with greater precision by reference to the franchise and its gradual extension to those not previously qualified to vote. In countries where the legislature is established as a central agency of government, the number of citizens entitled to vote for their representatives is a pointer indicating whether privilege or equality prevails.

The main precipitating cause in this nineteenth-century development was undoubtedly economic. The economic factor, however, assumed different guises in different places. In Britain the movement to broaden the franchise was an offshoot of the Industrial Revolution, which increased the social power of the urban middle class and converted a large section of the population into factor workers. In the agrarian community of the United States, as in Canada, Australia, and New Zealand, equalitarianism issued largely from the psychological impact on Europeans of emigrating from overcrowded lands to spacious undeveloped territories where new

---

[8]*Fundamental Principles of the Metaphysic of Ethics*, 10th ed., trans. T. K. Abbott (London: Longmans, Green & Co., 1929), p. 56.

vistas beyond the outer rim of settlement beckoned the enterprising. There, where each could find enough, and where muscle and nerve were each person's primary resource and stock of capital, that equality of conditions existed which makes for freedom.

Extension of Voting Rights in Britain

The impact of these changes on politics deserves description, since within a century they were responsible for writing a spectacular new chapter in the history of the state. I shall begin with the British experience for several reasons. In the nineteenth century she was the world's most powerful nation; she was ahead of others in industrialization, and was extending the institutions of democracy. At the time of her mortal clash with Napoleonic France, Britain already possessed a potent legislature, but one that represented only a minority of the population. The House of Lords, filled for life by hereditary peers, was the entrenched stronghold of the landowning aristocracy who, along with a minority of merchant-financiers, enjoyed a virtual monopoly of wealth, prestige, and political skill. The control of governmental power by this oligarchy embraced a House of Commons whose personnel were in large part the kinsmen of the nobility and were elected from antiquated districts by voters with ancestral or property qualifications. That this system did not preclude the possibility of opposition to the government is proven by the rise of the party system toward the end of the seventeenth century, by the conflicts between Whigs and Tories, and by the careers of such men as the two Pitts, Burke, Fox, and Canning. But institutional change was necessary if Britain intended to absorb industrial urbanism into its politics at home and to organize its gigantic empire abroad. A decade and a half of agitation after the defeat of Napoleon led to the enactment of the first Reform Act in 1832. Its general aim was to initiate a closer correspondence between Parliament and the people by redistributing the electoral districts and enlarging the franchise. A property qualification was retained, but the amount was set lower than before, resulting in the enfranchisement of the urban middle class. The electorate in 1833 was 75 percent larger than two years earlier, but it was still a mere 4.4 percent of the whole population, as table 2 indicates.

During the middle decades of the nineteenth century, the suffrage remained as it was defined in 1832. As late as 1866, less than 6 percent of the British population were registered as voters. Government was of the people; but it was conducted by a minority and, in the main, for that minority. The two major barriers excluding the majority of adults were wealth and sex. When would the electoral law abandon the disqualifications of poverty and femininity? The middle class could not avoid the issue of sharing with the work-

TABLE 2. The Growth of the British Electorate

DATE OF LAW EXTENDING SUFFRAGE	REGISTERED VOTERS		POPULATION AT NEAREST CENSUS		PERCENTAGE OF VOTERS TO POPULATION
	DATE	NUMBER (000'S OMITTED)	DATE	NUMBER (000'S OMITTED)	
1832	1830	440	1831	16,261	2.7
	1833	725			4.4
1867	1866	1,200	1861	23,128	5.6
	1869	2,250	1871	26,072	8.6
1884	1883	2,590	1881	29,710	9.9
	1886	5,000			16.8
1918	1910	7,200	1911	40,831	17.6
	1918	19,500	1921	42,769	45.6
1928	1924	20,650	1921	42,769	48.3
	1929	28,500	1931	44,795	63.6
1969	1966	36,000	1961	52,675	68.0
	1970	40,000	1971	55,347	72.0

ing class the privileges which they themselves had wrested from the aristocracy. In the agitation for reform, which shook British politics to its foundations from 1830 to 1832, the working class supported middle-class demands without insisting prematurely on a share for themselves. But eventually they were bound to press for theirs. It then remained to be seen whether the middle class would reciprocate their support or would, as radicals of yesterday who had gained their desires, become the conservatives of tomorrow. Such queries erupted in the revolutionary year of 1848, when autocratic regimes were challenged or overthrown on the continent of Europe and new constitutions were proposed or established in France, Prussia, Austria, the Italian states, and elsewhere. At a critical stage in those movements, the middle class took alarm at working-class aspirations and swung to the conservative side. Thus the liberal blossoming of Germany's Frankfurt Assembly, elected in 1848 by universal manhood suffrage, ran to seed in the Bismarckian reaction. In France, the liberal-democratic constitution of November, 1848, which contained a similar suffrage, gave way to the empire of Napoleon III. Hence, a British historian has tersely commented: "The year 1848 was the turning point at which modern history failed to turn."[9]

In Britain itself the year 1848 did not witness the same upheaval as occurred across the English Channel. This was because the British had been wise enough or fortunate enough to conduct in the seventeenth cen-

[9]G. M. Trevelyan, *British History in the Nineteenth Century* (New York: Longmans, Green & Co., 1922), p. 292.

tury the kind of political revolution that others were attempting in the nineteenth;[10] and also because the reformers had won the crisis of 1832. All that happened of moment in 1848 was that the Chartists, who had been pressing for further changes (including universal adult suffrage), reached the climax of their movement in the peaceful presentation of their Charter to Parliament. Liberalism was then forced to decide whether its acceptance of Bentham's precept would be extended in practice to an all-inclusive doctrine of citizenship. If the desire of the working class for equal voting rights were conceded, the middle class would have to welcome as full participants in the political process those who were poorer, less educated, and on a lower social level than themselves. The conflict in their reasons and emotions is typified in the candid avowals of the liberal philosopher John Stuart Mill. When his *Principles of Political Economy* was published in 1848, he stated with characteristic frankness:

> Of the working class of Western Europe at least it may be pronounced certain, that the patriarchal or fraternal system of government is one to which they will not again be subject. . . . The poor have come out of leading strings, and cannot any longer be governed like children. . . . The prospect of the future depends on the degree in which they can be made rational beings. There is no reason to believe that prospect other than hopeful.[11]

To him, the ultimate goal was not debatable. Only the timing was in question; and he, for one, was prepared to consider the maturity of the working class to be conditional upon its education.

These same anxieties were repeatedly voiced in the years immediately preceding and following the second extension of the franchise in 1867. When Mill's *Considerations on Representative Government* appeared in 1861, he again expressed his fears: "But even in this democracy, absolute power, if they chose to exercise it, would rest with the numerical majority; and these would be composed exclusively of a single class, alike in biases, prepossessions and general modes of thinking, and a class, to say no more, not the most highly cultivated."[12] Similarly Walter Bagehot, who added a new introduction to the second edition of his *English Constitution* in 1872, commented with even more candor: "As a theoretical writer I can venture to say, what no elected member of Parliament, Conservative or Liberal, can venture to say, that I am exceedingly afraid of the ignorant multitude of the new constituencies. . . . Their supremacy in the state they now are, means the supremacy of ignorance over instruction, and of numbers over

---

[10]Macaulay, in a passage of his *History of England* that was penned in 1848, compares British and Continental experiences in a series of rhetorical contrasts that exude no little complacency, vol. 1, p. 412.

[11]John Stuart Mill, *Principles of Political Economy* (Boston: Little, Brown and Company, 1848), vol. 2, part 4, chap. 7, sec. 1.

[12]*Considerations on Representative Government* (Everyman's Library), pp. 276–77.

knowledge."[13] Nevertheless, British democracy took the plunge into the deep seas of mass enfranchisement. In 1867 the vote was first accorded to members of the urban working class; within less than two decades it was granted to their rural confreres. Two years after the Act of 1884, the enrolled voters numbered some five million, roughly 17 percent of the population.[14]

Once the barriers were breached, the sequel of the story was a foregone conclusion. In the final struggle, the focus shifted from the laborers to the ladies. Feminists had already argued their cause, as had Mill; and a nation which romanticized its queen could not long or consistently deny to women a place in government. After the turn of the century, the suffragettes added a militant warhead to the movement, gaining their victory as one of the political offshoots of World War I. The Acts of 1918 and 1928 marked the culmination in a century of orderly evolution toward the ultimate goal of universal adult suffrage. The only significant changes since then were the Acts of 1948 and 1969. The former abolished the last remaining instances of plural voting, under which owners of business premises or holders of the higher university degrees were able to vote twice. The latter lowered the age of eligibility from 21 to 18. Hence, in the election of 1987, the registered British electorate was 43,600,000, of whom over 32 millions (75 percent) actually voted.

The Suffrage in American Democracy

In the two centuries since the Constitution came into force, the experience of the United States has been parallel to the British, with one country or the other taking the lead in the equalization of voting privileges. But the American development has been more complicated than the British. This is due in part to the greater heterogeneity of America's population, containing a large racial minority, and owing much of its increase to the immigration of adults whose mother tongue was not English and whose assimilation took time. In part, the complication has arisen from the relation between the electoral laws and the federal system. The regional diversities present in America from its founding precluded the drafting of uniform qualifications for the franchise in 1787. Instead, the Philadelphia convention adopted a provision which applied to national elections whatever franchise was used by the respective states for electing the lower houses of their own

---

[13]Walter Bagehot, *The English Constitution*, World's Classics (London: Oxford University Press, 1928), pp. 272, 276.

[14]Enrollment of voters, be it remembered, was voluntary. There were many who could qualify to vote under the law, but who for some decades neglected to register.

legislatures.[15] Thus, each extension of the suffrage within a state simultaneously broadened it at the federal level.[16] For this reason, and also because every state relies on voluntary methods of registering voters, the growth of the American electorate cannot be traced as precisely as in Britain. We can say how many were registered to vote and how many did vote in a presidential contest, but not how many were qualified to vote under the various state electoral laws.

In 1787–1788, when elections were held to choose the delegates who would ratify or reject the United States Constitution in state conventions, only a small percentage participated of the nation then numbering almost four millions. "It seems a safe guess to say," wrote Charles A. Beard, "that not more than 5 percent of the population in general, or in round numbers, 160,000 voters, expressed an opinion one way or another on the Constitution. . . . We may reasonably conjecture that of the estimated 160,000 who voted in the election of delegates, not more than 100,000 men favored the adoption of the Constitution at the time it was put into effect— about one in six of the adult males."[17] In the presidential election of 1984, however, when the total population was around 235 millions, there were 174 million citizens of voting age. Of these, 116 millions were registered to vote, and 93 millions cast their ballots on election day.[18] What happened between 1787 and 1984, besides the increase of population, to make this possible?

Two centuries ago, three principal barriers, other than age, excluded the majority of Americans from the polls. These were wealth, color, and sex. The history of the equalization of the franchise is the story of the progressive reduction of these barriers. Initially all states confined the franchise to the well-to-do. Sometimes the method was to insist that the voter must own a minimum amount of property. Sometimes the tax assessment was used as the criterion. Such limitations, in vogue along the eastern seaboard, lost their meaning when population moved west and carved out new territories which were then admitted as states. Here was free land for the taking. Here everyone who worked could acquire some property. Here

[15]"The House of Representatives shall be composed of members chosen every second year by the people of the several States, and the electors in each State shall have the qualifications requisite for electors of the most numerous branch of the State legislature." *United States Constitution*, Art. I, Sec. 2.

[16]Conversely, any restriction of the franchise within a state automatically narrowed the federal franchise.

[17]Charles A. Beard, *An Economic Interpretation of the Constitution of the United States* (New York: The Macmillan Co., 1935), p. 250.

[18]This means that actual voters in 1984 numbered only 53 percent of the population of voting age. The significance of this fact is discussed in chapter 9. See the section on "The Ins and the Outs."

were intrepid and hardy souls who would not accept a lower class citizenship. The barriers of wealth, like the walls of Jericho, fell before the trumpet blast of the all-leveling frontier, and under the fluid social conditions of the early nineteenth century new ramparts could not long be sustained. Benthamism, firmly planted in the West, spread back to the East, bringing constitutional change and electoral amendment. As Tocqueville presciently remarked:

> The further electoral rights are extended, the greater is the need for extending them; for after each concession the strength of the democracy increases, and its demands increase with its strength. . . . The exception at last becomes the rule, concession follows concession, and no stop can be made short of universal suffrage.[19]

In 1832, nearly 10 percent of America's population voted in the election which gave Andrew Jackson a second term. When Lincoln won his first term, actual voters were 15 percent of the population, a favorable comparison to the 5½ percent then registered in Britain.

The failure of property to provide a defense line in the resistance of quality to equality was followed by inroads first on the race barrier and then on sex. Where the West had led the attempts to nullify the electoral predominance of the wealthy, it was the North that began minimizing the political relevance of distinctions in race and color. In the "birth certificate" of the United States was inscribed the clause: "*all* men are created equal." These words, written by a southerner, were now to receive a literal and liberal interpretation. Although northern states prohibited slavery, they did not universally grant Negroes the right to vote. By the time of the Civil War, this right was available to black citizens in only four New England states, where their number was small. Of the legal changes resulting from the war, the most important were the three new amendments to the Constitution. The thirteenth abolished slavery, making all American territory "free soil." The fourteenth clarified the meaning of American citizenship which was at issue in the Dred Scott case, basing it primarily on birth within the United States irrespective of parentage. The fifteenth spelled out the political rights of citizens. It affirmed that the right to vote could not be denied by the federal government or by a state for reasons of "race, color or previous condition of servitude." Thus had the Constitution, one century later, caught up with the philosophy of the Declaration of Independence.

What was yet to be determined was whether "all men" included "all women." Here again it was the West that proved itself the radical innovator. The women who braved the discomforts and dangers of the frontier earned the respect of their menfolk. Moreover, in the area between the

---

[19]A. de Tocqueville, *Democracy in America*, trans. Henry Reeve, part 1, chap. 4.

Mississippi and the Pacific women were fewer than men, and their scarcity enhanced their value. It was in the West, therefore, that American women were enfranchised first. The movement to nationalize what the states were doing piecemeal was stimulated by the events of World War I, which brought more women into public life and economic activity. The climax came in 1919 with the adoption of the Nineteenth Amendment.

The phrasing of the Fifteenth and Nineteenth Amendments, however, is significantly negative. To declare that the right of citizens to vote may *not* be denied or abridged on account of race, color, previous condition of servitude, or sex, implies that this right may legally be denied or abridged on some other ground. Various methods, in fact, have been employed constitutionally for excluding some citizens from the polling booth. The age limitation is one example.[20] Another method, the requirement of a certain length of residence in the voting district, is justifiable as a means of ensuring proper registration and enrollment of voters, thereby impeding some fraudulent practices. The literacy tests, which used to exist in some states, were defended on the ground that whoever exercises the precious right of the franchise in a democracy must be able to read in order to vote intelligently. This argument applied with special force to a nation where many citizens were immigrants who became naturalized. But such tests were indefensible if the state failed to provide adequate public facilities for everybody to obtain the requisite knowledge, or if the system was administered with the ulterior aim of establishing some preconceived pattern of discrimination. In 1970 all such tests were made illegal. Such a pattern was also evident in the poll tax imposed as a condition of voting in several southern states. That tax was designed to exclude poorer citizens of any color, and it helped some unsavory political machines to prolong their stay in office. In 1964,[21] however, the Twenty-Fourth Amendment to the Constitution barred such taxes as prerequisites for voting in any federal elections, and in 1966 the Supreme Court extended the ban to state elections.[22]

Political Equality vs. Racial Segregation

Within a quarter of a century, therefore, after World War II, to the extent that federal law could provide, the prerequisites for voting had been equalized in the United States for every citizen above the minimum age. That was the close of one chapter; it was not the end of the story. Other episodes continue to this day, and they abound with complexity. Definite progress has been recorded in some spheres, but in others there is some retrogression. What has happened since the mid-fifties is worth reviewing, since the

[20]But no particular age—neither 21 nor 18—is sacrosanct.
[21]At that time five southern states still had a poll tax.
[22]*Harper* v. *Virginia State Board of Elections*, 383 U.S. 663.

American experience casts light, not only on this issue, but on some general characteristics of politics.

After a moral principle has become a national law, the way to local conformance and enforcement can still be long. A national majority may find it impossible to persuade, and difficult to coerce, opponents who are concentrated in local majorities. Those who remain opposed can devise means, both within and outside the law, of delaying, circumventing, and obstructing. On its face, the law may look fair. But the administrator can speak with a forked tongue. In something so vital as registering a citizen to vote the official procedures can be simple for some, but harassing to others. And if all else fails, society at large has extralegal weapons against those who would replace old customs with new laws. Economic boycott, loss of employment, social ostracism, and physical violence can all be used with political effect.

Thus the recent history of this revolution in human relations raises large questions for the student of politics. The British have a saying: "You can't make men moral by Act of Parliament." Is that true? Can a government be an effective agent for social change? How do you go about transforming attitudes and relationships which for centuries have become entrenched in vested interests and traditional belief?

Experience thus far in the United States suggests two conclusions. One is that politics can be the potent catalyst in a social revolution, but the changes in the intended direction are not continuous, nor is their pace constant. First comes an advance, after which resistance builds. Regression then follows, though this does not return all the way to the point of departure. Second, a revolution in something basic will be manysided, since its ramifications extend throughout the social order whose several sectors are intertwined. Hence, movement must proceed on more than one front, if gains are to have reality and permanence. Consider in this light the attempts to establish equality of opportunity for black Americans.

For the politics of a democracy, voting is fundamental. A person registered to vote is a force to be reckoned with. He and she will be courted by candidates. As the squeaking wheel gets the grease, voters with a gripe are granted remedies. Legislators and administrators will heed the demands of social groups which are organized to voice their interests, and any leaders who can "deliver" their votes wield influence. By contrast, those who are not registered are virtually nonpersons. Lacking political leverage, they are less likely to see their wishes incorporated into policy.

Despite the plain intent of the federal Constitution, black enfranchisement at first proceeded slowly because of social resistance. In 1960, nine decades after the Fifteenth Amendment was adopted, a mere 29 percent of black citizens of voting age were inscribed on the electoral registers of the eleven states of the South.[23] But in 1965 Congress enacted a

---

[23]Of the whites of voting age, 61 percent were then registered.

Voting Rights Act, and the progress in the following years was truly remarkable. In 1984, as many as 66 percent of blacks of voting age were registered in the South and in the country as a whole.[24] The black voter could no longer be ignored. As one direct consequence, there is a lengthening list of major cities which have, or have had, black mayors: among them, Chicago, Los Angeles, Philadelphia, Detroit, Atlanta, and New Orleans. Furthermore, there is now a Black Caucus in the House of Representatives, and in the presidential elections of 1984 and 1988 a black candidate, Jesse Jackson, was a force to be reckoned with.

The Revolution in Race Relations

But people do not live by politics alone. More is required than an occasional trip to the polls if individuals are to maintain their essential dignity. Being multifaceted, equality has many applications. Outside the polling booth it is pertinent to the home and neighborhood, the factory and office, the school and university, the streetcar and airplane, the restroom and restaurant. Any discrimination between human beings because they differ in race is obnoxious—and humiliating to those treated as inferiors—whether it be manifested in politics, education, employment, housing, or local services. In the body social as in the body politic, black persons, who are more than one-tenth of all Americans, were traditionally forced to remain a group apart. Northerners criticized the South, but turned a blind eye to their own cities, where blacks are involuntarily segregated in ghettos by economic pressure and white prejudice.[25] As blacks migrated from the South, the size of the ghettos grew and, along with it, their social disorganization. In the major metropolitan areas, whites have been moving to the suburbs, leaving the blighted central core to the blacks—many of them poor and poorly educated.[26] Not yet fully assimilated into the community, generally

---

[24]The corresponding figures for whites were 75 percent in the South, 70 percent in all the United States.

[25]"Segregation and poverty have created in the racial ghetto a destructive environment totally unknown to most white Americans. What white Americans have never fully understood—but what the Negro can never forget—is that white society is deeply implicated in the ghetto. White institutions created it, white institutions maintain it, and white society condones it." *Report of the National Advisory Commission on Civil Disorders* (New York: Bantam Books, 1968), p. 2.

[26]On these points, the statistical data speak eloquently. "In 1910, 91 percent of the nation's 9.8 million Negroes lived in the South and only 27 percent lived in cities of 2,500 persons or more. Between 1910 and 1966 the total Negro population more than doubled, reaching 21.5 million, and the number living in metropolitan areas rose more than fivefold (from 2.6 million to 14.8 million). The number outside the South rose elevenfold (from 880,000 to 9.7 million)." Ibid., p. 12. The 1980 census counted 26.5 million blacks. Of these, 12.5 million (47 percent) lived outside the South; 22.5 million (85 percent) lived in urban areas.

relegated to a low social status, blacks form the largest of the minorities[27]—others being the Indians and the Hispanics[28]—to which thus far the political ideals of America have been extended only in part.

All this is now challenged and changing. We are in midcourse of a social revolution which is uprooting vested interests, weeding out exclusive privilege, and pruning ancient prejudice. More is at stake here than an enlargement of electoral registers or a reordering of social habits. The integrity of our civic conscience is being tested. On our example, as shown by our actions, will depend our influence in the world.

The drive for equality in race relations has become one of the sweeping global movements of this century. The case for its recognition, brutally denied by German National Socialists and South African Nationalists, affirms the inherent worth of all humanity to which distinctions of race, per se, have no relevance. The equalitarian principle insists that a person's opportunities be based on the capacities of each individual and not on the group to which one was born or happens to belong. The task for our generation is to break down the barriers of segregation, both legal and social, and to treat individuals as their capacities merit. It is the consensus of most anthropologists and sociologists that, in comparing whole groups of different race, there is no proof that any particular race is inherently superior or inferior. Measurable differences do occur between the average performance of one group and that of another, but these should be attributed primarily to socially fostered discrimination which enlarged for some persons, as it narrowed for others, the avenues leading to education, income, and advancement. When such discrimination is removed, however, persons from formerly underprivileged groups can advance by their abilities in much the same way as the rest.

Educational Equality

Understandably, the educational system has been a testing ground for such principles and for the programs derived from them. Schools and universities have therefore been a central target in the black drive for equality. When these are financed from public funds, their policies are matters of general concern. Any discrimination by public bodies along racial lines negates the Fourteenth Amendment, which prohibits a state from denying "the equal protection of the laws" to any person within its jurisdiction. Although the intent and spirit of this famous formula are clear enough, after the amendment was added to the Constitution 86 years elapsed be-

---

[27]Discrimination against women, who are the majority of America's population nowadays, is discussed later in this chapter.

[28]In 1984 only 40 percent of Americans of Spanish origin were registered to vote.

fore it was unequivocally interpreted in so vital a sphere as the education of school children. In 1896 the Supreme Court adopted the "separate, but equal" doctrine that in public transportation the different races must be given equal facilities, which could, however, be separate so long as they were equal.[29] A few years later, that concept was applied to schools, and the policy of the South was to forestall social mingling between the races by providing parallel, and supposedly equal, services.

That policy, however, always rested on a fiction. Theoretically the Constitution was observed by pretending that separate facilities could be equal and really were. The facts did not support this contention. Not only did the parallel facilities differ in quality, but the act of segregation itself set up an intentional barrier affecting the psychology of individuals and the ethos of society. Equality is a myth when two races live side by side, but only one of them draws the boundaries and decides how both shall coexist. The inescapable result is a relation of superiors to inferiors; and when those on one side of this "equation" monopolize the social advantages, a judge who disregards the reality makes a mockery of justice. This truth was cogently stated by a unanimous Supreme Court in 1954, when it required the racial integration of the public schools.[30] Chief Justice Warren dispersed the fog of fiction with this simple good sense:

> Segregation of white and colored children in public schools has a detrimental effect upon the colored children. The impact is greater when it has the sanction of the law; for the policy of separating the races is usually interpreted as denoting the inferiority of the Negro group. . . . Separate educational facilities are inherently unequal.

Few judicial pronouncements in modern times have offered so conspicuous an example of the gap between declaring a principle and enforcing it. The ensuing controversy embroiled all three branches of the federal, state, and city governments, as well as the two political parties, the police, and the army. The crux of the problem has been to overcome the stubborn refusal of many whites (public officials and private individuals alike) to accept the social integration of races as required by the supreme law of the land and expounded by its supreme tribunal. That compliance would be neither easy nor automatic was recognized by the Supreme Court from the outset. It takes time to alter social practices long fixed in institutions and attitudes. Private associations, too, that are to be shorn of privileges do not yield promptly, even to public authority. For this the Supreme Court made due allowance when it invited the officials of the areas concerned to prepare their plans for changing "separate, but equal" facilities into "inte-

---

[29]*Plessy* v. *Ferguson,* 163 U.S. 537.
[30]*Brown* v. *Board of Education,* 349 U.S. 294.

grated and equal," requiring however that the change be consummated "with all deliberate speed."

For a decade after that decision, blacks were asking which seemed to be more deliberate—the federal speed or the local resistance. By the end of 1964, in the 11 states of the South, only 64,000 blacks out of a total of almost three million (a mere 2.13 percent) were enrolled in biracial schools.[31] What such figures cannot convey, of course, is the struggle required in producing even that amount of integration. Starting in 1957 at Little Rock, Arkansas, and continuing with successive incidents in Virginia, Louisiana, Alabama, and Mississippi, the local officials, legislatures, and governors defied the authority of the federal government. In some instances they did not comply until confronted with superior force. Presidents Eisenhower and Kennedy had to send the army into a high school and a university to enforce the orders of the federal courts.

After 1965, however, the public schools were integrated much more rapidly—particularly in the South. Throughout the United States in 1968, 23 percent of the black students at the elementary and secondary levels were enrolled in schools where whites made up more than half the total. Sixty-four percent were still members of a student body that was over nine-tenths black. By 1970, those percentages had changed to 33 and 43, respectively. In the 11 states of the South the gains were faster than in the nation as a whole. There, the corresponding figures were as follows: 18 percent of the black students attended schools where over half were white in 1968, compared with 39 percent in 1970. Meanwhile, the numbers belonging to a student body of which more than nine-tenths were of the minority race had decreased from 78 percent in 1968 to 33 percent two years later.[32]

In comparison with such impressive changes in the South, the focus of the struggle for school integration shifted in the 1970s to the North and the West. There, too, traditionally much of the public education has been racially segregated in practice. This has been due to neither the laws nor officialdom, but to the social and economic structure. If a school serves a neighborhood, and if all who live there belong to the same race, *de facto* that school will be segregated. Also, if the teachers, the teacher-pupil ratio, and the facilities in the central core of a large city are of lower standard, their students have less chance of admission to higher education and to the professions and better-paying jobs. Since it takes so long to alter a deeply rooted pattern of segregated housing, some communities have sought instant integration of their schools by public authority, busing children from one district to another and thereby requiring the school system to make up

---

[31]Data from Southern Education Reporting Service, Nashville, Tennessee, cited in *New York Times* (Special Education Survey), 13 January 1965, p. 75. By 1966 the total had risen to 690,000; the percentage, to 16.9.

[32]Data from *Digest of Educational Statistics*, 1972, p. 157. The source is a press release from the Department of Health, Education and Welfare, 18 June 1971.

for social injustices which the realtors and mortgage companies helped to perpetuate. This method initially encountered profound hostility, even violent opposition, from white parents, as in South Boston, when the schools opened in the fall of 1974. To these sentiments politicans of the right wing—such as Nixon, Ford, and Reagan—responded by seeking to reverse the court rulings which had made busing mandatory.

Overall, the results in 30 years of court-ordered integration are spotty. There are a number of cities in the North and West where busing now works with relative smoothness and where integration is more of a reality then was once the case. But, busing or no, the latest demographic trends in the central metropolitan areas are reintroducing segregation *de facto.* Blacks, together with Hispanics and Asians, now constitute a majority of the children in the public schools of most of the larger cities. Many of the white families which can afford the fees have sent their children to private schools. The causes of this extend far beyond education. They are entrenched in the economy and in still-surviving patterns of social discrimination. Can liberal-minded schools and universities apply the principle that the youth of all races are created equal when wealth and status are distributed unequally?

Economic and Social Equality

To bring social justice to a house divided against itself, solutions must be sought simultaneously on many fronts. Equality, in a word, is indivisible. You cannot have it anywhere unless you achieve it everywhere. Juridical equality of rights, for instance, will have little practical effect if incomes are distributed unequally, since money is the key that unlocks many doors.[33] Why insist that a housing tract or hotel, a golf club or restaurant, be integrated if members of a minority group cannot pay the bill? How can a black student attend a university whose cost for one year would equal the total family earnings?

The economic status of blacks improved somewhat in the period from 1960 to 1980. But the gains are still outweighed by the inequality that persists, and their foundation is fragile. Blacks suffered in the 1980s as a result of the Reagan administration's economic policies and the cuts imposed on welfare programs (such as food stamps for the poorer families). A report which was published in 1985 made these comparisons: "Black children are twice as likely as white children to die in the first year of life, three times as likely to be poor, four times more likely not to live with either

---

[33]Anatole France referred in *Le Lys Rouge* to "the law whose majestic equality forbids rich and poor alike to sleep under the bridges, beg in the streets, and steal for bread."

parent, and five times as likely to be on welfare."[34] The economic circumstances of Hispanic Americans, many of whom are wholly or partly Indian, also worsened during these years. In 1979, Hispanic families below the poverty line were 21.8 percent of the total. In 1985 they were 29 percent. Two Hispanic children out of five were then living in poverty.[35]

Although many contemporary manifestations of inequality are grounded in racial differences and the feelings these engender, the situation contains other aspects besides the racial. So wide is the social distance, so severe the economic separation, that race becomes compounded with class in a social structure which superimposes group upon group in a manner repugnant to the ultimate individualism of the American ethic. A circularity thus links the conditions to be changed and the remedies proposed. If the members of a disadvantaged minority are to qualify for the professions and for jobs requiring higher skill, they need a better education. To attain this, the segregated system must be broken down. Integrated schools properly presuppose, especially at the primary level, that housing is integrated. But renting or buying a house or apartment in the more desirable neighborhoods costs more money, which requires a higher income. There is no one lever, not even the right to vote, that can remove all obstacles at once.

In a revolution which is social as well as political, the underprivileged—impatient now and aroused—follow a strategy of advancing on all fronts at once. Their methods have ranged the gamut from the constitutional to the lawless. In the 1960s the rage of the ghettos exploded with violence. We witnessed the burning and pillage of the Watts district of Los Angeles, prolonged racial upheaval in Detroit, and the assassination of Martin Luther King. As extremes always nourish one another, so in this tragic story violence bred counterviolence, and the racism of one side fed its opposites. A white backlash developed during the 1970s. This manifested itself in the flight of families from the city centers to the suburbs, particularly families with children of school age or the elderly who sought protection against burglary and assault. There has also been a mushrooming of right-wing organizations, some of which are racist, while some are rooted in the religious fundamentalism which is ever a fertile soil for irrational prejudices. As a result, in the early 1980s segregation was on the increase again in certain sectors of our society.

It is hard to form a balanced judgment about a large and complex country where the facts are contradictory and the record is uneven. But when I compare these United States with those of a generation ago, overall

[34]From a study by the Children's Defense Fund in Washington, D.C. Reported by the *Washington Post* and reprinted in the *San Francisco Chronicle,* 4 June 1985.

[35]From an analysis of Census Bureau data, conducted by the Center on Budget and Policy Priorities. *Christian Science Monitor,* 4 September 1986.

the change for the better in the sphere of race relations is genuine and profound. The major accomplishment has been the shift in public opinion in favor of forms of integration which the majority would never have accepted before the watershed decade of 1954 to 1964. Because of this, it has been possible for a black to sit on the Supreme Court and in the Senate. As Kennedy needed Protestant and Jewish votes to be elected President, so in Chicago—a city with bitter racial divisions—Harold Washington could not have won the mayoralty if he had not received one-fifth of the white votes. Moreover, those who would generalize too sharply about the United States might pause to remember such a phenomenon as Hawaii. Placed "at the crossroads of the Pacific," the fiftieth state contains a living laboratory whose ethnic and racial groups know that they must coexist and, on the whole, are combining fruitfully. This has been possible precisely because the principle of equality was applied by public policy to peoples of great diversity. Assuredly there is prejudice among us, but there has also been a growth of tolerance and fairness.

India's Untouchables

The American experience in attempting to equalize opportunities for its oldest and most visible minority may be compared with India's problems in removing the stigma of untouchability. Indeed, the parallel between Untouchables and Negroes has been drawn in official Indian documents. Although the two situations are not identical, they share enough in common to justify being bracketed in this discussion.

The Untouchables have been called "the largest oppressed minority in the world."[36] Numbering over 100 millions, or 15 percent of the population, their position has resembled that of America's blacks in that they were traditionally relegated to the lowest level in the social structure. In every particular—whether political, economic, or educational—their treatment was the worst of whatever the system had to offer. The main difference in the Indian case, one which endows it with its unique character, is that this inequality is based on the Hindu scriptures and is backed by religious sanction.[37] That fact alone enormously complicates the difficulties in the way of removing the barriers to equality.

Ever since Aryan invaders subdued the earlier darker-skinned inhabitants in the North, Hindu society has been stratified into castes which defined a person's occupation and were hereditary. At the bottom of the heap were those assigned to the filthiest physical tasks which, according to Hindu belief, polluted all who undertook them. Since this pollution could

[36]*The Economist* (London), 2 April 1983, p. 56.
[37]See chapter 4, section on "Discrimination through Religion."

be transmitted by contact, the lowest grade of humans were outcasts. They were forbidden to touch a member of a higher caste, to draw water from the same well, or even to enter their temples.

To challenge such beliefs and practices is plainly to embark on social revolution at the most fundamental level, since eradicating untouchability means striking at caste itself—in other words, at what has been the constituting principle of Hindu civilization for more than two millennia. To substitute new practices for old, government can be an effective agent, since it wields the legal machinery which regulates society. If consistently applied, law can eventually change custom. But to alter the beliefs which underpin the practice, new beliefs are required. This need belongs elsewhere. It lies in the realm of the spirit. It is a task for the mind or for faith.

That was exactly the vision of Mohandas K. Gandhi, the principal leader of the Hindus in India's struggle for independence. His goal was not only to end British rule by the ethical means of nonviolent resistance, but to build a just society afterward. Hence, he condemned the continuing degradation of the Untouchables whom he named *Harijans* or "children of God." The same doctrine inspired Jawaharlal Nehru, the first Prime Minister of independent India. When the Constitution was written for the new Republic, the chairman of the drafting committee, Dr. B. R. Ambedkar, was a Harijan. Early in its political life, the Nehru government proved the seriousness of its intentions by securing the passage in 1955 of the Untouchability Offenses Act—a piece of legislation comparable in spirit and purpose to the civil rights laws of the United States Congress. That was a generation ago. What results have been achieved?

Progress and Reaction

In reviewing the evidence and forming a judgment, one is constantly struck by the closeness of the parallel between India and the United States. Even when due allowance is made for the obvious differences—the greater size of India's population and its more complex makeup, the depth and extent of the poverty of a large proportion, the need to combat religious tabus— the two experiences have been, overall, remarkably similar.

India's social revolution was energized by Gandhi's spiritual leadership, aided by Western affirmations of the "Rights of Man," but it has been organized through central power. Obedient to the principles of its newly adopted Constitution, not only did Delhi enact the needed laws, but it initiated policies to rectify past injustices and make equality real. Huge sums of money were allocated to the education of Untouchables, including the provision of university scholarships; their economic rehabilitation was actively fostered; and numerous jobs were reserved for them in public employment. In other words, what the United States calls "affirmative action" has its Indian counterpart. Also like blacks, the Harijans have taken full advantage of a democratic system to improve their lot by political action. For this, they have tried two alternatives: one, a political party of their own (named Republican), and the other, participation in the dominant Congress party where they can bargain for benefits by offering their votes.

But India, too, has faced no lack of obstacles and opposition. The interests vested in the caste system and exploiting the misery of the oppressed have not lightly surrendered the citadels of privilege. A backlash has developed of sufficient strength to weaken the application of central policies or even to nullify them. Progress there has been in the direction of equality, but severe discrimination also persists.

It is in the cities that gains have been most notable. There the population is more mobile; society, more fluid. Absorbed in the urban environment, the erstwhile Untouchable is less visible and can become anonymous. A change of clothes—and one is assimilated! Even if appointed initially to a job reserved for outcasts, a later transfer to another position conceals the evidence of origin. In a crowded bus, moreover, one and all must perforce rub shoulders. The city and its economy are dissolvent acids, obliterating the texts of the ancient Vedas.

Quite otherwise is the countryside. There, where society is more static and each person is known in the village, the writ of the center is heeded less. The landlords are the power that counts. Many are Brahmans and wish to retain their status and luxuriate in its perquisites. Remove untouchability, and with it you threaten the entire fabric of the caste system. And their opposition is reinforced by fundamentalists in the Hindu priesthood, who refuse to deviate from their holy scriptures. In consequence, since the law and the government are against them, these conservative upholders of traditional inequality resort to extralegal means—to the very violence which Mahatma Gandhi so deeply abhorred. Untouchables are frequently intimidated by physical assaults. Even murders are not uncommon.[38] But against Hinduism, too, so diverse a country presents the means of escape. Cast out from that faith, the pariahs—the word is Indian—can convert to another. They may become Sikhs or Jains, Muslims or Christians or Buddhists.[39] As always in human affairs, when a monopoly is broken, some freedom is possible.

The Fair Sex and the Unfair

But what is to be said about the form of discrimination which has been the most pervasive in all civilizations and the most persistent through historical time, the discrimination which is not directed at a minority but has been

---

[38]"In three years, says *The Indian Express*, 40,000 cases of atrocities committed against Harijans . . . have been listed." André Fontaine, *Le Monde*, 25 March 1983. If that number has been reported, the actual figure must be larger.

[39]Ambedkar himself became a Buddhist, as did many of his followers.

habitually practiced by one half of the human species at the expense of the other? Irrespective of race, religion, or culture, men have traditionally treated women as inferiors. The physical differences between male and female have served as the foundation for a superstructure of discrimination. Human society has conventionally allotted separate roles to each sex, which have some of the characteristics of a caste in that they are predetermined and inescapable. Childcare, cooking, keeping house were considered the work of the female; political activity, higher education, the learned professions, paid employment, and social leadership were the preserve of the male. Some economic activities were shared, particularly in rural areas where peasant women would work in the fields alongside the men. But the more skilled tasks, and the direction, remained in male hands.

To this discrimination, the organized religions of all major faiths have added the weight of their authority. Indeed, their holy texts, written by men, were quoted to endow earthly injustice with heavenly sanctity.[40] What is more, to each sex was ascribed a catalog of psychological traits supposedly rooted in physiology. Females were portrayed as gentle, submissive, and compassionate;[41] males, as tough, pugnacious, and competitive. These groupings of qualities were then postulated as natural to each sex, with the result that a sensitive man or a strong woman was frowned on as contrary to nature.

To men and women alike, this structure of belief did untold harm, because in fact no necessary correlation exists between the biological differences in sex and such assumed psychological contrasts. Assuredly, individual men and women vary in their gentleness or toughness, sensitivity or callousness, and the rest. But such traits differ in degree; they are distributed in both sexes along a continuum. It is perfectly natural for either a man or a woman to manifest any of these to any degree in his or her personality. What is unnatural is the network of stereotypes and institutions which society has erected upon the myth that leadership is a male prerogative. Using that notion to justify their predominance, men have proceeded to "man" the institutions—the word is significant. And the old illusions die hard. On the issue of male superiority, Freud is at one with the popes; black male militants do not differ from the Klansmen. In consequence, millions of males and females have been twisted and forced into social roles which often contradict their individual natures. Much alienation and neurosis, many mental breakdowns have been the result. Moreover, the males who reached the top of the social hierarchy did so by

[40]E.g., the role of Eve in *Genesis*, or the sexist utterances of St. Paul.

[41]Such was the characterization of the female when the man was being kind. Misogynists, however, have drawn their pictures of women as gossipy, scheming, shrewish, hysterical, stupid, and flighty.

exalting and exercising power—a low value in ethics, but one they associated with masculinity. Especially is this manifest in the political sphere, where, as noted earlier, the preoccupation with power became a perversion.

Thus has the vertical division between the sexes been converted into a horizontal stratification within the social hierarchy. The entire complex of male-staffed institutions of every manner and description—governments, churches, business firms, trade unions, the legal system, the universities—combined for centuries to keep women subordinate and dependent. All in all, this adds up to a sad commentary on our progress toward a higher level of civilization. For, as John Stuart Mill has written, "historians and philosophers have been led to adopt their [women's] elevation or debasement as on the whole the surest test and most correct measure of the civilization of a people or an age."[42]

How much has been lost throughout the centuries by this deliberate denial of equal opportunities to half of the human race is impossible to calculate. Not only were women prevented from developing their capacities and achieving creative fulfillment, but they were often reduced to a condition akin to slavery. Social custom, reinforced by legal and economic imperatives, decreed that women live their lives under the control and in the custody of a man—first of their father, and then, if they married, of their husband. In fact, a woman was conventionally treated as an item of property. In law, she was classified as a chattel; in some countries, she could actually be sold. If her father or husband was brutal and mistreated her physically, there was no redress. And if a woman was too "uppity," society at large resorted to the final solution. Between the fourteenth and seventeenth centuries, approximately a million persons were burned or hanged as "witches," some 90 percent of them women. And this was done at the decree of churchmen, Catholic and Protestant, who administered the religion of Jesus!

In countries with democratic regimes, the movement for women's emancipation first directed its attention to obtaining the franchise. Once this was achieved, it became apparent, as the black minority has also discovered, that voting, though essential, is but the beginning. Even when equality of opportunity is established in law, it exists only in form unless and until the surrounding social context is changed, and that does not happen without a revolution in prevailing attitudes. Many white males reacted to black equality with fear; equality for women they countered with ridicule. The movement for women's liberation,[43] therefore, propelled with a new vigor and determination in the 1960s, addressed itself to both

---

[42]From *The Subjection of Women.*

[43]Two of its landmark books were Simone de Beauvoir's *The Second Sex* and Betty Friedan's *The Feminine Mystique.*

sides of the problem—to the removal of the impediments, both cultural and institutional, which have barred women from so many vocations and positions, and, positively, to their creative participation with men on a basis of full equality and respect. Further than that, the drive to liberate women, seen in reverse, was at the same time aimed at the freeing of men. For when all members of both sexes attain equal respect and opportunity as individuals, men too will at last be liberated from the constrictive roles which for millennia have twisted their natures as markedly as women's.

In many respects, the changes since the mid sixties have followed a course similar to that observable in race relations and in the campaign against untouchability. Women have advanced positively in certain countries and in some sectors of society. But overall the picture is spotty, and a reactionary resistance has been able to slow the rate of change.

At the political level, which is the most visible, a handful of women have attained a public prominence previously unmatched except by strong-minded queens. One could in this respect compare Indira Gandhi, Golda Meir, and Margaret Thatcher with Catherine of Russia, Elizabeth I of England, and Maria Theresa of Austria. All of these—premiers and queens alike—demonstrated in their exercise of power, both at home and abroad, the same qualities as their male counterparts. Or at any rate they showed no evidence of acting with a different ethic.[44] At the next level of public life, women have been elected for more than 50 years to legislative bodies. Here their numbers fluctuate, but they are invariably a small minority. An occasional woman finds herself appointed to a cabinet office, and in the United States one now sits on the bench of the Supreme Court. American cities have also elected more women as mayors—for instance, in Chicago, San Francisco, Houston, and Dallas—while in a few states women have been elected governors.

But these cases, however one adds them, still amount only to tokenism. Genuine equality between the sexes, resulting in true integration, is a long way off. Were proof of this needed, one has only to recall the fate of the Equal Rights Amendment proposed for the Constitution of the United States. This was defeated by a well-organized and well-financed opposition composed of conservative women who were satisfied with their legal and economic dependence, of religious fundamentalists such as the Mormons, and of the corporate interests which did not want the government to compel them to pay and promote their women employees on the same basis as men.

How precarious the economic status of women remains was further proven during the depression of the early eighties. Being among those most recently hired, women like minority men soon lost their employment.

---

[44]As Prime Minister of Norway, however, Gro Harlem Brundtland demonstrated that a woman leader could be imbued with different values.

Simultaneously in the United States, public programs intended to assist the financially weak were drastically cut by the Reagan administration. The economic inequality of American women in 1982 was graphically summarized in this statement:

> There are 9.4 million American families headed by single women. Fully 34.6 percent of them live below the national poverty level compared with 11.2 percent of all families living in poverty. . . . Women earn on the average only 59 cents for each dollar earned by men. . . . Today, women and in many cases women with children are: 75 percent of all people living in poverty; 69 percent of all food-stamp recipients; 67 percent of all Legal Service clients; 66 percent of all residents of subsidized housing; 61 percent of those depending on Medicaid.[45]

And that is the situation existing in the wealthiest of the world's larger countries!

But you could pick almost any country today ranged on a scale from the very best (those in Scandinavia) to the very worst, and you could cite abundant evidence of sexual discrimination. Observe the personnel entrenched at the top in virtually all of today's governments, churches, corporations, trade unions, or universities. There is no glossing over the visible conclusion that contemporary civilization remains sexist. What is more, you will find the same pattern in the secretariats of the United Nations and its related organs. Indeed, injustice against women is generally worse in the world's less developed areas or wherever a fundamentalist religion is dominant. A blatant recent example of the latter is Khomeini's regime in Iran. But there are others who act the same, both in the Islamic culture and elsewhere, less stridently.

Inequality dies hard. Seldom do the privileged surrender their advantages without a struggle. Reviewing the exclusive and inclusive notions of citizenship, one may conclude these two chapters with the reminder that most political history records the work of oligarchies. Customarily, a few have governed the many for the benefit of the few; the general rule of humanity has been the rule of privilege. Examples of the contrary have been the exceptions. To proclaim that all are fundamentally equal, then to seek to translate this into practice, is abnormal. But since the trend in this direction has been more pronounced during the present century than in any of the past, one may expect that what once was rare may yet become the norm.

There is an aspect of the modern revolution which distinguishes our time and differentiates it from the past, namely the reversal in basic priorities. Previously when the few dominated the many for their own advan-

---

[45]From "Expanding the Role of Women in Our Economy" by Representative Geraldine A. Ferraro, chairwoman of the Task Force on Women's Economic Issues. Quoted in *The Washington Spectator*, vol. 9, no. IX, 1 March 1983, pp. 2–3.

tage, the propriety of this arrangement was seldom questioned. But nowadays the assumption is more widely spread that everybody counts and that governments must somehow serve the needs of all. This shift in values is the precondition for every other change, since no program to equalize opportunities can begin until thinking makes it so. The implications of this shift are seen today in the fact that wherever oligarchy (whether traditional or new) still prevails, it is on the defensive. This means that it must justify its privileges in a manner which was not previously required, or it attempts to conceal them, or it pretends that the opposite is the case.

Hope is therefore reasonably justified about the eventual outcome of this issue. The number of countries where practically all adults are entitled to take part in the election of their government has been growing. Never before, to paraphrase Churchill, have so many had so much opportunity to choose so few. Wherever the mass of the people may participate in the electoral process and freely choose between genuine alternatives, the formulas of Kant and Bentham, and the universal humanity of the great Declarations, can at last be converted from ideal to reality.

6

Second Issue—Part 1

The State and Society

The Unity of Society

States exist because people want the services they can provide. To know what the state is, therefore, we must look at what its government does. Hence we turn from the citizens it serves to the character of its services. All associations, as we saw, are differentiated by the functions they perform. In the case of the state, those functions admit many possibilities which are debatable since the range of choice is wide. Thus controversy extends beyond what the state does to what it might do. We inject into discussions of the state our preferences for what activities properly belong to it. This makes the study of governmental functions both descriptive and normative. For the state is what its functions are, as influenced by our conceptions of what they ought to be.

If we are to choose rationally, we must grasp the issues involved in the debate over what activities are appropriate to the state. Why do we struggle to extend the functions of government or confine them? Since the state evolves within society, how does it relate to other associations? The answer can be attempted by continuing the discussion begun in chapter 2. There, I stressed that cooperation between human beings gives rise to a plurality of groups, and that individuals associate and reassociate in varying patterns according to the aims they share or the ambitions over which they clash. The fact that each of us belongs to many groups within a complex society creates a competition among our goals and loyalties. The outward schism between the groups that compose society is reproduced internally by what Toynbee calls "schism in the soul." If people are to live at peace with themselves, if there is to be harmony among groups, two requirements must be met. Subjectively, human beings have to feel that what unites them is superior to what separates them. Objectively, they need some institution to organize those feelings. For the term *society* to be more than a vague generalization, something must bind the mixture. Can that "something" be identified?

Pluralism Versus Monism

The relations between the groupings in society have been viewed in opposite ways. Some thinkers stress that associations spring spontaneously from the free play of human activity. They are not summoned by fiat, nor do they stem from a single source. In their origins they are independent of one another; and, as the stimuli to associate differ, so do the associations. Therefore, it is concluded, they must be able to operate with the same freedom as allowed them to be formed. Since to be free they must be equal, all should be considered coordinate. No association can arrogate to itself the prerogative of superiority over the rest. The strivings of humanity, it is argued, cannot be folded within the embrace of one supreme good or final end. People reach out for ends in the plural, not for a single end; and as their purposes are plural, so must be the structure of society.[1]

To the pluralists comes the rejoinder of the monists. In their view, society is, or should be, a unity; and for it to be unified, there must be a binding tie. Granted that human drives spontaneously generate a host of groupings; but however independently born, these cannot function independently. As they pursue their aims, groups impinge on one another, creating a need for harmony and order. Individuals are confused by the conflicting claims on their allegiance of distinct and sometimes rival associations. The remedy is to discover some higher good which includes and transcends the lesser. Then, one association must be recognized as responsible for attaining it. To this let the remaining associations be subordinated. Thus can society become and remain unitary in purpose as in organization.[2]

[1] For examples of this viewpoint, consult Harold J. Laski, *Grammar of Politics*, 3rd ed. (London: George Allen and Unwin, 1934), pp. 25–28, 37; or Robert M. MacIver, *The Modern State* (New York: Oxford University Press, 1926), pp. 7, 182.

[2] The monists, curiously enough, exhibit contrasts no less marked than the pluralists. Witness Aristotle, in the paragraph with which he commences the *Politics*, and Mussolini in *The Social and Political Doctrine of Fascism*.

Each of these views is strong where the other is weak. One stresses the role of society as a creative matrix of varied behavior. To advocates of this way of thinking, any proposal for central control or unified direction spells death to the kind of society they idealize. Spontaneity, freedom, variety, autonomy—these they consider the cardinal virtues of groups and group action; and the society they applaud most is that in which such qualities are maximized. But the price of diversity is the impairment of unity. The more the pluralist exalts and exaggerates the independence of associations, the more "the great society"[3] vanishes—until, as with the Chesire cat, a face lingers on without a body, then a grin without a face, and lastly the grin fades away.

Contrariwise is the position of the monists. They are all for unity and for the virtues they hope will accompany it—order, harmony, and singleness of purpose. To attain these is impossible, as they see it, unless the many cohere around one focus. Nor does this coherence result from subjective attitudes alone. To unify society, it is not enough for people to feel that they belong together. The sentiment must be fortified with organization which establishes orderly and harmonious relations between groups by institutional procedures. Though this consummation be devoutly wished by monists, they too encounter difficulties which stem from their position. For they invite the question whether their insistence upon unity is so excessive that groups, other than the supreme unifying agency, will lose meaning, character, and identity to the extent that their autonomy is impaired. The penalty for unity can be the imposition of uniformity.

Moreover, each of these views confronts a difficulty which is the result of its special position. Both philosophies stand unequivocally against something: the pluralist, against organized unity; the monist, against anarchic diversity. But, in a constructive sense, for what kind of society does each view positively contend?

The pluralist may argue for a multiplicity of coordinate associations, whose mutual interplay will cancel out the dangers of excessive power by any one group.[4] But, following the potentialities inherent in this logic, you may go further. Approving the subdivision of society into its groups, you may also approve the fragmentation of groups into their individual members. At the logical extreme, therefore, the truest pluralists are individualists. Such thinkers give the primacy to the individual; and in the name of individuality will resist the pressures from the groups in which they combine and the society which would unify the groups. Pluralism, so conceived, is the plurality of autonomous individuals, rather than that of autonomous associations. Conversely, the pluralist may veer in the other direction. Though conceding the need for individuals to be grouped and organized, one may be dubious about the possibilities of maintaining equi-

---

[3]This is the title of a book by Graham Wallas, published in 1914.
[4]Such, essentially, is Madison's conception of society in *The Federalist*, no. 10.

librium and order among too many associations. Why not then support the idea of a balance between two bodies roughly equal in weight and bulk? Distrustful of the monopoly that the monist accepts, one settles for dualism. Two great associations may be more stable than many, and safer than one. Indeed, as the discussion will show, the pluralistic argument for society has in some historical cases assumed a dualistic form.

Unity through the Family, Church, or Business

The monist, too, has problems. If you seek an integrating focus for society, you must designate what this should be. Which institution do you select to embrace or oversee the rest? And how can it accomplish that task?

That a choice exists, and that the answer is not cut-and-dried, is substantiated by historical evidence. Several social institutions, in fact, have functioned in the role of prime coordinator for society. One of these, at various places and times, was the family. In such a case kinship becomes the determinant of every relationship. Because human beings are connected in certain ways by birth, their other group activities are cast in the mold of heredity. Thus the family serves as the economic unit, where each works for all and receives a share of the total output. The family takes care of its weak, its aged, and its incapacitated. The family provides education, and, for religion, worships its ancestors. The family determines marital unions by alliance with other families. The family establishes rules and administers its discipline with rewards and punishments. Sometimes it even levies a death penalty on one of its members or wages war upon a neighboring family in the form of a blood feud or vendetta.

Similarly, religious associations have expanded beyond their primary function of worship and have encompassed the general direction of society under spiritual authority, as in a theocracy. When Calvin and Calvinists controlled Geneva in the seventeenth century or when the Jesuits ruled Paraguay in the eighteenth, a church-government regulated the conduct of individuals and groups in minute detail. Religious, no less than secular, bodies can declare and enforce the law by reference to divine sanction; maintain and direct an economic system as proprietors and managers; supervise the family by granting or withholding its rites; educate the youth; organize charities for the needy; and dominate the arts by control over their themes and forms. Religions can likewise launch crusades, proclaim "holy wars," and place armies in the field.[5] Men have bled and died for the Cross, the Crescent, or the *Mogen David*, as they have for Old Glory, the Union Jack, or the *Tricolore*. Nor need one turn to the past for examples.

---

[5]"Men never do evil so completely and cheerfully," wrote Pascal, "as when they do it from religious conviction."

Early in 1979, when Iran's government changed from the autocracy of the Shah to a theocracy under the Ayatollah Khomeini, a steady stream of fulminations issued from the city of Qom as orders to true believers and threats to the infidel. Expressing himself as spokesman for the Islamic faith, Khomeini was the lawgiver on all aspects of Iranian society.

Sometimes the paramount association is economic. A group formed for purposes of manufacturing or trade may discover in a certain *milieu* that it cannot fulfill these functions unless it extends its control over other institutions. Whether Napoleon was right in describing the British as "a nation of shopkeepers," or whether President Coolidge did full justice to his fellow countrymen with the remark that "the business of America is business," the fact remains that society can be integrated not by kinship or religion but by control of productive resources, by entrepreneurial technique—in Carlyle's phrase, by the "cash nexus." Indeed there have been corporations clothed in the full panoply of governments. The celebrated East India Company,[6] which ruled Britain's empire in India until 1858, is a conspicuous example. When business organizes society for business ends, it too can make and apply the law, establish an ethical code, and define the standards of right and wrong in relation to such concepts as "property," "profit," or "labor." By prescribing the conditions, hours, and wages of work, business can make or break the family. By its influence over occupations and careers, it can mold the policies and curricula of education. By paying artists and purchasing their products, it can regulate aesthetic style and taste. Lastly, to promote or preserve a commercial empire, business has mobilized military force and fought its battles at so much *per caput* and for such and such *percent*.[7]

These facts warrant an inference. Because the family, church, and corporation have made efforts of this kind with considerable success, it would appear that, in the absence of a coordinating institution, society contains a vacuum which there is an opportunity to fill. If various associations made the attempt, it is reasonable to assume that a need exists which they seek to satisfy, and that they can then be judged on how well they fill it. That need arises in part from the competition between associations and their rival claims on the allegiance of their members. The relations between groups demand regulation, supposedly by some superassociation. But there is more to it than that. If the unity of society is not an empty phrase, more will be required than a mechanism that merely mitigates the effects of

---

[6]In the course of his *Speech in the Impeachment of Warren Hastings*, 1788, Edmund Burke thus described the company: "The constitution of the company began in commerce, and ended in empire. . . . The India company came to be what it is—a great empire, carrying on, subordinately, a great commerce. . . . In fact, the East-India Company in Asia is a state in the disguise of a merchant." *Works*, 7 (Boston: Wells and Lilly, 1827), 29.

[7]Contemporary cases which approximate to this are many of the business corporations in Japan, whose paternalism envelops much of the life of their employees.

conflict. Since society is built more on cooperation than competition, a case can be argued for promoting harmony between groups.

As a group is more than the sum of its separate members, so is society more than the mere addition of the component groups. Some writers have described the structure of society as federal. This is a helpful analogy if it is understood in two senses: first, that society is not properly a collection of individuals, but rather of groups of individuals; and second, that the groups constitute more collectively than they would separately. Considered by itself, each association is concerned with human interests that are fractional, these fractions being called economic, educational, religious, and so on. Functioning in its primary sense, an economic association performs activities that are economic, a religious association pursues aims that are religious, and similarly with the rest. No one association, if all are coordinate in rank and limited in function, has the responsibility or means to see that these fragments of human life are fused into a whole. In other words, there is no way of ensuring that the economy functions, not as a thing apart, but as the economic aspect of society; that a school or university is no cloistered academy, but a training ground for the use of intelligence in the workaday world; that the particular, in short, be treated within the framework of the general.

Defects of a Single-Track Society

But the monist who seeks an integrated society, though possessing many weapons against the pluralist, still runs a risk. If any association is to succeed in coordinating society, it must evolve from a minor part to the leading role. It must broaden the necessarily narrow interest from which it started into a comprehensive concern for the whole. The question is whether an association will in fact be capable of growing to the stature of its wider responsibilities or will instead remain the prisoner of its origins and of the limits they impose. The problem can be illustrated by some examples that are by no means hypothetical. Suppose the institution that tries to coordinate society is the family.[8] A group created by kinship and sustained by living together must then be expected to transfer to other spheres the characteristics of its primary functions. Relations between human beings will correspond to those between husband and wife, or parents and child, or sibling and sibling. Authority will be parental in form. Status within the family circle will determine status within the social circle. Family dictates will be the overriding consideration in the economic realm. Thus the

---

[8]Some oriental cultures provide examples of the transfer of the family relationship to an entire society. See an analysis of this attempt in Japan by Robert A. Scalapino, *Democracy and the Party Movement in Prewar Japan* (Berkeley: University of California Press, 1953), pp. 120 ff.

ownership and inheritance of the family homestead, the provision for a son to marry and support a wife, production for subsistence only or for exchange—such matters will be settled by the prevailing conceptions of the family as the unifier of the social order. The great society will become an association of kinsfolk, writ large.[9]

Likewise, when the integrating agency is religious, its theology will extend to every secular activity. If the religion asserts that there is life after death, we shall be told to prepare ourselves in this world of mortal things for the eternity hereafter. The rules of daily conduct will be construed as a lifelong consecration to the Deity. The social contacts of the individual will be confined to the ranks of one's coreligionists. Those who do not belong to the established communion—call them heathen, pagan, gentile, infidel, heretic, or whatever—will be society's outcasts. They are "the stranger within thy gates," "the untouchables," "the internal proletariat,"[10] living witnesses of a house divided against itself, with religion as the divider. Holy Writ becomes law in the form of the Gospel, the Torah, the Koran, the Vedas, and the supreme lawgiver is the Holy Man, Prophet, or Son of God—A Gautama, Jesus, Mahomet, or Moses. Within this frame of reference, criticism of authority is equated with blasphemy; opposition itself is sin.

Similar in principle is the result that befalls the economic group seeking to integrate society. In this case the basic elements of the economic order will pervade the social system. Thus the rights that are vested in the ownership of property, and the human relationships arising from it—such factors of production as the control of natural resources, the use of tools and equipment, the structure of the wage system—all this will affect the rest of man's estate. Humanity will be preoccupied with material concerns, such as living standards, the distribution of goods, the struggle for acquisition, the maintenance of employment and of purchasing power. The world will be viewed as a market. Language itself will take its connotations from the categories of economics. "Enterprise" will be synonymous with "business"; ideas one seeks to impart will be commodities one "sells"; human beings will be specified as "managers," "consumers," "hands." The great society, if it knows no other god than Mammon, will strike the balance sheet of its civilization in pecuniary terms. For what shall it profit a man if he gain his own soul and lose a whole market?

The point of the foregoing paragraphs can be summarized thus: When an association that originates with a finite function broadens out to the indefinite horizons of society, it tends to apply to its larger task the criteria of its initial limits. To the extent that this is so, its efforts provide

---

[9]Many peoples have expressed this idea in the form of a story that they are descended from a common ancestor.

[10]This is A. J. Toynbee's phrase in his *Study of History.*

society with both integration and straitjacketing. To subordinate all aspects of life and all kinds of groups to the single principle of kinship, religion, or economics can yield an unwholesome monism. If its results then are to be beneficial, the unifying association must meet this test: While retaining its original functions, it must transcend them and change its own character. It cannot integrate society merely by refashioning every other association in its own image.

This survey of the arguments in issue between monists and pluralists and of the problems peculiar to each facilitates a better understanding of the controversy over the functions of the state. The analysis so far has indicated that the question of what activities are appropriate to the state is not narrowly political, but broadly social. It has also become clear that two questions are involved, since a choice must first be made between pluralism and monism; and, if the latter is preferred, a second choice must determine which association can best coordinate the whole. The answer to the second question is, in a vital sense, relevant to the first, because, if no association can fill the role of integrating, the case for pluralism wins by default. If, on the other hand, some one association is competent to do it, then the case for the monist is strengthened.

The State's Relation to Society

In this controversy the state is directly involved, because one inevitably asks: What activities is government to undertake? Somehow, the relations of the state to our other associations must be defined. If the pluralists are to prevail, they must explain (1) why it is necessary to limit the functions of the state, (2) where to place the limits, and (3) how a society holds together, or achieves integration, in the absence of a unifying agency. In order to win the argument, the monist must demonstrate (1) that society needs unifying, (2) that the state can do it, and (3) that any risks in confiding this duty to the state can be safely forestalled or are outweighed by the attendant advantages.

Both viewpoints have been expressed at various times by those who wished to advocate or resist some manifestation of governmental power. Nor have the rival philosophies been confined to theoretical debate. Under one guise or another, each has been translated into practice and has received concrete expression. Hence the discussion and evaluation of each can be based both on the reasoned hopes of their advocates and on the performance that results from their application in practice. Like the family, business, and church, the state has entered this field of controversy because there is an opportunity for it to grasp. If society is ready for integration, the state is as well placed to provide it as are associations based upon kinship, economics, or religion. Or possibly, it is even better placed because of its original, primary function. All human beings want protection. So, all of us depend on the association which provides it. Moreover, the state controls the force which ensures the protection. Through this same force, the government is able at times to impose itself upon the other institutions of society. Indeed the state can be more effectively monistic than businesses, families, or churches because of the sanctions it employs. Those who do not bow to family control may be excluded from the kin group. Those who defy their employers may lose one means of earning their bread and butter. Those who resist sacerdotal authority may be excommunicated. Such sanctions are not completely compulsive unless the victim is left with no other alternative. But in some societies a person may survive without a family, may earn a living in new ways, embrace a new faith, or do without one. Universally, however, the ultimate sanction of the state is a gun pointed at your heart. If the state has a monopoly of the available force, as is ordinarily the case, there is no choice but to submit or die.

Behind the modern debate over the proper sphere of governmental activity stretches a history of at least 25 centuries. For that reason the best way to understand current controversies about the functions of the state is to review them in chronological perspective. The story forms a sequence of alternating episodes, with the emphasis shifting from one pole to the other. The city-state of the Graeco-Roman period was primarily monistic in spirit and organization. The counterdoctrine, that the sphere of the state must be limited, was advanced by the Christian church after it became the official religion of the Roman Empire and a partner in the established order. This principle continued to prevail through the Middle Ages, but lost ground with the advent of the Reformation and the emergence of the nation-state. The ethos of the latter at its inception was as strongly monistic as the city-state had been. It remained so until the economic ferment of the Industrial Revolution once more brought into vogue the concept of the limited state, with business now cast in the role formerly played by the medieval church. The twentieth century, influenced in this matter as in others by the nineteenth, has both imitated and rejected its predecessor. In the ninth decade of this century, both viewpoints—that which insists on limits and that which does not—are still embattled. Neither is clearly dominant.

The successive periods may be roughly identified as follows:

Period 1, approximately from the tenth century B.C. to the fourth century A.D. Monistic State.

Period 2, from the fourth century A.D. to middle of the fifteenth century. Limited State.

Period 3, from the mid-fifteenth century to 1776. Monistic State.

Period 4, 1776 to 1914. Limited State.

Period 5, since 1914. Return to the Monistic State, but with resistance to its domination.

A survey of these periods[11] and a review of their problems will help to explain the advantages claimed for each doctrine and the difficulties attending its fulfillment.

The Graeco-Roman City-State: An Experiment in Monism

In its developed form, the *polis* or city-state-community, such as Sparta in the sixth century B.C. or Athens in the fifth, demanded complete allegiance of its citizens. All activities and associations were either controlled or liable to control by the state. Society—the sum total of all groups—was inseparable from the state. Even the Greek language, that flexible instrument for conveying the subtlest nuance of thought, had no word for society any more than it distinguished between state and city. The one word *polis* sufficed for city, state, and society combined. Within this context of ideas, the state was the paramount social institution when and wherever it chose to intervene. Thus, the economic field was subject to political ordering as the public interest seemed to require. Religion consisted of state worship of the patron hero, the city deity, and the pantheon of the Olympians. Many of the cultural achievements which made that age immortal were evoked or produced by state enterprise. Architects, sculptors, and painters—an Ictinus, Phidias, or Apelles—dedicated their genius to the temples and other civic buildings constructed by the state for its adornment. It was the public marketplace that served as classroom for the interrogations of Socrates; the citizens' assembly that inspired the oratory of Pericles or Demosthenes; the official festivals and contests that promoted the staging of dramas by the great playwrights.

Nevertheless, although that describes the general tendency, some aberrations or exceptions existed. Certain religious cults, such as the Eleusinian Mysteries, did not belong to official state ceremony. Some creative artists, the lyric poets for instance, produced their works to satisfy an inward urge rather than a public audience. In actuality, not everything was prescribed and ordered by the state, save possibly in Sparta and Crete. But if the state chose to extend its authority to any sphere, there was no rival institution strong enough to resist its advance and no social philosophy delimiting the bounds of state action. Indeed, the magisterial pronouncements of Plato and Aristotle are wholly couched in terms of the omnipotent *polis*. In their major treatises, these two touch on nearly all of the great issues that occupy the forefront of political theory and practice in the

---

[11]This breakdown into "periods" is offered with the necessary caution that any such subdivision contains an element of arbitrariness. The beginning and ending dates are averages, rather than precise points. Few periods, moreover, are all one thing or all another. Usually, contemporary instances of the opposite to the prevalent tendency can be discovered.

modern world. Significantly, though, they omit the questions of the relation of the state to society and the possible limits of state power. The reason for the omission is that such queries did not even arise in Greek experience. It never occurred to Plato and Aristotle to examine an alternative to monism. This they took for granted.

However, a clarification should be noted. Both Plato and Aristotle are monists in the sense that they view the state as supreme among human associations and set no bounds to its activities. But their monism is not identical. Or, to be more precise, the supremacy of the state is manifested differently. Aristotle asserts his monism in the opening paragraph of the *Politics*, where he calls the state the paramount association, embracing all the rest and pursuing the highest good. Yet this conception of the state does not lead him to undervalue, still less to abolish, the remaining associations. These retain their place within the fabric of society and even serve to strengthen the bonds of social cohesion. But if a conflict arises, it is to the state that all are subordinate. Plato differs from Aristotle in his utterly uncompromising emphasis on unity, which he believes is best safeguarded by the destruction of competing associations. All loyalties and affections are to be focused on and drawn toward one center. If other institutions, such as the family or the ownership of private property, are likely to distract the individual from a single-minded dedication to the public interest, the platonic guardians must have no share in them. The monistic state of Aristotle is one that permits other groups to exist, but stands supreme over them. The monistic state of Plato prefers to abolish the other groups and absorb their functions.

Apart from the preferences of philosophers, however, what were the social reasons why the practice and philosophy of the city-state were monistic? Two reasons suffice. One was the smallness of the city-state. With an area and population so confined, there was little room for parallel, coordinate systems. As the Greeks read the lessons of their own history, they could choose one of two alternatives: unity with order or faction fights with anarchy. Closeness of contact, and the pressure of small-sized communities, bred a view of the state as the paramount social organization. In the antithesis between the public and private sides of life, Greek spokesmen supported the former. Thus their term for private citizen, *idiotes,* has given us the modern "idiot," and Pericles could castigate those who took no part in civic affairs as useless to the community.[12] Besides smallness, a second reason for monism was the insecurity which plagued the Greeks in their interstate relations. Not only was there the possibility of war between Greek and non-Greek, but the little city-states themselves were often at each other's throats, and neighboring settlements were likely to be hereditary

---

[12]See the Funeral Oration in Thucydides' *Histories,* ii.

foes. Seeking protection from these perils, the Greeks were impelled to rally around the institution whose function was to protect.

If monism was encouraged by the smallness of the unit of government and facilitated by the absence of any association rivaling the state, it would be expected that, when these conditions disappeared, the monistic state would also disappear. Early signs of this possibility were discernible in the first philosophies which emerged after the absorption of the *polis* into the larger units of kingdoms or empires. The Stoics[13] and Epicureans rejected the assumptions of Plato and Aristotle. They sought to reconcile opposite extremes by finding a place for the individual within the immensity of the universe. Since the politics of the three centuries between the breakup of the empire of Alexander and the consolidation of that of Rome were chaotic and turbulent, many people viewed the state with pessimism, apprehension, or indifference. If the good life was unobtainable through politics, it must be sought in other ways. If the ambitions of governments were prejudicial to the public peace, peace of mind must be cultivated elsewhere. Hence followed a reassessment of the relative priorities of public and private activity, and philosophers now advised that all should compensate for the insecurities around them by seeking security within themselves.

As occurred with equalitarianism, a concept born in the minds of Greeks received institutional form through the acts of Romans. This happened after Rome had succeeded in expanding into an empire and Christianity had managed to capture Rome. Previously, when Rome was a small community beset by unfriendly neighbors, it was subject to the same internal and external forces as the city-states of Greece. No sphere of life was exempt from the power of the state, if there was occasion or demand for its exercise. None of the other groups composing society was in a position to withstand the state or claim an independent or higher allegiance. Family relations, religious cults, economic affairs, cultural advances—all could be brought within the ambit of official surveillance. That situation changed when the Roman Empire expanded to an unparalleled size. The tightly knit organization of a small community could not be transferred or reproduced across the large-scale dimensions of Rome's conquests. Given the means of communication then available between the central authority and peripheral regions, the extent of the area to be governed precluded any intensive direction of society by the state. As long as Rome's authority was firmly established in the spheres of military power, foreign relations, and finance, in other matters much diversity and autonomy were permitted to the provinces and municipalities.

[13]For the Stoics, see chapter 5, section on "The Classical Roots of the Doctrine of Equality."

Along with this change of scale, an empire that eventually stretched from Jordan to Scotland and from the German forests to the Sahara Desert came to embrace a host of religious faiths. Out of the welter of sects, cults, rites, and deities, Christianity emerged dominant. When the Emperor Constantine was converted, the *Imperium Romanum* entered into articles of union with the church. Considered in political terms, this partnership between the Cross and the Eagle brought gain and loss to both. The state gained, because the spiritual influence of the Christian faith could now be employed to unify the allegiance of Roman citizens. But simultaneously the state lost its monopoly. Accepting a partner, it admitted a separate and coordinate body to the citadel of power. The church likewise derived a benefit; but it also incurred a liability. Becoming an integral part of the established order, the church ceased to be a victim of persecution—henceforth it did the persecuting. Indeed it could, if necessary, invoke the secular arm as its ally against heretics and infidels. This power, however, brought disadvantages. Not only might the church be obliged to extend reciprocal aid and support its temporal partner, even if the latter were, to put it mildly, unsaintly; but the church could also become corrupted by its involvement in the preoccupations of its position. Dominance could even bring wealth, at least to the princes of the church, and therewith a tendency to corruption. It was Dante who wrote, with a reference to the supposed Donation of Constantine to Pope Silvester:

> Ah Constantine, what evil hast thou sired!
> Not thy conversion, but that price wherewith
> The first rich father thou has paid and hired![14]

The Christian Revolution: Church-State Dualism

Thus was inaugurated a new era in political history. What it signalized was a different solution to the problem of defining the functions of the state. Where the old order had been content with a doctrine that set no limit to these functions and made the boundaries of politics coextensive with the range of social conduct, the crux of the new order lay precisely in the effort to delimit the field of politics within the larger area of society and thus necessarily establish an adjacent field, which the state had no right to enter. The earlier concept of a society unified by the monistic state was rejected. It was replaced by the notion of a society split in two, with twin institutions separated by a frontier. Philosophy was now called upon to justify, and

---

[14]*Inferno*, Canto 19. 11. 115–17. My translation. In this Canto, Dante is attacking the clerics who sold ecclesiastical office and religious favors for monetary gain.

statesmanship to operate, a division of spheres. The issues posed by this endeavor were challenging. Reasons had to be discovered for the assertion that dualism was in some ways superior to unity; a line of demarcation had somewhere to be drawn; and finally the separate spheres and the government of each had somehow to be related to each other. These problems in all their ramifications occupied human ingenuity for over a thousand years.

Whenever it is argued that the power of the state be circumscribed, the proposal takes its specific form from the nature of the association which offers the challenge to monism. In this case, since religion assumed the offensive, it was the church that emerged as an institution coequal with the state. Relations between church and state now became the central issue for political theory and organization, which they had not been before. It is, therefore, to the social doctrines of Christianity, as these evolved from the fourth to the fourteenth century A.D., that we must turn for understanding the theory and tactics of the Dark and Middle Ages.

Like all systematic philosophies, Christianity assumed a view of human nature. Human beings were thought to be composed of two parts, body and soul. The body, an object of sense perception and known through sensory evidence, exists as a member of the world of material things. It is born, passes through the life cycle, then dies. The soul does not belong in the sensory realm. Belief in its existence is granted by divine revelation and must be accepted on faith. Joining the body when life begins, the soul will depart on the advent of death and is immortal. The soul is therefore on a higher plane than the body and is our most important possession. Hence in the scale of Christian values this world takes second place to the next. The care of the spirit, which is everlasting, has priority over the temporal and mundane. Our greatest concern, while alive on this earth, is to save our souls for eternity.

The dualism which runs through Christian thought and theology is evident in the saying of Jesus: "Render, therefore, unto Caesar the things that are Caesar's; and render unto God the things that are God's." The same pattern recurs in the treatise of Saint Augustine, *Concerning the City of God,* where an analogous distinction is drawn between two cities, the earthly and the heavenly. People must resist the temptations and avoid the perils of the earth. Let them seek the eternal bliss of the heavenly city by obeying the counsel to be perfect "even as your Father in Heaven is perfect." To apply these attitudes to actual government was the task initiated by one of the early popes, Gelasius I, and continued by various of his successors. Since every person contained two natures, one mortal and the other immortal, the organization of society—so the argument ran—must correspond to the dualism implanted in humanity by the Creator. The church should be the institution charged with the salvation of souls and the preparation in this life for the life everlasting. The state should have the responsibility for affairs of this world, for the mortal sphere pertaining to the body. Church and state should be constituted as separate authorities, each paramount within its own bailiwick and possessing its own government. But how were the twain, *sacerdotium* and *imperium*, the ecclesiastical power and the temporal, the spiritual and the secular, to be related? The Gelasian answer envisaged them as "two swords" that could not be grasped and wielded by one hand. As God had endowed us with a soul separate from the body, so must church and state exist independently of each other. It would therefore be as wrong for an emperor to exercise spiritual power as for a pope to hold secular sway. What God had put asunder, let no man put together.

It is evident that the application of these formulas depended on the validity of two assumptions: one, that the spheres of the ecclesiastical and temporal jurisdictions could in fact be separated; and the other, that the two institutions would respectively adhere to their coordinate status. Failure to fulfill either assumption would destroy dualism. How did the medieval Christian world meet these tests of its dogma?

The Theory of Dualism vs. the Conditions of Unity

The separation of the spiritual realm from the secular was more easily stated as an ideal than realized in actuality. The things that are Caesar's may be distinguishable metaphysically from the things that are God's, yet both are physically intertwined. Thus there were ceremonies and official acts of the state that were accompanied by prayer or required solemnizing by some religious affirmation. Treaties between rulers, for example, were signed and sworn under oath that called for the presence of the Bible and a priest. Governments were staffed by human beings who possessed souls and who, being Christians, were children of the church. The church could therefore call them to account if their governmental acts violated its canons of Christian duty. By the weapons of excommunication and interdict, the pope could even subdue a temporal ruler, as in the cases of the Emperor Henry IV and King John of England. The long drawn out investiture controversy revolved around the question: Should a bishop be invested with the insignia of his office by the secular authority of the area or by an ecclesiastical superior? Conversely, while the church was involved in various functions of the state, so was the state immersed in matters vital to the church. As its power waxed, the church became an integral part of the established order which the state protected.[15] The church acquired land and buildings and other forms of property. It employed large numbers of people, including serfs. It used the revenues from its possessions for its own needs and claimed to be exempt from contributing to the temporal

[15]For some evidence on this point, see Tocqueville, *Ancien Régime*, part 2, chapter 1.

treasury. If the state failed to maintain internal order, or was unable to protect its territories from invasion, the church ran the risk of looting and pillage. Hence in a thousand ways, lay matters were interlocked with spiritual. The two spheres were separated by an ideological, not an iron, curtan, and it was not practicable to make them self-contained.

Similar difficulties were encountered with the effort to place the two institutions on that footing of equality which the Gelasian theory enunciated. Each of the partners, as occasion permitted or demanded, pressed its attack on the other. Each, at one time or another, struck at the foundations of Gelasianism by attempting either to subordinate one sword to the other or to grasp both with one hand. In this tussle for supremacy between church and state, the initial advantage lay with the church, and the first major blows at the doctrine of Gelasius were dealt by his papal successors. There were various reasons why this happened. For one thing, the theoretical postulates of Christianity were not easily reconciled with the concept of equal jurisdictions. To a Christian the soul was clearly on a higher plane than the body, life in the hereafter more important than the life here and now, eternity more significant than threescore years and ten. Hence in the hierarchy of Christian values the church outranked the state. If churchmen argued that the spiritual sword should precede the temporal, who could gainsay such a contention? Furthermore, independently of theoretical beliefs, practical considerations favored unity over dualism. This was especially so in the troubled times following the breakdown of the Roman Empire in the West, when Teutonic peoples invaded its territories and carved out new kingdoms. While the secular power was at the worst in dissolution, or at the best in flux, often the sole rallying point for society proved to be the church. If there were instances when popes gratuitously clutched at both swords, there were also times when the church held both through the state's default.

The Papal Rejection of Dualism

The papal attacks on the Gelasian doctrine were occasioned by two of the most prolonged and harassing issues of the medieval period: one concerning the claim of secular rulers to invest bishops with the symbols of their office, the other arising over royal demands that the clergy pay taxes to the state treasury. During the former of these controversies, Pope Gregory VII, who eventually dominated over Emperor Henry IV, insisted that within the church the bishops were subordinate to the pope and that in church-state relations a defiant ruler could be excommunicated and his subjects absolved from their oaths of allegiance. This was tantamount to claiming for the papacy a power to depose a monarch, employable at the pope's discretion. Implicit in this, of course, was the view that of the two swords the *sacerdotium* was mightier than the *imperium,* a doctrine which, whether justifiable or not, was not Gelasian. But Gregory went further. Mindful of the distinction that St. Augustine had drawn between the city of God and the earthly city, he proceeded to suggest—which Augustine had not—that the city of God was synonymous with the church whereas the earthly city, or kingdom of the Devil, was identifiable with the state—a pair of equations which definitely concluded with debasing the secular sphere in the hierarchy of Christian values!

The later controversy over the taxing powers was, if anything, fiercer and more embittered. On its side, the church reached the ultimate in extravagant contentions as its relative position weakened. The leading protagonists in this struggle were Pope Boniface VIII and Philip the Fair, King of France. Armed with the doctrine enunciated earlier by Innocent IV that the pope enjoyed *plenitudo potestatis* ("total power"), Boniface moved into the logically final ground and expressly rejected dualism. In a bull entitled *Unam Sanctam,* whose initial word stressed unity, the Pope claimed both swords—though the temporal one could be delegated to the secular arm to be wielded at ecclesiastical bidding. This pronouncement sealed the papal rejection of the goal of a divided society.

Attack on Dualism by the State

The state's position in this controversy switched as its power changed relative to that of the church. If the temporal authorities were disorganized, as was not infrequently the case during the Dark Ages; if the empire, reconstituted by Charlemagne in A.D. 800, was more shadowy than real, and the emperor was insecure in his authority; if kings were weakened by the pretensions and powers of the feudal nobility; then the secular branch was scarcely so consolidated as to withstand a determined pope. Under such conditions the state was on the defensive, which forced its apologists to adhere fairly strictly to the doctrines of Gelasius. Acknowledging the monopoly of the church in the salvation of souls, the state's defenders had to assert that over temporal matters the ruler derived his power directly from God—not indirectly via the pope as an intermediary. In other words, the things that are Caesar's are entrusted to Caesar by divine dispensation. For the powers that be (and this means all of them) are ordained of God. On this assumption, the state could preserve its role as equal partner of the church.

In the later phases of the conflict, however, especially during the struggles between Boniface VIII and Philip and between Pope John XXII and the Emperor Ludwig of Bavaria, the weights were tipped in the balance on the secular side. This was due to the cumulative effect of political trends operating within the medieval system, which finally contributed to its downfall. One such trend was the gradual consolidation of monarchical power at the expense of the nobility.[16] Another, associated with it, was the dawning of national[17] sentiments—particularly evident when the French clergy supported King Philip of France on the tax question against the pope at Rome. A third was the political weakening of the papacy because of internal corruption and its lowered prestige in the period of the schism. Thus strengthened, the state was able to launch its own offensive, and therewith attack the Gelasian theory from the opposite flank. Its line of argument contended that the function of the church is to teach and preach. As an institution organized on this earth, the church falls within the category of worldly affairs. Hence its property is taxable by the state, while its personnel (the clergy) are merely one vocational group within society and, as such, are subject to the jurisdiction of laymen. Like the contrary attempt of Boniface VIII, this was a rejection of dualism. But the advocate of unification was now siding with the state, which cast itself in the paramount role.

All in all, the medieval experiment must be judged a failure. Dualism did not work. The two spheres were not kept separate. The two jurisdictions did not continue equal and coordinate. The two swords were not brandished in harmony and unison. Too often they clashed. Like a pair of unruly oxen harnessed to the same yoke, both parties sought to be rid of the Gelasian legacy. But the impasse that medievalism had reached by the early fifteenth century marked the end—not of the story, but only of an episode. A new epoch was arriving with new facts and formulas.

The Reconstruction of Unity

It is characteristic of the political process that, when a trend in one direction has reached a point of excess, a counteraction is likely. Sometimes the latter movement, too, will be developed to excess. With the breakdown of the attempt at dualism came a new effort to reinstate the older principle which predated Constantine's conversion. In place of two spheres, there would be one. Instead of the state performing limited functions which covered a fraction of society, its sphere was now to be as wide as society itself. In lieu of limits, the state's range of action was to be unbounded.

The yearning for unity was an understandable reaction to the insecurities and discords of a divided society. Many were tired of conflicting claims, clashing loyalties, and antagonistic systems. They preferred to accept, with all its risks, a single authority. Unity at least meant that you knew whose laws and which commands to obey. Hence it is that Thomas Hobbes,

---

[16]See chapter 10, section on "The Medieval Dispersion of Powers" and "Sovereignty and Absolutism in the Nation-State."

[17]See chapter 12, section on "The Cracks in Medieval Unity."

expounding the convenant on which a state and government are founded, urges the concentration of authority: "The only way to erect such a Common Power, as may be able to defend them from the invasion of Forraigners, and the injuries of one another, . . . is, to conferre all their power and strength upon *one* Man, or upon *one* Assembly of men, that may reduce all their wills, by plurality of voices, unto *one* will. . . ."[18] In keeping with this plea for unity, Hobbes views with suspicion, distrust, or outright antipathy the development within society of associations other than the state, since these may grow from subordinates of the central authority into rivals. Upon them he vents his displeasure in a wholesale indictment embracing "the Ghostly Authority" of the church, the accumulation of too much treasure by a few, the loyalty of an army to an ambitious general, "the immoderate greatness of a town," and also "the great number of Corporations, which are as it were many lesser commonwealths in the bowels of a greater, like wormes in the entrayles of a naturall man." For full measure he adds to his list "the Liberty of Disputing against absolute Power, by pretenders to Politicall Prudence; which though bred for the most part in the Lees of the people; yet animated by False Doctrines, are perpetually meddling with the Fundamentall Lawes, to the molestation of the Common-wealth; like the little Wormes, which Physicians call *Ascarides*."[19]

From the colorful language, a clear meaning emerges. Hobbes is predisposed against a plurality of associations on grounds akin to Plato's objection to the family and private property. The coexistence of other associations alongside the state he considers a weakness to both state and society, because it subjects each individual, as a member of many groups, to diverse affiliations and potentially rival allegiances. The Hobbesian cure-all for the disorders of pluralism is as drastic, uncompromising, and clear-cut as the Platonic. All power must go to the state, and, within the state, to its supreme ruling element. Rid yourselves, so runs his advice, of a multiplicity of associations. Rally around the great association. Finally, since few of his readers were rationalists, with a last flourish he inserts the keystone of religious faith into the archway of his "scientific" reasons for the foundation of the state: "This is the Generation of that great LEVIATHAN, or rather (to speak more reverently) of that *Mortall God*, to which wee owe under the *Immortal God*, our peace and defence."[20]

These excerpts from Hobbes have been cited as representative of the new trend because of the rigorous character of their logic. They have the merit of hewing the issue in sharp outline and high relief. But the ideas were not, of course, chiseled in thin air. They were excavated from the rock strata of facts, thrown up into new convolutions by the political earth-

[18]*Leviathan*, part 2, chap. 17 (Everyman's Library), p. 89. My italics. See chapter 29 (pp. 174–75) for his explicit rejection of church-state dualism.

[19]*Leviathan*, chapter 29.

[20]Ibid., chapter 17, p. 89. Italics and capitals in the original.

quakes of the sixteenth and seventeenth centuries. The violence of those circumstances was due to the breakdown of the Gelasian formula and the search for new solutions.

Uniformity or Toleration?

Since the church had been partner or rival of the state for a thousand years, and since church-state relations were in contention, it was this problem that the new era tackled first. The relative strength of the two institutions, already changing with the emergence of nationalism, altered decisively in the sixteenth century as the papacy weakened. In this respect, even more important than the internal decline of its organization (which could be, and later was, reconstructed) was the defection from Rome of large areas of Western Christendom. The Protestant Reformation, whose influence was felt most in north central and northwestern Europe and more among Teutonic and Scandinavian peoples than among Latins, established in a Christendom already divided between the Roman and Eastern Orthodox rites a further split within the West. Since that time, to be a Christian in Western Europe or its subsequent colonial offshoots did not necessarily mean acceptance of the Roman rite or allegiance to papal authority. The Catholic church, whose Greek name literally means "universal," no longer possessed a universal following. The result has been that for five centuries no one church in the West has enjoyed a monopoly of Christianity. Furthermore, when the dissolvent acids of Protestantism commenced their corrosion of the once monolithic church, the same chemistry could operate within the chinks and crevasses of Protestantism itself. The practice of dissent could react upon its instigators; and the divisive process started a chain reaction of sects and schisms. Lutherans, Anglicans, Presbyterians, Baptists, Quakers, Methodists, and others held out to puzzled humanity their many keys to the Kingdom.

The political consequences of a fragmented Christianity were momentous alike for citizens individually and for the state of which they were members. In spiritual matters the individual no longer faced the compulsions of monopoly. The doctrine that "there is no salvation outside the church"[21] lost most of its effect, since there was now a variety of churches, each proffering salvation. Excommunication lacked its former terror when there were other communions to join. The interdict, whereby medieval popes forbade obedience to a heretical ruler, became an obsolete weapon. Skepticism now had full scope in matters theological, since if many churches indicated different roads to heaven, the curious were bound to inquire which route was right.

What effect did this have on the state? In what ways was government

[21]*Extra ecclesiam nulla salus.*

impelled to readjust? The political novelty lay in the fact that Christianity, for the previous thousand years a unifying force in Western Europe, now became a disruptive agent. Previously, if a ruler accepted the church as a partner or as the superior, there would at least be relative harmony. But now a Christian ruler had to choose between different churches (it being assumed that one could not be non-Christian or atheist); and, once the personal choice was made, he or she must decide whether subjects could choose differently or must adhere to the same communion. Thus arose the political issue of whether people's religious beliefs were relevant to their citizenship and their allegiance to their sovereign. Could Protestants tolerate Catholics, or Catholics tolerate Protestants, as equally loyal members of the same state? Could one Protestant sect even tolerate another? Should the state, confronted with the fact of differences, exercise neutrality and ennoble the tolerance of diversity as an ideal of politics? Or should it require conformity to orthodoxy, if necessary, by imposing it and persecuting heretics? To find answers to these questions occupied two centuries during which throughout Europe blood was spilled, martyrs were tortured and burned, treasure was squandered, savage wars were fought, and bigotry reaped its bitter harvest of bestiality.

One answer—which was everywhere the first attempt, and in some places also the final outcome—proceeded on the assumptions that a person's religion is relevant to the ruler, that church and state must be identified by merger of their controlling authority, and that heresy is therefore treason. These doctrines were summarized in the terse Latin formula: *cujus regio, ejus religio* ("who controls the region, controls its religion"). Both Protestants, in areas where the Reformation was successful, and Catholics, where the Counter-Reformation held its ground, applied this formula to their adversaries. In England the Reformation was launched when Henry VIII, wanting a divorce, obtained the support of the Parliament for abolishing papal authority over the church, dissolved the monastic orders, and established a national church with himself at its head as "Defender of the Faith." These decisive events produced their aftereffects, as when Henry sought to exact from the clergy an oath of allegiance to himself as their spiritual superior; when Mary attempted to reinstate Catholicism; when policy was once more reversed under Elizabeth I, who authorized a new prayer book and a revised liturgy; and when James II, a century too late, again led England back to Rome and lost his throne to the final assertion of triumphant Protestantism.[22]

---

[22]The principle of the subordination of the church to the state is thus described by G. M. Trevelyan: "Bishop Jewel, the best exponent of the ideas of the early Elizabethan settlement, declared: 'This is our doctrine, that every soul, of what calling soever he be—be he monk, be he preacher, be he prophet, be he apostle—ought to be subject to King and magistrates.' The sphere of King and magistrates covered religion. All were agreed that there could be only one religion in the state, and all except Romanists and very rigorous Puritans were agreed that the state must decide what that religion should be." *Illustrated English Social History*, vol. 2 (London: Longmans, Green & Co., 1950), 34.

The dreadful cost of internecine strife between irreconcilables prompted England at last to apply an alternative answer: that the state, though officially committed to its own orthodoxy, could safely permit its subjects to profess different religious beliefs—always provided that this concession did not diminish their political allegiance. Through the eighteenth century only members of the Church of England were allowed by law to hold political office.[23] But in the 1820s the disabilities of other faiths were removed and all posts, save the monarchy, were opened to their adherents. Gradually, the principle of tolerance, at first a hard-won necessity, was elevated into a virtue. In the United States, from the beginnings of its independent nationhood, public guarantees of private religious freedom, as well as a ban upon establishing an official religion, were incorporated into the legal structure of the governmental system.[24] Jefferson in 1786 was the author of Virginia's notable *Act for Establishing Religious Freedom*. Its preamble affirmed that the state stands neutral where matters of faith are involved: "Our civil rights have no dependence on our religious opinions, more than our opinions in physics or geometry." A few years afterward, when the Bill of Rights was appended to the Constitution of the United States, the opening words of the first amendment declared: "Congress shall make no law respecting an establishment of religion, or prohibiting the free exercise thereof."

Monism Again:
The Theory of Sovereignty

The quest for a fresh formula to govern church-state relations did not lack results. In the sixteenth century a new principle took shape to express the departure from Gelasianism. This is the doctrine, so much touted from that time to the present, called sovereignty. An early exposition of it comes from the Frenchman Jean Bodin, who in 1576 published his *Six Books Concerning the Republic*. He writes: "Sovereignty is a power over citizens and subjects that is supreme and above the law."[25] In this phrasing, as in others, sovereignty is evidently a complex, embracing several ideas. Some of these, since sovereignty has many ramifications, fall under different headings among the five classic issues and will be discussed elsewhere.[26] But one aspect is central to the issue now being considered. In rejecting the view

---

[23] Annually, however, after 1727, Parliament passed Indemnity Acts, exempting from legal penalties those who held public office without swearing the necessary oath.

[24] Prior to independence, of course, the leading example of religious toleration, thanks to Penn and the Quakers, was to be found in Pennsylvania.

[25] *Maiestas est summa in cives ac subditos legibusque soluta potestas.*

[26] See chapters 10 and 13.

that the functions of the state should be exercised within a limited sphere, sovereignty asserted the limitless range of governmental activity. When sovereignty was pronounced to be one and indivisible, the state was intended to assume (or resume what it enjoyed in Graeco-Roman days) the general direction and supervision of society. The very force of the new insistence on unity was a measure of the reaction against dualism.

But a further clarification is necessary. When a king, like Henry VIII of England, proclaimed himself head of the church, he unified the two spheres and left the church in no position to set bounds to the sphere of politics. If the state was prepared to tolerate religious dissent, however, as later happened in Britain and the United States, did the abandonment of the demand for conformity imply that the state accepted limits to its power? The answer to this question, though arguable, is probably negative. Where the state tolerated diversity, it did so on one important condition, whether tacit or expressed. A dividing line was supposed to be drawn between matters of public and private concern. The churches—any number of them—were permitted their freedom, on condition that they confined their activities to worshiping the Deity and teaching religious doctrine. Belief in this field was ascribed to the private conscience, for which reason the state would keep its hands off. But in the public domain the state maintained its claim to be sovereign, and any church that departed from the private sphere and entered the public arena would run the risk and pay the penalty of grappling with Leviathan. Hence if toleration existed, it did so on political sufferance. The state stood neutral because the stings of the churches were drawn. They, for their part, exercised their freedom on condition of abstaining from political power. Any breach of this condition would call down on ecclesiastical heads the full weight of sovereignty, that is, of secular supremacy.

Thus the wheel had turned full circle. The first experiment in setting bounds to the functions of the state ended in a restoration of the status quo. From the Greek concept of the all-embracing *polis* to the Bodinian or Hobbesian theory of sovereignty, a connecting thread is woven across the centuries. But the first challenge to the omnipotent state was not the last. So, let us turn to the second attempt and observe how, when, and why the pluralist cudgels were brandished anew.

7

Politics and Economics

The Economists' Case for Limited Government

The second attempt to limit the functions of the state opened with different assumptions from the first, but ended with a curious and unforeseen resemblance. This was the effort to restrict the authority of government by appeal to the authority of the individual. Following the train of thought that government maintains order, order calls for law, law requires enforcement, enforcement demands coercion, and coercion is the enemy of freedom, one may conclude that government and liberty are antithetical. From this it could follow that any enlargements of the functions of government would mean a corresponding reduction of liberty, so that those who prize the latter would have to confine their government within limits. Then, once those limits were set, individual human beings would be free to apply their energies at will outside the sphere belonging to the state.

Historically this doctrine, which created a power vacuum in the areas where the state was denied access, preceded the Industrial Revolution. But that phenomenon released new forces that rushed to fill the void. During the nineteenth century the social order of many countries was transformed by a series of economic changes. New scientific discoveries, new techniques of production, new forms of corporate organization generated new wealth without the inhibitions of political direction. Such wealth, when amassed, formed a reservoir of power, and its owners challenged the rulers of the state for the leadership of society. In this indirect fashion, owing largely to the historical timing, the individualist doctrine, which the Renaissance and Reformation initiated, laid the ground for what became a second venture in dualism. There arose an economic theory, suited to the interests of businessmen, that preempted the individualistic argument and supplied its own bias to the notion of opposition to state authority. The effect of the doctrine—though seldom presented so explicitly—was a virtual bisection of society into a political order and an economic order, allotting to business a position within society coordinate with the government and carving out an economic sphere which should function as independently of the state as possible.

The similarity between this and the medieval system resides, of course, in the common presumption in favor of a limited government. The difference lies in the source of the challenge to the state's monopoly of authority. It is now economics which leads the assault, not religion. Economists, businessmen, bankers, manufacturers—not the clergy—now provide the main impetus toward pluralism. Hence it is in terms of economic policy, and over its relations with politics, that many arguments about the functions of the state are formulated. The state and the economy; government and business; politicians (or officials) and entrepreneurs; these, whether conceived as partners or rivals, resume the controversy where popes and emperors left off. In the second round, Leviathan grapples with Mammon.

As there was novelty in the problem that Christianity posed for the state from Constantine onward, so there was in this changed relationship of the political and economic orders. Prior to the eighteenth century the intimacy of the connection between politics and economics was not seriously questioned. The field of economics, originating as "household management" which it means literally, became the management of the community of households. As such, this was scarcely distinguishable from the government of the community. Issues of public policy and choices between alternative social values were undeniably implicit in the nature of the economy which the political order protected. The problems of the economy, though these embraced their technical aspects, were not considered separable from the sphere controlled by the state. Take any of the major economic questions prior to the Industrial Revolution—the tenure of land and its distribution, the accumulation of wealth, the provision of food supply, urban-rural relations, the pricing system, the direction of foreign trade, and so forth—these were treated as aspects of "political economy" dealing with subject matters that overlapped and finally fused. Opposition might be directed against specific instances of governmental power, and controversies might arise about the equity or expediency of certain policies. But that the power of the state extended over the general control of the economy was not an article of dispute.

State Control of the Economy in Antiquity

From Graeco-Roman antiquity to the eighteenth century the history of all European states provides testimony to support these generalizations. The list of economic functions that the state has performed in various places and periods is lengthy. Besides waging war, three major activities that long ago drew the government into commercial policy were communications, currency, and food supply. Of course, there was always a military motive behind the building of highways, as well as the need for speedier transmission of official edicts and diplomatic messages. Such reasons explain the lengthy Royal Road that the Persians constructed to link their inland capital of Susa with the Mediterranean seaboard of Asia Minor. Similar, but more spectacular, was the network of highways that the Romans flung across the provinces where their legions marched. But the roads, which were of service to cavalry, phalanx, or legion, were also usable by the caravan. Under state auspices they facilitated the flow of commerce and controlled it by dues and tolls. The issue of currency, too, was early undertaken by the state. When the direct barter of commodities was replaced by the use of a medium of exchange, or money, the state intervened for two compelling reasons. For there to be such a medium, people had to know it, accept it, and have confidence in it. Consequently it was best to employ a single medium, common to all transactions, and issued by authority with some recognizable stamp or imprint. Furthermore, to be accepted, it should consist of a material which was scarce, durable, and not too bulky. Thus metals were generally in demand for currency, and since their mining and coining were lucrative, the state found an added incentive to enter and then monopolize the business of moneymaking. The coins of Athens, Corinth, and other states with far-flung commercial interests spread extensively through the central and eastern Mediterranean. Wider still in later centuries was the dispersion of the *denarius,* financial symbol of Rome.

The concern of the state over food is explicable in terms partly economic, but largely political. When the city-state was the unit of government,[1] in addition to the natural dangers of crop failure due to drought or flood, the man-made perils of war exposed many communities to undernourishment or even starvation. Ordinarily a small city would obtain its wheat and olive oil from the adjacent rural area. When states were at war, the contending armies sought to destroy the standing wheat before it ripened and to cut the slow-maturing olive trees. Even in peacetime the largest cities were vulnerable because they imported their grain and oil from distant areas (the granaries being Sicily, North Africa, and what is now southwestern Russia). There was always the chance that political disor-

---

[1]See chapter 12, section on "The Optimum Area for the State."

ders abroad or piracy on the intervening seas might disrupt the supply. Hence ancient states took strict measures to control the food market by bulk purchases overseas, naval protection for transports, and regulating the domestic price. To avoid riot and insurrection among the poor, state policy frequently required the sale of wheat at subsidized low prices or even its free distribution. The politics of food, involving direct governmental intervention, was a dictate of humanitarianism, expediency, and plain necessity.

In the three fields just discussed, different factors with varying influence led to similar results. The motives for state intervention in communications were mainly military; in coinage, mainly economic; in food supply, mainly political. But regardless of variations in emphasis, the common feature was the accepted view that any widespread need occasioned and justified action by the government. All that was necessary was for the need to arise and be felt. Given these conditions, no obstacle was presented either in the form of ideas that the state ought not to enter this field or in the form of nongovernmental institutions powerful enough to do the job themselves and to resist the state.

Medievalism and Mercantilism

The infusion of Christian doctrine into the Graeco-Roman tradition did not change these principles. When the church argued for limits to secular power, it sought to define them within a theological context. As to economic problems, neither church nor state ignored their existence. But both stood on common ground in believing that the economy was part of the general ordering of this world and was therefore merged with, or subordinate to, the jurisdiction exercised by each in its respective sphere.[2] Now this did not mean that none of the issues dividing state and church had economic relevance. On the contrary, disputes over the ownership of land, the use of revenues from its produce, and the taxation of the clergy were economic as well as political, and they were certainly vital to both parties. But the issue was not whether economics formed an independent sphere, but whether church or state should govern particular segments of the economy; and each institution, facing the challenge of the other, became more anxious to control its own economic base.

---

[2]de Tocqueville supplies some striking examples of the economic activities of the church in *Ancien Régime*, part 2, chapter 1. Likewise, R. H. Tawney has written: "The Papacy was, in a sense, the greatest financial institution of the Middle Ages, and, as its fiscal system was elaborated, things became, not better, but worse. . . . Practically, the Church was an immense vested interest, implicated to the hilt in the economic fabric, especially on the side of agriculture and land tenure. Itself the greatest of landowners, it could no more quarrel with the feudal structure. . . ." *Religion and the Rise of Capitalism*, chapter 1, secs. 1 and 3.

The dominance in the medieval age of theological assumptions and a Christian ethic was a further obstacle to the autonomy of economic factors. If charging interest for a loan or exacting above a certain rate was branded "usury" and deemed "un-Christian," an economic matter was argued on moral grounds. Likewise, when prices rose too high for the poor to purchase the necessaries of life, controls could be justified by the concept of a "fair price" (*justum pretium*). In this doctrine, economic, legal, theological, and ethical considerations were intertwined. But the ethical category was the most important and was the criterion for setting an economic standard.

While the medieval world subordinated economics to ethics, and ethics to theology, in the following period economics was no less emphatically subject to calculations of political and military power. When, therefore, the medieval dogma of dualism was replaced by the politico-legal concept of sovereignty, a corresponding substitution took place in economic policy and theory. The new doctrines which superseded the medieval, and which provided in economics a counterpart to sovereignty in politics, have been generally known, since Adam Smith's critique, as *mercantilism*. This system of thought reacted against the restraints to which the medieval economy was subject—those on production, for instance, which the craft guilds imposed, plus the numerous blocks to commerce in the form of customs barriers between localities and tolls on rivers and highways. In order to augment the national wealth, the mercantile system considered it necessary to increase the volume of production and exchange, to which end the medieval restrictions had to be modified or eliminated and new restrictions had to be added. The new theory held that a surplus of exports over imports was a sign of strength, the surplus being measured by the importation of bullion from the purchasing countries. Hence an inflow of gold and silver to replace an outflow of goods was approved as the index of a prosperous economy.

To assess the economic pros and cons of such ideas is beyond the scope of the present inquiry. The political implications, however, are relevant. For the mercantilists the prime objective of policy was the furtherance of national power, and their emphasis was thus placed on national, in contrast to local or regional, interests. To this goal, so preeminently political in character, economic policy was supposed to contribute. The means that the mercantilist advocated, as distinct from the ends (that is, the stimulation of exports and the desire to accumulate bullion), could be argued as essentially economic propositions. But the employment of such means led to political consequences—to trade wars, struggles for markets and sources of raw materials, control of colonial settlements, and the rest. Hence under the aegis of mercantilism, economics was necessarily the serving maid of politics. One had only to demonstrate a connection between a particular economic policy and an advantage to national power, and there was no questioning the central assumption that the state had the right to intervene in any fashion in this or that sector of the economy. The difference between the medieval and the mercantilist economies lay not in the latter's emanicipation of the economic order from governmental controls, but rather in its substitution of one type of governmental control (particularly if nationwide in scope) for another.

Laissez-Faire—
The Economists' Declaration of Independence

Judged from the political standpoint, the sharpest break in the continuity of economic thought occurs in the swing from mercantilism to its successor. The latter has had many aliases: economic liberalism, conservative economics, classical economics, or laissez-faire. The last of these will be used here. As an economic doctrine, what novelty did laissez-faire impart to views about the state and society?

The central innovation was a bias against the state. Once that point and its implications are grasped, the rest follows with logical consistency. The historical reasons for that bias are as significant as the bias itself, and they explain the resulting consequences. For a point of departure, take the publication in 1690 of Locke's second *Treatise of Civil Government*. Writing to justify the peaceful English Revolution of 1688, Locke advocates a theory of the state which substitutes constitutionalism for arbitrary[3] power and limited government for absolute. To support this position, he assumes the existence of a law of nature that "belongs to men as men"[4] and not as citizens of a state. A natural social union, according to his belief, is chronologically prior, as it is logically prior, to the establishment of a political and legal union. In this state of nature, as he calls it, we are endowed with rights which, since they derive from natural law, are also natural. The collective name for these is *property*—an ambiguous usage, since Locke employs it both in an all-inclusive sense embracing "life, liberty, and estate" (where "estate" means material things one may acquire and use), and in a restricted sense, equating it with estate only and omitting life and liberty.[5] It is to enjoy our property (in either or both of those senses) more securely that we mutually contract to institute a government.[6] The legitimate powers of government are derived from that portion of our natural rights which we entrust to its care, and its functions are to preserve intact the

---

[3]For the meaning of these terms, see chapter 5, section on "The English, American, and French Revolutions."

[4]*Second Treatise of Civil Government*, chapter 2, sec. 14 (Everyman's Library), p. 124.

[5]For these conflicting usages, compare the passages in secs. 87, 123, 31; pp. 159, 180, 132.

[6]*Second Treatise of Civil Government*, secs. 85, 94, 138; pp. 158, 163–64, 187.

rights which we retain. Such suppositions glide readily to the evident conclusion that the scope of state activity is confined within the limits of the powers delegated to it. Should the state exceed those limits, it has passed out of bounds, becoming an invader of a domain where it had no right to enter.[7]

The concept that there is a domain which the state may not enter carries the corollary that some social activities are best conducted either by private individuals or by associations other than the state. (If there was not this corollary, it would be pointless to argue in favor of limiting the functions of the state.) To pursue this inference was the preoccupation of many thinkers from the mid-eighteenth century to the mid-nineteenth. The next step after Locke was taken by a French school, called Physiocrats. Their philosophy was conceived in reaction against the mercantilist system, designed and developed in France by Colbert, the finance minister of Louis XIV, and his successors. Whereas the basis of national wealth and strength appeared to mercantilists to reside in foreign commerce, favorable trade balances, and international movements of precious metals, to the Physiocrat it lay in the land, the basic productive resource and the chief original creator of wealth. Hence the prosperity of agriculture was the prime indicator of the national weal, and the interests of landholders overrode those of merchants. Such an outlook confirmed the Physiocrats in an antistate bias. For one thing, their solicitude for farming was linked with the contemporary, romantic appeal to "return to nature," since it was easy to identify farming as our "natural" occupation.[8] As Rousseau in that period assumed a contrast between primitive goodness in an idealized state of nature and corruption by society and the state at Paris and Versailles, so the economic doctrine of the Physiocrats employed the same concept for an assault upon the state.

To be precise, it was against the functions of the state as Colbert planned them that the Physiocrats protested—against restraints or requirements, both negative and positive, which the state imposed on the economy in the mercantile interest. The Physiocrats' reaction to this was a desire to curb the sphere of the state, to limit it within boundaries, and leave the (mainly agrarian) economy to the operation of "nature." Their specific protest was voiced in the cry: "Leave us alone to produce what we want and to send our products where and how we want" (*laissez nous faire, laissez nous passer*). Shortened into *laissez-faire,* this crisp injunction was tossed at the state: "Leave us alone!"

The further cultivation and final flowering of these principles took place in Britain and the United States in the last quarter of the eighteenth century and the first half of the nineteenth. The Bible of the British move-

[7]Ibid., sec. 135, pp. 184–85.
[8]The title *physiocrat* means "rule by nature."

ment was *The Wealth of Nations,* published by Adam Smith in 1776. The book was epoch-making because of its contribution to economic theory and to government policies. Nowadays its significance is best judged by the influences and trends which it set in motion, rather than by what Smith actually says, because the contents of the work embrace much that is out-dated or has been superseded. Roughly a quarter of it is devoted to an indictment of the faults of mercantilism, wherein some of the strictures are merited but others are exaggerated. Smith's theory of value, based on the cost of labor expended in the production of a commodity, was discarded by many of his followers in the second half of the nineteenth century and would today be accepted in its naked simplicity by few contemporary econ-omists. But such criticisms aside, the permanent importance of *The Wealth of Nations* may be found in its general picture of how a social order can function well. This picture was reproduced, filled in, and more sharply delineated by such successors as David Ricardo and John Stuart Mill. It became the leading doctrine in economic thought during most of the nine-teenth century, and epitomized the revolution in the attitudes of the econo-mist and businessman toward the state.

What was this picture? Essentially it depicted the individual as the true unit and society as an artificial aggregate of individuals in association. Assuming that all individuals desire their self-interest; that the latter, trans-lated into economic terms, means material enrichment; that each person is the best judge of the means appropriate to the goal—then it follows that. the larger the sphere of action left to the initiative of private persons, the better. Through the enterprise which involves taking risks in aggressive competition, individuals will reap the best rewards for themselves and, in the aggregate, for society as a whole. So strongly was Smith dedicated to this individualistic doctrine, and so thoroughly did he apply it, that his antipathy for collective endeavors extended not only to various state ac-tivities, but also to the institution of the joint stock company. The latter, which has become a major instrument of a modern capitalist economy, he deprecated as having limited usefulness and as functioning successfully only when it possesses a protected monopoly or conducts some routine operation.[9]

If these presuppositions were granted, Smith still had to demonstrate that the results of free competition between individuals could be not only beneficial, but also harmonious. For this he relied on a belief in "nature." The economic system, if left to the interplay of economic forces, would act in conformity with its own set of laws. Certain of these were based on psychological assumptions of universal human egoism (for example, Gresham's law that the bad money drives out the good, because people will

---

[9]*Wealth of Nations,* vol. 2, V, chap. 1, part 3, article 1 (Everyman's Library), pp. 242–45. Smith's attitude to the joint stock company was common to most English economists through the nineteenth century.

keep reliable currency and circulate the unreliable). Others were linked to the operation of physical factors also rooted in "nature" (for example, the law of diminishing returns, which tells the farmer that if he plants the same crop in the same field year after year, without replenishing the soil, the yields will eventually decrease). The analysis and elucidation of these laws formed the substance of economic science, a knowledge of which would assist people in conducting the economy according to nature.

The Bias against the State

Where did the state fit into this order of thinking? As with most doctrines that place their faith in nature, a contrast was implied between what is natural and what is man-made or artificial. Since nature, by definition, is right and good, human actions, unless conformable to nature, are likely to be wrong. If nature has its own laws, they must be beneficial. Human laws, when they contravene those of nature, are by that very fact harmful. From this point it is a short step to conclude that human laws have limited use since they are fruitful only if they assist nature and fruitless if they do not. The balance is so delicately poised, the interrelations so complex, between economic factors functioning as nature intends, that state direction is likely to disturb or destroy the natural equilibrium through clumsiness and misunderstanding. Hence a policy is adjudged wise when it enlarges the spheres of private activities and correspondingly restricts the range of governmental action. Such was the reasoning that led John Stuart Mill to write:

> In all the more advanced communities, the great majority of things are worse done by the intervention of government, than the individuals most interested in the matter would do them, or cause them to be done, if left to themselves. . . . The preceding are the principal reasons, of a general character, in favor of restricting to the narrowest compass the intervention of a public authority in the business of a community: and few will dispute the more than sufficiency of these reasons, to throw, in every instance, the burden of making out a strong case, not on those who resist, but on those who recommend, government interference. *Laissez faire,* in short, should be the general practice: every departure from it, unless required by some great good, is a certain evil.[10]

This revealing passage expresses the new thinking without equivocation. It asserts the superiority of private over public enterprise. It places on the state the onus of proving that its functions are justified. It supports, prima facie, any opposition to an extension of those functions. In a word, it typifies the bias against the state.[11]

Thus was launched a new attack on the monistic doctrine of the omnipotent state. The main assault on the citadel of power was, of course,

[10]*Principles of Political Economy,* 1st ed., V, chapter 11, secs. 5, 7.

[11]An even stronger bias was expressed by Herbert Spencer in his *Social Statics* (1850) and *Man versus the State* (1884).

the one conducted by business or in its name. In the medieval period, when the sphere of the state was curtailed by the claims of the church, the limits of political activity had been drawn along a line that simultaneously marked off the area of religious activity. Now the effect of circumscribing the powers of government was to leave the field to economic associations.[12] The strategy of the offensive against the state conformed largely therefore to the dictates of economic policy. If you could determine how much range was required by nature for the operation of its economic laws, you were by the same logic fixing the boundaries of the laws of government. The economic and political orders were thus considered to be coordinate, and a new species of dualism emerged as the substitute for monism.

As was to be expected, the main assault on the state was reinforced by a variety of flanking movements whose goal was not so much dualism as pluralism. Educational bodies, reasserting "academic freedom"; religious bodies, seizing the occasion to renew their opposition to secular supremacy; these and others, pooling their forces with the economic agitation, formulated theories of society in terms not of a simple dualism but of complex interrelations among many groups of which the state was only one.[13]

Nevertheless, in the modern statement of the issue, the argument based on economics and its case for dualism has overshadowed that based on a multiplicity of associations and their case for pluralism. The reasons for this tell us much about practical politics. For limits to be effectively imposed on the monistic state, more is required than the elaboration of a doctrine. A contrary power must be mobilized to confront the power of the state. Under no other circumstances will the state abdicate from its monistic professions. But to organize a counterforce capable of resisting the state is a political act, i.e., some other association has to marshal its resources and build a following. It was precisely because the church had attained this position by the fourth century A.D. that Constantine's conversion was assured, and state and church, in effect, established a partnership. If the church had not succeeded in mustering a widespread allegiance, it could not have effectively pressed the case for dualism. You have to create two institutions, or you waste your breath talking about two spheres. It was because this indispensable condition was repeated in the nineteenth century that dualism was converted from a potential of social theory into *realpolitik.*

[12]The parallelism between the medieval relation of state to church and the nineteenth-century relation of state to business is epigrammatically expressed by David Ogg, "The Scarlet Woman has been immured, and the Economic Man let loose," essay on "The Renaissance and Reformation" in *Great Events in History,* ed. G. R. S. Taylor (London: Cassell & Co., 1934), p. 335.

[13]Such pluralism is expounded in the late nineteenth-century viewpoints of the German theorist Von Gierke or the British legal historian Maitland. It is continued in the twentieth century by the French authority on jurisprudence and political science Duguit; by two Britishers, the political scientist Laski, and the economist Cole, in their earlier works; and by the American sociologist Robert M. MacIver.

Business Policy in Victoria's Britain

What reinforced the talk of laissez-faire economists was the new political reality, the rise of business firms powerful enough collectively to come to grips with the state. In Britain the writings of Smith, Ricardo, Mill, and Spencer coincided with the social ferment of the Industrial Revolution. Aided by an inventive technology, new methods of manufacturing transformed the industrial process and created a novel economic structure. Instead of the handicraft system, in which a textile worker, for example, owned a simple machine and used it at home, the new power-driven machinery involved a large outlay for plant and equipment. When the workers ceased to own their machines, they had to labor in factories belonging to their employers. The latter, requiring larger investments of capital, discovered in the joint stock company a flexible device for combining the savings of many individuals. Flying the corporate flag, the business firm sailed on the buoyant crest of the economic tide.

Being first with these techniques and forced by the Napoleonic Wars to expand industrial output, British manufacturers found themselves unrivaled in their domestic market and well placed for competing abroad. By their efforts Victoria's Britain became "the workshop of the world," trebled its population and established its control of the most extensive empire ever known. But this achievement was accompanied by demands from businessmen for emancipation, both from requirements imposed on commerce by mercantilism and from laws protecting the interests of landowners. These demands resulted in a concentrated attack on the protective tariff which boosted the price of homegrown wheat. After the Reform Act of 1832 transferred the control of the House of Commons to the urban middle class, the potato crop failures in Ireland brought about the Repeal of the Corn Laws in 1846. Three years later, by abrogating the Navigation Acts, which had restricted the external commerce of her colonies, Britain certified her adoption of "free trade." Henceforth, as long as Britain's manufacturers could undersell any competitors and as long as her navy dominated the oceans, in neat reciprocity Trade followed the Flag and the Flag followed Trade.

The same symbol of freedom, which in the case of foreign trade was invoked to justify abolition of a tariff on imports, was also applied to the domestic sphere, although in two different senses. In a negative sense, the entrepreneur claimed freedom from control, which meant control by the state, that being the only association capable of restraining him. Let the economic process function in obedience to laws, not of the state, but of economics—a plea that might be rephrased: Let the businessman be a law unto himself. Interpreted positively, freedom meant opportunity to take chances, experiment, and innovate. This was buttressed in the law courts by the doctrine of "freedom of contract," applied to a variety of economic relationships—for example, those of business partners, seller and purchaser, master and servant. The doctrine assumed the like freedom and equal capacity of the contracting parties, voluntarily agreeing as individuals to transactions for mutual advantage. In any case, either connotation of freedom, negative or positive, spelled a warning to the state: "Leave us alone!"

Jeffersonian Ideals and the American Frontier

The same antistate bias found fertile soil in the United States. But the reasons were not identical with those in Britain. The act of acquiring independence had involved resistance to a hereditary monarch, who still possessed wide discretion in picking his own ministers (for example, Lord North) and defiance of a Parliament in which the colonists were not represented. When a government of limited power, based on the Constitution, replaced a government which in American eyes had appeared authoritarian, the memories of opposition to King, Parliament, and royal governors left a determination to circumscribe the sphere of activity allotted to the state.[14] Hence when he wrote the Declaration of Independence, Thomas Jefferson, confronted with the same problem that Locke had faced, adopted a similar solution and used Lockian terms and thoughts. He speaks, therefore, of inalienable rights, which exist prior to the state. He assumes that, in joining the state, people surrender to it a fraction only of their rights, while retaining the rest. It then becomes the duty of government to employ its power to maintain inviolate the rights that are reserved. As a consequence, the power of the state must always be limited.

Besides these ethical and political arguments, Jefferson's thesis was strengthened by his economic philosophy. Although *The Wealth of Nations* was published in the same year as the Declaration, it is probable that in the ensuing decade and a half Jefferson derived his economic theories less from Adam Smith than from the French Physiocrats. Jefferson's personal predilection for an agrarian economy and the values of rural life chimed harmoniously with Physiocratic doctrines about agriculture and the landed interest. This preference was stated unequivocally in *Notes on Virginia*, "Query XIX":

> Those who labor in the earth are the chosen people of God, if ever He had a chosen people, whose breasts he has made His peculiar deposit for substantial and genuine virtue. . . . Generally speaking, the proportion which the aggregate of the other classes of citizen bears in any State to that of its husbandmen, is the proportion of its unsound to its healthy parts, and is a good enough

---

[14]See chapter 10, section on "Design of the American Constitution."

barometer whereby to measure its degree of corruption. While we have land to labor then, let us never wish to see our citizens occupied at a work-bench, or twirling a distaff. Carpenters, masons, smiths are wanting in husbandry; but, for the general operations of manufacture, let our workshops remain in Europe. . . . The mobs of great cities add just so much to the support of pure government, as sores do to the strength of the human body.

His stay in Europe, where he served as American Minister to France (1784–1789), and his residence in Paris and observation of its citizens, confirmed in Jefferson a distaste for large cities, which he regarded as politically unstable, economically parasitical, and socially corrupting. Thus, all elements in his makeup—the statesman, gentleman-farmer, and social philosopher—combined in the conclusion that a community of farmers, owning and working their own land, constitutes the best economic base for society. Let farmers, who live close to nature, be free to follow nature's laws. Let governments intervene only to protect and enlarge the range of private activities. For are not the best governed the least governed?

The conditions prevailing in the United States during the first half of the nineteenth century commended this theory to many Americans. In certain respects it corresponded with their actual mode of living. Not only had the United States succeeded in opposing an unrepresentative system, but independence enabled the young nation to populate a territory of continental dimensions. As settlers flooded west, Jeffersonism was reborn with each extension of the frontier. The pioneers who took the Indians' land were driven by the varied stimuli of quest for adventure, economic necessity, or religious belief. The West was an escape from a secure but humdrum existence, from poverty, from religious intolerance. Assuredly government agencies assisted this movement in countless respects. The federal authority negotiated the diplomatic treaties delimiting the international boundaries, extended the United States by military action against Mexicans and Indians, authorized grants of land from the public domain, organized territories and admitted new states, and helped to plan and underwrite the highways, railroads, and canals. But the expansion from the Atlantic to the Pacific was also an achievement of private persons and groups. The scouts and prospectors, lumbermen and cattlemen, trappers and traders, did not act under political directives or work to a state plan. They were the forerunners, blazing a trail along which others followed. Their efforts took them into regions inhabited by Indians and beyond the immediate sway of the Constitution of the United States. They were, therefore, accustomed to fend for themselves, to go armed, and to discharge as individuals some of those functions (for example, the protection of persons and property) that in a more settled society are done by state officials. Such conditions, however, were close to anarchy. When no agencies existed to enact and enforce the law, who could say which person was law-abiding and which the outlaw? As population grew in the West, the need increased for a system of order which only the government could provide.

Because the taming of the frontier was the work of both public and private enterprise, the pioneers came to believe that the role of the state, however indispensable, was limited. As the frontier moved west during the nineteenth century, the theory of laissez-faire reflected with some accuracy the psychology and the social realities of a transcontinental expansion. But this was not as true of the more developed eastern seaboard,[15] where Hamiltonian mercantilist notions continued influential. After the Civil War, however, at the time of the industrial expansion of the East and the Midwest, laissez-faire here too came into its own. As in Victoria's Britain, the leaders of American business were transforming the economy and were amassing capital, and, with it, the control that money brings. Hence they felt less dependent on public power and more disposed to rely on their own.

The Consequences of Industrial Capitalism

Both in the United States and in Britain, the laissez-faire doctrine, as was noted earlier, expressed a bias against the state. What consequences ensued when these ideas were put into practice? What resulted from the assumption that a good society is one in which governmental functions are confined to a minimum and economic activities enjoy maximum independence?

Some of the most notable changes are in the field of production. Never before has mankind come within reach of the abundance that has lain in its grasp during the last century. The techniques of mass production have increased the volume of commodities available to the consumer beyond levels previously known. Freeing the channels of trade inside the nation-state and freer trade across international boundaries together resulted in great extensions of the market, with accompanying benefits. What once were luxuries for the few have become staples for the many. In general, this has spelled itself out in changes which, from the material standpoint, have contributed to comfort and convenience, and in various countries have made possible the highest material standards of living in the world.[16]

These improvements, however, have been associated with other changes less beneficial. If risk taking, individual autonomy, and entrepreneurial initiative have served as stimulants to new endeavors, they

[15]For evidence, see Louis Hartz, *Economic Policy and Democratic Thought: Pennsylvania 1776–1860* (Cambridge, Mass.: Harvard University Press, 1948).

[16]Important as these gains are, it must not be forgotten that they were due not to the single factor of the laissez-faire doctrine, but to a combination of factors of which this was only one. In the nineteenth century the economic progress of Britain was attributable in large measure to the fact that she was first in the field with industrialization, and thus possessed a competitive advantage. The similar progress of the United States was facilitated by this country's rich endowment of natural resources that laid the foundation for agricultural and industrial wealth.

have also been responsible for some less pleasant aftereffects. The constructive achievements that laissez-faire capitalism has registered in production are not matched by an equal record in distribution. The main preoccupations of the economic system have been to organize production and to increase capital rather than to be concerned about the equities of distribution. As a consequence, even the wealthiest nations, such as Britain before 1914 or the United States since 1919, have contained a significant percentage of needy people, and the gulf dividing rich from poor became dangerously large. The same may be said another way: An immoderate emphasis on individual freedom accentuates inequalities between individuals.

Risk taking, similarly, can be responsible for unwelcome consequences. When millions of persons take their separate calculations of profit and loss and make decisions accordingly, their actions lead to a collective result to which all have contributed (though none has willed it) and which may turn out mutually ruinous. An example is the phenomenon known as the business cycle. Over many decades statisticians have traced a cyclical movement of the economy through a succession of phases. Market conditions offering opportunities for sales create an atmosphere of confidence, which encourages expansion and innovation. The desire to profit tempts businessmen to gamble on commitments beyond their immediate resources. The crash comes when too many have overextended themselves. The economy as a whole slumps into a prolonged depression, followed by a gradual recovery and then a return to the opening phase. Prosperity-depression-prosperity; growth-contraction-growth; this recurrent rhythm can be otherwise seen as a chronic condition of instability.

The application of laissez-faire doctrines, particularly to an economy in the course of change from a mainly agrarian to a mainly industrial base, has included many by-products which are not merely economic but, in the broadest sense, social. Industrialism alters the physical environment, reshapes everyday habits of living and working, and produces effects that become more drastic as planning and regulation diminish. Under shelter of the maxim "leave us alone," as it was practiced in Britain and the United States during the nineteenth century, the demands for manpower for the factories and all the services linked with them created huge cities where masses of people were overcrowded, overworked, underpaid, and underfed. The cities spread upon nature's landscape their blight of dirt and pollution, and upon their human inhabitants the blights of slums, disease, and squalor.[17] For many of the urban populace, and certainly for the poorest, life was a ceaseless drudgery. Theirs was the helpless feeling of imprisonment in a vast impersonal mechanism.

---

[17]For an analysis of modern urbanization, see Lewis Mumford, *The Culture of Cities* (New York: Harcourt Brace Jovanovich, 1970).

In large and wealthy countries, however, the most paradoxical result of laissez-faire has been its inability to live up to its own principles. The freedom on which the system prided itself permitted ample opportunities for any who started with an initial advantage, who were unscrupulous in their means, or who enjoyed exceptional luck, to become richer and more powerful than their fellows. Despite its good intentions, the doctrine of freedom paved the road to privilege. The presence, side by side, of rich and poor; the concentration of wealth and, with it, of social power; the organization of trusts, cartels, and monopolies; and the rise of holding companies and interlocking directorates negated the ideal of free competition among equal individuals. Indeed, to apply to huge corporations, owning assets that run into eight or nine digits, the rights and attributes of a single flesh-and-blood individual is a fiction that does violence to the facts.[18] The point that systems professing laissez-faire and dedicated to free competition among individuals have in reality diverged widely from their own doctrines has far-reaching implications. The central concept of laissez-faire, making a virtue of state inaction, formed an umbrella beneath whose shelter economic organizations could luxuriate. Since their activities were subject to few restraints, the largest and strongest pressed their advantage to dominate the small and weak. Thus society found itself at grips with the problem expressed by President Grover Cleveland: "It is a condition which confronts us, not a theory."[19] This condition was the simple fact that huge business corporations had come into existence wielding power by reason of the numbers they employed, the assets they owned, and the products they sold. In many branches of the economy, the paradoxical outcome of a doctrine that glorified the autonomous individual and simultaneously restricted the role of the state was to subordinate the great majority of individuals to these very corporations. Once established, moreover, they were hard to dislodge, and their ability to survive had the effect both of accentuating the differences between rich and poor and of further diminishing equality of opportunity.

The Power of Business in State and Society

In yet another respect did the results of laissez-faire belie one of its initial assumptions. Its proponents had called for limitations on the state and the maximum of independence for the economy, so that free and equal individuals could enjoy a large area for their enterprise. Practice, however, did

---

[18]For a critique of this practice, see Thurman Arnold, *The Folklore of Capitalism* (New Haven: Yale University Press, 1937; reprinted by Yale University Press, 1962).

[19]*Annual Message to Congress*, 1887. Cleveland was referring to the issue of free trade versus protection. But his words had a much wider application.

not conform to theory. For as it grew big, business spelled power—power in any sense: the amassing of wealth, control of people, dispensing of social influence, and, above all, mastery of the state. Such, indeed, was the ultimate and inescapable consequence of the success that business had achieved. The enforced contraction of the state did not leave society devoid of potent associations. When state power was dammed up, a vacuum was created into which other forces were free to flow. What resulted was not the extinction of power or even its limitation, but the substitution of one form for another— that is, of economic power for political. Individuals were still subject to controls. Only the controllers had changed.

Nor is that all. The substitution of economic for political power can be rephrased as the absorption of politics by economics, of the state by business. Power generated in the economic sphere was transformed into political power. Laissez-faire did not insist that the state wither away, but rather that its branches be pruned and its growth circumscribed; at the same time, business plants could spread around and above, cutting off the state from sunlight and water. In this way political considerations were subordinated to economic, and the powers of the state, when employed, were made to subserve what business deemed its interest. Hence the net result of the modern attempt to limit the functions of government and subdivide society into two or more spheres was akin to the comparable medieval endeavor to organize the secular and spiritual realms in parallel compartments. Both experiments proved unworkable; in neither instance was it possible to establish a clear line of demarcation. The medieval priest and the nineteenth-century businessman stepped beyond their original bounds of saving souls or capital, and their respective institutions, church and corporation, became involved in controlling the entire social order. Each in turn, as the moment appeared opportune, sought to establish the supremacy of his values over those of the state—the church with the claim that the hereafter was more important than the life now, and business with the assertion that a competitive system promoted freedom whereas government rested basically on coercion. Starting as pluralists or dualists, both ended as monists— the one seeking to unify society through the Gospel and the laws of God, the other through the division of labor and the law of supply and demand.

Nor does the similarity end there. The power wielded by the strongest of the medieval popes provoked a counterassertion of secular authority by emperors and kings, so that the aftermath of state-church dualism was the rise of the "sovereign" state. What has been the sequel to the nineteenth-century experiment in state-business dualism?

Karl Marx, the intellectual founder of the Communist movement, asserted that capitalism contained in itself the seeds of its own destruction. It would, he predicted, be destroyed from within through the irreconcilability of the classes it created. That the forecast has turned out inaccurate is proven by facts whose potentialities Marx underrated. He did not, for example, envisage the prospect that capitalism would develop a capacity for continuous adaptation in an evolutionary, rather than a revolutionary, manner. He did not expect that the owners and their employees—the relation between whom he described as the *Klassenkampf* or "class war"— might draw closer together instead of drifting asunder. Nor did he anticipate that liberal democracy, in his day largely a phenomenon of the middle class, would be extended to the working class. The suggestion that remedial measures might be employed to correct demonstrable abuses was alien to Marxian diagnosis and therapy. His cure for the disease was to kill the patient.

But to say that the "inevitable" revolution did not erupt in the most advanced industrial societies does not mean that the capitalist economy has persisted unchanged. On the contrary, change has been its one constant factor. What differentiates the history of modern peoples has been the character and extent of changes from which none has been exempt. The prediction of Marx would have been more accurate had he stated that industrial capitalism contained within itself the seeds of its own reconstitution. Let us explore the evidence for this view and see how those seeds were watered and nurtured.

Primarily it was industrialization which created the occasion and preconditions for new and momentous changes. Two of these set in motion a train of events directly relevant to politics. When technology produced ever more complex machines, more of the labor force had to be commensurately skilled. Many phases of manufacturing required the operator to tend and repair an intricate machine; to understand elaborate instructions, written as well as verbal; to calculate mathematically, and so on. In a word, industrialization demanded education, and mass production necessitated mass education. The investment tied down in a manufacturing plant could not prudently be entrusted to the unschooled.

The other innovation was the geographical redistribution of humanity. For the first time in history, countries that felt the full effects of the Industrial Revolution contained more people in the cities than on the land, more employees in factories and urban jobs than in farming, and higher densities of population per square mile. These changes led to a spreading contagion of adverse conditions: slum dwellings, unsanitary streets, high death rates, juvenile delinquency, sweatshops, and ignorance. But the physical overcrowding that aggravated these evils made it possible for their victims to combine in searching for remedies. Thus a second offshoot of industrialism was combination on a large scale. While laissez-faire doctrine emphasized the virtues of individuality, the growth of an industrial society negated that same value. Because it massed people together, industry paved the way for collectivism, first private and then public.

Emergence of Big Government

There were several ways of mustering opposition to the wealth and power which a few had amassed under the laissez-faire system. One method was to argue that, if the root of the trouble was the growth of overpowerful business corporations, the solution likewise must be found in the economic field. The proper counterpoise to an economic force was a rival economic force. In this light such organizations as the trade unions, farm groups, and the consumers' cooperative movement can be understood. Two of these in the sphere of production and the third in that of consumption were designed to offset the dominance of the captains of industry. The economic leverage which the unions or farmers could apply resided in their ability to withhold their labor or crops, and the strength of that leverage depended on the solidarity of their organization. If a union of workers or growers remained cohesive in demanding higher wages or prices, the consuming public would be hurt. In that case, was there any agency to arbitrate or overrule the differences?

From the logic of circumstances, the conclusion was obvious. The only institution able to adjust conflicts and prevent social harm was that which embraced everybody, which concerned itself with the general welfare, and which had power to enforce a settlement among the contestants—in other words, the state. Thus, by a converging of political pressures in its direction, the state was invoked as the chosen instrument to direct the forces of social change. But not the state as conceived by the philosophers of laissez-faire! Not the kind of state where good government was equated with little government! For the new state had to be strong. Its functions had to be formulated in positive terms. If changes originating in the economic sphere set up repercussions throughout the whole society, political solutions were required to mitigate their effects. Hence the attempt to carve out for economics a sphere of its own, operating under laws of its own, broke down. The social order was forced to reassert the primacy of politics over economics, of the state over business.

In the twentieth century, therefore, the political objective of every economic group is to capture the state. The more intense the economic struggle, the more strenuously do competitors seek to mobilize political power. No major interest in society shrinks from appealing to the state for preferential treatment when that would be to its advantage. Businessmen, who supposedly speak in character when complaining about government "interference" in the economy, will demand a customs tariff to protect their market or will regulate the supply of money or the rate of interest. Farmers welcome the workings of the state when its subsidies augment their income, and when dams supply water to their fields and electricity to their barns and houses. Labor unions object to controls on wages, but wish them imposed on prices. All theories to the contrary, every association which needs something otherwise unobtainable, or tries to buttress a weak competitive stance, seeks to enlarge those functions of government which serve its interest. If the appeal to Caesar be branded sin in the homilies of classical economics, none is so pure as to cast the first stone.

Moreover, do not forget that, simultaneously with the revolution in industry, in politics the democratic revolution was under way. Each interacted reciprocally with the other, as cause and effect. The liberal movement to extend participation in elections encouraged the growth of party organizations which bid for votes by expressing people's needs. Since democracy means "people's power," the natural consequence of more democracy was to replace the bias against the state with an appetite for its services.

Such are some of the reasons why in all countries touched by industrialism the functions of the state have expanded so broadly. But this enlarging role of the state in the economy has not been uniform. On the contrary, it has manifested itself in three relationships. First, the ownership and operation of an enterprise may be vested in the state rather than in private hands. This is socialism or nationalization. Second, the ownership and administration may remain private, but the state lays down conditions to which the private management must conform. As a further extension, the state may attempt to coordinate centrally the different aspects of the economy (investment, production, consumption, wages, prices, or profits) and may prescribe an overall plan to introduce equity into their relations and keep them stable. That is called a system of controls or regulation, or a planned or managed economy. Third, the state may accept the obligation for the welfare of its citizens by providing what are known as social services. To finance these it must obtain much of its revenue through taxation, taking a larger share from those who have more and thereby, in some measure, redistributing incomes. Let us review each of these state functions—ownership, regulation plus planning, and social services.

1. Pros and Cons of Public Ownership

State ownership and operation being no novelty, the only new point to determine is whether a specific enterprise should be state-run or not. Some government undertakings (coining money, for example) are so old and established that they no longer evoke the raising of an eyebrow. Some, such as the generation and sale of electric power, created furious controversy in the United States in the 1930s. In Britain, Henry VIII nationalized the Church, dissolved the monasteries, and grabbed their lands. Four centuries later, Prime Minister Attlee nationalized the coal mines and the railroads. But the Labourite, unlike the Tudor king, compensated the former owners. Is this not the same principle applied to different objects in different centuries by rather different methods? If the facts reveal any pattern, it is this: Arguments about whether the state should undertake a specific activity are waged more intensely according to the recency or rarity of its operation by the state and the strength of opposing private interests. In this, as in other matters political, yesterday's heresies often become tomorrow's orthodoxies.

The number and character of the enterprises which governments own and operate vary considerably. In the United States, besides the ubiquitous post office, the federal government makes loans to corporations and homeowners, produces and distributes electrical power, manufactures fertilizers, maintains national parks with tourist facilities, develops atomic energy, and sends satellites into space. Some states monopolize the retail sales of liquor; some operate harbor terminals; and North Dakota uniquely instituted its own bank, grain elevators, and crop insurance. Numerous cities own their transit system and supply gas, electricity, and water.

Everything, however, is dwarfed by the one government agency which influences the economy more profoundly than any other single organization—i.e., the Department of Defense. The military impact on civilian society in general and on the economy in particular became total during World War II, as a condition of survival. Since then, it has remained pervasive and in the 1980s it increased rapidly. Some figures will tell the story. In 1967 at the time of the Vietnam War, the assets of the Defense Department were reported at $184 billion—more than half the total value of federally owned property. One American in ten was then employed either by the Department directly or in a defense industry. In 1973, as much as $76.4 billion was spent on national defense, amounting to 30.6 percent of all federal expenditures.[20] All previous statistics were rapidly eclipsed, however, during the Reagan administration in the 1980s. As a candidate campaigning for office, Reagan had denounced government in general and federal programs in particular and had proclaimed that "you don't solve problems by throwing dollars at them." He then initiated the largest expenditures for military purposes in the peacetime history of the United States. Simultaneously, domestic poverty increased because of his cuts in federal programs designed to help the poor. During Reagan's administration more than two trillion dollars were allotted to defense, so that the percentage of the federal budget related to war rose from 25 percent to almost 40 percent. The diversion of funds to the manufacturers of armaments had the effect of broadening the influence in the United States of the "military-industrial complex," against whose encroachments his predecessor, President—and General—Eisenhower, had so presciently warned.[21]

The democracies of Western Europe have generally extended public ownership further than in the United States. There, it is normal for the

---

[20]*U.S. Statistical Abstract* for 1973, p. 256.

[21]In his Farewell Address to the American people, Eisenhower issued this warning: "In the councils of Government, we must guard against the acquisition of unwarranted influence, whether sought or unsought, by the military-industrial complex. The potential for the disastrous rise of misplaced power exists and will persist. We must never let the weight of this combination endanger our liberties or democratic processes." Reported in the *New York Times,* 18 January 1961.

central government to own and operate the post and telecommunications, gas and electricity and water, railroads and airlines. Beyond these, the pattern varies with the history or the economic situation of particular industries. Various European governments extract coal and oil, operate nuclear power plants, and have a share in the manufacture of steel, ships, and automobiles. In some of these cases, the paramount factor is political. Should the government buy or bail out a major firm which faces bankruptcy, when thousands of jobs and the economic health of an entire city are at stake? France faced this question with steel; Britain, with automobiles, steel, and ships; the United States, with Lockheed and Chrysler.

State ownership can be justified in several ways. One line of reasoning insists that whoever controls a substance like water or a service like transportation, on which everybody depends, will wield power over others. Therefore, such power should belong in public hands. A second argument contends that certain industries (coal, for example) are integral to the functioning of others. So, if you wish to plan the whole economy, ownership of a few "key" industries is a help. Third, some undertakings require so much capital—either to start a new industry or modernize an old one— that only the state has the necessary resources. Fourth, wherever a monopoly is appropriate (e.g., the telephone system in almost every country), the kind over which the public can have most control is presumably that which they own through the state. This argument, a political one, is valid only if the government is democratic. It does not apply to a dictatorship, where state ownership can only augment the dictator's power. Finally, some maintain that it is ethically superior and socially preferable to change the goal of the management from individual profit to public service.

The counterarguments stem from different preconceptions. Some of these concern the possible danger to individual freedom in fusing economic and political power. Even a state of limited functions is potent enough since it disposes of weapons of coercion. Entrust to the government functions which make it the arbiter of its citizens' livelihood, and you may be a few steps from tyranny. Others argue that an attempt by the state to run a business is foredoomed to failure, because the quest for individual profit is the most powerful of managerial incentives. A salaried state employee, they assert, will not be as efficient or as innovative as a private owner, and is subject to the restrictions imposed by a legislature of party politicans. Other objections are directed not so much at the feature of state ownership, as at the inherent difficulties of size. Whether in private or public organizations, largeness can be a liability and may be self-defeating because of its complex structure and elaborate procedure.[22] As size increases, and as an undertaking approaches or becomes a monopoly, eliminating competition may reduce efficiency.

---

[22]As is stated in *Small Is Beautiful* by E. F. Schumacher (New York: Harper & Row, 1973).

2. State Regulation and a Planned Economy

As with public ownership, regulation incites the most acrimonious controversy when the forms it assumes are novel and those at whom it is directed are powerful. Some examples will illustrate the point. Control of farm production, including the acreage sown, crops planted, animals raised or slaughtered; control of stock market transactions and sales of securities through examinations of company assets and prospectuses; control of investment and credit; control of prices, wages, hours of labor; of foreign exchange, along with the licensing of imports and exports; of land use together with building permits, zoning ordinances, and rent restrictions—these and more have been the battlefields of parties and pressure groups struggling for place, profit, and power. Current political controversy swirls around the more recent additions to that list: the conservation of the environment which involves restraining polluters and restricting the disposal of toxic wastes, as well as the regulation of nuclear power plants to safeguard the public. What pattern is woven into this network of regulation? What purposes are served by such controls? What is their rationale? Need we say more about controls except that they tend to expand indefinitely?

Their traditional justification represents the relation of the state to the economy as that of an umpire prescribing and enforcing the rules of a contest in which private individuals and groups are engaged. When the latter are left to their own devices, abuses will occur. Monopolies fleece the public. Competition becomes mutually ruinous. The weak are forced to the wall. The drive of an acquisitive society for individual gain can imperil the foundations of the commonweal. Thus arises the need for the state to brandish its big stick at the monopolies, to dull the throat-cutting edge of competition, to protect consumers from dishonest marketing, to shield the weak from extinction, and finally to succor that orphan child of individualism—the public interest. The gallant knight who leaps to the rescue and fends off the dragons is the regulatory agency, whether department, commission, or board.

A system in which the state regulates, but private persons own and operate, has been extolled as combining the best of both worlds. While private ownership contributes its vaunted efficiency, because of the profit motive and competitive[23] stimulus, state surveillance ensures that service to the public interest will be considered along with profit. Or again, regulation may be lauded as a happy compromise between the two extreme positions of outright public ownership and autonomous private ownership. Thus the regulated economy is pictured as a "middle way," lying between the aberrations of socialism on the left and of laissez-faire capitalism on the right. An additional argument emanates from socialists, who are prepared

---

[23]Except when the regulated undertaking enjoys a monopoly.

to confine public ownership within certain bounds, but desire to plan the economic system in order to prevent mass unemployment, improve living standards for the poorest, and stabilize the economy.

As the nature of controls is diverse, so are the criticisms they evoke. What some consider the advantages of regulation appear disadvantages to others. Thus if regulation is praised as a compromise, it is opposed by those to whom a halfway house is less satisfying than journey's end. Advocates of unrestricted laissez faire blame regulation by the state for hampering their initiative, while socialists claim that the public interest suffers if the state confines itself to laying down conditions and leaves their application to private operators. Thus instead of a union of public responsibility and private efficiency in harmonious wedlock, the results of divided authority can be jurisdictional deadlock. Furthermore, if regulation is justified as a means to a planned economy, many condemn it by rejecting the end. In their view, planning is administratively unworkable, economically inefficient, and politically dangerous. It increases the number of civil servants, subordinates economic calculations to political, and concentrates too much power in the state.

3. Social Services and General Welfare

Besides operating its own businesses and regulating those of others, the state administers social services. Under this heading are education, health, housing, and social security. Each has excited political controversy because the state's assumption of such responsibilities caused bigger public expenditures and conflict with private interests. When compulsory primary and secondary education was first organized under public authority, the private institutions, both lay and ecclesiastical, which hitherto had monopolized the field, did not welcome the entry of the state into their domain. Even nowadays, conflict between state and church schools continues in many countries. Health care has long fallen under state purview because disease knows no boundaries and major epidemics can lead to social upheaval. Modern urbanization requires public precautions in the provision of a safe water supply, disposal of sewage, sale of food, and isolation of victims of contagious disease. Battles were waged around proposals to organize a public medical service, a policy which invariably encounters opposition from the doctors. The same has happened in housing, when governments have financed low-cost homes in which private contractors and lending agencies have seen little profit. So, too, with social security, a field in which the comprehensive programs of modern states reduced the business of private insurance companies by offering everybody a minimum of protection.

The social service or welfare state, as it is sometimes called, came into being to mitigate the injustices of inequality. It would never have been necessary for the state to undertake such duties if there had not coexisted within the bosom of a single community those "two nations" of whom Disraeli wrote in *Sybil*—the rich and the poor. Through their wealth the rich could provide for the medication of their bodies and the education of their minds. They could reside in homes which were spacious and gracious. They could vacation at will and retire in comfort. The poor could do none of these. To the rich neither unemployment nor old age presented a financial crisis since the revenue from their capital did not cease to flow. To the poor the anticipated loss of earnings through age or unemployment was an everhaunting dread. Those to whom the price of private education, private medicine, private housing, and private insurance was prohibitive could obtain such services from only one source, a public agency. This meant an appeal to the state by the political process.

But what was the goal to be attained? Some called it equality, since they proposed to extend uniformly to all the benefits that wealth alone had been privileged to buy. Others named it social justice, for they thought that knowledge, health, a home, and economic security were everyone's right and were not to be rationed in proportion to property or income. Irrespective of label, however, the movement behind social services was concerned with raising the living standard of the less fortunate nearer to the more fortunate, and reducing the gap between "haves" and "have-nots." For the state to adopt such policies entailed the expenditure of large sums of money which could come only from the pockets of those whose wealth exceeded their needs. Consequently the extension of social services was accomplished through new taxes and higher tax rates, generally graduated on personal incomes. Thus financed, the social services redistributed income at least up to a point. Thereby, private wealth becomes subordinated to general welfare; the economics of inequality yields somewhat to egalitarian ethics; and politics is the instrument to bring this about. These objectives relate to the earlier discussion[24] where the functions of the state were seen to evolve progressively from its initial duty of ensuring protection to the provision of order and then of justice. But this latter ideal, a combination of Greek social theory with Roman legal practice, did not mark the end of the quest for a better life through political means. Christians preached the virtue of charity, which the church administered. Any system, however, in which religious agencies provided education, hospital care, or aid to paupers and aged could cover only part of society's need, because of limited finance and staff. Hence, if all the needy were to obtain relief and all the ignorant be educated, the task belonged to an institution able to mobilize the resources of the whole community. Thus the state entered the field, though not without challenge from churches, which did not relish the loss of their monopoly. Similar opposition was expressed by thinkers of the Herbert Spencer variety who saw in social services—and the taxes required to fi-

---

[24]In chapter 3, section on "Protection, Order, and Justice."

nance them—an interference in the "natural" operation of economic laws. As individuals, the laissez-faire economists might be moral and merciful, but, as a science, their economics was indifferent to ethics and callous to the suffering. When economics was reunited with politics, it was subjected again to ethics. In sum, when politics transferred education and charity from the church to the government, and called on economics to serve the public good, the state itself advanced beyond justice to well-being—the Good Life of Aristotle's concept.[25] For what else is the general welfare but humanized justice?

Reaction from the Right

The ultimate test of all theories is how they work out, not in logic, but in practice. I say that with the cautionary reminder that whenever a doctrine is adopted and applied, this happens in a specific historical context, i.e., amid the congeries of past traditions and present conditions of a particular country. These are the mold, as it were, into which abstractions and aspirations are poured as molten ore. From it, therefore, they acquire their shape.

The re-expansion of the powers of the state in the economy, vigorously reasoned and opposed from the 1870s to the 1930s, reached its high-water mark in the field of public policy during the first quarter of a century after the end of World War II (1945–1970). In that period, democratic states, no less than the authoritarian, spread their functions into the economic sphere in each of the three relationships just discussed. During the seventies, however, a perceptible opposition developed, taking the form of political movements whose avowed aim was to cut down the size and scope of their governments. Since public ownership, regulation and planning, and social services were programs sponsored by left-wing or liberal critics of capitalism, the reaction against them emanated from conservatives on the right.

Several factors united in the seventies to create an audience receptive to their message. It was easy to demonstrate that the newer functions of government, particularly the social services, cost large sums of money which were raised by increases of taxes. Burgeoning functions called for bigger staff, and hence a growing bureaucracy. Regulations were irksome to those whom they restrained, and many of the enterprises operated under public ownership were failing to show a profit. Add to this the particular circumstances of the early 1970s, when the principal producing countries decided to quadruple the price for crude oil, and then five years later

---

[25]"The Polis comes into being to maintain life, and exists fully when it maintains the good life." *Politics*, bk. 1.i.8, sec. 1252b.

to triple it again. The immediate result was a depression in the economies of the western, developed peoples, in which they suffered simultaneously from high inflation. high unemployment, and high rates of failure among businesses and banks.

A time of breakdown, especially in the economy, creates a willingness to change direction. Liberal policies were attacked by their critics as having failed. In their place, alternative nostrums were offered. These were a return to the old ideas which had expressed the conventional wisdom in the earlier period of laissez-faire capitalism. The doctrines of Adam Smith and David Ricardo were brought out of the freezer, thawed, and warmed up in the writings of their latter-day followers, master-minded by Milton Friedman whose monetarists recipes replaced the Keynesian diet.

Politically, all this expressed itself under the guise of neoconservatism. But that description was incorrect. Far from being new, this was essentially a rehash of old theory, fortified by strictures on the state-run programs developed since the depression of the 1930s and World War II. As for the philosophy being conservative, that too is a misnomer. Consider the views and the values of the politicans who came to the fore in the 1980s. Their predecessors who had led the right-wing in the fifties, such as Eisenhower and Macmillan, were conservative in the true sense. They did not abolish the reforms introduced by others, but sought to improve on them in constructive ways. By contrast, the leaders of that wing in the eighties, e.g., Thatcher and Reagan, were drawn from the far right. Their proper description would be not conservative, but reactionary—reverting back to earlier times and destroying in the process what was created to correct its inequities.

Both Britain and the United States acted in this fashion in the 1980s, and their example had many imitators. For Prime Minister Thatcher, *socialism* was a dirty word. Accordingly, anything so labeled must be utterly exorcised from the body politic. What she accomplished was to dismantle many of the regulations which had been imposed on business so as to protect the public, while she reduced the contributions of the state to public housing, education, health, and welfare. In addition, her Ministry sold back to private investors many of the economic enterprises which previous governments had nationalized. In fact, this policy, which received the label of privatisation, became the centerpiece of her program. It was portrayed to the public as designed to produce a profit through the stimulus of competition among private owners. In many instances, however, the result was not more competition, but merely the replacement of public monopolies by private ones, which the government under its right-wing direction refused to regulate as closely as before.

In the United States, where the circumstances were not quite the same, the Reagan-led reaction resembled Thatcher's in some features, but differed in certain major respects. Reagan, too, deregulated the business corporations to the farthest extent possible, leaving them freer to do what they wanted in competition with their rivals. This produced two consequences which were harmful to consumers. The government agencies which inspect the business firms so as to ensure minimum standards for the safety and quality of their products had their budgets slashed. Hence the public was less well protected. Furthermore, in various sectors of the economy the removal of regulatory controls left the more powerful firms freer to gobble up the weaker. Thus oligopolies emerged, and competition was, in fact, not increased, but reduced. Both of these harmful effects were particularly evident in the field of air transportation. This fell under the dominance of a few very large airlines, and these were so inadequately regulated that the travelling public was exposed to mounting inconvenience and risk.

Simultaneously, Reagan also cut back on federal appropriations for the social services to the extent that Congress would allow him. At the same time, however, as was previously noted, he ushered in an enormous increase in military expenditures. His priorities, therefore, can be described as substituting the warfare state for the welfare state. Meanwhile, in order to leave more spending power in the pockets of consumers, he greatly reduced the rates of federal taxation, especially on the wealthy. The results of what his own Vice President, George Bush, had once described as "voodoo economics" were dramatic. The federal budget sank into a continuous and mounting deficit, while simultaneously the United States incurred such a deficit in its external balance of payments that the nation which up to 1981 had been a creditor to other countries became within a few years the world's largest debtor.

Worse than that, the deliberate shift from socially oriented programs to the glorification of individualism, advertised in the name of freedom, generated a new birth of inequality. Eight years of reactionary policy in Washington and Westminister were a great boon to the rich and a devastating blow to the poor. British publicists regularly revived the use of Disraeli's phrase "the two nations" to refer to the ever-widening gulf in their country between social and economic classes. Unemployment, which stood at one and a quarter million when Thatcher took office, rose to over three millions under her stewardship. Likewise in Reagan's America, the numbers of poor increased—to the point where 40 percent of the children in New York City were estimated to be living in poverty. Western civilization, in the two major English-speaking democracies, paid a heavy social price in the 1980s for listening to the siren songs of a reorchestrated laissez faire.

Whither to the Year 2000?

And what of the future? In this chapter I have been describing the role of the state in the economy. Traditionally conceived in monistic terms, this was reformulated on pluralistic lines for a century and a half, and then swung back to monism after World War II. What is uncertain at present is whether the bias against the state, rekindled in the 1980s, is destined to endure or to be snuffed out as a merely temporary aberration. Although the outcome is not yet clear, my own belief is that the latter alternative is the more probable. All the imperatives of the coming decades will demand in my judgment stronger government, not weaker. We face a growing population, more complex technology and industrial organization, intensified struggles for scarcer resources, threats of pollution to our environment, global shifts in the balance of power, and the ever-present nightmare that a nuclear war could erupt. Can one contemplate confronting such problems without conceding to the state even more powers than it has already acquired? Is it not hiding one's head in the sand to envision that laissez faire will be born again? Leviathan is a reality with which we have to live.

But to say that is only to "solve" certain problems, while simultaneously embarking on another sea of troubles. What if the neomonistic state abuses its power? What if it be perverted into tyranny? Can we ensure that the actual government conforms to what the state ought to be? These questions lead to the third issue.

8

Third Issue—Part 1

Authority and the Authoritarians

The Justification of Authority

The choice of techniques whereby the government carries out its functions presents the third of the great issues of politics. If the ends of government are to evolve beyond protection, the means must also be transformed. For the selection of means affects the attainment of ends. Whatever goal one seeks, choosing the appropriate means is a condition of success, since methods shape results. The force needed to guarantee protection cannot by itself establish justice, still less ensure well-being. The state must, therefore, rise to the challenge of modifying its original methods, or its usefulness to society will be vitiated. The questions of whether this can be done, and how, create the issue.

Political decisions must be translated into governmental acts. These require enforcement, which admits of two alternatives; to impose coercive power or elicit a willing support. Thus the problem, raised in chapter 3, of the relation between force and consent becomes paramount. The selection of means helps to mold the attitudes of the governed and imparts to government much of its legitimacy and practical effectiveness. Those in office seek to convert power into authority, whereas the governed ask of authority that it serve their need: "By what right do you claim to do this?" "Whence comes your power?" "Who gives you authority?" These typical questions are more persistently raised about the state than about any other human association, because its functions produce such direct effects upon everybody and are so intimately related to life and welfare. Moreover, there comes a time when those in authority or their successors lose the popular support that once brought them to office. As their power slips, the authority that it supported must be transferred elsewhere. Can this be done peacefully? Who are to be the next inheritors of power? And how, if recognized, is their possession of it legitimized? It is precisely because of the character of the functions of government, and because abuse of power and conflicts over its transfer can be so murderous, that controversies occur about authorization. If the state were a "do-little" body, few would care to search the validity of its title deeds. But wherever so much power is concentrated, many will insist that might be adequately endowed with right.

Normally, we obey the state. That is, nearly all of us do so most of the time. For its part, the state expects this obedience, can ordinarily count upon it, and exacts penalties for disobedience. Why does this happen? Some psychologists explain our behavior as the product of our environment. Most of our conduct, as they see it, conforms to patterns designed for us, rather than by us. Parents, teachers, friends, peers, customers, clients, and employers combine to construct within us a strong pressure to conform. To that pressure we habitually respond both because we desire their approval and because swimming with the tide is always easier, as well as more agreeable, than battling against it.

But this explanation, even if correct, would only be partial. It does not explain two important matters. One is the fact of opposition to the state. Even if obedience to constituted authority is normal, every age has notable instances of protest, criticism, and resistance. How do we explain the dissenter, the nonconformist, the unorthodox, the heretic, the rebel, the martyr? History would have no record of revolutions, of movements for reform or independence, if its sole determinant were submission to established power. Second, let us not forget that conformists themselves look for reasoned justifications of what they are doing. Those who administer the state usually tell their fellow citizens or subjects that they must obey, and also that they should. The problem is, therefore, broader in scope than a description of how people behave. It involves the moral issue: Does the state rightfully command, and ought one to obey? By what means does power acquire an ethic and officialdom its legitimacy? What is it that distinguishes these persons bearing a gun—the soldier and the police officer or the gangster and the terrorist?

Domination vs. Accountability

The answers to such questions are based on diametrically opposing philosophies of the relation between government and the governed. If government is thought of as a procedure whereby a small number of persons issue orders to a much larger number who are their subjects and, as such, their inferiors, then authority is supposedly vested in the ruling class by virtue of their superiority, and is handed down to the mass of the community from on high. Civil government, so viewed, is likened to military discipline. As soldiers obey their commanding officers, so the people obey the state and are accountable to it. Rulers can no more be held to account by their subjects than a general by his army. The opposite doctrine reverses this relationship. It makes the rulers answerable for their actions instead of the people for theirs. The source of authority is the mass of the community who are considered as fellow citizens rather than as subjects. It is they who grant power, they who supervise its use, they who may revoke it. Authority is not something which a few impose upon many; it is what many temporarily delegate to a few.

But that word *many* is ambiguous. It is evident arithmetically that those who support a government are always more numerous than those who exercise its powers. The further question is whether the supporters are a majority of the whole community or not. In chapter 3, when discussing the difference between power and authority, I distinguished the varying amounts of consent that underpin the power.[1] That distinction is crucial to the choice which all regimes must make when they confront the Third Issue. The connection is this: Where the supporters of those in power are a minority of the whole, those in charge of government will rely more heavily on repression to control the majority. Hence, their methods will be what we call "authoritarian." But where those in power have the consent of a majority, repression is minimal or nonexistent. This difference is fundamental. It is one of the criteria dividing the dictatorships from the democracies. A test of a dictatorship is how severely the minority represses the majority; of a democracy, how liberally the majority tolerates the minority.

The results of this difference are far-reaching, for the character of the state and the structure of its government are directly related to this controversy about the origins of political power. According to whether authority is believed to flow from the governed or inhere in the governors, institutions will be differently constructed. In the latter case the ruling group will organize to maintain its supremacy and will repress opposition. It will employ techniques of intimidation and coercion. Not daring to allow any challenge to its preeminence, it will use the police, prisons, and army as central organs of administration. In all these respects it will constitute a dictatorship. If the guiding principle, on the other hand, is to assert popular control, means must be discovered for making officials govern on behalf of the people, and for keeping them within the limits of their powers. The people must choose certain of their number to act as agents for them all. Systems must be devised to enforce the responsibility of the government to the governed. For this purpose the state will be rooted in constitutionalism

---

[1]See chapter 3, sections on "Power and Authority" and "The Paradox of Power."

and the rule of law. It will institute an electoral process and welcome the existence of two or more parties which offer a variety of programs and leadership. The choice between these alternatives is the subject of this chapter and the next.

Types of Authoritarianism

When a government is founded on the opinion that its authority does not originate with those over whom it is exercised, some alternative source must be contrived. Two possibilities suggest themselves. Authority can be imagined to descend upon the government, like manna from heaven, as a gift of some higher power outside and above the government and the governed. Or it can be thought to inhere in the rulers by virtue of certain qualities with which they claim to be uniquely endowed.

1. Divine Right

The belief that the right to rule over other human beings comes from a higher than human source has lived long and dies hard. Nor need one search far for the reason why such an idea should have started. Often bewildered by the world around them, not understanding the operation of its physical laws, and therefore unable to live in harmony with their environment, people sought to erect frail shelters of security against the mysteries of a universe that dwarfed them. Before the age of experimental science they ventured to bend to their will the concealed and unknown forces whose effects they observed, but whose causes they did not comprehend. If drought were threatening the crops, with solemn ritual they poured water upon a stone, a symbolic act intended to draw rain from the reluctant skies. Desiring to be rid of some hated person, they fashioned an effigy which they then stabbed or mutilated, thinking thereby to bring on their enemy disaster and death.[2] But when the result did not conform to the hope, it seemed better to entreat the forces which one could not command. Prayer might accomplish what magic did not. In this case, however, since a favor was sought, one must obtain the good will of the power or powers to whom appeal was made. To attain this end certain observances were necessary. A person must be careful to give no offense to the Deities and incur no displeasure. Thus, one must live righteously, that is, in conformity with divine will, and must approach the godhead in a proper manner, that is, with the correct ritual. To know this will and ritual was of supreme importance. Indeed, in such matters as the conduct of war or the assurance of food supply, the life and death of the community were at stake. To placate and

---

[2]See James Frazer, *The Golden Bough*, one-volume abridgement (London: Macmillan & Co., 1941), chapter 3.

enlist the divine aid was therefore no casual affair but an act fundamental to the general welfare.[3]

These attitudes explain the frequent connection between government and religion or magic. Where much depends upon maintaining the right relation with the power pervading the universe, governmental responsibilities like war and welfare become intertwined with the ceremonies of witchcraft or worship. It calls for special skills, and therefore specialized personnel, to mediate on human behalf between the world that is seen and that which is unseen. Who holds the key to the mysteries that shape human fates, wields power.

Before modern times, when communication was severely restricted and few people ever had the occasion or the means to travel far from their homes, the reality with which most persons were directly acquainted was bounded by a close and closed horizon. Beyond that little which was known, the world shaded off into the myriad gradations of the vast unknown, all endowed with equal credibility. In this vein, Doris Mary Stenton has written of the belief in the supernatural which was so pervasive in the Middle Ages:

> The hard-headed practicality of the medieval people is nowhere more clearly shown than in their attitude to God and religion. They lived in a small world and knew nothing of its place in the universe. The conception of a globe revolving in space in a determinable relationship to other bodies had not dawned upon even the most advanced thinkers. Beyond the limits of their known world lay an unknown fringe of incalculable depth, sea or land, equally remote and full of perils. Their lives within the little medieval world were hard and brief and they accepted unquestioningly a religion that offered to the poor and hungry an eternity of satisfaction. Since so much of the world about them was unknown the invisibility of the next world did not trouble them. It was as real to them as remote lands to-day are real to the untravelled. They were equally assured of its existence.[4]

For the purpose of this analysis, it is unnecessary to inquire which kind of authority, human or superhuman, was the prior and superior. Indeed, the gaps and silences of prehistory do not allow a conclusive answer to the question: Did those who already possessed political power look for reinforcements from magic or religion, or did medicine men and priests project their influence into the general arena of government? All one can state with certainty is that human and superhuman authority have often been found in the closest relation to each other. The priest-king or god-ruler is widely spread among peoples at different levels of cultural development. Across centuries and the world, anthropologists and historians have discovered countless examples of rulers who perform magical or religious rites or are worshiped as living deities or trace back their lineage to a divine ancestor; of

[3]Ibid., chapter 4.

[4]Doris Mary Stenton, *English Society in the Early Middle Ages* (Baltimore: Penguin Books, 1951), p. 203.

prophets who announce they have heard the word of God and administer a code of divine commandments; of priests whom the faithful revere as custodians of the true faith and exponents of divine will. Until 1946 the emperors of Japan claimed to be descended from the Sun God. Homeric kings derived their lineage from Zeus the Thunderer, king of the gods. Those of the Roman emperors who did not arouse the ire of their subjects were customarily worshiped while alive (at least in the eastern half of the empire), and after death were officially deified with the title *Divus* and placed on the ceremonial roster of gods to whom prayer was due.[5] The Dalai Lama, who until 1950 reigned over Tibet from Lhasa, was regarded by his subjects as a living reincarnation of the Buddha. Alternatively, while the rulers' human character may be recognized, they may be considered as prophets or priests acting on behalf of the Deity, ruling by divine authority and thus mediating between God and man. In that sense, the people of Israel, when governed by Eli or Samuel, were a theocratic state. Their formal transition from theocracy to secular government is described in the Book of Samuel.[6] Other such theocracies were the city of Geneva under the control of Calvin, the Papal States in Italy before 1860, the Vatican since 1929, Iran since 1979.[7]

What consequence does this produce for the state? How is the authority to govern affected by being linked with a belief in power that is more than human? When humanity thinks its ruler is divine, or has a divine ancestor, or is divinely appointed, the relation of government to the governed can never approach equality. In the presence of deity or its representative, humans are made to bare the head or bow the knee, to listen submissively, to avert the eye, or gaze with awe and reverence[8]—all of which effectively precludes controls over government! How can a mere mortal demand an accounting from the godhead when criticism is named heresy and opposition is sin? Is not a law firmly founded when people believe it to be given by God, as when Hammurabi, king of Babylon, received the law from Shamash, or when Moses on Sinai was told the Ten Commandments from the mouth of Jehovah? Small wonder that royal monarchs in the sixteenth and seventeenth centuries fortified their authority with the doctrine of the "divine

---

[5]Hence the famous saying of the Emperor Vespasian on his deathbed: *Ut puto, divus fio.* ("I suppose I'm becoming a god.")

[6]I Sam. 8.

[7]A recent example is Iran. There, the political power of the Ayatollah Khomeini was enshrined in 1979 in the constitutional office of Faghi, or religious guardian, giving him ultimate authority over everybody else.

[8]Montezuma, whose position combined the functions of chief and priest, was accorded such deference by the Aztecs. Cortés described it thus: "The nobles always entered his palace barefoot, and those who were bidden to present themselves before him did so with bowed head and eyes fixed on the ground, their whole bearing expressing reverence; nor would they when speaking to him lift their eyes to his face, all of which was done to show their profound humiliation and respect." *Five Letters of Cortés to the Emperor,* trans. and ed. J. Bayard Morris (New York: W. W. Norton & Co., 1962), p. 97. This extract is from the second letter, dated 30 October 1520, describing his first conquest of Mexico.

right of kings." This theory, being then in vogue, was even put into the mouth of a murderer, King Claudius, whom Shakespeare allowed to exclaim:

> There's such divinity doth hedge a king,
> That treason can but peep to what it would,
> Acts little of his will.[9]

In real life, the deification of monarchy was unequivocally asserted by a reigning monarch, James I of England, in these words to Parliament: "Kings are justly called gods; for they exercise a manner of resemblance of Divine power upon earth. For if you will consider the attributes of God, you shall see how they agree in the person of a king."[10] Other rulers, without attempting so close an identification of themselves with deity, have used titles or asserted principles to invoke a divine sanctity and sanction for their office. The Fundamental Laws of the Russian Empire, issued in 1892, proclaimed in Article I: "The All-Russian Emperor is an autocratic and unlimited Monarch. . . . God Himself commands that his supreme power be obeyed, not only because of fear but also because of conscience." One may also recall such titles as Holy Roman Emperor and Most Christian Majesty; the careers of Joseph Smith and Brigham Young and the founding of the Mormon State of Deseret; and the role of the English monarch as the Head of the Church of England which once was politically relevant. From the standpoint of those who govern, the great advantage in deriving their authority from divine will is that opposition is made to seem so fruitless. Who dares resist the government is challenging a divine dispensation which mere mortals must accept and may not amend.

2. "Might Is Right"

A second method by which authority demands obedience is the appeal to force. The right of those in power is then defended by virtue of the fact that they are in power and possess the means to enforce their will. This view, instead of arguing that might is justified by the right it serves, inverts the relationship, deriving right from might. Thus we have such assertions as "Justice is the interest of the stronger"; "Obey the powers that be"; and "Whatever is, is right." The most that can be said for this point of view is that it offers the governed a counsel of expediency and prudence. But on all other grounds it is open to serious objections. Any doctrine is morally indefensible if it seeks to justify right by might. Countless crimes and cruelties have thus been explained away. Furthermore, to derive a government's authority from the force it commands is to invite any opponent to test its strength and challenge it with counterforce. Those who can overthrow the

---

[9]*Hamlet*, IV. 5. 122–24.

[10]Quoted in G. P. Gooch, *Political Thought in England, from Bacon to Halifax* (London: Williams and Norgate, 1914), p. 14.

existing order by violence are then entitled to succeed to its authority, and some will think the prize is worth the price.

Most states were created or have grown by violence. But the lapse of time can work a change in governments founded on force. A later generation will accept by habit and inertia what was imposed on its ancestors by conquest. The power that commands by terror today may reign by hereditary right tomorrow. Ibn Khaldun of Tunis was aware of such developments, which he had studied in the history of the Arab world, and drew this distinction between new and established states:

> Newly founded states can secure the obedience of their subjects only by much coercion and force. This is because the people have not had the time to get accustomed to the new and foreign rule. Once kingship has been established, however, and inherited by successive generations or dynasties, the people forget their original condition, the rulers are invested with the aura of leadership, and the subjects obey them almost as they obey the precepts of their religion, and fight for them as they would fight for their faith.[11]

An example of this transformation and of its practical results may be found in the earlier history of South America. The Incas built their empire in the Andes by the usual methods of conquest. But once their power was consolidated, the character of their rule altered, as did their subjects' submission. Consider the following description:

> When the Incas set out to visit their kingdom, it is told that they traveled with great pomp, riding in rich litters set upon smooth, long poles of the finest wood and adorned with gold and silver. . . . Around the litter and alongside it came the Inca's guard with the archers and halberdiers, and behind an equal number of lancers with their captains, and along the road and over the road itself went faithful runners seeing what there might be and giving word of the coming of the Inca. So many people came to see his passing that all the hills and slopes seemed covered with them, and all called down blessings upon him. He traveled four leagues each day, or as much as he wished; he stopped wherever he liked to inquire into the state of his kingdom; he willingly listened to those who came to him with complaints, righting wrongs and punishing those who had committed an injustice.[12]

3. Ancestral Lineage

Once this change has occurred, the feeling that submission to those in power is an unalterable feature of the established order can be endowed with its own justification and rationale. It can be asserted that the authority to govern issues neither from force nor from heaven, but from the past.[13]

---

[11]*An Arab Philosophy of History*, ed. Charles Issawi (London: John Murray, 1950), p. 110.

[12]This is taken from *The Incas of Pedro de Cieza de Léon*, trans. Harriet de Onis, ed. by Victor Wolfgang von Hagen (Norman: University of Oklahoma Press, 1959).

[13]In some cases one source of power may merge with another—for example, when people worship their own ancestors. This occurred in China under the state cult of Confucianism.

Government, as the argument runs, consists essentially in superiors giving orders to subjects. The continuity and stability of the state are best assured when human beings are ranked in classes and are assigned at birth the same status in society as their parents so that relationships continue unchanged in successive generations. Some are highborn, some lowborn. If my grandfather was the inferior of your grandfather, and my father of your father, then I am inferior to you and take your orders. Authority thus becomes a matter of hereditary right, an appendix to a birth certificate. The title to rule is a product of lineage and lapse of time.

Such a philosophy is not merely a conservative plea for the status quo. It is also the defense of a society divided into classes whose membership is determined—or rather predetermined—without any of us willing it so. Society thus visualized evolves as a seamless web woven to patterns of ancient design. By allotting to each of us our station in life, heredity selects our environment for us, and fixes it by the unalterable circumstance of parentage. It is then a simple matter to discover the source of authority. Authority is ancestral—and that is that. Clearly, this principle can operate only in a fairly static society. Furthermore, it can provide but one political advantage, namely stability of government and a sure procedure for the transfer of power, which, though desirable up to a point, is not the sole ideal for which the state exists. But in any case how does an authority founded on the past reply to critics who shout that the times are out of joint and that a sick society needs a new medicine and new doctors?

The Power of the Elite

The three methods just described have this in common: They justify the authority of those in power by reference to some external criterion—gods, guns, or grandparents. But if these methods fail, another way is possible. This is to argue that the authority of the few over the many derives from some quality of excellence which makes the minority inherently superior. Who are "the best" and what makes them such was discussed in chapter 4, where different elites were analyzed. They have been variously identified as the oldest, wisest, wealthiest, and so on. If sufficient people accept the view that fitness to govern is associated with one of these attributes, then those who have mustered enough years or knowledge or property owe their authority to this fact. In short, once the premises are conceded, the conclusion resolves itself into a tautology: The best know best how to govern. If so, how can their inferiors hold them accountable?

Throughout history, most governments have been authoritarian. Indeed, the commonest type of rule has been that of oligarchies, which impose their will by fiat. Why is this so? A priori, it might seem natural, even inevitable, that majorities should rule and that they should be the donors of authority and its source. After all, the weight of numbers is on their side, and that is no small advantage. But if history supports any generalization, it is the contrary. Normally, it has been easier for the few to dominate the many than the reverse, and this is as true in politics as in religion, economics, and the military. Most politics, in fact most social organization, has consisted in the subordination of the masses by a judicious blend of force and fraud. Force has meant the custody and use of weapons by a trained and disciplined few, since a small band, well-armed and organized, can usually overpower an ill-equipped, unorganized multitude. Fraud has been practiced by playing on the superstitions and fears of the ignorant, by the use of ideas as a technique of political supremacy, or by propaganda. Moreover, the mass of people in the past occupied a lowly social status and eked out a living which left little or no margin above subsistence. They were habituated to accept their condition as part of a predestined order. Custom, inertia, and ignorance have always combined to preserve the status quo.

To maintain traditional patterns has been easiest in periods when the rate of change was so slow that, to any one generation, society seemed to be cast in a rigid mold. The majority of mankind were then resigned to political servitude as their inescapable lot. Politics was physically distant from them and was conducted at a level above their daily affairs and preoccupations. The capital was remote from the farm and village; at the castle and the palace, arrogance dwelt in affluence. What was most wanted of rulers was that they not be oppressive.[14] When the state intruded into the lives of the common people, it generally came in an unpleasant guise. The government was the tax gatherer, soldier, or functionary. Politics, therefore, was conducted by a small cast on a limited stage. The populace were passive spectators of a play which they observed at a distance and whose action went over their heads.

The Modern Revolution

The political and social revolution of modern times has drastically altered the conditions under which authoritarianism can dominate. One change is fundamental to all else. The masses are no longer as passive as they once were. In the course of the past century they have grown self-conscious and gained in self-confidence. The numbers of those who are actively concerned and who actually take some part in the political process are larger than ever before. More and more people look to their government, make claims upon it, and expect its help. Twentieth-century politics is the politics of mass action. No more can governments rely on the passivity of subjects; they must face the activity of citizens.

[14]"The aim of the people is more honest than that of the nobility, the latter desiring to oppress, and the former merely to avoid oppression." Machiavelli, *The Prince*, chapter 9.

This numerical difference, together with the psychological change in relationships, does not mean that authoritarianism has ceased to be possible in the sense of a minority imposing its will on a majority. Far from it. The majority of humans still live under political dictatorships, as did our ancestors. What has altered, however, is the method which authoritarianism must employ in the contemporary world. It has had to adapt its techniques to this enlargement of scale. The few can still dominate the many through violence to body and mind. But in both spheres the means must be both more brutal and more subtle. What are the institutions, then, that have evolved to serve this purpose? How does modern authoritarianism resemble, and differ from, its predecessors?

Dictatorship in Modern Dress

Dictatorships of the twentieth century fall into three main groups. The type which most resembles the traditional autocracies is the military ruler. Since World War II this pest has spread on every continent except North America, and some have stayed in power unconscionably long. Western Europe has had three. Franco squatted despotically on Spain's back for a third of a century. Greece, the birthplace of democracy, fell prey to a brutal military junta from 1967 to 1974. And France in 1958, frustrated in its efforts to discover the general will, resigned itself to the will of the General—although de Gaulle, however autocratic, was no despot.

Latin America, where the army *caudillo* is endemic, has continued its outbreaks of the plague. The three southern states—Argentina, Brazil, and Chile—lay under the military heel during the 1970s. But early in the 1980s the Generals' rule collapsed in Brazil and Argentina of its own incompetence. Their economies, after initially booming under the impact of Friedmanite[15] policies designed in the interest of businessmen, were in shambles. Discredited by their failures and detested for their cruelties, the Generals withdrew to their barracks. The exception has been Chile, where a particularly brutal soldier, Pinochet, has stayed firmly in the saddle. Elsewhere, in the small and medium-sized states, militarism has continued to be the rule rather than the exception. Such names as Batista in Cuba, Trujillo in the Dominican Republic, Stroessner in Paraguay, and the Somozas in Nicaragua are reminders of the use of power—and its abuse—by the military. Since in these regimes the military held down the mass of the populace for the benefit of an oligarchy of wealthy owners of property, it is not surprising that after their overthrow some of their successors—

---

[15]In these countries, as in Pakistan and South Korea, many of the economists who served the military were trained in the monetarist ideas of the "Chicago School" where Milton Friedman dominated. Friedmanite policies of freeing businessmen to do what they wished chimed harmoniously with despotism which crushed unions and prevented political opposition.

e.g., in Cuba and Nicaragua—were Marxist. Several generations must elapse before Latin America can escape the incubus of the authoritarian traditions, both in state and church, of its Iberian past.

Much the same pattern can be traced across Asia, from the Middle East to the southeast. All the Arab states, with the exception of the tribal monarchies in Jordan and Saudi Arabia, have experienced military rule, as have most Islamic countries from Algeria and Libya to Pakistan and Indonesia. Chiang Kai-shek lost the Chinese civil war through corruption and incompetence, then ruled the Taiwanese until his death. Nor has the Buddhist world been exempt from the warlords, as Burma and Thailand attest. Israel, in fact, is the only[16] continuous democracy in all of Asia, but its culture is more occidental than oriental.

As for Africa, since the European empires were liquidated, in one new state after another the army has provided an instrument for governing. Those who emerged on top owed their training to the former imperial masters. Mobutu was trained in Zaire under the Belgians; Idi Amin in Uganda under the British; Bokassa in the Central African Republic under the French. Apart from the grosser instances of personal aggrandisement and plunder, the order which the soldiers have maintained has two objectives: the economic need for a long-range plan of development, and the fusing of tribal divisions in a national unity.

A second type of autocratic rule consists of exalting a single individual within the ruling group. This dominance of one may be due to that person's magnetism and popular following. In ex-colonial regimes it is often the leader of the resistance who on gaining independence becomes the new boss and clings to power as long as possible—witness Nkrumah in Ghana, Kenyatta in Kenya, Nyerere in Tanzania, Mugabe in Zimbabwe, Soekarno in Indonesia, Rhee in Korea. Some of these, Nkrumah and Rhee for example, repressed their domestic rivals or critics with the same severity as the imperial rulers had employed. One may then speculate on what is gained in substituting the home-grown despot for the alien proconsul.

The third type of modern dictatorship has little in common with traditional forms. Its aims are revolutionary in a more fundamental sense, and certain of its methods have been invented in this century. This kind of dictatorship seeks to refashion human society in terms of some ideology or doctrine. Its instrument of power and innovation is the state, and it employs the three techniques of terror, propaganda, and the single political party. The first of these is by no means novel, since brutal men in all centuries have dealt forcibly with opposition. But the modern species of terror is far more thoroughly organized. Propaganda, too, has some earlier analogies, at least to the extent that censorship negatively restricted the freedom of opinion. What distinguishes the modern version, however, is

---

[16]Japan has regularly conducted free elections which offer a genuine choice between parties, but has yet to experience their alternation in power. India temporarily abandoned democracy when Indira Ghandhi suspended constitutional guarantees.

the active propagation of halftruth and untruth, designed positively to direct people's thinking into certain molds.[17] The monopoly of political power by one dominant party is a feature unique to our time. It is precisely this organizational tool which has been engineered to cope with the problem of mass participation. The party is the instrument by which the masses are both driven and drawn, both controlled in disciplined subjection to the few and prodded to follow them as required.

These practices have been most systematically employed by the dictatorships of Right and Left, by the Fascists, Nazis, and Communists. Although these differ sharply in their philosophies and objectives and in the groups which support them, their methods are markedly similar. In fact, one can observe in chronological succession a borrowing, which has occurred between the extremes. The first in the field was Lenin, who organized the Bolsheviks to overthrow the Kerensky regime and then guided Russia through the revolution, civil war, and foreign intervention. His methods were imitated by Mussolini, whose Blackshirt militia overawed the feeble government of Italy in 1922. After 1925 the techniques of the Fascist regime came to resemble those of the Communists. Next was Adolf Hitler, whose Nazis emulated and vied with Communists and Fascists. They established their evil dominance over a nation that had greatly vaunted its enlightenment and *Kultur*. As the Germans do everything thoroughly, so in the use of brutality by the Nazis they sank to unprecedented barbarism. Finally in the Soviet Union the efficient and cold-blooded Stalin learned many lessons from Hitler and applied them internally against his own opponents. In the mid-1930s, and again in his last phase (1947–1953) when he became morbidly despotic, Stalin's system of terror was akin to Hitler's.

Fascism and Nazism

When Mussolini wrote an article on "The Political and Social Doctrine of Fascism," he asserted: "A party which entirely governs a nation is a fact entirely new to history, there are no possible references or parallels." Although this statement, referring to his own Fascists, conceals his debt to Lenin, Mussolini was correct to emphasize the function of the party in the conduct of the dictatorship. Both fascism and nazism considered themselves programs of action. They represented their mission as the regeneration of a people demoralized by division and defeat. Theirs were regimes of crisis, injecting into the cynical and the listless the political stimulant of enthusiastic nationalism. They were movements of combat, their adherents trained for battle, taught to hate, murdering the foes within, "blitzing" the enemies without. Democracy they despised as weakness. Discussion spelled

---

[17]The nearest parallels to this in previous systems are provided by the thought control of religious fanaticism—the Spanish Inquisition, for instance.

delay and the inability to agree. Reason was the fraud or cowardice of the intellectual. Instead of reason, they glorified will; instead of discussion, decision; instead of democracy, leadership. Leadership itself was the responsibility of the party, which took its cue from its Duce or Führer. Authority was exercised over the nation by the dominant group, as the leadership interpreted the nation's interest. The people did not delegate that authority, could not define it, dared not revoke it. Those who ran the party had mobilized force. Those who used such force gained power. Those who possessed power claimed authority.

Unswerving obedience to an ironclad autocracy was the ideal of the Nazi-Fascist state. In Italy and Germany under the regimes of Mussolini and Hitler the dictatorship of the party over the people was as intense as the preeminence within the party of the Duce or Führer. "Believe, obey, fight" was the motto prescribed by Mussolini for his countrymen. "In the name of God and of Italy I swear that I will obey the orders of the Leader without questioning"—this was part of the oath taken upon admission to the Fascist party. *Mein Kampf*, the bible of the Nazi movement, enunciated with grotesque clarity the contempt which Hitler felt for the mass of humanity and his determination to subject them to a disciplined inferiority. "A view of life," he proclaimed, "which, by rejecting the democratic mass idea endeavors to give this world to the best people, that means to the most superior men [the Germans], has logically to obey the same aristocratic principle also within this people and has to guarantee leadership and highest influence within the respective people to its best heads." Political organization therefore requires "Putting the heads above the masses" and "subjecting the masses to the heads." Mankind's interest "is not satisfied and is not served by the rule of the masses who are either unable to think or are inefficient, in any case not inspired." Such assumptions brought Hitler to formulate his principle of leadership. "The principle which once made the Prussian army the most marvelous instrument of the German people has to be some day in a transformed meaning the principle of the construction of our whole state constitution, authority of every leader towards below and responsibility towards above."[18] To carry out his beliefs and realize his ambition, Hitler gratuitously launched a World War. Before he was stopped, millions had died.

The Communist Dictatorship

Granted that their objectives are dissimilar, dictatorships of the far Left employ similar methods to those of the far Right, although in certain respects they display more skill. For communism patently carries out the

[18]These quotations are from "Personality and the Conception of the National State," *Mein Kampf*, trans. Alvin Johnson (New York: Reynal & Co., 1939), vol. 2, chapter 4, pp. 661, 665, 670.

principle that the masses must be goaded, curbed, and led by a disciplined few, and their instrument for accomplishing this is the single dominant party, concentrating in its grip a monopoly of legal authority. As a technique of government, the system originated with the revolutionary movement from the Left which grew out of the central root of Marxism. The first one to carry out this idea was Lenin. What he initiated was rigorously extended by Joseph Stalin, who chose to call himself "Lenin's faithful disciple." Holding the Marxian view that society was irreconcilably split into two economic classes, that the relationship between these can only be one of war, and that the revolt of the submerged class and its eventual triumph are inevitable,[19] Lenin concerned himself with the tactics for hastening the inevitable and guiding it into Communist channels. Since the revolutionary class (called the proletariat) was large, poorly educated, and politically inexperienced, its victory required, according to him, the aid of a smaller group, firmly disciplined and iron-willed, whose members could fathom and follow the laws of "scientific" Marxism.

Such was the Communist party which Lenin set out to build and which Stalin and his followers continued in the Soviet Union or reproduced elsewhere. Its character was described by Stalin at the time (1924) when he was its secretary-general. According to him the party "must first of all constitute the vanguard of the working class." As such, it "must take its stand at the head of the working class, it must see ahead of the working class, lead the proletariat and not trail behind the spontaneous movement." The similarity between a revolutionary struggle and war makes it necessary for the proletariat, like an army in the field, to have a general staff. "The Party," therefore, "is the Military staff of the proletariat." From these premises the conclusions follow that the party must be "the organized detachment of the working class"; that it is "the highest form of class organization of the proletariat"; that it serves as "the weapon of the dictatorship of the proletariat"; and that "the existence of factions is incompatible with Party unity and with its iron discipline."[20] When the "Stalin Constitution" was written and ratified in 1936, the principles outlined above were duly recorded in Article 126 as follows:

> The most active and politically conscious citizens in the ranks of the working class and other strata of the toilers unite in the Communist Party of the Soviet Union (Bolsheviks), which is the vanguard of the toilers in their struggle to strengthen and develop the socialist system and which represents the leading core of all organizations of the toilers, both public and state.

Using statements of this kind to explain his actions, Stalin established a remarkable triple dictatorship: that of himself over the Communist party,

---

[19]According to one wit, Marxism is the science that proves what must happen—and, when it doesn't, why it couldn't.

[20]The above quotations are from a lecture on "Foundations of Leninism" given by Stalin in 1924 and printed in many collections of Marxist writings.

that of the party over the peoples of the USSR, and that of the party in the USSR over organized Communist movements elsewhere in the world, with the one exception that eluded his grip, Yugoslavia.

Numerically the ratio of Communist party members to the population they govern is small. Their control is maintained by various devices—by a complete grip on the machinery of government at its highest levels, by placing their members at key points in the community (in factories, collective farms, educational bodies, and so forth) to direct and report on non-members, by a monopoly of all media for influencing opinion, by the prevention or punishment of overt criticism, and by the terrorist activities of a secret police. Most important of all to the party is the selection and training of its own personnel. Prospective members are carefully observed during a long period of probation and preparation. Once admitted to the party, the Communist's life is dedicated to a meticulous discipline of thought and action. Every now and then a purge is conducted to rid the party of any who are too weak, too half-hearted, or too independent for its tasks. Because of the Communist conception of their mission as an officer class directing a revolutionary upsurge of the masses of mankind, their ethical code knows no greater sin than disunity. Their bitterest hatred is therefore directed, not at those whom they call their class enemies, but at other Communists who differ or deviate from the high command (as Trotsky did) and at Socialists of a democratic brand who compete with Communists for the support of the working class. Finally, since a dictatorship thrives on continuing crisis, the Communist leaders have regularly sown suspicion among their subjects and implanted widespread fear of traitors within and spies without. If systematically conducted by a watchful secret police who are backed up by concentration and forced labor camps, this policy is calculated to keep the opponents of those in power disorganized, demoralized, and therefore harmless.

The most ruthless employer of these techniques was Stalin. After Lenin's death and the ensuing interregnum during which he crushed his opponents in the party, Stalin consolidated his own power and remained supreme for a quarter of a century. Lenin had never been scrupulous in his choice of methods and had dealt mercilessly with non-Communists. But he had tolerated discussion within the party and always felt some attachment to the "Old Bolsheviks," his fellow conspirators. Stalin, "the man of steel" as his pseudonym indicates, had none of these feelings. Aloof, secretive, and callous, he spared nobody. Communist and non-Communist, young and old—all had to toe the line. In a manner reminiscent of other Russian autocrats before him—Ivan the Terrible, for instance, or Peter the Great—he devoted his fantastic energies and powers of will and organization to strengthening his country. All else was subordinated to this aim. To achieve it, like Hitler, he killed by the millions when he deemed it necessary.[21]

[21]In the late 1930s a group of influential Britishers visited the USSR and were accorded an interview with Stalin. One of them, Lady Astor, asked the dictator: "How long will

Even after 1945, when the prestige of victory in World War II had ensured his power, Stalin actually tightened his grip on the Russian people instead of relaxing it. The party was reduced to what Trotsky had once contemptuously called "the dictatorship of the secretariat." The army was prevented from challenging him by honoring the marshals who had become popular heroes, and then relegating them to commands outside Moscow. All individuals who had access to Stalin were kept under watch by the secret police, whose activities were enlarged on the pretext of the cold war, which he himself did so much to foment. As far as possible, Russians were sealed off from contact with persons and opinions outside the Communist sphere. Moreover, what was sauce for the Russian goose was sauce for the satellite gander. The same Stalinist system, shielded by its iron curtain, was imposed on the peoples of Eastern Europe whose lands had fallen under the dominion of the Red Army. Only in one place did the results backfire. In Yugoslavia the equally strong-willed Communist ruler, Josip Broz Tito, successfully declared and consummated his independence—the only case in which Stalin failed to exterminate a foe.

Transfer of Power under Communism

Every political regime faces the need to maintain continuity and provide for an orderly succession. For a dictatorship this creates a special problem. Can a system born of crisis and revolution evolve into normalcy? Can it constitutionalize its own processes? Can it arrange for a transfer of power to new hands without reverting to internecine struggle? The danger to an oligarchy is particularly acute whenever one person accumulates great power. When that individual becomes feeble or dies, a vacuum is created. Feuding among the few at the top can so weaken the regime as to modify its authoritarianism. Hereditary monarchies, founded on legitimacy, adopted an automatic solution. How does the modern dictatorship provide for the smooth transfer of power?

In Fascist Italy and Nazi Germany this problem never arose. Both regimes were overthrown by military defeat in a war that they themselves instigated. But the Russian Communists have now confronted this problem six times—after the deaths of Lenin, Stalin, Brezhnev, Andropov, and Chernenko, and after the ouster of Khrushchev. I shall discuss the circumstances in these cases because of the light they throw on the transfer of power in an authoritarian regime. Certain patterns emerge, as will be seen. Sometimes, after one all-powerful individual passes from the scene, there is

---

you go on killing people?" "As long as it is necessary," was Stalin's reply. Solzhenitsyn has described and documented the far-flung activities of the Soviet secret police under Lenin and Stalin in his book *The Gulag Archipelago*. He has estimated that the number of their victims vastly exceeded those destroyed under the czars or by Hitler.

a relaxation of control, a loosening of the grip from the top, because the newcomer is not yet firmly in charge. Sometimes, the power may be shared among a few leading personalities. But eventually, one of these thrusts himself up as Number One. In the struggle for preeminence, the rivals turn to their advantage the resources of whatever is their power base within the system, which can be the party machine, the government bureaucracy, or the military. But in the competition for support, they contend for the policies they favor, both domestic and external, while criticizing those with which their rivals are identified.

The first leadership crisis occurred when Lenin died (1924), early in the history of the regime. Russia at that time had barely survived the ordeals of foreign war, revolution, civil war, and intervention. The country was isolated internationally and was still in the very early phase of rebuilding and development. The domestic opposition to the Communists had been crushed, but the Communist party was full of "Old Bolsheviks," the veterans of the revolutionary era. For three years (1924–1927) the party was torn by internal arguments about theory and program. The chief domestic issue concerned the future direction of the economy. Under Lenin's New Economic Policy, a limited amount of capitalism had been reintroduced in order to stimulate production after the fighting ended. The party's right wing, under Bukharin, Tomsky, and Rykov, favored extending this policy further. Trotsky, however, led a left wing, where he was joined by Kamenev and Zinoviev, in proposing rapid industrialization under state auspices and a collectivized agriculture. At the same time he espoused a foreign policy of "permanent revolution," arguing that socialism could not survive in one country and that Communist revolutions must be fomented elsewhere.

Stalin had no theory, but he had two clear objectives. He wanted to build the power of Russia and his own power within Russia, to which latter end he utilized efficiently his opportunities as the Party's general secretary. Recognizing Trotsky as his leading adversary, he decided to destroy him first. For this, he turned to his advantage the collapse of Russian policy in China, as evidenced by the dismissal of Borodin and the victories of Chiang Kai-shek over the Chinese left. With the support of the right wing, he advocated against Trotsky and his adherents the policy of "socialism in a single country." In 1927 the party dutifully expelled Trotsky, Kamenev, and Zinoviev. Next year, however, Stalin turned against the Right. Arguing now for a five-year plan of rapid industrial development and collectivization of agriculture, he reversed the New Economic Policy and secured the expulsion of Tomsky, Bukharin, and Rykov. All these others he subsequently readmitted on his own terms, except for Trotsky whom he really feared and drove into exile.[22] Thus, by playing off one group against the

[22]Many years later Trotsky was murdered in Mexico by Stalin's agents. In 1938, Bukharin, Rykov, and other leading Communists were tried and convicted of conspiring

other, and picking policies from each side as they strengthened Russia and himself, within a few years Stalin ruled supreme. During his long sway, which lasted until 1953, because of the fear he induced, the adulation of his individual personality went to lengths that far exceeded the deference paid to Lenin. The truth of this is well attested by those who had most cause to hate Stalin—the men near him. At the Twentieth Party Congress in 1956, his successors spoke revealingly of the terror that had reigned at the top. Nor did they conceal their dislike for his despotic excesses. Mikoyan, then first deputy premier, stated: "In the course of about 20 years we, in fact, had no collective leadership. The cult of personality, condemned already by Marx and afterward by Lenin, flourished, and this, of course, could not but exert an extremely negative influence on the situation within the party and on its work."[23] Speaking in the same vein, Khrushchev delivered a lengthy report indicting Stalin for acts of despotism. "It is clear," he said, "that here Stalin showed in a whole series of cases his intolerance, his brutality and his abuse of power. Instead of proving his political correctness and mobilizing the masses, he often chose the path of repression and physical annihilation, not only against actual enemies, but also against individuals who had not committed any crimes against the party and the Soviet Government."[24]

The Khrushchev Period

When the dictator died, his heirs confronted a new situation that required delicate handling if their own power was to continue unimpaired and their regime was to advance in strength. Internally, the Russian people were more secure than in the 1920s. But they had been denied consumer goods and were sealed off from communication with the world beyond their borders. In the Communist party few of the "Old Bolsheviks" remained. Practically all those at the top, and everyone in the middle ranks, were of the generation that knew only Stalin. The army leaders were anxious to have more of a say, as were the new intelligentsia, the scientists, and the experts in technology, on whom the Soviet Union depended for its further progress. Moreover, the government was deeply involved in a network of relations with other Communist regimes, on which Stalin's fist had lain so roughly.

The internal struggle for power after 1953 revolved around two axes: choice of policies and rivalries between individuals and institutions. In policy, the choice was whether to continue Stalin's programs and methods,

---

against the regime and were executed. Fifty years later, the Soviet Supreme Court reversed their conviction and exonerated them of all charges.

[23] As quoted in the *New York Times*, 19 February 1956, p. 26.

[24] The text of the entire report, with commentary, is published in *Khrushchev and Stalin's Ghost*, by Bertram D. Wolfe (New York: Frederick A. Praeger, 1957). This extract is on p. 116.

or relax or reverse them. Depending on this decision, one person or group would emerge predominant. There were three institutions in the Soviet system that could produce the new leadership: the party, the government functionaries, or the army. The man who bested his rivals was Khrushchev. To consolidate his position took five years (1953–1958)—one year longer than it had taken Stalin—after which he remained Number One in Russia until his overthrow in October 1964. Let us see how he did it.

On Stalin's death, Malenkov became chairman of the government. Closely associated with him were two other powerful figures—Beria, the head of the secret police, and Molotov, the foreign secretary and long-time associate of Stalin. Meanwhile, the Party line emphasized the change from the former "cult of personality" to the new "collective leadership." Khrushchev was strategically placed as general secretary of the party, and the army marshals, of whom Zhukov was the best known, were seeking to assert themselves. All sides now began the political game of Russian roulette. Only one shot was fired, however. Its victim was Beria. As chief of the secret police responsible for internal security, he had his own military force, which his "colleagues" feared and the army resented. He also had dossiers on everybody else, which he could draw on whenever he saw fit. Since he was a threat to the others, they closed ranks, with support from inside the army, and struck at him first. He was executed—the only one, as far as is known, to whom this happened in the post-Stalin period.

For nearly two years Malenkov stayed in the chair, but insecurely, because he was under pressure from Molotov in foreign policy and from Khrushchev on the domestic front. How much of the budget to divert from armaments and heavy industry to consumer goods? How to increase agricultural production? How to deal with the regimes of Eastern Europe? How to handle China? Whether to continue the cold war with the United States? On all these questions divisions occurred between a right wing of Stalinists and what might be called the revisionists. Malenkov, who tended to represent the government functionaries and the technological experts, could not withstand the power of the party apparatus. Eventually, he resigned and was demoted. His place as the formal head of the government was next taken by Bulganin, with Khrushchev looming large at his side. For about three years these two paraded in tandem, both inside Russia and abroad. But increasingly, the ebullient Khrushchev stole the show from the stuffy Bulganin.

A mixed policy now developed. Relaxation continued in Russia, as Stalin's monolith began to crack. More voices were heard; a freer movement of persons, and even ideas, was cautiously permitted. Bulganin and Khrushchev placated the army, restoring the wartime hero Marshal Zhukov to Moscow and admitting him to the Party Presidium. Attention was given to consumer needs; the satellite regimes were treated more gently; a reconciliation was sought with Tito. For a dictatorship in transition, the beginnings of freedom are a time of danger. The new taste whets the appetite of those who like the flavor. Hence, in October 1956, a full-scale revolt broke out in Budapest. The Hungarians deposed their Communist regime and installed one that was not Communist. At this threat to Russian hegemony, the Soviet leaders reverted to Stalinism. The Red Army reentered Budapest and reenthroned the dictatorship of "the proletariat," the local arrangements being handled by the Soviet ambassador to Budapest, one Yuri Andropov.

In the aftermath of those events, the struggle for power was renewed in Moscow. Khrushchev's rivals now had a case against him. He was endangering the solidarity of the Soviet empire. Then, something amazing happened. In June 1957, Khrushchev found himself outvoted in the Party Presidium. Normally that would have been the end. But this was no normal man. With tough resilience, he struck back—appealing the decision from the Presidium to the larger parent body, the Central Committee. As it happened, this was well stacked with his supporters, for he had used his time as general secretary well. Vindicated at the higher level, he then counterattacked the "antiparty" group (that is, anti-Khrushchev). Out went Molotov, and with him the remaining hardline Stalinsts. Malenkov was shunted to an assignment in Siberia. Bulganin, who had wavered, was retired. Khrushchev installed himself as chairman of the government. Only one man remained as a potential challenger. Marshal Zhukov had thrown his weight on Khrushchev's side in June 1957. The Red Army, it could be assumed, would follow him if he gave the lead. Therefore he must be in no position to do it in the future. The next year, Zhukov was dispatched on a visit to Belgrade. While out of the country, he was replaced. On his return home, he learned that he had been dropped.

Continuity and Change in the Soviet Union

Khrushchev managed to stay at the pinnacle for six years. Domestically Russia was changing, as were its external relations. What had been the tightly closed society of Stalin's despotism showed signs of opening. There was less repression, less terror, less self-imposed isolation. More Russians traveled abroad; more foreigners visited Russia. The cold war was becoming a "hot peace." The government showed concern over the need to raise the living standards of its people. Although censorship continued and the press and radio were still strictly controlled by the state (that is, by the party), a "public opinion" was emerging. This was also evident in the relations between Russia and the other Communist regimes. Whereas previously Moscow spoke and the rest stayed silent, now there were dialogues. Not only Belgrade but also Warsaw and Bucharest were talking out and talking back. What is more, the latter two were even talking to each other.

A new term described the new reality. The monolith of Stalin's day was gone. In its place was "polycentrism."

Into this more flexible situation, Khrushchev flung the force of his unique personality. Gregarious and garrulous, boastful and bombastic, he was also an adventurous experimenter and prone to gamble. This latter trait proved his undoing, for too many of his gambles failed. Abroad, his policies failed in Cuba, the Congo, and China. At home, he failed in his effort to increase agricultural production, while his worthy aim of appropriating more funds for consumer needs antagonized the military. Thus his critics had ample material to use against him, and they were fortified in the knowledge that the army would not move in his defense. For the second occasion, therefore, they outvoted him—and this time there was no appeal. On October 15, 1964, Moscow announced to an astonished Soviet people that Khrushchev had been deposed.

The date is significant. In Britain on that very same day, the voters went to the polls and cast their ballots in a general election. Out of 35,894,000 registered voters, as many as 27,650,000 participated in choosing among the competing parties. So close was the outcome that not until the middle of the following day was the popular decision finally confirmed—that Wilson and Labour would replace Douglas-Home and the Conservatives. In the Soviet Union, by contrast, out of a population then numbering 210,000,000, two or three dozen persons at the top of the party hierarchy, presumably with the backing of the army leaders, engineered Khrushchev's ouster in the utmost secrecy. The difference between the democratic and nondemocratic modes of transferring power could not be more dramatically underscored.

But it must still be emphasized that for Russia the events of October 1964 marked a major improvement on past practice. Like Malenkov, who was demoted but stayed alive,[25] Khrushchev lived on in retirement for nine years until he died of natural causes. The rules of Russian roulette were changing. In another respect, however, continuity was more evident than change. After Khrushchev had achieved the supreme power, he too was exalted above the men around him,[26] a process which they must have resented. In all one-party regimes it is customary for one person to dominate. Communism, too, conforms to this law of Caesarism.

[25]Even after his demotion, Malenkov was sufficiently trusted by his successors to be sent on a visit to Great Britain. The late Hugh Gaitskell, at that time leader of the Labour party, told me of having had this conversation with him. "Do you know, Mr. Malenkov," asked Gaitskell, "why it is that all of us here are so interested in you?" "No," replied the Russian, "why is it?" "Because you're alive!" was the reply. Gaitskell said that Malenkov enjoyed this and laughed, then remarked in seriousness: "Do realize that this is a different Russia now."

[26]In the second edition of this book, published in 1960, I wrote: "As a consequence, when a party congress convened early in 1959, the patent political fact was the return to the supremacy of one man. In fact, the 'cult of personality,' for which Khrushchev had criticized Stalin, was beginning to reappear in the form of a new boss." On Friday, 16 October 1964, the day after the announcement of Khrushchev's dismissal, a *Pravda* editorial criticized "the ideology and practice of the personality cult" and demanded "collective leadership."

Brezhnev über Alles

The truth in this generalization can again be illustrated by the next episode. Once more the Russian Communist Party faced the question of whether its leadership would be collegial or that of one individual. Once more, they started collegially, but ended with the dominance of one. At first, the new leadership consisted of two men, coequal in outward appearance: Brezhnev in charge of the party apparatus and relations with other Communist regimes, and Kosygin, an expert in industrial management, heading the machinery of government and serving also as the arch-diplomat in contacts with the Western and Third worlds. With this pair at the helm, the USSR had to adjust to the urgent issues of the late sixties: the demand of its citizens for higher living standards and a freer intellectual fare, the increased enmity of China, the restiveness of Eastern Europe as manifested in Romania and Czechoslovakia, and the groping toward a tacit coexistence with the United States.

Until 1968 it seemed that a cautious liberalization would prevail. But in the summer of that year came a turning point, and the direction chosen was backward. Confronted by the radical measures which the new leadership of the Czechoslovak Communist party was inaugurating under Dubcek, and spurred on by the self-protecting fears of the Polish and East German autocrats, the Russians moved to the Right—in Prague as well as Moscow. The manner of their occupation of Czechoslovakia was strikingly parallel to Hitler's actions in 1938–1939, even to the extent of including East German troops among the initial invading force. The strategy behind this move was not hard to decipher. The men in the Kremlin had set their faces against those changes which would have spelled a greater diversity of policies and opinion. Increasingly preoccupied with the challenge of China, the Bear was preparing for a duel with the Dragon by solidifying its grip on the region in its rear and by stifling dissident voices at home.[27]

These tendencies were intensified in the early seventies—a period when the Soviet government was forced to choose between alternative directions at home and abroad. The major external threat was the new power of China, which was openly competing against the Soviet Union in the Communist countries and was actively bidding for the leadership of the Third World. At the same time there were acute territorial conflicts, embroiling the two governments in central Asia and along their common boundary. Since the most dangerous opposition to their hegemony came from eastern Asia, the Soviet leadership decided in favor of stability in the West. This meant a rapprochement with West Germany and tacit understandings with the United States. The architect of these policies was Brezhnev, who emerged as the supreme figure in the Soviet hierarchy, increasingly taking over the conduct of foreign relations from Kosygin.

[27]For Sino-Soviet relations, see the discussion in chapter 13, section on "Divisions within East and West."

Consequently, following in the footsteps of the man whom he earlier helped to depose, he went on visits, as Khrushchev had done, to Eastern Europe, Paris, and Washington. Once again, this was the general secretary of the Communist party who bested his rivals.

What is more, the party leaders who had refused to countenance a liberalization of the Czech regime became more brutal in suppressing criticism at home. Some of the most gifted of the Soviet intelligentsia were in open revolt during the seventies. Scientists, artists, writers, and independent thinkers were demanding reforms in their system. As a means to this end, they sought the freedom to express their opinions and voice their dissent. Against all this, Brezhnev reacted harshly. The only change from Stalin's terror was a refinement of technique. There were no mass trials, sudden purges, or executions. But the critics were deprived of their livelihood, were socially ostracized, and were publicly vilified. Moreover, medicine and psychiatry were brought into use as instruments of the police state. By Brezhnev's standards, anyone who was dissatisfied must be insane. Consequently, dissenters were incarcerated in mental hospitals where the psychoanalysts aided and abetted the secret police. Important figures, however, such as Solzhenitsyn, had to be treated carefully since they were protected by their international reputations. Some of them were allowed to leave Russia with their families—a sign that Party power was incompatible with intellectual independence. Brezhnev managed to stay on top until his death in 1982 at the age of 76. Evidently he had learned from Khrushchev's mistakes. At home, the regime avoided risks and played it safe. Indeed, in Brezhnev's later years, immobility was the rule. Abroad, however. Soviet influence was extended wherever an opportunity presented itself—as in Vietnam, South Yemen, Angola, Afghanistan.[28] Brezhnev's legacy to his successors was a combination of public inertia and a stagnating economy together with extensive and expensive commitments abroad.

Gorbachev, A New Kind of Leader

This time the transition to a new leadership occupied two and a half years because of initial bad luck followed by a poor choice. The bad luck was the death after only 15 months of the first of Brezhnev's successors, Yuri Andropov. Here was a man whose intelligence outshone all who had held the top position since Lenin. His background and prior service also stamped him out as different. He had directed the KGB, which operates the secret police inside Russia and conducts espionage outside. In addition, he had close links with the army. So, while being a party member and having served in its secretariat, his primary power base rested elsewhere—

[28]These gains were offset by losses, e.g., in Egypt and Somalia.

in the security agencies. In his brief tenure, two actions he took were forward-looking. He launched a campaign to stimulate the economy, cracking down both on corrupt managers and on absentee workers. Besides that, he chose as his principal aide, and thus brought into prominence, a younger man, one Mikhail Gorbachev.

When Andropov died in February 1984, a bad choice was made. The majority of the Party's Central Committee still consisted of aging *apparatchiki,* put there by Brezhnev. Andropov had managed to somersault over them, but this time they had their way by selecting one of their group, Konstantin Chernenko, then age 72. Chernenko was an undistinguished party hack who had risen high by serving Brezhnev faithfully. Obviously, his was a stopgap appointment until a choice could be made among the next generation. In this case, the waiting interval was short since Chernenko died after only 13 months. But that whole sequence of events had revealed the problems of an authoritarian system where one party is paramount and one person leads it. Brezhnev's final two years were a time of internal paralysis. Andropov was able to be effective for only six months. Inaction persisted with Chernenko. Altogether, Russia lost four years. It was natural to suppose that when the leadership question would finally be settled, the new person would be impatient to institute changes.

To a stale Kremlin, reeking with the atmosphere of retirement home and hospital, the advent of Mikhail Gorbachev was a healthy breeze of bracing fresh air. Indeed, if any individual could personify the start of a new era, Gorbachev had the necessary qualifications. Born in 1931, his adult life was subsequent to World War II and Stalin's despotism; having climbed to the peak by the age of 54, he might expect to stay in control for two decades. A law graduate of Moscow University, he brought a different kind of training to bear on the problems of government. In personality, too, and style, he was unlike any of his predecessors. Quick-witted, fluent of speech, with a well-stocked mind and a ready smile, this was not another dour, unprepossessing Russian leader of whom the world had seen so many. Both he and his wife, herself a university teacher, gave every appearance of being modern, sophisticated, and intelligent.

At home and abroad, the new touch was quickly felt. Gorbachev's program for revitalizing Russia is summed up in his two key concepts: restructuring *(perestroika)* and openness *(glasnost).* Restructuring has the aim of raising the low rates of productivity in the economy. Gorbachev not only cracked down on absenteeism, a task barely begun by Andropov, but also fought against the chronic alcoholism which reduced efficiency in the workplace. Beyond that, however, he introduced proposals which, if carried into effect, would mean abandoning some of the centralized controls which Stalin had imposed. Agricultural production was to be stimulated by permitting the farmers an opportunity to produce and sell outside of the state-run program. Factories, too, were to be freer in making their own decisions about what to produce as well as in obtaining their raw materials. Most radical of all, the central fixing of prices and their lowering by means of subsidies on essentials were scheduled to disappear over a wide range of commodities. Thus, in ways not yet fully spelled out, certain features of a market economy were somehow to be combined with socialism.

For this to happen, the Russian people were encouraged to confront the shortcomings of the existing system and to engage in open discussion of its processes and personnel. That was the purpose of *glasnost*. Being himself a man with a lively mind, Gorbachev understood that Russia needed its intellectuals and that they needed greater freedom to think and to discuss. Some prominent critics of the regime, such as Orlov and Scharansky, were allowed to emigrate, while the noted physicist, Sakharov, was set free from internal exile. That was a message calculated to appeal to those whose creativity had been stifled for so long. Similarly in foreign affairs a new approach, more sensitive to world opinion, began to animate the Russian diplomacy. The West was courted with a succession of proposals for reduction of arms, while reconciliation was sought with China. In Afghanistan, where the Soviet military occupation had reached an impasse, Gorbachev decided to bring the troops home.

Together with big hopes, these initiatives also raised big questions. As in the Khrushchev years, when a long hard winter is followed by a thaw, in what direction will the currents flow? When questioning and experimentation are encouraged in an authoritarian system, how far can they go without a challenge to the regime? The introduction of economic reforms was certain to cause a stressful transition and thus provoke opposition. If price fixing was to cease, inflation would start. If inefficient enterprises were to close down, unemployment would occur, at least temporarily. The workers would be expected to work harder, while the planners would lose their power. Could the economic system become more flexible without the political system following suit? Would traditional Russian conservatism be stronger than the dynamism of *glasnost*? Would the Party revolutionize itself and tolerate public criticism? The world will watch the outcome.

Poland: From Polonaise to Marche Militaire

What can happen when a threat confronts the Party's dominance over the system may be illustrated by the experience of Russia's next-door western neighbor. For a year and a half Poland underwent an extraordinary upheaval with which its Communist Party was unable to cope. Equally unprecedented was the outcome, since it was unlike anything that has happened in a Communist regime. When the Party lost its grip, Communism gave way to Caesarism. Let us examine the sequence of events and their consequences.

Whatever their form of government, the Poles are bedevilled by two perennial problems—one geographical, the other cultural—whose contradictions impede their resolution. Their homeland on the northern plain of eastern Europe is squeezed between two peoples, the Germans and the Russians, who have been formidably powerful since the eighteenth century and whose access to one another runs across Polish territory. Culture compounds geography in that the Poles possess a split personality. As Slavs they are linked to Eastern Europe, while as Catholics they are pulled to the West. How does a nation survive under these conditions?

Since World War II, the control of Poland has been essential to the Russians' security on their eastern frontier, having been invaded from that direction three times in 13 decades. To supply their forward divisions in East Germany, they must be certain that Poland's highways and railroads will not be cut. Hence they have only tolerated a Communist regime under a party subservient to Moscow. But the Polish people are stubbornly nationalistic, which leads them to behave more as romantics than as realists. The Communist party failed in managing the economy of the largest population of the Soviet satellites in Eastern Europe. Consequently it encountered not only a rural resistance, but the active revolt of coal miners in the south and of workers at the Gdansk shipyards in the north. Mass demonstrations, strikes, and riots erupted on more than one occasion, particularly whenever the government raised the prices of basic foodstuffs. In 1970 the party leaders called on the soldiers to restore order, with the result that hundreds were killed or arrested. In the aftermath a change took place at the top. Out went Gomulka; in came Gierek.

During the seventies there were two developments which prepared the ground for the cataclysm of 1980–1981. Both illustrate the effect of external influences on Poland's internal affairs. In Rome, the College of Cardinals, when electing a new pope, broke with a centuries-old tradition by picking a non-Italian. He was the Cardinal of Cracow, Jan Wojtyla, who took the title of John Paul II. The Polish people are over 90 percent Catholic and are deeply attached to their church through which they can express an alternative allegiance whenever they detest their regime. Having a Pole as head of this international church reinforced their national pride, besides supplying some external leverage against the rule of the Communist Party.

The other big change in the seventies was economic. Gierek had launched a program of growth to remedy the shortages which afflicted Polish consumers. To finance the new enterprises he had obtained loans not only from Moscow, but also from Western banks. But by the end of the decade, all countries, Poland included, were suffering from a worldwide depression. The Polish consumers rebelled—and this time, when the government raised the price of meat, the response was unprecedented. In August 1980, the workers at the Lenin shipyard in Gdansk went on strike and their example spread across industrial Poland. What began as a list of economic demands quickly erupted into political confrontation on a grand scale. By halting production, the workers brought the Party to its knees. When this stage was over, they had extracted a concession which no Communist regime within the Soviet sphere had granted before: the right to form their own union independently of the government.

Two reasons explain their success. One was the extent and intensity of dislike for the regime which gave the workers their solidarity and their new union its name. The second reason was the emergence at the right moment of a unique personality, Lech Walesa, an electrical worker at Gdansk, whose bold leadership gave unity to the opposition. These two factors, the power of Solidarity and the effectiveness of its leader, dominated the Polish scene for the next year. At its height, the union had nearly ten million members and won concession after concession from a government which had become morally and politically bankrupt. In point of fact, the Communist Party started disintegrating. It lost a fifth of its membership and was unable to attract new recruits of stature. Inevitably the leadership, widely assailed for corruption and incompetence, changed again. Gierek was dumped; in came Kania. General Wojciech Jaruzelski, an army man who was also a party member, became Minister of Defense and later was also made Premier. When the Party held a congress in July 1981, its delegates had been chosen in relatively free elections and they were able to insist on secret balloting for the positions of leadership. Not long after, three more generals were added to the government.

Throughout all this, impalpable but omnipresent, there loomed the Church. As the one institution which was independent of the Party, the Church had long been a focus of resistance to the regime—all the more needed because the Party was identified with subservience to Moscow. But the Church had limited its aims to matters which concerned it directly: the right to worship and to provide religious education. When bargaining with the Party, it did not make demands which could threaten the regime's existence. Solidarity's emergence aroused in the Church an ambivalent response. For one thing, the Church could not but be pleased by the erosion of the monistic state, particularly when run by Communists. On the other hand, the hierarchy feared that, if the union pushed the Party too far, the worst would ensue. To Poles, the worst meant only one thing: Russian tanks in the streets of their cities, as had happened in Poznan in 1953, in Budapest in 1956, then in Prague in 1968. Moreover, the manifest popular strength of Solidarity meant that the Church was no longer the sole vehicle for expressing opposition to the regime, which amounted to a relative diminution of clerical power. In such calculations the Papacy was deeply involved. The last that a Polish Pope wanted was to give the Russians their excuse to intervene. Moreover, Walesa himself and many of his followers were devout Catholics and heeded papal guidance.

Matters came to a head late in 1981. The Party, under Kania, made still more concessions to Solidarity, even granting to the noncollectivized peasants the right to organize their own agricultural union. But the economy continued to slump as production declined and consumers found less to buy. Solidarity then committed the tactical error of pushing too hard. Its congress adopted a radical program which proposed, along with free elections and a loosening of censorship, a referendum on how Poland should be ruled. This touched on Moscow's raw nerve, since it challenged the Party's predominance and thus could imperil the extension of Soviet military control to East Germany. The Party responded by changing leaders again. This time the choice for general secretary was General Jaruzelski. He planned for two months, then struck like lightning.[29] Martial law was declared; Solidarity's leaders were arrested; its offices were closed; its organization was broken. One blow of the mailed fist smashed in a day all the rights achieved in a year of popular upheaval. Walesa was eventually released after more than a year's detention, but he was kept under surveillance.

What sort of Poland has emerged from this fiery ordeal? On the surface, the country now appears passive and submissive. Order has been restored—the order of the barracks. The General stayed firmly in charge, relaxing his grip when he felt it safe to do so. The Party was shaken up and a new union was officially recognized as a substitute for the outlawed Solidarity. Eventually, amnesty was granted to those of Solidarity's leaders who had continued their struggle underground. But the economy has not responded because the morale of the "workers and peasants" was broken.

Meanwhile, the Church retained its influence unscathed. The Polish Pope could resolve his ambiguities by giving his blessing to Walesa, but throwing Solidarity to the wolves. As long as the Russians did not march in, and the institutional interests of the Church were safeguarded, John Paul II could deal with Jaruzelski. Effectively, the choice for Poland remained as heretofore: It lay between the Red Army and the Black Madonna.

China: Governing One Billion

Uniquely interesting as it is, the case of Poland does not by itself supply a sufficient parallel to Soviet communism, since the Polish climate is darkened by the Russian shadow. Of countries with a communist regime, only one other is powerful enough and independent enough to be bracketed with the Soviet Union for purposes of comparison. From China perhaps we can learn whether Moscow's experience is special to Russia or generic to

---

[29]Speculation continues over the role of the Russians at that time. Were they actually going to intervene? Was Jaruzelski perhaps the patriot who acted to forestall them? Or did the Russians, despairing of the Polish Communists and preferring not to intervene themselves, advise the general to act in their place?

communism. Immense in population, and uniquely the product of humanity's longest-enduring continuous civilization, China has the capacity to differ. What, then, has been the history of power in Communist China? Is the pattern akin to the Soviet, or not?

The salient fact in China's case is the lengthy reign of Mao Zedong. Becoming party leader in 1935 during the "long march" from the south to the northwest, he remained supreme until his death in 1976. For 14 years he led his side in the civil war against the Kuomintang; for 27 more, he ruled China. Was any emperor in earlier dynasties more autocratically secure than he? It was as if Lenin had survived to lead the Russians until 1944. Consequently, although earlier maneuvering for the succession was evident, almost a generation elapsed before China faced the actual problem of the transfer of power.

Nevertheless, although Mao's authority remained constant, there were several abrupt reversals of policy during his reign. Inevitably rival groups competed with alternative programs, and the victors of the moment used their advantage to pillory their opponents. Throughout the shifts of the party line the central issue was the direction of China's social revolution, on which depended the choice of means. Granted the need to industrialize and to revolutionize land ownership and food production, should these programs be centrally planned and directed on the Stalinist model, or decentralized under local control? Were differential rewards, and therefore unequal life-styles, to be accepted? Was a large bureaucracy of administrators and experts desirable? Could diverse opinions be freely expressed, or did one man voice the general will? Should China seek outside help or build from its own resources? And what, if anything, of the Confucian tradition should be retained?

Initially China relied heavily on the Soviet Union for technical assistance and loans, which brought an accompanying influx of Russian experts and advisors. But their overbearing ways provoked the same negative reaction in Beijing as in Belgrade, Cairo, Jakarta, and other capitals. Nor would the Chinese leaders submit to the Russians' determination to keep them subordinate in the councils of international communism. Rifts widened into a rupture, which became total after 1961 when Khrushchev "lost" China. Mao then settled for self-reliance at home, while openly competing with the Russians for support in the Third World.

How One Flower Bloomed

Another early policy which did not last was the liberalism of the mid-1950s. Himself a poet and calligrapher, Mao had appealed to intellectuals by proclaiming: "Let a hundred flowers bloom; let a hundred schools contend." Evidently he had not anticipated the eagerness of the response. When the flowers blossomed in profusion, the Chairman started pruning the garden. Quickly a censored uniformity was reimposed. Across the length and breadth of the "Middle Kingdom" Mao's thoughts were studied and quoted as Scripture. Complacently, the great calligrapher observed: "The outstanding thing about China's people is that they are poor and blank. On a blank sheet of paper, free from any mark, the freshest and most beautiful characters can be written."[30]

The next episode, bizarre in the extreme, was the Cultural Revolution of 1966 to 1969. The Communist Party had then been ruling China for a decade and a half. What form of government, what type of society, was beginning to emerge? Was the revolution a continuing process? Or was a new order being established, and with it a new Establishment?[31] These were matters of genuine concern to the chief architect of the new regime, who had drawn his own conclusions from the Russian parallel and from Chinese history. He rejected the Stalinist model of a highly centralized system staffed by an ever more stratified bureaucracy. That way, thought Mao, was to lose the popular élan. Even when directed by the Party, the dictatorship of the secretariat could not lead to anything but conservative ossification. Of all countries on earth, China had enough experience with the rule of the mandarins, which it had invented, to know what vices accompany the virtues of meritocracy. What was to be done? Answer—appeal from Stalin to Trotsky, from the Confucians to the populists. Save the revolution in all its pristine purity—by unleashing the Red Guards!

Considering the ends in view, no means could have been less appropriate. For three years, the authorities—meaning Mao and the extreme Left of the Party—set out to attack any idea, institution, or person associated with China's Confucianism, Russia's Stalinism, or Western imperialism. This resulted in an intensive campaign of propaganda, the closing or incapacitating of the universities, vandalism of monuments of the past, and public humiliation and physical assaults on domestic and foreign "devils." The chosen agents were young Communists who were encouraged to terrorize and destroy, and who rampaged without check. Senior-ranking Communists, such as Liu Shaoqi and Deng Xiaoping, were abused, demoted, arrested. After a few years of this, China was approaching a standstill. Finding himself the chairman of his own chaos, Mao was persuaded by other counselors to call a halt. Zhou Enlai, the responsible moderate, emerged as the guiding spirit, and with him new policies took shape.

---

[30]Quoted by Sydney Liu, *San Francisco Sunday Examiner and Chronicle*, 21 December 1969.

[31]This question echoed the earlier concern of the Yugoslav Marxist Milovan Djilas, whose book *The New Class* so angered Tito.

Apotheosis and the Apostles

Still under the aegis of a Mao approaching the age of 80 but sublimated finally to demigod, the Chinese leadership focused on Russia's expanding power as a threat to their security in northeastern Asia. This meant that they had to come to terms with the technology of the West; otherwise they could not develop their science, modernize their industry, and arm their military, within less than a generation. The result was to abandon an isolation so complete that their one foreign friend had been the government of Albania. Overtures were made to France, to Japan, to the United States. At a banquet in the Great Hall of the People in Beijing, Nixon, the vocal anti-Communist, ate his own words by quoting those of Chairman Mao.

Presiding over this shift of direction were new directors. The Trotskyite radicals, with their regional power base in Shanghai, lost control at the center, even though one of their number was the wife of Mao Zedong. Lin Biao, the Defense Minister and well placed for succession, was outmaneuvered and eliminated in the crash of a plane whose course, had it continued, would have led to the Soviet Union. In 1976, the Old Guard of China's communist revolution reached the mortal end—Zhou Enlai in January and Mao, already apotheosized, in September. Zhou's place as Premier was filled by Hua Guofeng. After Mao's death Hua acted swiftly against his rivals on the Left, who were now vilified as the "Gang of Four" and arrested. Deng Xiaoping—exalted, disgraced, then exalted again—became vice-premier and organizer of the opening to the West. There followed a period of relative liberalization similar to what the Russians experienced after Stalin's death. But as in Russia, when innovation (technological, economic, and social) stimulated discussion and the voicing of political dissent, the authorities reneged. The flowers that bloomed too soon were cut. "Democracy Wall" in Beijing, where posters could be freely displayed, was literally whitewashed.

What followed in the early 1980s were shifts in power which accompanied changes in policy. The stated aim of the post-Mao leadership was to accomplish by 2000 A.D., if possible, "the four modernizations"—in agriculture, industry, defense, and science and technology. How could this be done? Not on the Stalinist model of central direction through an all-pervasive state bureaucracy, nor by the Trotskyite populism of the Cultural Revolution which had terrorized the intellectuals. More appropriate, it seemed, was the introduction into the economy of some non-Communist principles which would accompany the new technology imported from North America, Western Europe, and Japan. The first sector of society to feel the benefit of the innovations was agriculture. Its productivity was literally vital in a country which had to feed one billion people, four-fifths of whom lived and worked outside the cities. The essence of the novelty was that the peasants would make contracts to produce an agreed amount and sell it to the government, after which they could sell whatever surplus they produced on their own initiative. The results, manifest within a few years, were tantamount to an agrarian revolution. Productivity skyrocketed, and with it the peasants' "profit." Their earnings were quickly exchanged for such desirable consumer items as bicycles, radios, washing machines, television sets, trucks, and housing—all of which together stimulated urban manufacturing.

To change the industrial sector was a more complicated matter. In very small enterprises, individuals were allowed to operate their own businesses, taking the risk of making a profit or incurring a loss. But in the larger industries—those requiring sophisticated machines and processes and a major investment of capital—it was a more complicated matter to test the managers' skill and the workers' output. So they embarked on various experiments. The system of centralized planning became more flexible. More decisions were permitted at the plant level. Joint enterprises with foreign corporations were encouraged, especially in certain regions designated as areas for development. Many Chinese traveled abroad, to study or train. More outsiders were welcomed in China to introduce their techniques. All in all, the atmosphere in the China of the eighties was that of an age-old civilization infused with a new dynamism and fluid and flexible with its experiments.

That raised the big question. Could these innovations of science, technology, and economic processes be absorbed without corresponding innovations in the political system? How would the dominance of a single party be affected? Could the four modernizations be accomplished by changes of the party's personnel, organization, and philosophy? Or would it be necessary to revolutionize the system yet further?

China's answer to this question has still to be decided. The astounding fact is that the major changes since the death of Mao were launched by a man born in 1904 who, whether the future shows him to have been right or wrong, injected a rare flexibility into the leadership. Deng Xiaoping's outstanding quality, over and above the tenacity which enabled him to survive, has been a nonideological pragmatism. This is expressed in his remark: "If we can increase production, it doesn't matter whether operations are run privately—it doesn't matter if a cat is black or white, as long as it catches mice." The same flexibility was evident in negotiating with Britain about the future of Hong Kong. With Taiwan ultimately in mind, China's new leaders proclaimed the formula: "One country, two systems." One can imagine what Mao or Stalin would have said to that!

In one way or another, the political issue concerning the mode of governance will have to be settled. By the end of the eighties, the customary strains of a sharp transition were already evident. With the increase of purchasing power, and the removal of certain subsidies, inflation was taking hold. Those on fixed wages or salaries were feeling the disparity between their incomes and the earnings of those venturing into the private market. Moreover, those on whose brains China depended—the intellectuals, artists, writers, scientists, and students—were restive under restraints. University students demonstrated en masse in December 1986, with demands for "freedom and democracy," and they were able to quote the views of some academic administrators and professors in their support. To this the authorities reacted with a decisive reassertion of the Party's power. Academics who had raised inconvenient questions were demoted or transferred. Marxist orthodoxy was reimposed on the students, as a condition of their receiving higher education. The Party's General Secretary, Hu Yaobang, who had tolerated an opening to liberalism, was fired. Moreover, it was made clear that foreign ideas or practices which might lead to an erosion of the Party's leadership would not be tolerated.

This crackdown from the still surviving Old Guard expressed the Chinese dilemma. Could the country modernize its economy and revitalize its culture, education included, but retain its monolithic party structure? Must not political changes accompany social and economic changes? How fast and how far the new China will advance hinges on its answers to those questions.

The Stigmata of Dictatorship

Authoritarianism leaves its imprint on politics in many ways. An oligarchy separates ruler from subject, but merges government and state. Lest its authority be challenged, the ruling class monopolizes power, excluding others from participation. It is then simple for those in control of the government to assert that they indeed constitute the state, thus obliterating the difference. Any attempt to change the government becomes an effort to overthrow the state, and opponents of those in power can be punished as traitors. By contrast, when the government is viewed as a group of officials authorized to act in the name of the state for a limited time only and with limited powers, then the state may be considered to continue in existence despite changes of government.

The traditional aristocracies, in periods when they held a monopoly of governmental power, regarded the state as their property. Thus the people who were their subjects "belonged" to the privileged class by virtue of an inherited status—in much the same way as a mansion, land, crops, and cattle belonged to the individual noble. A similar outlook pervades the one-party state of the twentieth century. The party elite in a dictatorship absorbs the state instead of merely acting on its behalf. The party does more than take over the government. It abolishes whatever institutions might compete for authority with the party organs—as the Russian Communists abolished the Duma, and Mussolini, the Chamber of Deputies. Or, if it does not destroy, the party emasculates its rivals, permitting them a shadowy existence—as Hitler allowed the Reichstag to linger on and as the Communists under Stalin treated their own Soviets. The state thereby becomes the adjunct of the party. Only in this one respect can the state be said to wither away: Its life is sucked from it by the party's cancerous growth.

The classic vice of all authoritarian systems is their assumption of the superiority and infallibility of those in power. Such pretensions are not justified by the facts of history. Though some absolute rulers have been benevolent, though some oligarchies have performed acts of wise statesmanship, these systems generally produce too much stupidity, waste, and cruelty to merit the favor of humanity. Dictatorship exaggerates the worthiness of a few and demeans or brutalizes the remainder. With unwarranted arrogance, it identifies the general well-being of the community with the special interest of the ruling group. Even when philosophers, like Hegel, devote their services to its cause, the claims of absolutism remain bogus. Stripped of the veneer and camouflage, dictatorship is essentially a regime of privilege. As such, since it cannot evoke consent from the underprivileged, it must hold sway by force and secrecy. The dominant group coheres for fear of losing its special advantages. These it is able to prolong because in practice the mobilized force of an equipped and disciplined minority is often superior to the potential of an unorganized majority. Dictatorship thus succeeds in diverting a portion of the force, which the whole community needs for its protection, to protect the government from the governed. Hence arise the familiar characteristics of the "police state," which is simply an arrested stage of political development. That is a state that begins with the elementary need of protection and has advanced as far as establishing order.

But to advance beyond order to the next stage, that of justice, confronts the authoritarians with a dilemma which their methods of governing prevent them from resolving. In effect, the few in control have struck a tacit bargain with the many whom they control. What they are saying is that it is possible to have either security or freedom, but not both.[32] They offer security under their protection, in return for which the governed relinquish the expectation of certain freedoms of action. That is why the mass of the population normally accept their conditions with acquiescence, since in some of the Communist regimes those conditions are an improvement on what existed before. When education, medical facilities, social security, and jobs are extended to people among whom poverty has been endemic, the civil liberties which we so prize in the West may appear the less urgent priority.

This explains why, in Russia or Cuba for example, the regime itself is

[32]This is the point of the Grand Inquisitor's speech in Dostoevsky's *The Brothers Karamazov*. Ordinary people, he argues, do not value freedom. They want bread and will obey anyone who offers it.

not challenged although dissatisfaction may be voiced at particular programs or persons. It also explains why those authoritarian regimes which do not adequately fulfill their side of the bargain, fall into trouble. When there is widespread public perception of the fact that the few are gorging too much for themselves while the many are receiving inadequate food or security, then the mass of the people can be aroused to act and to overthrow their rulers—armies, police, and prisons notwithstanding. Witness what happened in recent times in Iran, in Nicaragua, and in the Philippines. Witness the attempted explosions in Poland, Hungary, and Czechoslovakia. Eventually, the regimes of the dictators collapse of their own internal immorality.

And what of the alternative? What of the regimes where freedom receives the priority? What kind of bargain do they strike, and what are its terms? Let us turn to chapter 9.

9

Third Issue—Part 2

The Freedom of the Governed

Foundations of Freedom

What is the alternative to dictatorship? By what means can the authority of government be made subject to consent? How is it possible to grant powers for use and still prevent their abuse? The beginning of an answer is to reject the doctrine that the government is the source of authority and to embrace the contrary notion that authority derives from the mass of the people who entrust the government with powers to be exercised on their behalf. Although the choice between these two political poles and their resulting forms of organization is a critical issue of the present century, the decision that confronts humanity is not new. A long tradition supports the view that authority is somehow delegated by the governed to their government, although states founded on this principle have been rarities and continue to be the exception rather than the rule. The assertion of the principle, however, would have had little effect on practice unless institutional means were developed for curbing those in authority. The doctrine that government should be responsible has to be studied in the light of historical efforts to make it so.

The Athenian Democracy

In the first democracy an elaborate system ensured that the people, or *demos,* would be self-governing and would control its officials. From the mid-fifth century B.C. to the mid-fourth, Athenian government rested on the belief that all power belonged to the people, who exercised it by a many-sided participation in public affairs. The price of Athenian citizenship was activity and versatility. Among a citizen's duties were service in the army or navy, attendance at festivals, and jury work in the courts. Most important of all was his participation at the Assembly's monthly meetings, where he helped to enact laws and decrees, settle questions of high policy, conduct foreign relations, and authorize the finances. The work of the Assembly, however, needed supplementing by administrative officials. These were selected in one of two ways. The Assembly filled by election offices that required special qualifications and expert knowledge. In other cases, where anyone of average intelligence could apply ordinary judgment, the Athenians employed a method distinctive to their democracy—the lot. At the head of a department or agency, they placed a board of citizens picked by lot annually. Such a system served many purposes. It ensured that government was conducted, in a literal way, *by* the people. It contributed to public education by enlarging the direct acquaintance of citizens with governmental problems. Through rotation in office, it spread a sense of civic responsibility.

Certain safeguards were added to forestall the appointment of anybody manifestly unfit and to prevent abuse of power. Before they could assume their posts, those whom the lot selected were made to pass a scrutiny which was both qualifying test and loyalty clearance. Then ten times during the year, at the regular meetings of the Assembly, the populace could vote approval or censure of their officials—censure being followed by an indictment in the law courts, tantamount to impeachment. Finally, when the officeholder's year of service ended, he presented to a special board of auditors the accounts for any public monies of which he was collector, custodian, or disburser. This last requirement—the accountability of the official as enforced by a postaudit—constituted, in Athenian eyes, the ultimate weapon of popular control. When their statesmen and philosophers contrasted their political institutions with those of oligarchy or monarchy, the two features they stressed most were appointment by lot and postaudit. Both practices, in their view, prevented the rise of a bureaucracy as an uncontrollable corps of officialdom.

There was another risk, however, to which Athenian democracy was liable. Where matters of such weight were determined at the Assembly of the citizens, much depended on the judgment displayed by the leading orators. Decisions were reached by majority vote after free and open discussion, and a proposal could be adopted on the motion, not of some holder of public office, but of any private citizen with a popular following. In the absence of further safeguards, policies might be settled or reversed by snap votes; majorities could be incited by ranting orators; the heat of factional fights might inflame the community. To counteract these dangers, of which they learned through bitter experience, the Athenians instituted two more safety devices. One was the drastic expedient called ostracism. When internal dissension between ambitious politicians imperiled the unity of the state, the Assembly could adopt a motion to ostracize. This was followed in two months' time by a special election where, provided at least 6000 participated, whoever received a majority of adverse ballots was banished for ten years, after which he could return and resume all his civil, political, and property rights. A second way in which the Assembly sought protection against divisive leaders and indeed against its own worse judgment was by distinguishing laws of general application from decrees dealing with particulars. No law could be amended or repealed without due notice and procedural safeguards. Decrees also had to satisfy procedural checks as well as conform to law. The Athenians enforced these principles in the courts. Within a year of the passage of any law or decree, its proposer could be indicted on a charge of unconstitutionality, the penalties for which were severe. Thus an all-powerful Assembly attempted to guarantee a government under law.

There is more than experimental novelty and a unique structure to give merit to this Athenian constitution. Its ideals were tinged with realism. The Athenians were not content solely to proclaim the fine-sounding doctrines of citizen participation, official accountability, and rule of law. Such ideas would have been insufficient to mold political behavior, were they not reinforced with appropriate institutions and procedures. It was the latter that put teeth into theory and made democracy effective. How vital it is to install the necessary machinery, if ideas are to operate in practice, can be better understood by noting the contrast with other systems that neglected adequately to translate some well-meant formulas into hard fact.

The Roman Sacrifice of Liberty to Empire

For a contrast, consider the record of Rome. Between the expulsion of the monarchy at the end of the sixth century B.C. and the establishment of the Augustan Principate five centuries later, Rome was a republic. During this period, the Romans accomplished some remarkable achievements. They laid the groundwork for a system of civil and criminal law which is basic to the jurisprudence and legal codes of many modern nations. By the prowess of their redoubtable legions they absorbed within a single empire all the lands and peoples surrounding the Mediterranean. Under the dominion of Rome southern and western Europe, North Africa, and much of the Middle East experienced a greater measure of political unity than that region had known before or has known since. But these organizers of law and legions; these architects of highways, aqueducts, and central heating; these Caesars and Ciceros whose craftmanship left Rome the eternal city and Latin a universal language—these men could not for all their political talent construct a democracy. The tradition associated with Rome was and is authoritarian. The major concepts that typify the Roman contribution to politics are expressed in these Latin-derived words: "power"—*potestas,* "authority"—*auctoritas,* "empire"—*imperium.*

The principles of the republican constitution were potentially democratic. Wanting to avoid a repetition of the tyranny of some of their kings, the Romans deliberately separated powers and distributed them among various assemblies and offices which were a check on each other. From the consuls on down, their officials were elected by assemblies of citizens, and for a year at a time. Legislation, too, had to be voted on by the citizens, whose approval converted a proposed bill into an authoritative law. From this it would seem clear that the Romans intended their government to be subordinate to the governed. But circumstances combined to defeat the intention. The republic seldom enjoyed the luxury of a long peace. Its response to the challenge of nearby peoples launched it on a tide of military conquest. Acceptance of an imperial mission, however, brought an enlargement of size and power for which Rome's earlier institutions proved inadequate. The need for continuous direction of policy and for central supervision of outlying provinces was ill met by the poorly organized popular assemblies and annually changing magistrates.

Only one institution attempted to fill the need, the Senate. But when this body—a tightly knit oligarchy of past and present officeholders and noble families—was itself split through the growing division of Roman society into opposed classes, the state was torn apart by internal conspiracies and civil war. The last century of the republic's existence (133–31 B.C.) was a catalog of revolution, counterrevolution, and *coup d' état.* Unable to control its commanders in the field, the Senate lay successively at the mercy of Marius, Sulla, Pompey, Caesar, and Anthony and finally succumbed to Augustus. The system founded by Augustus became an autocracy centralized in the person of the emperor, who maintained his position by placating the mob in the streets of Rome and controlling the legions in the capital and on the frontiers of the empire. Only as a memory from the past did the theory linger on that an emperor received his authority in a law conferring the imperial prerogatives at the beginning of his reign. That law, however, was enacted merely out of deference to an ancient form. It altered not a whit the political realities of absolutism.

A striking parallel may be observed in the medieval period. The political structure of feudalism exhibited a glaring contrast between its doctrines—that government is limited by law and rulers are responsible for their actions—and the absence of effective means of enforcement. Though they acknowledged the principle that they should serve the common good, medieval governments fought shy of control by the common people. There is a historical explanation for this. The Germanic tribes, which burst the ramparts of the Roman Empire in the fifth and sixth centuries A.D. and sliced its sprawling territories into kingdoms, had formerly developed some institutions of a primitive democracy in the forests of Germany. But the urge that drove them west and south was itself the result of pressure on central Europe from some other peoples farther east—the pressure of Asians, like the Huns, foraging for new supplies of food and plundering as they went. This migration of people, the *Völkerwanderung*, had a profound effect on forms of government. A tribe on the march, or one that has to repel invaders, must militarize itself to survive; thus it becomes authoritarian. When in addition the Goths, Franks, Vandals, and the rest gradually imbibed the influence of the civilization they had overrun, they sought to assimilate their own kingdoms to the pattern of imperial Rome. The democratic folkways of the German forests, like the traditions of the Roman republic, thenceforth continued to exist in a mythical realm of inherited ideas to which the daily facts gave the lie.

The Medieval Order: Fictions and Facts

The medieval world which emerged from the Dark Ages fairly bristled with notions of law as a restraint on government. Being a Christian, a ruler must conform to the law of God. Being custodian of the community's way of life, he must uphold and preserve its immemorial customs, to which indeed he owed his own powers and privileges. But was there anyone to say whether a ruler had in fact violated divine or human law, and if so, how could he be called to account? The possibility of curbing a ruler depended, as always, on the existence of organized opposition. In the Middle Ages, this might spring from two sources.

One of these was the church. If it appeared that a ruler sinned against divine law, the church could direct against him its two powerful weapons—excommunication and interdict. When employed by a masterful pope, these devices could bring to heel a king, like John of England, or even an emperor, as Henry IV. Such clerical resistance to royal or imperial power, though it imposed a limitation on the state, did not necessarily constitute a gain from the standpoint of democratic or popular control. When the papacy won, all that happened was the temporary subordination of secular to ecclesiastical authority, the latter being as authoritarian in spirit and structure as the former. Hence, toward the close of the Middle Ages a movement developed for the reform of church government. Associated with the names of the Italian, Marsiglio of Padua, and the Englishman, William of Occam, this was called the Conciliar Movement because its aim was to place at the head of the church a general council of elected delegates representing not only the clergy but all Christian believers. The Conciliarists came near to their goal at the end of the Great Schism when, in order to heal the breach in the church and overhaul its organization, two councils were convoked which met respectively at Constance (1414–1418) and Basel (1431–1449). However, in the face of opposition from the pope, the cardinals, and the higher clergy generally, this attempt to democratize the structure of the church failed. The "Petrine theory" of papal power, placing supreme authority in the pope who governs in consultation with the college of cardinals, was emphatically asserted. In consequence, as George H. Sabine has written: "The pope in the fifteenth century established himself as the first of the absolute monarchs, and the theory of papal absolutism became the archetype of the theory of monarchical absolutism."[1]

The Struggle between Kings and Nobles

Besides the church the other quarter from which effective opposition to a king could come in the Middle Ages was the nobility. Much of the political history of those centuries consisted in struggles between the nobles and their monarch, each trying to curb the other. When the nobles stood together, they could wring concessions from a king. A notable instance was the triumph of the English barons in compelling King John to sign the Great Charter of 1215 which reaffirmed their ancient rights and privileges against royal encroachment. Still more successful was the Polish nobility, whose prolonged resistance reduced the institution of monarchy to a weak figurehead. In their case, however, "success" had suicidal consequences, since the Polish state in the absence of strong direction fell easy prey to Russian and Prussian expansion and was erased from the map. Sometimes a powerful nobleman opposed the reigning monarch in order to dispossess him of the crown and place it on his own or a kinsman's head. Usually the rivalries between great aristocrats and their clans sowed a bitter crop of strife and bloodshed. The Wars of the Roses, which for three decades split medieval England into hostile camps, were sparked by the clashing ambitions of the Houses of Lancaster and York, as were the political aims of papacy and empire respectively championed on the Continent by Guelphs and Ghibellines.

From this welter of discord, into which the loose-knit character of

---

[1]George H. Sabine and Thomas L. Thorson, *History of Political Theory,* 4th ed. (New York: Holt, Rinehart & Winston, 1973), p. 305. See the whole of chapter 17 in that book.

feudalism had plunged society, there emerged in one country an achievement which endured. In England during the thirteenth century the institution of Parliament took shape and acquired, at the hands of Simon de Montfort (1265) and King Edward I (1295), the form and functions that differentiated it from the earlier Great Council. During the thirteenth and fourteenth centuries that form was set into the definite mold of two chambers, one of which, the House of Lords, contained the higher nobility and higher clergy while the second, the House of Commons, represented the lesser nobles (for example, knights of the shire) and commoners.

The functions of Parliament are a more complicated story. The reason for its existence in the Middle Ages may be found in two circumstances. The "loyal, trusty, and well-beloved subjects" of the king normally had various grievances of which they wished to complain. These could be more effectively voiced and would carry more weight if expressed through a regularized procedure. While subjects needed to approach the king for redressing their wrongs, he had a motive for approaching them, since he wanted their money. Originally the king's government was considered a branch of his household. As any great landowner managed his estates and supervised the affairs of his tenantry, so was a king supposed to govern the realm and protect its inhabitants. Affairs of state were handled by secretaries and other palace officials who in a literal sense were servants of the crown, while the costs of administration were defrayed out of the king's personal wealth. In all this, no attempt was made to separate public from private. Or rather, the concept of public interest had disappeared in the smothering embrace of private relationships. Public officials were court functionaries; the public treasury, a private purse.

Such a situation could continue only so long as the functions of the central government were few and their costs remained small. Everything changed, however, when kings endeavored to extend their authority to new fields (for example, the provision of a uniform, national system of justice) and when they embarked on that costliest of all governmental activities—war. To pacify the Welsh, contain the Scots, crush the Irish, and conquer the French[2] meant retaining and supplying large armies in the field. No longer could a king "live off his own" as tradition expected. He must now ask his subjects to contribute in his service not only their lives but that other dear possession, their money. Here then was a situation with the makings of a bargain advantageous to both sides. If the king were to appropriate his subjects' money without their consent, they would have a new and serious grievance. If he requested them, however, to agree to contribute, was not the time opportune for them to ask him to remedy their wrongs, which might lead to legislative action or changes in executive policy? Furthermore, when seeking money, the king would have to satisfy the

[2]For example, the protracted campaigns of the Hundred Years' War (1337–1453).

taxpayers who wished to know how equitably it would be collected and for what purposes it would be spent. Hence Parliament received its start in life from the coupling of two original functions—the power of the purse and the need for a public forum for the ventilation of grievances. From these roots there later grew such other duties as the enactment of law. discussion of public policy, and control of the executive.

Rise of the English Parliament

Great institutions grow slowly, however, and, like big trees that add a new ring annually, accumulate their layers of precedents. Four centuries elapsed between Edward I's Model Parliament of 1295 and the final victory of parliamentarians over royalists in 1688. What was it that took so much time? The answer lies in a social and economic, as well as a political, explanation. When Parliament was constructed to represent wealth and social superiority, when the dominant interest in the economy was the possession of land, and when the nobles were among the biggest landowners, then an addition to the powers of Parliament with its proportionate weakening of the crown could only mean government of the people by the nobility for the nobility, and it was doubtful whether anything was to be gained by rejecting the king's yoke in favor of that. On the contrary, from the standpoint of the mass of the population there was much to be said in favor of a weak nobility and a powerful king, since when a king abused his power, his oppression was likely to bear hardest on the nobles, the nearest rivals to his preeminence.

The politics of this situation was reinforced by the economic developments of the fifteenth century. At that time the structure of feudalism, centering on the ownership and produce of the land, was challenged by a contrary interest. An expansion of handicraft industries was accompanied by increase in domestic and foreign commerce. Enterprises of this character stimulated and strengthened the craft guilds, associations of merchants, and credit and banking institutions. For mutual convenience these clustered within the walls of the trading city[3] (*Handelsstadt*), which was the focal point in the system of production, distribution, and communication. Such cities began to influence the political process. They sought the preservation of order (because warfare disrupted trade) and their emancipation from rural supremacy. On both scores urbanism pitted itself against the feudal aristocracy, whose discords disturbed the peace and whose wealth was drawn from the soil. The monarchy, natural foe of the nobility, was the natural ally of the urban *burghers* or burgesses. The grant to cities of royal

[3]Witness the growth in importance of the Hanseatic League (including in its membership Hamburg, Bremen, Lübeck, Bergen, Danzig, and others), the cities of northern Italy (like Venice, Milan. and Florence), and Antwerp, Amsterdam, and London.

charters of incorporation, as in England, enabled them to be self-governing, that is, to be rid of feudal government by the nobles who dominated the countryside. Consequently it was this urban "middle" class that rallied to the crown, helped to replace the decentralized disorder of feudalism by unified central power, embodied the new concept of sovereignty[4] in the person of the sovereign (a word that became synonymous with "king"), and reaped the economic benefits of the centrally directed policies of mercantilism.[5] In England as in France the monarchy became absolute because there were material interests approving the powers it wielded.

The Revolution in England

It is the style of political change, as was observed earlier,[6] to proceed from excess in one direction to counterexcess in the other. Feudal disunity gave way to royal absolutism, which in turn outlasted its original justification and, by abuses of its own, invoked new opposition. A monarch who was steering a dangerous course—witness Henry VIII piloting the English Reformation or Queen Elizabeth I holding the Spaniards at bay with zigzags of dalliance and defiance—wisely employed the institution of Parliament for enlisting public support, and Parliament's members, their appetite for authority whetted with each taste, would not willingly be denied a further share once the immediacy of crisis was past. The cooperation between Parliament and the crown, fairly well maintained by Tudor monarchs, broke down under their unhappy successors, the Stuarts. A variety of circumstances turned a rift into a revolution. Chief blunders on the royal side were the decisions of Charles I to dispense altogether with Parliament, to levy taxes without parliamentary consent, and to administer secret and arbitrary "justice" in the Court of the Star Chamber. The price England paid was a civil war (1641–1651). Charles paid by defeat and the loss of his head. Even this example did not deter King James II, 30 years later, from attempting to restore Catholicism to a predominantly Protestant people. Again an aroused Parliament formed the focus of opposition. In 1688 a second revolution was won without bloodshed, the King fleeing with his neck intact. Parliament then invited William of Orange and his wife Mary to occupy the throne and in an Act of Settlement laid down the terms and limits by which the monarchy has since been bound.

Thus was consecrated the first of the modern revolutions which delivered a new birth of freedom. By the end of the seventeenth century England had secured the essentials of political liberty by creating at the apex

---

[4]See chapter 6, section on "Monism Again: The Theory of Sovereignty."
[5]See chapter 7, section on "Medievalism and Mercantilism."
[6]See chapter 6, section on "The Reconstruction of Unity."

of its government an institution representative of the governed. In this way the English people established for themselves, and by their example demonstrated to others, a method through which the effectiveness of power could be legitimized with the moral sanction of consent. Then, with parliamentary supremacy assured, the theoretical explanation followed. In 1690 John Locke published his two *Treatises of Civil Government.* The first he devoted to the negative task of destroying the fatuous doctrine of the divine right of kings. In the second he constructed a positive theory to take its place. Governments, he asserted, may rightfully exercise only those powers to which the people give their consent. Authority is conferred as a trust, being simply "a fiduciary power to act for certain ends."[7] The wishes of the community are represented and formulated by the legislature, which ranks supreme among the organs of the state. Should those in power abuse their trust and a conflict break out between the government and the governed, the latter retain the ultimate weapon of revolution, since they can never surrender the right to save themselves.[8] In any such dispute between the citizen body and authority, no third party can serve as judge. The people are always their own final court of appeal.

The supremacy of Parliament, resulting from military victory in the civil war and political triumph in 1688, accorded well with these doctrines—subject to one proviso. It was one thing to assert that the monarchy should henceforth be limited, not absolute, and that Parliament (the legislature) should be paramount over the crown (the executive). It was something else to assume that the dominance of Parliament was the same as control by all the people. At the time when Locke wrote, the franchise was limited to property owners who were a small fraction of the population. Nor did Locke propose to change that. Thus the consent of the governed boiled down to the interests of a class. Nevertheless, wittingly or unwittingly, Locke had sown a seed, and there was no stopping its growth. What is more, there were other soils, besides that of England, in which it could take root. This was what an English government learned in 1776.

Principles of the American Revolution

"To secure these rights, Governments are instituted among Men, deriving their just powers from the consent of the governed." The key words in this sentence are "just" and "consent." Jefferson's problem, when he drafted the Declaration of Independence, was similar to that which Locke had faced a century before. He was expounding the right to rebel against authority that was unresponsive to the governed. Since liberty was a su-

---

[7]*Second Treatise of Civil Government,* chapter 13, sec. 149.
[8]Ibid.

preme good, he wanted a society of free men. These, he recognized. must accept certain restraints on their behavior and must enforce their rules on offenders. Like the other fathers of the American Revolution, Jefferson was no anarchist. His purpose was not to sweep all government away, but to create authority that could be held to account. How was this to be done? Was it possible to argue for freedom and yet acquiesce in some coercion?

Jefferson began by reasserting that the consent of the governed is the foundation of all legitimate government. Consent alone gives moral sanction and legal validity to the physical force employed by the state. Powers derived from consent, therefore, are just. But what if a government acts in defiance of consent? "Whenever any form of government becomes destructive of these ends," continues the Declaration, "it is the right of the people to alter or to abolish it, and to institute new government, laying its foundation on such principles and organizing its powers in such form, as to them shall seem most likely to effect their safety and happiness."

These ideas have never ceased to yield inspiration. Their expression in this form was a turning point in modern political history, and their subsequent influence has been profound. Yet the concepts enshrined in the Declaration are not free from difficulties, either philosophical or practical. Designed for a solution to existing problems, they inaugurated new ones.

Consider some implications of the doctrine of consent. Besides the ethical force of the argument that consent lends morality to the actions of government, it made sense in the seventeenth and eighteenth centuries to contend that, when people stayed in a community, the fact of their remaining implied their consent to its functions. Englishmen who disliked their government could emigrate across the Atlantic. Colonists who wished, after 1776, to remain under the British crown could move north to Canada. Where there was some freedom of movement, the doctrine of consent was not a pious fiction. It contained some realism. But in the twentieth century, the world is not so open. Millions, having no alternative and being unable to emigrate, must live under a regime to which they do not consent.

Moreover, consent implies agreement, but agreement about what? Is it about procedures (for example, elections, voting, and majority decisions), whereby we assent in advance to abide by any result that emerges from the procedures? Or is it agreement about ends and goals? That is to say, do we agree in preferring a certain social order, a group of values, a civilization? And do we then regard it as a duty of government not to do whatever would violate such values? In the former case, there can be no restriction on how the procedures are used, provided that a "due process" is followed. In the latter case, the restrictions are definite, since the community is committed to certain goals. These will be modified only as we come to prefer new values or alter the interpretation of the old ones.

Plainly consent, if stated as an absolute, will not be completely realized in practice. Since unanimity never exists in big political issues, somebody's consent has to be forfeited whenever a majority has its way at the expense of a minority. On occasion, it may be in society's interest for the majority to prevail, and for the minority to submit. But cannot majorities also be oppressive? And, if so, is not the minority then entitled to resist? In other words, consent is not the sole pillar of a free society, though it is certainly one of the pillars that are fundamental. Ensuring the freedom of the governed is not the apparently simple process of discovering what the people will and then doing it. On most matters there are many wills, since human beings, belonging to many groups, have so many interests. Because in actuality the support sustaining a government will at times be that of a majority, at other times that of a minority, the governed need alternately protection by government and protection from it. To assert the inalienable right of a people to regain their freedom by revolution is excellent doctrine. But it describes an ultimate weapon for use in the last resort. Revolution can be a method—fully justified when it is directed against a despotism—of founding a government in the first instance. It is not a means of continuous popular control over regular government activities. For this, something else is required, and it is to the credit of Jefferson's generation that they not only formulated the principles, but also constructed workable institutions which have yielded results in practice. The foundations of the latter were laid between 1787 and 1803.[9]

Supremacy of the Constitution

In the American solution to this problem of giving government the power to serve, but denying it the power to dominate, the distinctive feature is the role assigned to the Constitution. The English Revolution left Parliament supreme; the American Revolution resulted in the supremacy of the Constitution. How is this ensured? Various measures guarantee that the Constitution will be paramount. It was drafted by a special convention of delegates, with Washington presiding. Its adoption was referred to the states, all of which, except Rhode Island, elected delegates to special conventions which voted on the issue of ratification. Since going into effect, the status of the Constitution has remained unique. The preamble announces that "We, the People . . . do ordain and establish this Constitution," thereby affirming that the government is founded on the popular will. While the people create the Constitution, the latter creates the institutions of government. All these—Congress, President, and Supreme Court, as well as the constitutions of the states—are subordinate to the Constitution of the United

---

[9]1803 was the date of the decision in *Marbury* v. *Madison.*

States, to laws conforming to it, and to treaties made under its authority, which together comprise "the supreme law of the land."[10]

Besides being asserted, the supremacy of the Constitution must be enforced. How is this accomplished? First, by requiring that all government officials—federal, state, and local, elected and appointed—take an oath or affirmation to support the Constitution. Second, by judicial procedures and penalties, including impeachment, in case any official betrays the people's trust. Third, by requiring a special method, distinct from the ordinary process of legislation, for amending the Constitution's written text. Fourth, by judicial review of legislation, through which any statute enacted by the legislature and approved by the chief executive or repassed over a veto may be challenged as unconstitutional. A case will then be heard in the courts, where the judiciary determine whether the contested statute is to be obeyed as law or regarded as null and void.

The Rule of Law

These principles are a special derivation from the broader concept of "the rule of law." The main requirements of that famous doctrine are as follows:

1. Governments shall exercise their powers in conformity with known laws enacted through a regular procedure.
2. No laws shall convert into offenses actions that were lawful when they were performed.
3. No one may be convicted on any charge save after a fair trial in open court.
4. The judiciary, when applying the generalities of the law to particular cases, must be independent of external pressure and control.

Such maxims, while arguable on theoretical grounds, have grown from the facts of experience. Each was formulated in contrast with the proven practices of many governments in the past and present. When a state does not enthrone the rule of law, the governed have no adequate protection against the whims of those in power. Tyranny, despotism, or dictatorship exists when a government makes and unmakes the law without permitting public criticism or challenge; when it imprisons an individual without public hearing and an equal opportunity for defense; when judges decide cases under the intimidating shadow of executive power; and when laws are enforced arbitrarily, so as to discriminate on grounds of political or personal favoritism between citizens who deserve like treatment.

The constitution that Massachusetts adopted in 1776 contained the hope "that it may be a government of laws and not of men." That antithesis cannot be taken literally. No legal system can operate automatically without

---

[10]*United States Constitution,* Article VI.

human discretion. Laws, unlike some individuals, are not self-made. Still less are they self-enforcing. Human beings must draft, enact, interpret, and apply the law, scaling down the broad classification to the narrow particulars. But though the Massachusetts formula is rhetorical exaggeration, the antithesis emphasizes an important distinction. A state may be organized with curbs on its activities. Or it may flout restraint. In the former case, the government's power is harnessed and bridled; in the latter, it is absolute and uncontrollable.

Conformance of Law to Custom, Nature, or Utility

To impose the restraint of law on government has been tried in various ways, each with its merits and difficulties. An example is the notion that law is the product of immemorial custom. As the deposits of millions of microorganisms eventually surround an island with a coral reef, so millions of human acts repeated in habitual patterns construct a ring of custom around a community and its governance. Custom is then a barrier confining officials within limits, and law is the accretion of practices which custom has confirmed. Discover the usages of the past, and you find the law of the present. This done, the duty of government is to preserve unbroken the links which connect the chain of custom. Such a view is adequate to maintain a stable continuity in an imperceptibly changing society. But it ill accords with circumstances of rapid flux when experiment and flexibility are more needed than tradition.

Another device for subordinating the state to legal restraint is the belief in a law of nature or reason. Once the assumption is accepted that such a law exists, which is a matter of faith rather than reason, various consequences can be deduced—for instance, that nature embodies principles that can be understood by reason, that these are universal in scope and eternal in duration, that the state governs well when it assists the individual in conforming to natural law, and that acts which violate such law are invalid. This "higher law" theory, like the doctrine that derives law from custom, is appropriately adapted to a certain goal. By appealing to a higher law (that is, higher than that proclaimed by the state) people may justify resistance to authority or outright revolution, since it is always psychologically necessary for those who resist or rebel to make their opponents, not themselves, appear in the wrong. Alternatively, the higher law doctrine suits the needs of other institutions which fear the state or are its rivals, for these can affirm that humanity does not live by politics alone and that in nature's house there are many mansions. With such reasons, both churches and corporations have welcomed the notion of a natural law.

But its philosophy abounds with unsolved problems. How do we know which principles are natural or what is reason's law? When different interpretations are offered, which is correct? Because of these uncertainties, the practical effects of appealing to natural law can be unfortunate. Those who flee from one type of authority, that of the state and its laws, seek refuge in the arms of another, for example, that of the priest, pastor, or entrepreneur. The law of nature is then respectively translated into the law of nature's God, as clerical authority affirms it, or the natural laws of economics, as some economist expounds them. Alternatively, those who shrink from substituting new authoritarianism for old will escape into the relativism that rejects every interpretation of natural law on the ground that anybody's guess may be right and none can be proven. In this case there is a flight from reason; decisions are reached through force, and the more powerful proclaim themselves the rightful.

A third formula for using law to restrain government is the maxim of Jeremy Bentham and the Utilitarians—that governments must promote the greatest happiness of the greatest number. The Utilitarians were the British reformers of the early nineteenth century who, seeking to modernize their political machinery and legal code, applied to every law and institution the test: What is its utility? Whatever statute or executive act helped to increase the sum total of happiness in the community was considered good. Whatever diminished that stock of happiness must be removed or reformed. A government merited support or opposition according to how it influenced happiness. Such a yardstick subjects the state to a different standard. To appraise a government's action by its degree of conformity to custom or nature means referring to the source of authority. To test an act by its relation to happiness means studying its effects and comparing one set of results with another. Thus the latter approach is empirical. Applied in practice, however, Bentham's formula fails, because it is impossible to measure a quantity of happiness. People have wrangled endlessly about whether a particular governmental action, compared with possible untried alternatives, produces more happiness or less.

Constitutions and Constitutionalism

Besides these ways of restraining government by law, there is the more general argument that the state will not tyrannize over its citizens if it is imbued with respect for constitutionalism. What does this mean? A distinction should be made between "constitutionalism" and "the constitution." A constitution is the basic design of the structure and powers of the state and the rights and duties of its citizens. In that sense there is a constitution in every state with an established government—in the United States, Canada, and Britain, as well as in Nazi Germany, Franco Spain, and Stalin's Russia. To say that a state possesses a constitution implies nothing about its democratic or dictatorial character. Constitutionalism, however, is a term with specific implications. It is bound up with the notion of restraining power by the rule of law; it embraces the idea that a government should not be permitted to do whatever its officials please, but should conduct itself by agreed and equitable procedures. The purpose of this restriction on its freedom of action is, of course, to safeguard a fundamental area of freedom for its citizens. For tyranny exists wherever power is total.

Clear though it is that constitutionalism is incompatible with dictatorship, and that political freedom requires a curb on power, the nature of these limits calls for more discussion. Just as it is one thing to harness a horse and another to hobble it, so it is one thing to control a government and another to cripple it. The difference may be one of degree or emphasis, but it is all-important. It stems from contrasted attitudes toward power. Some are so fearful of its abuses that their picture of constitutionalism is a series of prohibitions. Their rule of law develops into a roll of negatives. To devise checks, controls, restraints, and limitations becomes the essence of constitutionalism and the prime guarantee of human freedom. But is it really necessary to lean so far backwards? May not this overattention to abuses defeat its own purpose? Since government is indispensable and no one can govern without power, it is evident that constitutionalism should first be concerned with how power must be used, then with the prevention of its abuse. The state should be envisaged as a canal through which political power may flow, releasing its energy for the benefit of mankind, rather than as a dam to hold it back. After all, the first aim of any philosophy of government is to figure out what the state must do, not what it should be prohibited from doing. Nor is it to be forgotten that, while tyrannical governments destroy freedom, other governments may enlarge it. Many of the functions undertaken by the modern state are designed to make opportunities more nearly equal for everybody and to protect weaker individuals from the rapacity of the strong.

But there is a still more basic objection to those who develop their photograph of constitutionalism in the negative and neglect to print the positive. If constitutionalism is approved on the ground that it restrains government, the inquiry is thrown one stage further back. Constitutionalism itself is the result of other factors. What are these?· Essentially they are political, which switches the discussion onto another track. Hitherto in this chapter the problem of making government accountable to the governed has been treated in a predominantly legal light—in terms of the rule of law, of legal curbs on power, of constitutionalism—so that political freedom appears as the consequence of a certain legal situation. But this is an illusion, for the image has been turned upside down. Although there is always some interaction between law and politics, it is primarily politics that controls and determines law. It is not the rule of law or respect for constitutionalism that gives birth to a politically free society, but rather the politics of freedom that creates the sanction for constitutionalism and law. What has been called "the firmament of law"[11] is not self-supporting. It is propped up on political pillars. Without them, it would topple.

The Political Roots of the American Constitutional System

To understand this, let us take a closer look at the government of the United States. The Constitution stands at the center and is the chief symbol of the American form of government. The year 1989, in which the eighth edition of this book is being published, has a special significance in history. It was 200 years ago that the Constitution, drafted in 1787, went into operation with the election of the first Congress and the inauguration of George Washington as the first President. In the course of two centuries, this document has evolved in an organic relationship with the country whose needs it serves. The repetition of precedents, arising from similar responses to similar circumstances, has produced a body of custom, and this in turn has grown into living traditions which enfold the written text as the bark surrounds a tree trunk. Moreover, because the Constitution has survived for two centuries and has accompanied the American people from the infancy of Independence to the maturity of full-grown power, it has also taken on meanings which are more symbolic than literal. Let us examine some of its complexities.

Because the Constitution is a supreme law and contains a list of judicially enforceable rights, and because of the practice of judicial review of legislation, it has become customary to think of the Constitution as a document to be construed in legal fashion.[12] But this is to overlook the political context which ascribes to law its significance and to judges their status. Under the Constitution the ultimate power is lodged not with the Supreme Court but with the people. It is "We, the people" who "ordain and establish" the Constitution. It is the people's elected representatives who amend it and may express their disapproval of a Supreme Court decision by an amendment.[13] It is the political branches of the government, the President and the Senate, that nominate and confirm appointees to the Court and, by

---

[11]Robert M. MacIver in *The Web of Government*, rev. ed. (New York: The Free Press, 1965), chapter 4.

[12]A cynic has observed that "a government of laws, not of men" becomes a government of lawyers, not of men.

[13]There are several instances of amendments which reversed decisions of the Supreme Court. To wit, the Eleventh, which recorded the indignation of the states at *Chisholm* v. *Georgia;* the Thirteenth, Fourteenth, and Fifteenth, which repudiated the principles of the Dred Scott case; and the Sixteenth, which overthrew the opinion of the Court concerning federal inability to levy income tax.

choosing its personnel, influence the trend of future decisions. Where the rule of law exists, it is because a political will wants to have it so.

This point is reinforced by a further reflection. As practicing politicians know and students of government soon discover, many features of the American system of government cannot be learned from reading the Constitution. The latter is a compact document, its brevity being one of its merits. On few issues does it elaborate in any detail, and those are mostly concerned with electoral machinery or the procedure for a presidential veto of legislation. For the rest, as a Constitution should be, it is broad in scope and general in its terms. Since the Bill of Rights (the first ten amendments) was added in 1791, the text has been changed only 16 times in two centuries. But the nation has altered beyond recognition. From four million persons living in 13 states along the Atlantic seaboard with an agrarian economy and a precarious military position, this Union has expanded to 245 millions spread across 50 states from the Atlantic far into the Pacific and from the Arctic Circle to the Tropic of Cancer, exhibiting a highly developed industrial technology, administering distant bases and possessions, and wielding a mighty aggregate of military strength. Of these changes there is scarcely a trace in the text of the Constitution. But such social transformations cannot fail to affect the basic design of the powers and structure of government and the rights and duties of citizens—to repeat the definition offered earlier.[14] It stands to reason therefore that these effects have been registered in other ways than by the formal method of constitutional amendment. If so, what are they?

The first is legislative enactment. Much of the output of Congress, admittedly, is of no fundamental importance. Legislation runs the gamut from private bills that concern a particular person to measures affecting the prosperity and security of the nation and the world. Certain of these statutes, as judged by their subject matter, occupy a crucial position in the governmental process. Laws that organize the federal courts, that establish the major departments, that provide a program of social security, that regulate the franchise or the conduct of elections—these deal with matters no less fundamental than some sections of the Constitution itself. The continuous labors of 100 Congresses have done much to shape the primary patterns of American government.

The same may be said of the Supreme Court. Because the Founding Fathers were writing a Constitution rather than a statute, they drafted many clauses in language so broad as to permit diversity of definition and detail. In countless instances the Court had to supply the guiding principles for Congress and the executive branch to follow. Consider the federal powers over interstate commerce and general welfare.[15] Their terse word-

[14]See the section on "Constitutions and Constitutionalism," in this chapter.

[15]In its list of subjects on which Congress may legislate, Article I, section 8 of the Constitution includes the powers "to regulate commerce . . . among the several States" and "to lay and collect taxes . . . and provide for the common defense and general welfare of the United States."

ing has left room for wide possibilities, as can be seen in the decisions which the Court has rendered. When they interpret these powers—as with due process, equal protection, or free speech—the judges are in effect amending the Constitution by giving its generalities more precision. Judge-made definitions have added essential portions to the foundations which the Constitution laid.[16]

Nor is this all. Many fundamental facts in the American system of government can be explained only in political, not in legal, terms. Some sections of the Constitution have not been applied in practice because political considerations prevented their enforcement. Thus the Fourteenth Amendment declares, in section 2, that if a state denies voting rights to any of its citizens, the congressional representation to which its population entitles that state shall be proportionately reduced. Until 1958 no effect was given to that provision because, had it been strictly enforced, both major parties and many states, northern as well as southern, would have lost representation. By "gentlemen's agreement," therefore, the Constitution was tacitly ignored. At long last, however, the Civil Rights Laws of 1957 and 1964 attempted to cope with this problem. The Commission created by the Act of 1957 probed for two decades into districts where blacks were systematically prevented from registering to vote and initiated action in the courts against the responsible local authorities.[17]

This becomes plainer when one reflects on other features of American government which have developed into customary political practice and of which the Constitution remains innocent. Many examples can be cited, but none is more revealing than the rise and organization of political parties. The party system that grew in the nineteenth century was antithetical to the ideals of those who drafted the United States Constitution. Thus the institutions they constructed did not anticipate the emergence of parties, were not designed to admit them, and have not always dovetailed with them in a harmonious fit. What is more, James Madison and other leading spirits of his generation viewed government by parties as an evil, since they habitually described their eighteenth-century equivalents by the unfavorable term *factions*. Modern democracy, however, has taken the parties into the inner sanctum of power, and its political process is now unthinkable without them. Voting for a president by means of a college of electors; the organization, procedures, and output of Congress; cooperation or friction between chief executive and legislature; the people's choice of policies and

---

[16]Many doctrines have been enunciated by the Court that, until modified by a later majority of judges, have controlled the legislative and executive branches—for example, the doctrines of "original package," "business affected with a public interest," "the flow of commerce," "clear and present danger," "separate, but equal," and so forth.

[17]In the 1980s, however, during the Reagan administration the Commission was systematically crippled and became a nullity. Also in those years, the Justice Department adopted interpretations (e.g., on the subjects of affirmative action, bussing, and reversed discrimination) which were inimical to racial minorities.

personalities; none of these would be as they are if parties did not profoundly influence the result. No small slice of American government is composed of political customs whose content is as important and enduring as what is written in the Constitution.

Hence we need a realistic approach to the problem of explaining what a constitution is and does. The pattern of government in the United States can be compared to a river created by the confluence of four streams. First is the document entitled the Constitution. Second is legislation. The third consists of judicial opinions. The fourth is political custom. A convenient term to embrace the four would be "the constitutional system." This is what underpins the entire structure of government; its strength rests on the bedrock of political power, not on the sands of legal formulas.

The Politics of the British Constitution

If more evidence is needed to sustain this view, it can be gathered from Britain. To many writers on politics the British form of government appears a paradox, especially when compared with the United States. Some striking differences exist between the two constitutional systems. In Britain there is no document analogous to the United States Constitution. Parliament, unlike Congress, is empowered to make any kind of law it chooses.[18] The courts have no authority to nullify legislation. From the purely legal standpoint, therefore, it is impossible in Britain to specify which rules, procedures, and institutions are part of the constitution and which are not; and a constitutional lawyer, reasoning only from legal assumptions, can never satisfactorily explain the nature of the constitution and its sanctions. Much nonsense has consequently been written about Britain by those who, starting with false premises, arrive at wrong conclusions. Thus Tocqueville asserted that because of the legal supremacy of Parliament, which may change the constitution at any time by simple legislative act, there is in reality no constitution at all.[19] An odd argument this one, since it involves defining a constitution so narrowly, restricting it to those states where the power of the legislature is limited by a superior law.

Equally odd was the reasoning of A. V. Dicey, the English jurist who distinguished between what he called the law of the constitution and its conventions (that is, customs). The former consists of rules enforced by the courts; the latter, of rules binding through political usage. Political rules

---

[18]With one important exception. Since Britain joined the European Community in 1973, Parliament's lawmaking power has been subordinated to the requirements of the Treaty of Rome, and British courts must nullify an Act of Parliament that contravenes the Treaty.

[19]Alexis de Tocqueville, *Democracy in America*, part 1, trans. Henry Reeve (New York: J. & H. G. Langley, 1841), chapter 6, p. 103.

are obeyed, he said, because, if they were not, a breach of law would follow—which satisfies a lawyer's logic, but is untrue in many cases.[20] For the British constitution is a political instrument, not a legal charter. What the British call their constitution is the consensus, reached by the end of the seventeenth century, about the principles to which their government should conform and the institutions which make it effective. That consensus is political because it embodies the will of an overwhelming majority in favor of a particular structure of government. This will may be expressed in various ways. One is for Parliament to enact a statute, or for the courts to render a decision acceptable to Parliament, in which case a political will is dressed in the outer raiments of law. Another way leaves it to usage to build a set of rules, creating the expectation that what was done under like circumstances in the past will ordinarily be followed in the present. Each method has merits. To write a political agreement into legal form results in greater precision if the wording is detailed and exact, and this may reduce the area of controversy. To leave decisions to the formulation of custom may permit a change to be speedily accomplished in a time of crisis without the need for conforming to legal procedures which can be cumbrous.

The British and American Systems Compared

A comparison of the British and American systems permits a more accurate view of constitutions. Misunderstanding of both has given rise to false contrasts and exaggerated distinctions. Thus, the American constitution has been described as written; the British, as unwritten. If taken literally, that is incorrect; if figuratively, the meaning is unclear. The truth is that both systems include portions committed to writing and portions that are not. The statutes and judicial opinions, as well as the text of the Constitution of the United States, are written—as if the form were the decisive factor in determining the character of a constitution! That certain topics receive written statement, while others are left to informal understanding, is not of itself a profound difference. What surely matters more is what content receives expression in one medium or the other.

Another contrast calls the British system flexible, the American rigid. The point at issue here is not trivial. It concerns the ease or difficulty of the method by which the constitution is changed. The belief, however, in the flexibility of the one vis-à-vis the rigidity of the other is a fallacious inference. The British constitution, it is argued, consists of two parts—law

---

[20]See his *Law of the Constitution*, 8th ed. (London: Macmillan and Co., 1931), chapter 15, pp. 441ff. There have been, for example, a few instances of somebody briefly serving as a Minister without a seat in either House of Parliament. This broke political custom, but not the law.

and custom. The law may be changed at any time by ordinary Act of Parliament. Custom, too, may be altered by statute, or by the simple device of departing from precedent. In either case, change is possible. The American Constitution, however, consists of the document drafted in 1787 and amended 26 times since then. The process of amending the text of the Constitution presents a formidable obstacle to innovation.

The errors and omissions in this argument are numerous. It rests on a myopic view of the American Constitution, excluding from sight the statutes, judicial opinions, and political usages, which in a broader and more realistic sense are integral parts of the constitutional system. It further assumes that amendments to the Constitution of the United States can be obtained only with the greatest difficulty; that in political reality Parliament will dare to proceed as far as its legal powers extend; and that rules of custom are more readily modified than rules of law. None of these assumptions is wholly correct. When the people of the United States decided after a dozen years of nationwide prohibition that the experiment was unworkable, they adopted the Twenty-First Amendment easily and speedily. On the other hand, the custom that no president should serve more than two terms was maintained for a century and a half with a rigidity which only the menace of Hitler and the greatness of Franklin D. Roosevelt could shatter.[21] As for the use by Parliament of its theoretically unlimited authority, obstacles and limitations do exist—but they are of a political, rather than a juridical, nature.

This does not mean that on the subject of rigidity or flexibility the two constitutional systems are indistinguishable. Genuine distinctions may be drawn, but the reasons for them have been wrongly stated. Any portion of a constitutional system, legal or customary, is likely to be rigid if expressed in minute detail and supported by an organized sentiment. Conversely, any provision, legal or customary, can be flexible if its terms are vague or general and if sentiment in its favor is lukewarm or disorganized.

Some examples will illustrate these points. A rigid feature of the American Constitution is the clause prescribing a four-year term for the president and an election for a new term in every fourth year. Never yet in peace or in war[22] have the American people deviated from the requirement of conducting the presidential election at identical and regular intervals. Only by amendment to the Constitution could a president's term be shortened or lengthened and a special election held. Rigidity on this point is mainly due to the exactitude with which the Constitution expresses itself. On the other hand, where the wording is general and imprecise, this same Constitution (though "written"!) can prove conveniently flexible. The

---

[21]What was a rule of custom eventually became a rule of the Constitution by the adoption of the Twenty-Second Amendment.

[22]E.g., in 1864 and 1944.

interstate commerce clause, for instance, has been subject to vastly varying interpretations, each reflecting the changing views of the majority of voters, congressmen, or judges.

The same can be said of the rules produced through custom. I mentioned that the Constitution is entirely silent about parties, yet they have profoundly influenced its operation. Contrast their effect on electing the president and on voting in the legislature. The president is not elected directly by the people, but by members of a college elected in the 50 states for that specific purpose. When people wish to vote for their party's candidate, they vote in fact for others of the same party who then cast their ballots in the electoral college for their party's presidential nominee. Nothing in federal[23] law compels the members of the college to vote for the party's choice. Political obligation, however, requires them to do so. They perform this one duty as expected, whereupon their office terminates.

How different is the voting in Congress! Senators and representatives are elected under a party label and continue during their term to be party members. But neither they nor their constituents consider them obliged to vote with the majority of their party on every issue or to support every measure proposed by a president of their own party. Indeed, on many a legislative decision, a minority of Republicans will be found voting with the majority of Democrats, and vice versa. What this means is that the party system requires discipline on the one specific matter of getting its candidate into the White House, since control of the presidency is vital to the power of the party. The parties do not yet, however, regard the enactment of legislation or the acceptance of a president's program as equally vital. They therefore tolerate some independence in the halls of Congress. Thus rules of custom, like rules of law, may be rigid or flexible according to the precision with which they are formulated and the force of opinion behind them.[24]

The French Experience

Another comparison confirms the point that control over the government rests ultimately on political sanctions. In the United Kingdom and the United States the constitutions have stood the test of time, and usually they

---

[23]The laws of some states, however, place certain restrictions on presidential electors.

[24]Nixon's enforced resignation in 1974 illustrates my point. Charges of illegalities were leveled at his campaign for reelection in 1972. His own guilt or innocence centered on the burglary at the Democratic Party's campaign offices in the Watergate building. Did he know of this in advance? Did he authorize the subsequent attempted cover-up? It took a year and a half for the courts, the Congress, and the press to extract in public the information which proved that Nixon had broken the law. When it became certain that Congress would use its constitutional power to impeach him, he resigned. Thereupon, his successor, President Ford, granted him an absolute pardon.

work, because behind them lies the consensus of a community whose union outweighs its divisions. But observe what happens when the picture is reversed. When disunities transcend agreement, not only is it impossible to establish constitutionalism but a constitution itself cannot function properly. Where the needed political underpinnings are absent, the legal superstructure will sag and bend out of alignment. A pertinent example is France. Since 1789 the French have experienced 14^{25} regimes, some quite short-lived. The longest, the Third Republic, lasted from 1875 to 1940, but collapsed in military defeat. The average duration for a constitution, through the Fourth Republic, was 13 years. Why was this?

The reasons do not lie primarily in the institutions which the French have tried to operate. As the figures imply, France has run the gamut of constitutional experiments, but none of those adopted thus far gained enough support to endure. This was equally true of legislative supremacy, executive supremacy, and the cabinet system.

During the Third and Fourth Republics, 1875–1940 and 1946–1958, it was evident that the root of the political malady lay deeper than the structure of government. Some attributed the blame to the party system, whose turbulence and inner discords made crisis endemic and agreement abnormal. But the party system was an effect more than a cause. Its own chaotic character was symptomatic of a more fundamental malady, the cleavages within French society, whose number and crisscrossing made widespread and long-term combinations impossible. The French Revolution not only came later than the English, but left deep scars which took time to efface. The representatives of the old order were weakened but not crushed. Aristocrats and others of authoritarian bent despised the unglamorous Republic and its talkative democracy. The army leaders, bred in discipline, saw politics as anarchy. Patriotic as Frenchmen, they were often disloyal to the regime they were supposed to defend. The church, identified with the traditional order, found in the secular state a disturbing competitor and in the accompanying rationalistic philosophies a challenge to its dogma. The economic transformation, which industrialism required, was absorbed more slowly by the French than by Americans, British, Germans, and Japanese. Most French people did not take readily to large-scale organization. Basically individualistic, they had always been artisans first and mass-producers second. They felt comfortable in the small enterprise, whether in farming, commerce, or manufacturing. When forced into a big organization, their individualism rendered them impotent and mutually discordant.[26] Then in reaction and resignation, they would finally accept

[25]I exclude the Vichy regime of 1940–1944, since that was a puppet government set up in half of France under German military occupation.

[26]Signs have increased, however, since the 1960s that certain French business firms have adapted successfully to the requirements of large-scale organization. The underlying causes lay in the economics of the new technology (especially in electronics, aircraft, and

an authoritarian system—witness their army, church, and empire. Large-scale democratic organization they had not yet devised. In France, therefore, the majorities needed not only for stable government but for a constitutional consensus, were lacking. Negative majorities—that is, a vote against something—were always forthcoming.[27] Positive majorities, in favor of something, were hard to elicit. Under these conditions, the competitive factors outweighed the cooperative. Interests, pressure groups, organizations, and parties struggled among themselves—but without the wider harmonies that keep divisiveness in check. Whether the future will be an improvement, we wait to see. By 1989, the constitution chosen by de Gaulle for the Fifth Republic had already lasted twice as long as the average. It had three conservative presidents in succession, followed in 1981 by a socialist. That is a good augury, since it demonstrates a trend away from multipartism toward a two-party alternation. Moreover, the fact that Left and Right can operate the same institutions may indicate the emergence of a consensus which heretofore was lacking. Should that turn out to be the case, France may at last succeed in extricating itself from the dilemma it faced for so long—either multipartism or Bonapartism.

Once again, does not the French experience illustrate that politics will determine the constitution, the restraints of law, the orderly alternation in power of changing majorities, and all the rest? In the political process reposes our governmental salvation—or damnation.

The Key to Freedom

By what political method can the people control the powers they grant? How can a populace that reposes trust in its officials be sure they will not overstep the limits of their authority? One clue is suggested by the events discussed in chapters 6 and 7. The efforts of medieval popes and modern corporation presidents to curb the power of the state produced competing institutions that rivaled the state in the interests they mobilized and the loyalty they exacted. The peculiar significance of those ventures lay in the attempt to construct within society, but outside the political framework, an association capable of resisting the state. When dualism led to discord, and discord to conflict, the unity of the social order was eventually reaffirmed under the aegis of the political order. The triumphant assertion, however,

---

automobiles) and the stimulus provided by the policies and potentialities of the Common Market. The same has been true in agriculture. By 1980 France had many fewer farms and farmers than in 1950.

[27]When the Constitution of the Fourth Republic was adopted in 1946, only a minority of the registered electorate voted for it. Those who voted against it, plus the large number who abstained, formed a majority.

of the primacy of the state over the rest of society could permit a tyrannical abuse of power, if no corrective existed. The secret of the new solution has been to limit political power not from outside, but from within; to make the state safe for its citizens not by an external but by an inner check.

The method by which this is done is ingenious. It consists of an argument in various stages. Stage one asserts that the state belongs to all its members, whether they are of the government or of the governed. This is a rejection of the authoritarian, elitist view that the rulers are the state and that the people are subjects who belong to them. The contrary belief is contained in the two famous terms, "republic"[28] and "commonwealth." Both have essentially the same meaning: The state belongs to the public who own it as wealth shared in common. The second stage is a corollary of the first. If the state is the property of the whole people, including both government and governed, a distinction exists between the state and its government. The government is not identical with the state. It consists of a few chosen from the whole people who act in the name of the state and on its behalf and for a while dispose of its authority. The implication is that the same state can have a succession of different governments. These may change while the state continues.

But how can the government change and one group of rulers take the place of another? By a device which is perhaps the most notable of modern contributions to the art of politics: the party system. In itself, the existence of parties is not new. What is novel is the organization of modern parties, their place in the political process, and our attitude toward them. Two centuries ago parties were viewed with disfavor as a menace to the unity of the state. Because people had conspired to resist despotic kings, party was tinged with the taint of treason. Around the party, because schisms had split the church, hung the whiff of heresy. The name of faction, which a party was often called, was unsavory in early America, as Washington warned in his Farewell Address.

Since then, the growth of democracy has changed our perspective.[29] While no one would deny that a system of government by alternating parties is imperfect, a superior method of ensuring political freedom has yet to be found. So strong is this conviction in democratic countries that the existence of more than one party has become an essential criterion to distinguish a regime of liberty from dictatorship. For where there is an opportunity of choice, there is some freedom. Where no choice exists, there is coercion. Hence when the nature of the state is appraised, an all-important test is whether more than one party is tolerated. When the connection between party politics and freedom is studied, the difference

---

[28]From the Latin *res publica*, "a public possession."

[29]I have discussed this in my work *The Democratic Civilization* (New York: Oxford University Press, 1964), chapter 11.

between a two-party and a multiparty system appears far less significant than the gulf between one-party government and any system containing more than one. Indeed if language has any meaning, the term *one-party system* is a misnomer. By definition, a party is a part of the whole and therefore implies the presence of an alternative. To speak of the one-party state is a contradiction in terms. Such a state, whether Fascist or Communist, exhibits a monopoly of power. Its proper name is dictatorship.

The Requirement of Two or More Parties

A system containing two or more parties is a major step in the attainment of political maturity. Historically the emergence of the modern party has accompanied the growth of the modern electorate. Indeed, it was the latter that made the former possible. As the right to vote was extended throughout the nineteenth century, party organizations, which previously had been based mainly on legislative cliques, undertook to attract and mobilize the ever-increasing electorate. Parties then acquired their new character. They became mass organizations, linking together a large body of citizens with their representatives in the legislature; they developed institutions of their own, and to fight and win elections, they besought financial contributions. In this way the parties responded to a genuine need. Without them, the millions who comprised the new electorate would have become a disorganized crowd, unable to formulate their aims or debate the vast issues they confronted. By means of parties, the voters obtained a medium that, to state it in no stronger terms, afforded a chance for coherent action and, hopefully, responsible policies.

Nothing in the entire conception of the party system is as crucial as the requirement that there be more than one party. This condition sanctions the right of criticism and opposition as a legitimate and necessary element in the political process. The government of Britain symbolizes this situation with a unique terminology. There the ministry is officially styled Her Majesty's Government. In like manner the minority party is Her Majesty's Opposition—its loyal duty being to oppose in the name of the crown what the majority is loyally doing in the crown's name. The result of this remarkable concept is that resistance to power—if its methods are peaceful—is brought within the constitutional order. No longer need those who seek a change of government launch a revolution. No longer does the prevention of tyranny depend on constructing outside the state institutions capable of opposing it. By the coexistence of two or more parties, the means of curbing an overpowerful government is built within the political order. The parties in opposition supply today's equivalent of the captains of industry and finance in the era of unregulated capitalism or the popes and cardinals of a still earlier age. But the relation of the state to society, and the nature of the state itself, are vitally different when the check on the abuse of power exists inside the political order, not outside. Freedom is not primarily the legal concept that jurists depict. Nor is it, as Robert M. MacIver holds, solely the consequence of a pluralistic[30] society. In the modern state, freedom is basically political. It permits and is then perpetuated by a two- or multiparty system.

The Ins and the Outs

Saying this, however, does not exhaust the complexity of the relation between a party that governs and one that opposes. The peculiarity of this relationship is that the party in power does not eliminate those opposed to it, and the latter, while opposing, obey the declared will of the majority of the moment. Each side recognizes that it is a member of a system requiring, as a permanent feature, the existence of an opponent. Each accepts the principle of "live and let live" in the knowledge that the system allows each in turn its fair share of power. The corollary to this is that alternation must in fact occur—i.e., at some point of time, those in power leave office and are replaced by those in opposition. The reason why this is essential to a genuine democracy is that the certainty of such alternation imposes restraints on those wielding power for the time being.[31] In addition, if one groups holds office continuously for too long, corruption and arrogance set in. When this happens, cynicism pervades the general public and civic morale breaks down.

Alternation cannot occur, however, unless the scales are evenly balanced between the two sides. A free election is not necessarily a fair election. Indeed, we have had evidence since the 1970s of a new threat to democracy. This arises from a combination of factors—the numbers entitled to vote, the cost of campaigning, and the artifice of novel techniques of communication. Already this tendency has reached serious proportions in the United States where the electorate is huge, the interests involved are rich and powerful, and technology is so advanced. Here it is that the politics of democracy now suffers from invasion by the economics of the market. America's commercial culture, obsessed with the need to sell, has relied on advertising to entice potential buyers, and the advertisers have drawn heavily on the research of behavioral psychologists. What results is a

[30]For the meaning of this term, see chapter 6. See MacIver's *The Web of Government* (New York: The Free Press, 1965), chapters 8, 13.

[31]Such regimes as those of Japan or Mexico cannot, therefore. yet be considered fully democratic. Various parties do coexist in those political systems and elections are held regularly. But one party has held power continuously, either alone or in a coalition which it controls. Never yet has the opposition obtained office. As a consequence, the dominant party has become corrupted by its long tenure of office.

massive system of manipulating consumers by blending truth, half-truth, and untruth. For this, the most potent of media lies ready to hand. It is television—immediate in impact and, with its fleeting images, escaping critical analysis. When employed in a political campaign by the skilled practitioners of "public relations," candidates for office and party programs are packaged and "sold" as are laxatives and deodorants. And all of this costs billions of dollars, which the wealthy contribute. Thus can the oligarchy of the corporate rich prostitute the democracy of the mass.

These dangers, which have become very real, illustrate that general characteristic of the political process which I noted earlier. Conditions generate problems; these receive solutions, which then become problems requiring further solutions. The electoral system, as it evolved during the nineteenth century, contained many flaws which had to be corrected, and eventually were. New flaws are evident now, but built into the system itself is the opportunity for their correction. What is needed is political action to place legal curbs on the power of wealth and bridle the monster of television advertising in the public interest. That in turn will require a consensus between the political parties that the individualist concept of freedom must be tempered by the social value of fairness.

This raises, of course, the very large point that parties thus prepared to alternate in office do not disagree on everything. Overriding their differences on other matters is a consensus about the basic features of the system to which they belong. This is only another way, however, of describing the Constitution, which, as I stressed earlier, is essentially a political instrument. Its contents include those principles and procedures about which the parties are in the main agreed. Conversely, the parties give their general support to the constitutional system that embodies some of their wishes and guarantees each its place. A revolutionary party is, of course, one that wholly rejects these fundamentals and operates, whether from outside or inside the constitutional system, in order to destroy it.

The situation where parties cooperate in some matters, but compete in others, is precisely the crux of the problem discussed in chapter 2. There, I suggested that individuals and groups are thrown into social relationships by the contrasted, yet complementary, influences of cooperation and competition. The relation between parties and their constitution, and the manner in which government and opposition reciprocally contribute to freedom and to constitutionalism, afford an example of competition within a framework of cooperation. The forces operating at the core of the political process are based on the same principles as give rise to the formation of groups and the development of society itself.

Moreover, the possibility of cooperating and yet competing within the same framework is linked politically with certain requirements as to means and ends. If people are to coexist through constitutionalism, they must abandon violence. Otherwise, might prevails—whether this be the majority crushing a minority or a resolute minority intimidating an unorganized majority. Since the 1960s many countries rediscovered amid domestic turmoil a truth that had been forgotten since the thirties, that violence employed by any side begets its counterviolence. Once this happens, a community is drawn into a spiraling sequence of conspiratorial coercion, mob reaction, and police repression.

But to prevent recourse to violence, something positive is required. All individuals and groups in the society must be treated according to a common standard of justice in the sense that their basic substantive rights are respected and enforced. Whoever feel that they are denied justice and that the system of government is not responsive to their legitimate claims will be disposed to attack it with violence; that is, they will resort to extra-constitutional means. In that case, "law and order" are imposed by those who enjoy their benefits upon those who do not. Society will avoid disorders only when the order that the power of the state underpins by force is recognized as universally just—or as capable of achieving justice through flexible adaptation.

Flaws in the "Iron Law" of Oligarchy

To this argument, however, an objection has been raised which, if valid, strikes at the root. Against authoritarian doctrines that subject the governed to a ruling elite, the principle of freedom proclaims that the governed must and can control their rulers. For this to be realized in practice, the many have to be able to control the few. But can they? Some have denied that they can. There are influential thinkers who hold that all social activity requires organization; that organization evokes leadership by a few; that leaders must be in command over their followers; that so it has always been and ever shall be. Vilfredo Pareto is author of the saying: "In fact, with or without universal suffrage, it is always an oligarchy which governs, and which knows how to give whatever expression it likes to the 'popular will'." Roberto Michels formulated what he called "the iron law of oligarchy," asserting that in every human association power gravitates by an inevitable tendency into the hands of a few. By the force they wield, the fear they instill, the prestige they possess, and the propaganda they spread, the superior few outwit and overawe the mass. "Majority rule," "responsibility to the people," "popular sovereignty," and similar phrases are illusions which cunning rulers offer their unwitting dupes.

This view is backed by enough plausible evidence to have gained many adherents. Nobody would deny that all human institutions abound with examples of oligarchical rule. Scan the records of churches, clerical orders, armies, navies, universities, business corporations, trade unions, governments, political parties, civil services, and you find the same pattern of controlling cliques, power monopolies, and autocratic bossism. Our social history includes several upheavals against tyrannical authority that were designed to set people free but did not always turn out as planned. The Gospel of Jesus was a challenge to the might of Rome. Its teaching was pacifist and equalitarian; its ultimate political ideal, anarchist. But in a later century the church became wedded to power and then did what it deemed necessary to maintain its power. The French Revolution was initially dedicated to the principles of liberty, equality, and fraternity. Yet its attempts to usher in a new birth of freedom delivered the military autocrat Napoleon. The Bolshevik Revolution was once greeted with the plaudits of many an idealist who hailed it as a landmark in human liberation. But Stalin's relentless rule forged the fetters of a new despotism.

What does this add up to? That the larger part of the government of mankind has been oligarchic? That many a movement conceived in freedom has degenerated into its opposite? This much is true and cannot be gainsaid. When Michels spoke of an iron law, however, he was asserting its universal applicability. In one sweeping formula he sought to summarize the whole range of mankind's experience in constructing institutions to serve their needs. But is it true that all organizations have been, and must be, oligarchic? Apart from two exceptions—the military and civil services, both of which are universally built in hierarchical style from the top down—every institution offers some instances of control by their members. One may grant that democratic governments are imperfect and do not yet attain their own ideal. Nevertheless, to dismiss as a sham the record in countries great and small—in the United States, Switzerland, Great Britain, Norway, or New Zealand—does violence to truth.

The fact that power in any community tends to gravitate to a few and that authority is ordinarily exercised by a minority does not refute the possibility or genuineness of democracy. What makes the vital difference between dictatorship and freedom, between responsible and irresponsible power, is the method whereby authority is acquired, the conditions under which it is wielded, and the manner in which it is forfeited. The nature of power is changed—not merely its external apparatus, but its inner character—when its holders must run the gauntlet of periodic elections and respond to the charges and criticisms of a free press. Nor are such phrases as majority rule and popular control empty of all meaning. A system that invites its citizens to believe in these principles often ends by bringing the beliefs to life, for people will demand of their government that it pay more than lip service to its professions. Moreover, there is the corrosive effect upon the iron law of oligarchy of a two-party or multiparty system. It is not so difficult for a Fascist or Communist party in a one-party state—or any monopoly for that matter—to be authoritarian. But where a choice exists, the knowledge that people may select an alternative is itself a check against oligarchy. A party's rival is likely to create trouble for a controlling clique by encouraging its followers to rebel against their leadership, and such revolts, outside of a police state, are not so easy to suppress. Those who formulated this iron law did not pay enough attention to the mutual interaction of competing organizations.[32] For nothing does so much to keep us free as the chance to choose.

Civil Liberties

Where the opportunity exists to choose between two or more parties and to oppose a government within a constitutional framework, certain related liberties are found that negate or mitigate the strength of oligarchy. The state can be subordinated to popular control, instead of the people being subservient to the state, when freedom of association and the right to criticize are preserved inviolate. Without freedom of association one could not organize a group of like-minded individuals as an alternative to those in power. Without the right to criticize, genuine debate of public issues could never be conducted. These rights are in turn buttressed by accompanying freedoms which prevent enslavement of one's person or one's mind. Freedom from arbitrary arrest and secret trial, from seizure of one's belongings or cruel and unusual punishments, these and similar rights protect the liberty of the person. Equally important are the particular rights that add up to liberty of thought in general: the right of access to information and to publish without censorship, the right to read whatever one wishes, and the right of free speech.

For those who cherish the values of a free society, such rights are as indispensable as the air we breathe. The reasons for them are written in clear type in the annals of every police state, old and new, and in the long uneven record of humanity's intellectual progress. There would be no Bill of Rights in the United States today or its equivalent in any other democracy if dissident minorities and individuals had not clashed with past wielders of power in the name of truths they held to be self-evident. There would be none of our modern achievements in pure and applied science, no betterment in our methods of living together in organized society, if sone of our ancestors had not been willing at times to express unconventional ideas or challenge the established mores. The memory of Socrates before his Athenian accusers; of Jesus before Pilate; of the destruction of the library at Alexandria; of Roger Bacon, Copernicus, Galileo, and Darwin, whose scientific method demolished untruths sanctioned by the re-

---

[32]This holds true even when the competing organizations are themselves structured on nondemocratic principles. Acton makes the telling point that the modern democratic state evolved neither out of the medieval state nor from the medieval church, but from the struggle between the two. The fact is that, whenever an alternative exists, there is some element of freedom. It is monopolies which are coercive.

ligious orthodoxy of their time; of Spinoza excommunicated by his synagogue; of beliefs in sorcery and burning of "witches"; of propaganda and persecution as practiced by Joseph Stalin, Joseph Goebbels, and the Japanese thought controllers before 1945—these are salutary warnings to prove that the repression of individuals does not determine which ideas shall perish and which prevail.

But though political liberty depends on these accompanying freedoms, it is no simple task to dovetail them in the structure of the state. If a passion for order, pushed too far, can degenerate into authoritarianism, so can a zeal for liberty become license by excess. All rights involve responsibilities, and no right exercised within society is absolute. This is true, for example, of freedom of speech. On the principle that my right to swing my arm ends where the other fellow's nose begins, so must the right of free speech avoid infringement of the rights of others. Hence it is appropriate to have laws against libel and slander, or against incitement to violence.

Added to the difficulty of definition is that of enforcement. The rights of a citizen may be invaded by other citizens or by the government. They may therefore require protection by the government or against it. Rights produce their impact upon government, as does government upon rights, through the medium of institutions or agencies. How vigilantly these operate, how they are staffed, what precedents they develop, to what pressures they bow—this can make all the difference between paying lip service to freedom and actually practicing it. Traditionally, the branch of government that has encroached the most on civil rights has been the one whose opportunity is greatest—the executive. That was so under the regimes of absolute monarchy and continues to be true of the modern dictatorship. Naturally, since the executive administers the law and has military force, police, and prisons at its disposal, threats to liberty will always come from this source if such powers be abused.

For that reason, in countries where civil liberties have nurtured political freedom, the other branches—the legislature and judiciary—are often called on to champion the rights of citizens against executive invasion. But institutional history may so vary from one state to another as to place a different emphasis on the respective roles of legislators and judges. In the United States, where the hierarchy of law subordinates a statute to the Constitution, where the Constitution contains a Bill of Rights, and where it is the judges who say what the Constitution is,[33] the courts form the inner citadel in which the defense of civil liberties is conducted. Political factors, moreover, reinforce this arrangement. The courts—and more particularly the federal judiciary headed by the Supreme Court—are generally respected for their impartiality and scrupulousness. The same reputation is not enjoyed by Congress or the state legislatures. In general, the legislative

---

[33]This is the observation of the late Charles Evans Hughes. former chief justice.

branch has shown considerably less zeal to uphold civil rights than the judicial. Not infrequently it endangers them.

Finally, there is the problem of determining the ultimate sanction which guarantees that civil rights will be operative. Though it is valuable to spell out basic rights in classic formulas and constitutional definitions, those are not self-enforcing. Many a constitution has been drafted to include the finest sounding liberties that in practice were not worth the paper on which they were written. Nor does the secret of the defense of rights lie solely in such institutions as courts and legislatures, indispensable though these be. For institutions, like rights, will vary in effectiveness; courts may function under the shadow of intimidation; and legislatures may be maintained as a convenient fiction. The truth is that institutions are strong to the extent that a large enough section of the public feels keenly enough to have them so. Exactly the same applies to civil liberties. If enough people are sufficiently determined to preserve and exercise their rights, those rights will be exercised and preserved, and the institutions will then be found to do the job. But where that determination is lacking, no court, no congress, no parliament can fill the gap. The ultimate sanction, therefore, of all civil liberties resides in the source that creates the constitution initially and renders it effective—the political will of the people. Freedom in any society is what the people earn and guard for themselves.

10

Fourth Issue—Part 1

Concentration of Power vs. Dispersion of Powers

Power, Functions, and Institutions

Regardless of where authority originates—whether from the people or the government—questions arise about its organization and use. As the electricity generated at a dam is distributed by a network of transmission lines, so is the current of political power conducted from its source to the outlets where the functions of government are plugged in. The machinery for this consists of an elaborate set of institutions whose pattern may be variously designed. The issue is: What pattern to choose?

To understand what is involved, two earlier points are relevant—first, that people have needs which the state must satisfy, and second, that power seeks recognition as authority. These factors have a common bearing on an identical problem. Both the provision of services by the state and the structuring of its authority have the effect of stimulating the growth of institutions. Law enactment, for instance, produces a law-making body—the legislature; the quest for justice creates a system of courts; the mail is handled by a post office; and so on. Similar consequences follow from the mobilization of power, since the latter generates institutions to obtain results. The Roman Senate and Emperor; Britain's Parliament and Cabinet; the American Congress, President, and Supreme Court; Japan's Shogun; the Nazi *führer;* Italy's *duce;* the Politburo of the Communist Party in the Soviet Union—these are some institutions where the power produced by society is channelled and exercised.

Thus the machinery of government varies in design according to the needs of its consumers or the plans of its architects. The framework which fits prosperity and full employment may be ill-adapted to a depression. A structure suited to the tempo of peace will be streamlined amid the urgencies of war. If those in power desire to act with a minimum of delay or forestall challenges to their supremacy, they will weaken or destroy any institution where opposition can rally. This will involve concentrating authority to facilitate decisions, together with unimpeded communication from those who decide to those who execute. But if the overriding aim of constitution builders is to put brakes on the government, restrict its functions, and prevent abuse of power, institutions will be constructed on different principles. In any case, the ever-present problem, irrespective of the kind of government, is to devise machinery appropriate to whatever functions people expect from their state and to mesh political power with governmental institutions. In fact, the strongest institutions are those which are genuinely supported because they serve the citizens' needs and thus reflect the realities of power. But woe betide an institution that retains the outer shell of authority in which the kernel of power has shriveled up! Where revolutions occur—that is, where one form of political power is substituted for another—there is generally some change in the functions of government and always an overhaul of its institutions.

Centralism or Localism, Separation of Powers or Integration?

There are two angles for viewing the concentration or dispersion of authority. One kind of power relationship exists between a central government possessing jurisdiction over the whole territory of the state and the various localities into which it is subdivided. In some states local government is merely an extension of the center, and local officials are like the fingers at the end of a long arm controlled by a single brain. In other states local governments enjoy independence of central direction in varying degrees. A second power circuit arises from the relations between the various agencies constituted on the same level. It is possible to have one focal institution, to which the rest are inferior. Or powers can be distributed among several coordinate branches so designed as to maintain an equilibrium. The choice between strength at the center and strength in the localities is the difference between centralization and decentralization; the alternatives of having one integrating agency or several coordinate agencies form the contrast between integrating powers and separating them.

The Contrast between Athens and Rome

In politics, such questions are constant. They were raised long ago, which is proof enough, were proof required, that they comprise an issue basic to governments everywhere. In this respect the politics of antiquity provides a preview for modern controversies. There was a period when Athens itself fell under a *tyrannos*, Peisistratus, who gathered all power in his hands. After his system collapsed under his sons, a major stride was taken toward achieving popular self-government through the citizens' assembly. Its authority was limited, however, by the veto of a court, the Areopagus, which represented oligarchical influences. A more democratic system was instituted in the middle of the fifth century B.C., when the Areopagus was stripped of many functions and the power to declare legislation enacted by the people unconstitutional was transferred to the ordinary law courts where juries formed a microcosm of the citizen body. Thus a decision approved by a majority of the Assembly could be taken on appeal to the majority of a jury—an appeal presumably from the people drunk to the people sober. With this exception—that a sample of the people serving as a jury could be a check upon all the people serving as legislators—the structure of Athenian government was tightly consolidated under the authority of the Assembly.

The Roman experience contrasts with the Athenian.[1] The Romans vividly remembered the despotic rule of their last king, Tarquin the Haughty. After they drove him out, so intense was the feeling against the title of *rex* (king) and any type of one-man rule, that the Roman constitution evolved with a pattern in which authority was elaborately subdivided and distributed. Instead of one popular assembly, several coexisted with different functions and powers. Instead of one consul (the highest of the annually elected officials), there were two with equal status who could check each other's actions. And as if this were not enough, to protect the plebians from the upper class (the patricians), ten tribunes were instituted with power to veto a consul or any lesser official. Hovering between the assemblies and the magistracies was the Senate, possessing slight authority *de jure* but vast influence *de facto*. With such a system, small wonder that when the Romans faced an emergency, usually of a military nature, their constitution provided for a temporary integration of powers. This was done by appointing a *dictator* who for six months was the supreme commander of the army and dominated the civil government through martial law.

These arrangements were inadequate to govern an extensive empire. Neither the annually elected officials nor the assemblies nor even the Sen-

---

[1]This paragraph summarizes the results of a constitutional development spread over three centuries.

ate could maintain a continuous policy or keep a rein on commanders at a distance. A repetition of civil turmoil led to the drastic expedient of converting a republic into an empire under an emperor. The wheel thus turned full cycle. After failing with a dispersion of powers, Rome went to the extreme limits of integration.

Over the issue of centralism versus decentralism the experience of the Greek states also contrasted with that of Rome. The area of a *polis* was ordinarily so compact that problems of internal decentralization were scarcely pressing. Larger states, like Athens, did contain smaller units (the *demes*) for purposes analogous to local government. But these units were strictly subordinate to central jurisdiction. In fact, this emphasis on centralism contributed to the ultimate downfall of the city-state system, since the Greeks were unable to invent a workable method of consolidating their small states into a larger and stronger unit.[2] To this problem, however, the Romans found a solution. The vexed issue of how the central government could control the governors of imperial provinces was settled, as has been seen, by the emergence of an emperorship which engulfed the divided institutions of the Republic. But along with integration at the center, the emperors made it their policy to promote a measure of autonomy (or local self-government) in the cities of their empire. While fundamental questions of foreign relations, military security, and to some extent finance were reserved for the jurisdiction of Rome and its proconsuls within the province, on a wide variety of other matters local diversity and discretion were tolerated. The grant of special privileges of home rule to the *municipia* was one of Rome's outstanding accomplishments and partially explains the long duration of its empire.

The Medieval Dispersion of Powers

The Roman way of combining some decentralization with strong integration at the center was abandoned after that empire collapsed. Though municipal autonomy was permitted and encouraged at a time when the empire was firmly knit, Roman rule tilted the balance to the side of central supremacy. Medieval Europe, however, developed a social and political organization in which the scales dipped on the other side. Decentralization was the chief characteristic of that period, despite its theory of universal unity. Indeed, few facts impress the student of medieval government more forcibly than the contrast between the strength of localism and the weakness (sometimes impotence) at the center. To this end some of the weightiest forces in medieval society jointly contributed. The principal resource in the feudal economy was land, whose ownership and tenure were closely

[2]See chapter 12, section on "Anarchy and Imperialism in Classical Greece."

linked with the character of feudalism. Much of the land was parceled out in large-sized estates which were assigned as the property of a nobleman. Agricultural labor was done by tenants who occupied the lord's land, paying their rent in services and kind. In rural England under the manorial system[3] these formed a community which was largely, though not completely, self-sufficient. All tenants owed allegiance to the lord, while he owed them protection. For the nobility, besides being landowners, were also a political and military elite. The lord extended his influence to protect the vassals dependent on him. If able to bear arms, he was expected to don the heavy suit of mail, which only the wealthy could possess and which made the armored knight on his mount the heavy tank of medieval battlefields. Since the nobility occupied a strategic role in the administration of justice and in the mustering and supply of armies, since good highways were infrequent or nonexistent, and since the economy was organized around tightly knit local units, the political structure was not so much a state as a collection of estates.

Consequently, in the struggle between king and nobles—the key conflict of medieval politics[4]—the decentralized fragments were normally more powerful than the institution which represented centralism. As for the government that did exist at the center, the king, though he bulked largest, was by no means omnipotent. Wherever any council or parliament or estates-general was organized, even though its functions might be mainly consultative and its structure rudimentary, such a body was likely to limit the king, since in it the nobility were the mainstay. Furthermore, the presence of the church, in the Middle Ages a virtual state within the state, posed another obstacle to an ambitious monarch.

Sovereignty and Absolutism in the Nation-State

When the medieval order yielded to the nation-state, and a feudal economy to a mercantilist, the attempt was made in theory and practice to construct the government on opposite principles. In place of localism, the accent was put on centralization, drawing its breath of life from the new sentiment of nationality. To achieve this, it was, of course, necessary for the king to triumph over the aristocracy, a feat accomplished in every state that made the transition from medievalism. But royal supremacy over the nobles brought a further consequence besides centralization. The power redounding to the king at the center was concentrated in his office. Monarchy became the magnet, attracting local loyalties to the capital and the court, and

---

[3]For a detailed study, see E. Lipson, *The Economic History of England*, 12th ed., vol. 1 (Harper & Row; Barnes & Noble, 1959), chapters 1–2.

[4]See chapter 9, section on "The Struggle between Kings and Nobles."

overriding the separatist tendencies of competing institutions. Hence, with centralization came integration. From both, the king was the gainer. Theorists justified these facts by the new doctrine of "sovereignty."[5] The consolidation of power, which this term signified, meant the recognition of one supreme will, paramount over other central agencies and local particularisms. The identification of the symbol of sovereignty with the office of monarchy was easily brought about. The king was "the sovereign" personified. What could be more simple?

Thus was inaugurated in Europe a period in which monarchy attained its zenith, accumulating so much power as to merit the description "absolute." Never was this absolutism more fittingly epitomized than by Louis XIV of France, the Sun King, in his remark "L'Etat, c'est moi," a comment whose boast of personal preeminence exceeds even the claim of Adolf Hitler: "For 24 hours I was the supreme court of Germany," or the statement "I am the law," attributed to a sometime mayor of Jersey City.

But as often occurs in politics, what was originally justified in response to public need can degenerate with lapse of time. Exaltation of the monarch, who served as a foil to the obnoxious nobility, outlasted its usefulness when the power of the nobles was reduced or when an incompetent sat on the throne. In various countries, therefore, resistance developed to royal absolutism and to the identification of sovereignty with monarchy. This opposition culminated in the three revolutions out of which the modern democratic state was born. What bearing did these have on the issue of concentration versus dispersion of power?

Parliamentary Supremacy in Britain

The English Revolution, lasting from 1640 to 1688, was the earliest, and provided an example for others to copy or alter. It was from the membership of the House of Commons and within its chamber that much of the protest was voiced against the autocracy of Charles I. Parliament thus spearheaded the rebellion against the king. But an army was needed to fight Charles and his supporters. The occasion found Oliver Cromwell, who organized the "New Model Army" on the parliamentary side. When the battle was fought, however, and Charles had been executed, Parliament was closed down by its new master, who preferred to govern without assistance from the legislature. Not until after Cromwell's death, the restoration of the Stuarts, and their final expulsion in 1688, was the supremacy of Parliament over the crown irrevocably established. What was thus accomplished politically then received legal recognition. The sovereignty that

---

[5]See chapter 6, section on "Monism Again: The Theory of Sovereignty," and chapter 9, section on "Rise of the English Parliament."

once belonged to the monarch was transferred to Parliament, which thereby became the omnipotent lawmaker. Integration continued, therefore, to be the keynote of the British political system, but with the important difference that the supreme institution was henceforth a legislature, not a monarch. The supporting theory was stated by Locke: "In a constituted commonwealth standing upon its own basis and acting according to its own nature, that is, acting for the preservation of the community, there can be but one supreme power, which is the legislative, to which all the rest are and must be subordinate. . . ."[6]

Nor was legislative supremacy diminished when the judiciary received permanence of tenure by the Act of Settlement of 1700. During the struggles of the mid-seventeenth century, the relation of the judges to king and Parliament was much debated. Against a royalist like Bacon, who contended that judges were "lions *under* the throne," Chief Justice Coke argued for judicial review of the constitutionality of parliamentary acts and royal actions. To him the principles of the common law imposed a restraint on both, and it was for the judiciary to expound those principles. Parliament, however, after its successful rebellion against the monarchy, insisted on subordinating judges to itself, while still requiring that they be independent of the executive. Judges were neither to be intimidated by the crown or its agents nor be subjected to pressure in deciding particular cases. But they must accept as definitive the law which Parliament enacted and were never to invoke some other law as higher.[7] That principle stayed in force until 1973 when Britain joined the European Economic Community, thereby according the Rome Treaty a higher status than an Act of Parliament.

The French Pattern of Unified Power

The French Revolution, though it postdated the American, can be discussed next, because in this respect the pattern of its institutions resembled the British. Through the many stages of France's revolutionary agony runs one persistent theme—the concentration of all power in a single supreme body. Whether that were the Convention or the Directory made little difference from the standpoint of integration. The new rulers of France were conducting revolution, whose temper and tempo do not brook opposition, delays, or checks and balances. One critical difference did exist, however, between the British and French situations. The European repercussions of France's revolution exposed that country to invasion, and before long its domestic upheaval embroiled the nation in foreign war. Whereas the English Revolution produced a civil war and required an autocrat to lead

---

[6]*Second Treatise of Civil Government,* chapter 13, sec. 149.
[7]See chapter 9, section on "The Revolution in England."

Parliament to victory, the revolution in France, which lacked the advantages of an island, led to conflict with its neighbors and discovered the military genius of Bonaparte. His dictatorship, however, was imposed for longer on the French than that of Cromwell on the English, first because the survival of the nation was more imperiled by foreign than civil war, and then because of Napoleon's far-reaching ambitions. So deeply was the mark of Napoleonic statecraft imprinted on the government of France that when his empire was replaced by constitutional monarchy, and that in turn by a democratic republic (1875–1940), the principles of integration and centralization remained. Both of the constitutions which France has tried since 1945, despite their differences in spirit and structure, have been similar in this respect. The Fourth Republic embodied the principle of legislative predominance. Its regime was a *gouvernement d'assemblée*. Equally strongly, and by reaction against the executive weakness of the Fourth, the Fifth Republic—created by General de Gaulle—reverted to the Bonapartist type in its aims and administration. The nucleus of power became the presidency. Animated by the *mystique* of a France revivified, de Gaulle ruled his country with a blend of personal prestige and popular referenda. Others were allowed to talk, but he alone decided. Understandably, the three presidents who followed him—Pompidou, Giscard d'Estaing, and Mitterrand—were less autocratic. Neither in personality nor in their political base did they possess his strength. Nevertheless, in marked contrast with France's recent past, the presidency continued to be the focal institution of the regime.

Or so it was until 1986. The legislative elections of that year produced a result which had not previously occurred under the Gaullist Constitution. Until then, the President, whether of the Right or the Left, had always had the support of the majority of the Assembly. Now, however, the French found themselves confronting a situation with which Americans are all too familiar. The President, a Socialist, belonged to the Left, while the parties of the Right had recaptured the legislature. There ensued, instead of presidential leadership, a division of power between the President (Mitterrand) and a Prime Minister (Chirac) drawn from the conservative end of the political spectrum. For this novelty, the French found a name: They called it "cohabitation." That lasted two years. In 1988, after Mitterrand won a second consecutive term, the ensuing legislative elections resulted in no majority. The future of relations between President and Assembly is still unclear.

It would appear, therefore, that the French were belatedly putting into practice the ideas of Montesquieu rather than those of Rousseau. But although Montesquieu had traditionally been ignored by his fellow countrymen when they drafted their constitutions, he was not without influence. For his were the ideas which helped in 1787 to shape the government of the new republic of the United States.

Separation of Powers in the United States

The American Revolution resembled the British and French in being directed against an authority uncontrollable by the governed. Moreover, in practically all the state constitutions adopted within the first decade of independence, as in the machinery set up by the Articles of Confederation, the clear objective was legislative supremacy. That the legislature should have been chosen for this role is understandable in the light of the part played by the colonial assemblies in resisting British authority. "Thus in a typical revolutionary manner," writes William Anderson, "all powers of government were brought for the time under a single control, that of the convention or congress in each state. Perhaps in no other way could the quick and decisive measures have been taken that were needed to sever the bonds with Great Britain. Surely it was no time for a separation of powers and checks and balances in government."[8]

A short experience with legislative predominance, however, convinced the country's leading spirits that concentration of power in any one institution is fraught with abuse. Consequently, it was Jefferson who wrote thus about the first constitution of Virginia: "All the powers of government, legislative, executive, and judiciary, result to the legislative body. The concentrating these in the same hands is precisely the definition of despotic government. It will be no alleviation that these powers will be exercised by a plurality of hands, and not by a single one. One hundred and seventy-three despots would surely be as oppressive as one."[9] The same point was observed by Madison, who warned: "The legislative department is everywhere extending the sphere of its activity, and drawing all power into its impetuous vortex. . . . They [the founders of our republic] seem never to have recollected the danger from legislative usurpations, which by assembling all power in the same hands, must lead to the same tyranny as is threatened by executive usurpations."[10]

If concentration of power was the evil to be avoided, was there, besides executive or legislative omnipotence, some third possibility? The answer was the introduction of what has come to be called the separation of powers. The republic of the United States has followed the model of the republic of Rome in the respect that its institutions have been intentionally constructed with the aim of dispersing authority. Let us see how this came about and what the results have been.

Prior to its adoption as the architectural design of American government, the doctrine of a separation of powers had evolved in long, slow

---

[8]*American Government* (New York: Holt, Rinehart & Winston, 1938), pp. 39–40.
[9]*Notes on the State of Virginia,* Query XIII.
[10]*The Federalist,* no. 48.

sequence. Its origins are in Aristotle, who distinguishes three "parts," or branches, of government—the deliberative, executive, and judicial.[11] Aristotle, who is generalizing, from Athenian practice confines himself to a description of their personnel, organization, and functions, and leaves it at that. The modern phase of the doctrine opens in seventeenth-century England and belongs to the inquiry into the fundamentals of politics stimulated by the Puritan revolution. Locke argued that three powers exist in every commonwealth. These he called legislative, executive, and federative—the last being equivalent to the conduct of foreign relations.[12] The executive and federative powers, he pointed out, "are always almost united," to which union he expressed no objection. But it was otherwise with the relation of the executive power to the legislative. The latter "in well-ordered commonwealths, where the good of the whole is so considered as it ought," is placed in the hands of an assembly that convenes at intervals. But since the administration and enforcement of law is a continuous task, a power distinct from the legislative must remain "always in being." In practice, therefore, "the legislative and executive power come often to be separated." In principle, however, there is also a good reason why this should be so "because it may be too great temptation to human frailty, apt to grasp at power, for the same persons who have the power of making laws to have also in their hands the power to execute them."

The Ideas of Montesquieu

It was this insight that formed the theme in the next development of the doctrine. The French writer Montesquieu visited England in the middle of the eighteenth century and compared favorably the independence of the judges and the strength of Parliament with the subordination of the judiciary to the French monarchy and the virtual extinction of the Estates-General. Not foreseeing the rise of the cabinet system in Britain, and wanting to substitute individual liberty for royal absolutism in France, Montesquieu advocated the separation of powers as a device to make government safe for the governed. The division of powers that he envisaged was similar to Locke's conception. But in his insistence that they must be entrusted respectively to different personnel he went considerably beyond his predecessor.

> In every government there are three sorts of power: the legislative; the executive in respect to things dependent on the law of nations; and the executive in regard to matters that depend on the civil law. By virtue of the first, the

[11]*Politics*, iv, chapters 14–16.
[12]*Second Treatise of Civil Government*, chapter 12, secs. 143–48.

prince or magistrate enacts temporary or perpetual laws, and amends or abrogates those that have already been enacted. By the second, he makes peace or war, sends or receives embassies, establishes the public security, and provides against invasions. By the third, he punishes criminals, or determines the disputes that arise between individuals. The latter we shall call the judiciary power, and the other simply the executive power of the state. . . . When the legislative and executive powers are united in the same person, or in the same body of magistrates, there can be no liberty; because apprehensions may arise, lest the same monarch or senate should enact tyrannical laws, to execute them in a tyrannical manner. Again, there is no liberty, if the judiciary power be not separated from the legislative and executive. Were it joined with the legislative, the life and liberty of the subject would be exposed to arbitrary control; for the judge would be then the legislator. Were it joined to the executive power, the judge might behave with violence and oppression. There would be an end of everything were the same man or the same body, whether of the nobles or of the people, to exercise those three powers, that of enacting laws, that of executing the public resolutions, and of trying the causes of individuals.[13]

While the framers of the American Constitution were profoundly influenced by Montesquieu,[14] their own experience reinforced the persuasiveness of his theory. The governmental system with which they had the longest and closest acquaintance—that of the colonial period—embodied a species of separation. Prior to 1776 the executive branch under its governor was distinct from the legislature, and controversies between them were rampant in the two decades prior to independence. The statesmen of that day were equally familiar with the principle of judicial review (at least when applied to an inferior legislative body), since the validity of colonial enactments could be challenged before a British court, the Judicial Committee of the Privy Council. History, therefore, united with philosophy in writing a separation of powers into the federal Constitution.

Design of the American Constitution

To be precise, however, the separation of powers was not stated explicitly in the Constitution. For an exposition of the principle one must turn to the constitution of Massachusetts, which affirms: "In the government of this commonwealth, the legislative department shall never exercise the executive and judicial powers, or either of them; the executive shall never exercise the legislative and judicial powers, or either of them; the judicial shall never exercise the legislative and executive powers, or either of them; to

[13]*Spirit of the Laws*, XI, 6, ed. Franz Neumann, trans. Thomas Nugent (New York: Hafner Publishing Co., 1949), pp. 151–52.
[14]Note Madison's remark in *The Federalist*, no. 47: "The oracle who is always consulted and cited on this subject is the celebrated Montesquieu."

the end that it may be a government of laws and not of men."[15] In the United States Constitution the principle is more implied than asserted. Hence a need arises to understand what kind of separation is intended. Clarity is obscured, however, by the use of the ambiguous term *powers*. The meaning of the doctrine can be better analyzed if one drops the reference to powers and distinguishes between *branches* of government and their *functions*. A branch is an organization of agencies with their personnel. The services they undertake are their functions.

If this distinction is borne in mind, the doctrine can be redefined and its logic expressed as follows. The activities of government group themselves into three divisions. Observation may verify that these divisions exist, for they arise not from preconceived theory but from the character of the functions. It is one thing to legislate, another to administer, a third to judge. How can these three activities be embodied in the institutions of the state? If separation is the intent, a government should consist of three branches, each having its own personnel. Assign to one of these the entire function of lawmaking; to a second, the whole of administration; to a third, all the judicial process. Thus by creating three distinct branches for the three functions, the structure of government will incorporate the principle of separation.

To what extent was this achieved in the federal government of the United States? The Constitution certainly does establish three branches and staffs each of them with separate personnel. Expressly, it prevents any legislator from simultaneously holding either an executive or a judicial office.[16] Simultaneous tenure of executive and judicial offices, however, is not explicitly forbidden. But on this score the text could safely be silent because judicial independence of the executive, secured in England in 1700, had already entered into the American tradition and, being no longer controversial, did not need to be written down. The question whether a senator or representative could administer an agency was still unsettled. Therefore the solution had to be written.

The threefold division of functions, however, was not designed to correspond unambiguously with the organization of the three branches. Instead of assigning a whole function to a single branch, the Constitution distributed them. The bulk of each function was apportioned to one branch, but smaller slices were given to each of the other branches. In legislation, for example, most of the lawmaking power was placed in the Congress. But the president received a share in the powers to recommend measures, to summon Congress into special session, and to veto their bills. The Supreme Court, likewise, by exercising the power of judicial review, asserted its claim to a portion of the legislative function. Similarly with the

---

[15] Preamble to the Massachusetts Constitution, Sec. 30.
[16] *United States Constitution*, Art. I, Sec. 6.

judicial process, though most of this is undertaken by the courts, Congress acts in a judicial capacity in cases of impeachment, where the House is empowered to prosecute and the Senate sits in judgment. The president, too, can intervene in the business of the courts through his power of pardon for all offenses except treason and by nominating the judges.

Hence the term *separation of powers* oversimplifies a complex set of facts. Though many have misunderstood the doctrine, the leading lights at the Philadelphia convention did not deceive themselves about what they were doing.[17] Because portions of each function were distributed among agencies with different personnel, the "separation of powers" was intended to result in a system of checks and balances. Ordinarily, unless the members of the three branches cooperated harmoniously, none of the principal functions of government could be adequately performed. Conversely, a branch or pair of branches that sought to overstep their constitutional authority could be restrained by the refusal of a third to connive.

The Tradition vs. Modern Dynamics

It was only to be expected that an institutional framework which emerged from the political upheavals of the seventeenth and eighteenth centuries must undergo later adaptation. As the age of Jefferson, Napoleon, and Nelson receded into history, Western societies faced fresh problems, or new forms of old ones. An industrial revolution, geared to a novel technology which harnessed unprecedented quantities of energy for manufacturing, upset the equilibrium of primarily agrarian economies. The extension of occidental influence around the world, first under European and then under American leadership; the ambition of new states such as Germany or of such old ones as Japan; the impact of two global wars; the revolutions in Russia and China; the emergence of independent states in Africa; the growth of a mass franchise and demands for social reform; all these were bound to impose a strain on structures designed originally for different loads.

Two other factors were responsible, however, for more immediate effects on the relation between legislature, executive, and judiciary. These were the sheer increase in the functions of government and the rise of organized parties with a mass following. As the state enlarged its activities, the burden on all branches increased. Lawmaking bodies had to decide new issues of public policy, discuss fresh objects of expenditure and modes of revenue, and grant the statutory authority. The courts found their dockets crowded as they were called on to interpret legislation and review ad-

[17]For example, Madison in *The Federalist*, nos. 47–48.

ministrative acts. But the greatest expansion occurred in the executive branch, for there lay the responsibility of translating policy into practice. Every new service the voters thrust upon the state, every additional power the government sought, ended in executive expansion. New programs brought more agencies into being, thus multiplying the number of civil servants. Huge sums of public money were theirs to disburse. Broad legal powers were entrusted to their discretion. In their files and records a vast store of specialized information was garnered. The administrator's status was converted from that of amateur to professional, skilled in managing the relations between people.

These changes resulted in shifting the foundations on which the doctrine of the separation of powers was built. Locke had conceived of the relation between the three powers in terms of legislative supremacy. Montesquieu and Madison preferred an equilibrium between three coordinate branches. Despite such differences, however, all of them joined in opposing executive predominance, which they associated with royal absolutism. But though no longer linked with monarchy, executive predominance or something close to it has prevailed in the twentieth century. This is to be explained not only by the contrast between the small number who compose a legislature or a judiciary and the huge staffs engaged in administration, but by some further advantages possessed by the latter. The strength of a judiciary, for example, lies in the mastery of the content of law, which requires trained practitioners and familiarity with complicated texts. On these counts the civil service based on the merit system of appointment and promotion—that great innovation of the late nineteenth century—has nothing to yield to the judges! The complexity of public administration, its large-scale character, its technical content and intricate procedures, its opportunities for a life-long career and the system of recruitment and promotion by merit, have made public employment a profession comparable to the practice of law. Neither is more nor less scientific than the other; to the uninitiated, both are mysteries.

The role of legislator, by contrast, has not become so professionalized. Attaining office by public election, the legislators serve the majority of their constituents; and since the support of the latter may switch, the legislature offers no guarantee of steady employment. Although that service, if continued long enough, trains a person in the work of government, the relation of legislator to civil servant is that of part-time amateur to full-time expert. On one side are political backing, legal powers, financial authority; on the other, specialized technical competence. A legislature supervises, watches, inquires, and castigates. But if the state, in the final analysis, is what its functions are, a government becomes what its functionaries do. It is the administrator who makes or mars the policy. Power, in daily practice, resides in the hands that execute and enforce. Small wonder, therefore, that much modern government has come to be realistically described as bureaucracy,[18] or rule by the bureaus.

In still another respect have modern developments upset the original concept of the separation of powers. Besides changing the relation of the three branches, the needs of modern government have blurred the distinctions between the three functions. Administration and adjudication, for instance, no longer seem as different as they once were. Both judges and administrators apply broad rules of law to individual cases, each possessing within limits some discretion in fitting the particular facts under the general principle. Bureaus and courts alike are engaged in the same task of law enforcement,[19] the essential difference being that the former take the initiative in administering the law whereas the latter must wait until a dispute arises and one party seeks a judicial settlement. Nor is the function of lawmaking as dissimilar from that of law enforcing as it was once thought to be. Owing to the intricacy of modern social problems, the formulation of general principles and the administration of concrete facts are no longer clear-cut or sharply separable. Many intermediate steps must be taken before broad rules are narrowed down to the particulars.

A realistic way to visualize the process of contemporary government is to think of concentric circles. Each circle represents a field of choice among a number of possible policies. When one of these is adopted, the next smaller circle provides for a new choice—limited and bounded, of course, by the previous decision—and so on. Most legislation now has to be supplemented by rules, regulations, or orders, which spell out the generalities of a statute. Certainly at the higher levels of any department, the work of officials is primarily concerned with matters of policy, on which subject they render advice to members of the legislature and give instructions to their subordinates. Between a whole people adopting a constitution and one mail carrier delivering one letter to one address, there are rings within rings of diminishing fields of choice and narrowing decisions. The molds have broken in which the thoughts of Locke, Montesquieu, and Madison were cast; their contents have spilled together.[20]

---

[18]Like the term *politician, bureaucracy* has acquired some unfavorable connotations. But it can be used neutrally and descriptively, as above.

[19]Courts in earlier periods performed many administrative services, and still perform some.

[20]A familiar example of this is the so-called regulatory agency (for example, the Securities and Exchange Commission). Under an act of Congress these issue rules, enforce them, and serve as tribunals to hear disputes and complaints. Their work, exemplifying the unity of the governmental process, marks a fusion of powers rather than a separation.

Effect of Political Parties on Institutions

The rise of the executive branch to preeminence, however, and the blurring of the traditional division of functions are not due solely to the increase of governmental activities. Besides the organization of the career civil service a second novelty of the nineteenth century was the political party with its mass following. Parties had no place in the calculations of those who espoused the doctrine of the separation of powers.[21] But their impact on the separation was bound to be felt after the extension of the franchise had encouraged the electorate to mobilize under the banner of parties and thus compete for control of the state. Being a newcomer to the political scene, the mass party lacked restraining inhibitions about the sacrosanctity of separation. Avid for power, it was less scrupulous about the nicety of distinctions between powers. It would not willingly exempt any segment of authority from its grasp. What constitution framers had trisected and put asunder, the party was prepared to reunite.

Thus, from Jackson's era to Cleveland's, the American parties made their onslaught on the institutions of government. Jobs in public offices were the spoils of political warfare, to be looted after an electoral victory and used to grease the party machine. Simultaneously, the civil service was filled with partisan employees of uncertain tenure and dubious qualifications. Almost the same treatment was accorded to the judiciary. The party wanted to control the courts because of their role in law enforcement plus their power to review legislation. Where judges were elected to the bench, as in many state and local governments, the parties determined the selection of candidates and ensured the support of the voters. Or, if the judges were appointed, the party could influence the chief executive who made the nomination and the senate which confirmed. The capture of the legislature, and of elective posts in the executive branch, was achieved through the electoral system, where the parties maintained a firm grip on nominating procedures and methods of balloting. The extreme point in these developments was reached when the party fell under a boss. Often without even holding public office, a boss was able by his mastery of the party machine to achieve a concentration of power that violated the fundamental concepts of American democracy.

Fortunately, the popular reaction to the scandals, which in this instance, as usual, accompanied excessive power, ushered in a trend of reforms designed to purify the processes of government and restore to the people their birthright of political authority. Slowly, but surely and inexorably, the evil of bossism, entrenched in many sectors of American public life, was attacked and, if not completely eradicated, at least reduced to

---

[21]See chapter 9, section on "The Key to Freedom."

smaller and safer proportions. Slowly but surely, around two institutions, the civil service and the courts, a *cordon sanitaire* of political neutrality has been drawn. Since law must be applied by both bodies with fairness and honesty, there is no room for spoilsmen in the bureau or partisans on the bench. Administrators and judges must be kept independent of party pressure—in one case through security of tenure and appointment by merit, in the other by nonpartisan election or selection.

While dams were thus erected to hold back the floodwaters of party power, alternative channels had to be provided into which the new pressures could flow beneficially. Since parties brought politics in their train, any place in the governmental system that fitted one was appropriate for the other. Plainly then, the correct fields for parties to penetrate and occupy were the legislature and the elective offices of the executive branch. These areas were rightfully theirs. Few[22] would want to see the parties ejected from the institutions that represent and translate the preferences of the voting public on broad issues of economic and social policy. But that being so, if it were permissible for the parties to capture the presidency and governorships and to organize majority and minority caucuses in Congress and the state legislatures, the structural separation of the executive and legislative branches was certain to be modified by the party tie. Though discipline within the party may not always be strong, though there may be opposition to the leadership of the chief executive, nevertheless a common interest of a sort—even if it is no more than the desire to keep their side in power—unites all those who bear the same label. Unless they hang together, they are more likely to hang separately!

Government by Party and Civil Service

Thus a study of the party system and its consequences suggests that modern government can be viewed in a fresh way. In the eighteenth century government was explained in terms of three powers with their corresponding branches. The nineteenth century, under the stimulus of expansion both in the electorate and in government activities, witnessed the formation of two potent institutions—the political party and the civil service based on the merit system. When these were superimposed on the preexisting trio of branches, the junction of two such newcomers with the three older bodies produced initial friction because the older institutional framework had to accommodate itself to the intruders. In the twentieth century the governmental process has consisted increasingly of a partnership between party and civil service. These between them have harnessed administrative tech-

---

[22]Exceptions are the states of Nebraska and Minnesota, whose constitutions require nonpartisan elections of members of the legislature.

niques to political strength, and it is in their hands that effective power lies. Most of the work of the modern state is accomplished by party and civil service together.

New Role of the American Presidency and Governorship

In the United States clear evidence of the joint impact of party and civil service is revealed in the modern status of most presidents and governors. When the potentials of each office are developed, its occupant ceases to be a chief executive in the narrow sense, and becomes in addition a party leader, chief legislator,[23] and mobilizer of public opinion. This is an accurate description of the role played by outstanding presidents, such as Wilson and the two Roosevelts, and by successful governors, like the elder La Follette of Wisconsin, Smith and Rockefeller of New York, and Warren of California.[24] Their leadership has been dual, since it was felt in both branches, the legislative and executive. To them may be applied the words which Water Bagehot used to describe the British cabinet in the mid-nineteenth century: "a *hyphen* which joins, a *buckle* which fastens, the legislative part of the state to the executive part of the state."[25]

Various circumstances have combined to thrust the chief executive, whether of a state or of the United States, into a more prominent role. A new dynamism was infused into politics by a continent-wide expansion, rapid industrialization, and the mounting demands of underprivileged people for a more secure status. As a consequence, people who had some common interest to promote formed pressure groups to influence legislative action. Issues of public policy were aired in public debate. Party organizations had to decide what course of action to endorse—or of inaction, since dodging or straddling an issue was itself a decision. Inevitably this situation created the opportunity for a person or agency to give a lead. It was possible for that leadership to emanate from the legislature, but difficult, because in a bicameral body there were usually several members in each house with independent influence who competed for the limelight. Thus a tactical advantage lay with the chief executive, since the White House or governor's mansion had only one occupant, who could always command an audience and evoke a following. For this, the constitutional powers of the office provided a springboard. Presidents and governors

[23]This is a phrase used by Howard L. McBain in *The Living Constitution* (New York: The Macmillan Co., 1937), chapter 4.
[24]See my work *The American Governor: From Figurehead to Leader* (University of Chicago Press, 1939; reprinted by Greenwood Press, 1969).
[25]*The English Constitution.* World's Classics edition (London: Oxford University Press, 1928), p. 12. Italics in original.

took part in legislation through their powers to send messages, recommend measures, summon special sessions, and veto bills. In addition, they could harness other techniques to supplement their strategy. By the use of patronage, jobs could be traded for votes.[26] By appeals to the voters through oratory, the press, radio, and television, chief executives have dramatized their programs and compelled consideration of their views. In this way, the presidency and governorship became the focal offices in national and state politics whereby the force of public opinion and the power of the party system have been funneled into the structure of the Constitution.

But leadership is a two-edged sword. Whether the results are good or bad depends on the direction sought and the methods employed. And these flow in turn from the qualities of the person leading, not primarily from his or her strength, but from corruption or integrity, folly or wisdom. In the state governments, there are abundant examples to illustrate the point. California found a statesman in Warren, but leadership of the opposite kind in Reagan. Hatfield and McCall were strong and enlightened in Oregon, whereas Faubus in Arkansas and Wallace in Alabama, although equally strong, were pernicious. Power in politics is not enough; it must be used with wisdom.

It is at the federal level, however, that the potency is greatest, as is the potential for weal or woe. Presidential power has increased so vastly since World War II as to disrupt the equilibrium between the three branches. There were times in the past when the legislature or the judiciary overstepped its bounds. In the 1880s Woodrow Wilson criticized Congress for arrogating too much power. Half a century later, when the Supreme Court was nullifying one statute after another, the feeling spread that the judges had gone too far. Most recent is the aggrandizement of the presidency, whose growth since World War II has become cancerous. I use that term intentionally, for I believe that, if the office continues as it has been under Johnson, Nixon, and Reagan, democracy in the United States will be destroyed.

The abuses of presidential power, most glaringly displayed by those three, have their source in the position which the United States has come to occupy in world affairs since 1945. The combination of industrial and technological capacity, military might, and financial strength brought into being an American empire whose institutional expression has been termed the Imperial Presidency.[27] The consequential effects in the operations of the American government have been pervasive and profound. What has developed in the executive branch since 1945 is a dual system. The national government has functioned at two levels simultaneously—one visible, the

---

[26]This technique was formerly more effective than it is now because of the extension of civil service protection to large numbers of government jobs.

[27]The title of a book by Arthur Schlesinger, Jr.

other invisible; one democratic, the other undemocratic; one within the law, the other outside the law. The visible portion consists of the three traditional branches and those executive agencies which operate in the public eye and are open to scrutiny. The invisible part lies below the surface, as hidden as possible. Its activities are clandestine; its watchword is secrecy; its professed objective is to ensure national security as defined by itself. Here are conducted the espionage, the counter insurgency, the covert operations of several departments. Those generally known are the National Security Council, the Central Intelligence Agency, the Federal Bureau of Investigation, the National Security Agency, and branches of the Pentagon. Their activities have included political assassinations, the training and deployment of their own armed forces, and the overthrow of foreign governments. At times, the foreign policy thus pursued is the diametrical opposite of the official policy proclaimed in public at the visible level.

Central to this whole deplorable development has been the presidency, because it is here that the supreme executive authority is located over the two levels, visible and invisible. Increasingly since the 1960s, the White House has acted on a double standard of morality. Presidents have regularly lied to the American people, while their National Security Advisors and Secretaries of State and Defense strove to conceal what the invisible government was doing.[28]

Acting in this fashion, Lyndon Johnson launched a large-scale war in Vietnam which was never declared by the Congress as the Constitution requires. Richard Nixon extended this war by bombing targets in Cambodia and deliberately falsifying the military records. What is more, he employed the personnel and resources of the invisible government in undercover activities so as to undermine his domestic political opponents, thereby assuring his reelection as President in 1972.[29] Ronald Reagan pursued a relentless campaign to overthrow the Sandinista regime which had replaced the Somozas in Nicaragua. When Congress by law prohibited American military aid to the so-called "Contras," his administration con-

---

[28]Nixon concealed the bombing of Cambodia from his own Secretary of Defense. Reagan similarly kept his Secretary of State in the dark about many aspects of the tortuous negotiations to sell arms to Iran in exchange for Americans held hostage by terrorists.

[29]How serious has been the growing power of the secret police in the United States can be gathered from a comment of Richard Nixon's, revealed in *The White House Transcripts* (New York: New York Times/Bantam Books, 1974), pp. 77–78. In a conversation with John Dean on 28 February 1973, Nixon was speaking thus of the power vacuum at the head of the FBI since the death of J. Edgar Hoover. "Well, Hoover performed. He would have fought. That was the point. He would have defied a few people. He would have scared them to death. He has a file on everybody." The potentiality in these files for political blackmail is dangerously clear. The *modus operandi* of the invisible government is documented in ample detail by Seymour M. Hersh in *The Price of Power: Kissinger in the Nixon White House* (Summit Books, 1983). See also Bob Woodward's *Veil: The Secret Wars of the CIA* (Simon & Schuster: New York, 1987).

tinued for two years to support their military campaign through the actions of its own officials and by encouraging private donors and foreign governments to pay for weapons. In addition, funds obtained from the sale of arms to Iran, which was itself illegal,[30] were then diverted in a further illegality to finance the Contras. The principle that the United States has a government of laws, not of men, has been covertly subverted by at least three Presidents, who together dealt serious blows to the American constitutional system. These abuses of presidential power since the mid-sixties threaten democracy at its source. Of all forms of government, democracy depends most on the popular feeling that those elected to office can be trusted. That trust vanishes when the public learns that the government has pursued policies in secret which it has sought to cover up with lies and which were in some instances illegal. The Imperial Presidency stands in contradiction to the Constitution.

Cabinet Dominance in Britain

A comparison of the American with the British development is instructive. It is one of the ironies of political science that Montesquieu based his doctrine of the separation of powers in large part on his study of the British system, where he believed it to be embodied. He omitted to notice, or failed to consider significant, the rise of the cabinet in the reigns of George I and II, and the emergence under Sir Robert Walpole of the prime minister as the cabinet's presiding officer. It was the cabinet, however, that became the power center of British government and made the fusion, rather than separation, of powers its focal principle.[31] In the course of two and a half centuries the cabinet has risen to preeminence because of the same factors as have modified the American system—the extension of the suffrage and of governmental functions, the organization of the party and the civil service, and the leadership until 1945 of a worldwide empire.

There are three stages through which the cabinet has passed. The first lasted from the accession of George I in 1714 to shortly after the close of the Napoleonic Wars in 1815. During that period the cabinet successfully emancipated itself from royal domination. In so doing it was aided by the

[30]At that time, the United States was prohibited by law from supplying arms to governments engaging in terrorist activities. Iran was one of the countries on the State Department's publicly announced list of terrorist regimes. How much Reagan himself was involved, directly or indirectly, in the diversion of funds to the Contras will never be proven. Crucial documents were deliberately destroyed in the National Security Council by Lieutenant-Colonel Oliver North. Moreover, the key figure, William Casey, Director of the CIA, died early in the inquiries. Of the statements on this subject by witnesses to the congressional investigating committee, some were contradictory; some were implausible (e.g., those of Admiral John Poindexter, the former National Security Advisor).

[31]The only exception to this statement is that the judiciary, though subordinate to Parliament, is independent of the executive.

lucky accident that the first George, a German prince from Hanover, did not speak English and ceased to preside at cabinet meetings. This duty was then left to a leading, or prime, minister. With the monarch absent, ministers were a little safer in opposing his wishes and could reinforce one another by assuming collective responsibility for decisions. When George III, who was English-born, sought to revive the royal power, the failure of his policies in 1776 and his illness in the later years of his reign enabled the cabinet to reassert its supremacy over the crown.

The second stage opened with the beginnings of parliamentary and electoral reform in the early 1830s. In the middle of that century the extension of the franchise encouraged the growth of a party structure among the voters, whose allegiance, particularly when newly enfranchised, the parties were eager to capture. Increasingly, therefore, candidates were elected to Parliament because of their affiliation with a party and support for its program. This process, however, took time to consummate because economic and social conditions were fluid and the population and the electorate were expanding. Hence, although party discipline was crystallizing within the legislature, there were still minority blocs and numerous independents whose political eddyings could determine the rise or fall of governments. Cabinets in this period, therefore, were dependent on the House of Commons and it was there that they could be made or unmade.

The third stage commenced around 1884, when adult male franchise was attained. The consequent increase of the electorate made stronger party organization both desirable and imperative. Because campaigning in a larger constituency cost more money, local candidates depended on central endorsement and assistance. Since the central organization of the party was controlled by its parliamentary leaders, they had the wherewithal to influence the votes of the parliamentary rank and file. As the two-party system became more firmly established, and the number of independents in the legislature dwindled into insignificance, the majority and minority in Parliament were predetermined by the effectiveness of party discipline. Only in the rare event of a split within the major party, or during the temporary existence of a three-party system,[32] can Parliament now reassert its power to make the cabinet. The rule in modern times has been that the people decide at the polls which party shall have a legislative majority, and

---

[32]This occurred in Britain in the 1920s, when the Liberals were declining and Labor was gaining strength. Half a century later the Liberals revived because of public disillusionment with the two major parties. In the general election of February 1974, they received one-fifth of all the votes, but succeeded in capturing only 14 of the 635 seats. Neither they, nor anyone else, held the balance of power. That election was the first since 1929 that failed to produce a parliamentary majority. In the early 1980s, some of the right wing of the Labor Party, alienated by left-wing militancy, resigned and then formed a Social Democratic Party which entered into an electoral alliance with the Liberals. This centrist alliance received 22.5 percent of the votes in the 1987 election, but because of the mechanics of the electoral system won only 22 seats. In 1988 the majority of the Social Democrats merged with the Liberals in a new party.

the party leaders decide the composition of the cabinet. Normally, a twentieth-century British Parliament records the popular choice in much the same way as the electoral college ratifies the American people's choice of a president.

Nor is this all. The cabinet's functions are not limited to the legislative sphere. They embrace the executive branch by virtue of the fact that members of the cabinet are ministers of the crown. Severally, they are responsible for administering the various departments of state. Collectively, they must weave together the countless strands of administration and decide the broadest issues of national policy. To accomplish this, they have at their command the skill and resources of the civil service, which staffs the agencies that ministers direct. The role of the cabinet, therefore, is essentially dual. In that body resides the ultimate responsibility of leadership in the legislative and executive spheres alike. The cabinet has proven itself a flexible institution (though currently overworked), where the potencies of party and civil service are fused.

Within the cabinet the office of the prime minister has acquired a significance which at times suggests analogies with the presidency. Not all British Ministries function the same way, any more than Administrations do in the United States. Both institutions contain a minimum of constitutional authority, which is supplemented in varying degrees by the political strength of the president or premier, by that individual's personal magnetism or lack of it, by energy or passivity. Who presides makes a difference, and both offices have their political history of alternative strength and weakness. A cabinet containing many powerful politicians and strong personalities may need a moderate conciliator in the chair. At other times, dynamic qualities will come to the fore, the nation can be bound by one person's spell, and the cabinet (not without some resistance) follows along. Disraeli and Gladstone, Lloyd George and Churchill, mark the high peaks where the premier is as preeminent as the greatest of presidents. On the other hand, the case of Margaret Thatcher, like that of Ronald Reagan, demonstrates what harm can occur when leadership is strong but not wise.

But personalities apart, another set of dynamics—those of a long-term political change—has thrust the premiers into the forefront, even when a particular incumbent fell below the stature of the greatest. Changes in telecommunications and air transport since 1950 made it easy for heads of government to consult regularly by telephone and to meet face-to-face whenever the situation required. At the same time, the solutions for major economic and diplomatic questions have lain outside the sphere of any single government and have therefore prompted joint measures between several governments.[33] In consequence, the most important external nego-

---

[33]On this trend, as it concerns the declining viability of the nation-state, see the discussion in chapter 13, section on "Region-States in the Making?" and chapter 11, section on "The Individual in Revolt."

tiations are now conducted directly between prime ministers and their equivalents. This has meant, of course, a relative downgrading of the other principal figures in the cabinet—the foreign secretary, chancellor of the exchequer, and secretary of defense.

A century ago the American and British systems were poles apart. More recently, however, they have tended to converge toward a common denominator. This does not mean, of course, that the distinctions have been obliterated. There is still a crucial contrast between a leadership exercised within the legislature and one exerted from outside. There are divergences due to dissimilar electoral patterns, since in the United States it is possible for the party opposed to a president or governor to have the majority in one house or even in both. Furthermore, the relatively disciplined character of the British parties make parliamentary action more predictable than the actions of American legislatures. Also, the dismissal of a prime minister who has botched the job and lost support in the party and the country is far easier to accomplish in Great Britain (witness the substitution of Churchill for Chamberlain in 1940, or that of Macmillan for Eden in 1956) than is the removal of the president in the United States, where the impeachment process is both cumbrous and archaic, as the Nixon case exemplifies. Nevertheless, the similarities between the two systems are now at least as significant as their differences, and at certain periods—still admittedly the exception rather than the rule—they function alike. Franklin D. Roosevelt's relations with Congress early in his first term strongly resembled a prime minister's relation to the House of Commons. Conversely, during the war years from 1940 to 1944, Churchill's relation to the Commons—which he attended infrequently and where he spoke only on major occasions—was not unlike the contact between Congress and the president. Affected by the same influences, both systems have changed, and it is arguable that they may evolve into a new hybrid uniting some features of each.

The Legislature and the Courts

At this point, however, a word of caution is necessary if misunderstanding is to be avoided. To say that the party and civil service have been superimposed on the three branches does not mean that the latter have been replaced or obliterated. Likewise, the argument that presidents and governors have risen to a new peak of power, or that the cabinet has become preeminent over crown and Parliament, does not imply that legislatures and courts are nullities and no longer perform a useful function. It is true that there has been a change in relative power, but it is not true that institutions, now less influential than they once were, have been discarded.

Courts of law continue to be indispensable bulwarks of personal freedom, since they offer a tribunal where citizens who are involved in a dispute or who have a case against their government may sue for justice. To this end it is essential that courts be immune from outside pressure, that they prevent an arbitrary use of executive power, and that, under the American system, they prohibit violations of the Constitution by a legislative majority or a self-willed President. If courts be guardians of personal freedom, it is the legislature that safeguards political freedom. In systems of government which place a premium on discussion, criticism, and opposition, the interplay of rival parties is deemed valuable and constructive. The institution designed for this purpose is the legislature. Here the parties meet and are tested in public debate as it is intended they should. Here alternative policies are proposed and analyzed, and popular grievances are ventilated. The party and the civil service could wield their power and perform their jobs without the presence of a judiciary and legislature. But their regime would not be one of liberty; even if it were efficient at the outset, it would, if history is a safe guide, end in corruption.

Ultimately, therefore, it is on the legislature that political freedom depends, since it is here that government and the opposition to government are both rightfully represented. The legislature constitutes the public forum where the power of leadership confronts the power of criticism. Much is at stake, therefore, in how the legislature discharges its responsibilities. If the legislature does not merit the people's respect, if it succumbs to the pressure of special interests, if it fails to strike a balance between the roles of a rubber stamp or a negative obstructionist, then it does democracy no service, since it forfeits its claim to be the unique institution differentiating democracy from dictatorship.

The Power Pattern of Dictatorship

Dictatorship differs from democracy not in degree, but in kind. What I have discussed in this chapter are variations of the democratic pattern ranging along a scale where powers are dispersed at one end and concentrated at the other. When the latter trend is carried to the nth degree, however, it becomes a characteristic of a dictatorial regime. On this point the modern examples not only resemble the tyrannies and despotisms of the past, but in some respects outdo them because the techniques of oppression available today are far crueler.

In twentieth-century dictatorships, the executive government is carried on through the twin media of a single party or the army plus the civil service. But these institutions, though employed by democracy and dictatorship alike, differ radically in the two contexts. The spirit and status of a party are completely changed when only one exists legally and therefore possesses a monopoly. Likewise the army or the civil service in a one-party state cannot maintain the political neutrality that is expected when two or more parties alternate in office.

A dictatorship goes to extreme lengths in subjecting other branches to the domination of the executive. In any case with political relevance, the courts may not render a decision contrary to the will of the party leadership. Judges must be mice under the throne. So too with the legislature, which in a dictatorship is a superfluous and dangerous institution, since it could be a rallying point for opposition. Dictators, it is true, frequently permit the outward form of a legislative body to survive. But the form has no content. By packing it with party stalwarts, convoking it at long intervals, and controlling its agenda and procedure, the dictator turns it into a receptive sounding board for his own and his party's propaganda. Such was the fate of the Italian Parliament after 1925 and the German Reichstag after 1933. Similar has been the history of the Soviets in Russia. Those representative assemblies were constructed in 1917 by the revolutionary movement both as an instrument of opposition to czarism and as a nucleus for a new government. But because they were elected bodies, the Soviets contained within themselves a seed of democracy which Stalin did not permit to grow. Under his rule, therefore, the Soviets were reduced to a nullity. Any possibility of their independence was throttled by the stranglehold that the Communist party secured over them.

As examples of power concentrated to its utmost, compare the autocracy of the Russian czars before 1905, the dictatorship of Stalin in the USSR, Hitler's regime in Germany, Mussolini's Fascist system in Italy, and the oligarchy of militarists, bureaucrats, and businessmen who dominated Japan from 1931 to 1945. In more recent decades, examples abound of individuals who have aggrandized themselves at the expense of their rivals, crushing their opposition with force and grabbing all power for themselves. Nor have such dictators been only military men or Communists; nor have they arisen only in older states where the system was traditional. The Ghanaians won their independence from the colonial control of Great Britain. But Kwame Nkrumah proceeded to imprison his political opponents, to dismiss judges whose decisions he did not like, to censor the press, and to conduct a campaign of personal glorification, until retribution caught up with him. In the Republic of Haiti, a former doctor maintained a brutal tyranny over a people who were mostly backward, poor, and illiterate. Idi Amin, Bokassa, Pol Pot are names from recent times to remind us that Plato's depiction of Greek tyrants in the *Republic* or Dante's characterization of their Italian equivalents in the *Inferno* were no mere fantasies of a poetic imagination. When political power is totally unrestrained, its capacity for utter evil creates hell on earth.

To sum up, two quotations will serve. Said James Madison: "The accumulation of all powers, legislative, executive, and judiciary, in the same hands, whether of one, a few, or many, and whether hereditary, self-appointed, or elective, may justly be pronounced the very definition of tyranny."[34] The head of the government of a newly independent state described himself thus: "I am the boss and anyone who does not know that is a fool. I decide everything without consulting anybody and that is how things will be done in Malawi. Anyone who does not like that can get out."[35]

[34]*The Federalist,* no. 47.

[35]A quotation from Dr. H. Kamuzu Banda, prime minister of Malawi (formerly Nyasaland). *New York Times,* 20 September 1964. He was still in power in 1987.

11

Fourth Issue—Part 2

Localism, Centralism, and Federalism

Areas and Government

No modern government, not even the smallest, can transact all its affairs in one place. Because the territorial range of the state is coextensive with society, wherever individuals have contacts, situations will arise which call for government on the spot. Thus a modern political system, whatever its nature, requires a local administration. Two questions must then be settled: What functions should be assigned to which level? Which authorities should be preponderant, the central or the local?

The issue posed in these questions has several ramifications which are fundamental to statecraft. Ever since governments were organized territorially, their structure has necessarily been influenced by area. The state is conditioned by geography as much as by history. Its operations extend not only through time, but through space. Hence the problem recurs of relating its functions, institutions, and jurisdiction to the area it occupies. This is no easy puzzle to solve because the fittest boundaries from the standpoint of one function are seldom appropriate for another. A large city will obtain its water supply from one place; its electricity and other forms of power may come from a second; its sewage will, or should, be disposed of in a third. A transportation system connecting the sections of a city and linking it with adjacent suburbs will assume one shape; but the organization of districts for schools or the prevention of air pollution or crime may require yet other contours. Food for the urban population will be drawn from nearby farms, and from distant flour mills, stockyards, fruit orchards, and fishing grounds. The livelihood of the city dweller, who must find employment in a factory, business office, or retail store, depends on the intricate relationships of complex economic mechanisms whose boundaries may be national or international. Finally, the military defense, which in the Middle Ages was provided by the stout stone wall around the city's perimeter, depends today on submarines or on satellites encircling the globe. In short, each function of government, plotted geographically, projects itself on a map corresponding to its own needs; and if the maps were superimposed, no two would coincide.

How can we best adapt the structure of the state to interests and services which are spread out in such different patterns? The answer is a common-sense solution. Since it would be impossible to organize separate governmental systems with different areas for every function, and since identical areas would be unworkable, a compromise must be adopted. This consists in distinguishing needs or problems of general concern from those whose range is essentially limited. Hence the familiar division between a central agency and units of more circumscribed range.

The Community of Interest

Besides this argument of convenience, the case for separating local authorities from central is reinforced by further considerations. It is undeniable that proximity creates a community of interests. People who live in the same neighborhood have many ties. They are equally concerned about sanitation and public health, about water and similar essentials, about transportation to and from their work, about shopping and recreational facilities. The inhabitants of the same area are in constant contact. They meet face-to-face and communicate directly. Their daily activities bring them together; their children go to the same school or playground; most of their friends live within easy reach. In such circumstances, many elements basic to the community are present, for a community consists in a sense of solidarity evoked by common interests and shared experience.

But it is also possible for that feeling of oneness to extend beyond the finite area of face-to-face relationships, provided common interests exist and similar experiences are perceived. People are united, for instance, by the problems of growing and selling the same crop. Thus the Old South paid homage to "King Cotton," as do Canadian prairie farmers to wheat and São Paulo *fazendeiros* to coffee. Membership in the same religion may serve as a bond, as with Catholics, Jews, or Moslems, who are scattered among different localities, nations, or continents. So may people be drawn together who speak the same language, or have similar systems of government, or belong to one cultural tradition. Politically, all such wider unions—or extended communities—are reinforced when the territory they occupy forms a physical continuum. What gave the Old South its strength and made secession seem practicable was the compactness of the cotton kingdom. What consolidates the French-speaking Canadians, besides their church, is their concentration in the Province of Quebec. An extended community is always stronger when its members are contiguous than when they are dispersed. For like reasons, because proximity makes organization easier, a concentrated minority is generally more effective than a scattered one of the same size. If this were not so, it would be impossible to explain the separation of Ulster from Eire, Norway from Sweden, Israel from the Arab states, or Pakistan from India.[1] Pakistan itself broke up after two decades, its eastern portion becoming the state of Bangladesh. This occurred because Bengal and the Punjab, though united by religion, differed in language and other aspects of culture as well as in economic development. It was impossible to organize a common government for two distinct regions separated by a thousand miles of Indian territory. Community depends on communication. "Decentralization," "local autonomy," "states' rights"—such terms and all that they imply are derived from the fact that in politics proximity makes a difference.

Boundaries and Psychology

Moreover, a political boundary itself contributes to a sense of solidarity. It would be erroneous to assume that a community of interests is a result, transferred to politics, of causes that always originate in other social groupings. One of the most important of the experiences that unite a group is that they share the same government. The structure of the state has no less intimate an effect on the organization of society than society has on the state. When territorial areas are demarcated so that jurisdictions and services may be organized, symbolic associations tend to cluster around the same boundaries. Cooperative sentiments of pride and loyalty, along with competitive attitudes of jealous rivalry, attach themselves readily to spatial units. Both large and small cities can evoke in their inhabitants a city-centered patriotism. People then become conscious of their identity as Londoners, Parisians, New Yorkers, Bostonians. Or they may identify

---

[1]However, the geographical concentration of the minority, though vital in all these cases, is not the sole explanation of such splits. Sometimes the resistance which the local minority offers to the majority is fortified by a potent group outside. The support of Protestant Britain was indispensable to Ulster; that of the Moslem peoples in the Middle East, to Pakistan; that of American and British Jewry, to Israel.

themselves with some wider, yet politically articulated, areas. A county, perhaps, or a province, or a state within a union acquires an individual character: Witness the traditions and folklore of the Vermonter, the Texan, the Bernese, the Gascon, the Castilian, the Yorkshireman. Or the area may broaden out into regional dimensions, as long as it is endowed with recognizable features, real or supposed; for example, New England, Dixie, the Highlands, the Midi, the *Sertāo*[2] the Outback.[3]

It is the purpose of boundaries to divide. Physical separation lends itself to psychological alienation. All who are on "your" side of the line belong to "your" group; those beyond it do not. This feeling is heightened by the opposition that can arise mutually between different communities. A pair of cities may develop a rivalry, as in the cases of San Francisco and Los Angeles, Toronto and Montreal, Sydney and Melbourne, Madrid and Barcelona. So may a pair of counties like Yorkshire and Lancashire in England; or two cantons, such as Bern and Zurich; or two provinces, like Ontario and Quebec; or two sections, like North and South. It is precisely because of the psychological significance of boundary lines that common speech confers a symbolic meaning, of deeper import than their literal one, on such terms as "crossing the Rubicon,"[4] "beyond the Pale,"[5] "the Chinese Wall," "the Mason-Dixon line," and "the Iron Curtain."[6]

Local Liberties vs. Centralized Dictatorship

Local loyalties, regional rivalries, and separatist sentiments, where they exist in force, are barriers to unity and therefore to centralization. But a further factor, sometimes working in conjunction with these influences and sometimes operating independently, also produces a decentralizing effect. It is the fear that power is always susceptible to abuse, and that any accumulation of power not counterbalanced by an independent power can become dangerous. This is the core of the argument against monism, since the net result of ecclesiastical or business autonomy was to create social structures largely exempt from the control of the state and therefore capable of resisting or obstructing it. This is equally the logic of the separation of powers, since

[2]The arid area of northeastern Brazil.

[3]The interior of Australia.

[4]This river formed the boundary line between Italy proper and the province of Cisalpine Gaul. In 50 B.C., Caesar led his army south across it, which the governor of a province was forbidden to do. Thereby he declared war on the central authorities in Rome.

[5]When English power was expanding in the Middle Ages, the area where English law and jurisdiction prevailed (for example, in France, Scotland, or Ireland) was called the Pale. Those outside it were not subject to England. The same term was used to describe the area in Russia where Jews were allowed to settle by the edict of 1792.

[6]Compare the expression that used to describe the gulf between social and economic classes in an urban community, "the other side of the tracks." Nowadays, when freeways cut a swath through a city, they divide its population as the railway used to do.

there can be no omnipotent state to fear if the institutional structure of the government is dispersed in the form of coordinate branches. Likewise, this is the rationale of a preference for federalism and for "local liberties," the assumption being that Leviathan's grip is weaker when its skeleton is loose-jointed. Local or state governments, on this theory, can be made partly independent of the center, so that they may provide focuses of resistance if tyranny should ever be established there.

The nature of such tyrannies has been too vividly exemplified in modern times to doubt their character. Modern dictatorships are a product of aggressions, attaining control by violence. Because their regimes are founded primarily on force, not on right, they remain insecure even after they have come to power. Hence they continue to vent their aggressiveness against their opponents and any institutions where opposition can rally. If the government at the center is dictatorial, it is obvious that local parties can become a medium for criticism and local government a vehicle for opposition. To prevent this from happening is important to the modern dictatorship, which never feels safe unless its control is total. Thus the authoritarian regime eliminates any traces of local autonomy and subordinates all local authorities to the central will.

That autocracy is unlikely to permit decentralization is exemplified equally in both extremes of Right and Left. Before Mussolini's supremacy was established in Italy, the system of local self-government, despite its shortcomings, was an outlet for local feeling. This was particularly so in the regions of Tuscany and Lombardy, where famous cities flourished, where geniuses had lived and worked, and where historic events were cradled. The dictator, however, prizes dependence in his fellow citizens, not independence. The Municipal Council of Milan, for instance, had been controlled by Mussolini's political opponents, the Socialists. This he could not permit. So he abolished the locally elected councillors and substituted an official, the *Podesta*, appointed from, and responsible to, the center. The same practice commended itself to Adolf Hitler, an authoritarian centralist by temperament and conviction. In the German Empire, which Bismarck made by blood and iron, and in the Weimar Republic, which the moderate left and center parties created after World War I, the structure of the state was federal. But Hitler would have none of it. As he consolidated his power after the summer of 1934, he proceeded to abolish the Lands (or states) that had composed the federal system. Then, applying the *Führerprinzip*, he organized the German government from the top downward, appointing in each region and district a hierarchy of officials (*Gauleiters* and others) whose power derived from his.[7]

---

[7]It should be noted that in the Italian Fascist and German Nazi cases, this excessive centralism represented in part a reaction to the lateness of both countries in achieving national unification. See chapter 12, section on "The Problem in Europe."

In the Soviet Union, the Communist dictatorship, as Stalin practiced it, conformed to the same tendency. In semblance, at least, a federal structure was adopted which contrasted with the centralization of the Romanoffs. Moreover, in reaction against the czarist policy of "Russification"—a requirement of cultural uniformity imposed on the Poles and other minorities—the Bolsheviks initially sponsored a program of cultural diversity. But circumstances conspired to suppress these decentralizing influences.[8] In the economic sphere a centralizing factor of great importance was the series of plans, prepared and directed in Moscow, and encompassing the entire Soviet Union. To these national plans the policies of the component "republics" and "autonomous states" were subordinated. At the same time, the monopoly of power by a single party prevented that interplay between the Union and its components which is so characteristic of federal politics. In the face of the discipline of the Communist party and its hierarchical command, no unit of government could deviate from the central line. Finally there was the incalculable force of Stalin's personality, which did not brook opposition and would not see authority delegated. A Georgian from the Caucasus, Stalin had made himself supreme over all the Russians, and, like many a leader who emerges from a minority group on the border, he evolved into the supercentralist.

The Special Case of Yugoslavia

The exception among Communist regimes is the case of Yugoslavia, and it is worth examining. When Tito proceeded to govern Yugoslavia after the defeat of the Nazi invaders, he first sought his inspiration in Moscow and imitated the Stalinist model. In practice, however, Stalinism broke down for reasons both economic and political. With their diversity of cultures, languages, and religions, the Yugoslavs did not take readily to the centralism which Stalin's methods demanded. Industrial production did not revive as expected, and the attempts at enforced collectivization of the peasants were a failure. Politically, this proud and independent people resented the domineering attitudes of Russian "advisors" in Belgrade. In 1948, when three-quarters of his foreign trade was directed East and the Red Army was on the Romanian border less than a hundred miles from Belgrade, Tito had the courage to dismiss the Russians and break with Stalin. The Georgian despot declared that he would bend his little finger, and Tito would fall. But in this instance he had not correctly assessed either the man or the situation.

Since then, and aided by the United States after 1950, the Yugoslavs

[8]Soviet publicists themselves recognized this aspect of the facts by describing their system as "democratic centralism." Centralism it certainly is; democratic it is not.

have experimented along their own lines. What they have thus far developed is something different. It is not the same as the Communist systems to the east of them, nor does it resemble the practices of North America or Western Europe. In eclectic fashion, they have pioneered a mixed political economy whose blend is original. To understand and appraise it, one should review the intention and the results to date.

The essential feature of the Yugoslav experiment is the insistence that every social activity or economic enterprise—be it a factory, hotel, orchestra, or housing development—should belong collectively to, and be managed by, the persons who work in it. This is the principle of ownership and control by the producers of a commodity or service, which is how socialism is interpreted in Yugoslavia.[9] In order to convert this principle from theory to reality, the Yugoslavs concluded that their system requires maximum decentralization. Popular ownership and operation would be more genuine if the local community—not the central government—were in charge. Consequently, the system they introduced was built, somewhat like the Swiss, from the local level up.

It is rare for practice to conform to principle. What then is the situation in Yugoslavia? Do the realities match the theory? The answer is that the match is only partial. If traced on paper, the actual evolution of policy would not be a straight line, curve, or spiral, but a zigzag. The Yugoslavs have experimented with something which is difficult anywhere and is novel in the light of their past traditions. To encourage the citizens of a local area, or the members of a particular enterprise, to share personal responsibility for policies and to supervise their administration intelligently and conscientiously, is a tremendous task in civic education. The public must be well informed, and the directors of enterprises require training and experience. Since Yugoslavia was deficient in both respects, mistakes were made. But making mistakes and learning to draw the right lessons from them are aspects of the process of self-government. At any rate, the country has faced the implications of transforming a mass of subjects into communities of citizens.

Besides the problems of converting theory into practice, the Yugoslav system contains inherent contradictions. There are factors of a political nature which militate against some of the intentions previously described. Although the avowed aim of the regime is to decentralize and to rely on local initiative, centralized planning continues. Nor is this avoidable. In various aspects of its social and economic development, Yugoslavia has far to go before it catches up with the countries of Western Europe. The responsibility for adopting measures to strengthen the country as a whole has necessarily fallen on the government at the center. At the same time, internal conditions have varied considerably because of the contrasting

---

[9]As distinguished from its interpretation in Russia, where the owner is the state.

legacies that Yugoslavia inherited from the Hapsburg and Ottoman empires and the destruction of different areas in two world wars. Slovenia and Croatia, for example, are considerably more advanced than Macedonia and Montenegro. But to achieve an internal redistribution, using the resources of the more developed regions for the benefit of the less developed, requires central power, central planning, and central budgeting. Under these circumstances, the desire for control of economic enterprises at the local level may not be readily reconciled with the priorities and programs that the national government seeks to establish.

A similar contradiction has permeated the politics of the system. It has been normal for Communist parties to be centrally disciplined and to be directed from the top. Also, in Communist practice, Marxist theories notwithstanding, the subjective cult of an individual personality has loomed larger than objective laws of historical development. How does this fit in with the Yugoslav emphasis on community initiative, flexible experimentation, and local responsibility? The answer is that their system is neither one thing nor the other. The contemporary regime is still in the course of transition and exhibits opposing tendencies. Both within the Communist party and outside, spokesmen advocate alternative lines of future development. For three and a half decades, one man and one party were politically preeminent. Tito emerged the victor in a war which was civil as well as foreign, and after it was over, he conducted a genuine revolution. During those periods and when Stalin was seeking his destruction, his government dealt roughly with opposition. But once his power was consolidated and his position was secured, his rule underwent a subtle evolution. He gained a wide respect and popularity for the valid reasons that he had defied both Hitler and Stalin, preserved his country's independence, and accomplished more than anybody else to unify it. In addition, as a Croat, he was sensitive to the internal diversities of so complex a society and well understood that centralized uniformity or domination by a single group would be inconsistent with Yugoslav realities.[10] Hence he, the autocrat, encouraged the policy of decentralization.

Under these conditions, the Communist party also modified itself. To express its distaste for a centralized monolith of the Stalinist type, it changed its name from party to league. Within its ranks, distinct groups evolved in the 1960s arguing—even in public—for different policies. Some contended that the Communists should retain their monopoly as the unifying, directing force in the government, the economy, and society at large. Others believed they should withdraw from positions of control and increasingly share their power, functioning as a source of ideas, enthusiasm, and criticism. Tito himself responded to these discussions in a manner that

---

[10]I once heard a Yugoslav scholar say: "Yugoslavia is a country with six republics, five cultures, four languages, three religions, two alphabets, and one party."

not only showed extraordinary flexibility for a man in his seventies, but also indicated a statesmanlike resolve to safeguard the future. When he ousted Rankovic and his entourage, he stopped a tendency that could have restored the Stalinist model of an authoritarian police state. Then, after the Soviet occupation of Czechoslovakia, he reorganized the personnel and structure of the Communist party by promoting younger individuals into the top leadership.

Subsequently, however, his course again zigzagged in reverse. When dissident Croats, operating in and out of Yugoslavia, launched an overt terrorist campaign against his regime, Tito reacted with vehemence, discerning a threat to the fragile unity of Yugoslavia as well as to his personal authority. In the course of that reaction, much of his earlier tolerance was sloughed off. Critics were punished; the Communist leadership in Croatia was purged; questioning intellectuals among the professors and students found their freedom severely limited.

After 35 years of continuous supremacy, Tito died in 1980. The system which he bequeathed was designed for two purposes: to prevent any other one individual from wielding as much power as he had, and to institutionalize at the top the internal diversities of Yugoslav society. Leadership would be collegial as in Switzerland. The members of the executive committee would represent the component republics and they would rotate in the chair.

It is too early as yet to pass judgment on these arrangements. But some preliminary comments may be made. As with other countries, Yugoslavia suffered in the global depression of the early 1980s. The government responded with an austerity program, demanding sacrifices of its citizens. The national regime has already had to counter the inherently centrifugal character of the varied religions and ethnic groups, as was discovered in the outburst of resentments among the Albanian minority in Kosovo. Also, the Muscovite Bear used the occasion of Tito's demise to initiate a season of courtship, seeking to woo back into its embrace these errant southern Slavs. The only sure prediction is that this unique Marxist experiment has a full complement of problems ahead.

Freedom at, or from, the Center?

Yugoslavia resembles Switzerland in being the exception to many generalizations. Centralism is so common wherever a single party or person predominates that one wonders whether this combination reflects a natural affinity and whether centralism and liberty are incompatible. Some argue that political freedom demands substantial decentralization. Both statesmen and scholars have developed the theme that local self-government spells local liberties, which add up to the sum of national liberty. History supplies evidence for this view. In England, for example, the grant of corporate privileges to London and lesser cities, and the growth of a rural administration in which the country gentry (as distinct from the higher nobility) played a major role were factors that encouraged a sturdy spirit of resistance to anything smacking of oppression from the center. Moreover, in local politics and administration many persons discovered a preparatory training ground where they were initiated into the art of government before deploying the experience thus gained at the national level. These are considerations too important to be overlooked.

But in a broader perspective one notes that sin is no monopoly of the center, nor virtue of the localities. Examples of despotism emanating at the center can be matched by as many cases of local dictatorship. "There are village tyrants as well as village Hampdens."[11] People have often sought the aid of a distant protector to defend them from a nearby oppressor. The local bully—whether landowner, bishop, captain of industry, or political boss—could not always be resisted by the people of the locality where he dominated. If they were to be freed, he had to be overawed by some greater power from outside. In short, dictatorship can reign at the center; but so can freedom. There can be local tyrannies; or alternatively, local liberties. Local independence may defy a central dictator; and freedom, centrally organized, can defeat a local autocrat. Political chemistry is a rich amalgam of the same basic elements in diverse formulas that are combined in new compounds.

Unitary and Federal States

Though modern dictatorships prefer a centralized structure, it does not follow that contemporary democratic states are decentralized to the same degree. Wide differences exist and are expressed in contrasted institutional patterns. The most familiar is the distinction between unitary states and federal. In the former the government is organized on two levels only—national and local, the latter comprising both urban and rural authorities. A federal state has three levels instead of two, since between the national government and the local ones there is an intermediate layer, designated as states in the United States or Australia, as provinces in Canada, or as cantons in Switzerland. Intergovernmental relationships are therefore more complex in federal systems than unitary. In the latter, only central-local and interlocal relations exist. But in the former, the relationships are federal-state, federal-local, and state-local, as well as federal-state-local and

---

[11]Justice Jackson, in *West Virginia State Board of Education v. Barnette*, 319 U.S. 624 (1943). Gray in his "Elegy Written in a Country Churchyard" spoke of: "Some village Hampden that . . . the little tyrant of his fields withstood."

interstate and interlocal. Hence, delimiting the jurisdictions and meshing them together is far more intricate. Federal systems are thus more legalistic, more "jurisdiction-minded," and slower to act.

But caution is needed, lest these generalizations become oversimplified and inaccurate. Besides the distinction between federal and unitary, further differences occur within each category. Unitary states can be highly centralized, for example Denmark and New Zealand; or centralized to a lesser degree, as is Britain. A federal union can be decentralized in the manner of the United States or Switzerland; or it may distribute powers in favor of the center, as in Canada.

Centralization in Britain

A review of some contrasted types will make these points clearer. Great Britain is a democratic state whose structure is both unitary and centralized. How important are its local governments and what functions do they perform? A product of ancient traditions continuously readapted to social change, the design of British local government has never been uniform, simple, or logically consistent. Its outline combines the practicable and the desirable, the old and the new. Certain features in this blend endow the system with its general character. One is the differentiation between the metropolitan areas, where population and industry are highly concentrated, and the rest. A second dominant trait is the dependence of local governments on financial aid from the center, and their legal subordination to Parliament. A third factor is the principle by which functions are distributed between the two levels. Let us see what bearing this has on the dispersion or concentration of power in the British system.

Even when the structure of the state is specifically designed to avoid excessive centralization, it is impossible to determine the best allocation of powers with certainty. In Britain decisions about what functions "belong" to the national or local level have been influenced by social clustering, political pressure, fiscal resources, and historical tradition. In certain cases a dividing line between local and national concerns can be drawn without too much difficulty. Maintaining a fire brigade, for example, or providing public transport for an urban population inside municipal limits is clearly appropriate to local authority. On the other hand, the organization of a police force to protect persons and property—a function which could be either central or local—has remained under local control,[12] largely through a series of historical circumstances hardening into tradition. Modern social

---

[12]The nature of modern crime detection, however, and the problems of apprehending criminals have enlarged the activities of Scotland Yard as a nationwide police service. In addition, through its grants to local bodies, the Home Office prescribes general standards to which the local police must conform.

and economic changes have evoked a national concern in matters where the original emphasis was primarily local. In a complex of contributing factors, the root cause can be traced to the expansion of industry with its consequent stimulus to population growth and urban concentration. Britain has 24 percent of the population of the United States in an area equal to the state of Oregon. Even within that small space, a high proportion of the people are densely congested in the London area, the Midlands, the industrial North, and the "waist" of Scotland. The larger cities not only increased in size, but their suburbs and satellites sprawled into the nearby countryside. Their economic urgencies and opportunities, acting as a magnet, drew the rural economy into their orbit. The culture of the capital, transmitted by newspapers,[13] magazines, books, radio and television, has pervaded the village. The automobile—that "magic carpet" of the modern family—brings urban tourists, sightseers, and vacationers to "Ye Olde Tea Shoppe" and the parish church. Equally, it permits Farmer Giles to take his wife and children for an outing so that they may savor the throngs, hubbub, and sooty air of city streets.

Economics, congestion, and mobility have necessitated many readjustments in central-local relations. Programs of public assistance to the poor, for example, were once regarded as a local responsibility. But when it became evident that poverty (especially if associated with inadequate education or prolonged unemployment) was mainly a function of the national economy, and when the areas hardest hit by a business depression were unable to offer sufficient public relief to needy families from local resources, the conclusion followed that the responsibility for assistance must be spread over the entire community. For these reasons, many a governmental service has literally been "nationalized." Some functions have been wholly transferred from local to national jurisdiction. In other instances a partnership has evolved whereby national and local governments cooperate in a specific activity (for example, education or housing).

Under such a system the partners are not, and never can be, equal. A government of the whole is inevitably more powerful than those representing segments, irrespective of whether it deals with the parts severally or collectively. The realities of their relationship, as these exist in political power and financial resources, are mirrored in the law of the United Kingdom. Only one institution in Britain has the legal authority to decide how to distribute governmental functions between the center and the localities, and when to add or take away. That institution is necessarily the supreme lawmaking body, Parliament. At law, every local government is subject to the Parliament—which created most of them, can reorganize any of them, and has clothed them all with their legal authority and defined their areas

---

[13]Britain's small territorial expanse and the integration of the railways, motorways, and air routes that radiate from the capital permit the London morning newspapers to circulate throughout the country.

and powers. In this sense, because of the legal omnipotence of Parliament, the form of the British system is highly centralized. Moreover, the difficulty of financing the social services has reinforced the centralizing principles of constitutional law. The increase in governmental functions has been felt at both levels, local as well as national. But many of the newer local activities cost more than local resources can afford, particularly in the less wealthy areas where the need for governmental aid is greater. With most sources of taxation engrossed by the national treasury, there is a limit to the revenues of local bodies, which must thus depend on annual grants from the center. These are given with conditions about programs and standards determined in Westminster and Whitehall.

In the quarter of a century since 1965, the basic question of what kinds of local government were appropriate and what their relations should be to the center was fully reexamined. As a result, the basic pattern was redesigned, although not in such a fashion as to reduce the grip which London maintains over the rest of the United Kingdom. The need for some kind of restructuring was linked with Britain's relative economic decline in comparison with other leading industrial societies. That was itself reflected internally in the depression which had overtaken the major industries of an earlier period—namely, coal mining, steel, railways, ship building, and textiles. Since these tended to be concentrated geographically, certain cities and regions (particularly in the Midlands and the North) were falling behind the more prosperous South. The bases of power of the two major political parties were also linked to these shifts, since Labour had traditionally derived much of its voting support from the strongholds of the older industries, while the Conservatives had a bigger following in the southern region. As it turned out, ideas for reform which were initiated under a Labour government were later carried out by Conservative governments, with modifications which suited their policies. After a Royal Commission, appointed by Labour, had reported in 1969, the Conservative Heath Ministry put through Parliament the Local Government Act of 1972.

Under the new design, the dominant unit became the county, with broad powers extending to general planning, coordination of transport, most highways, police and fire fighting, education, and so on. Counties are subdivided into smaller districts which are responsible for housing, building regulations, garbage collection, and the protection of the environment. London and six of the counties where people and industry are most congested are designated as metropolitan. There, the subordinate districts have some of the powers (education for example) assigned elsewhere to the counties. Below and within the districts are the smallest units, 8000 parishes, created to safeguard local interests. At the opposite end are regional authorities, broader than counties, exercising responsibility for public water supply, and sewage.

The issue of central power versus decentralization received a new twist in the sixties and seventies. Public opinion crystallized around the fact that so much of the power and wealth of the United Kingdom was concentrated in the London area. The proposed remedy was to redistribute some of the capital's perquisites to other parts of the country. The natural place to begin was in the component parts which had been united to form the kingdom, a notion reinforced by the separate historical and cultural traditions of Wales and Scotland plus their distance from the southeast. Thus the ancient drama of Celtic resistance to the Anglo-Saxon was reenacted once more in modern dress. Sentiments of Welsh and Scottish nationalism acquired a political momentum with which the two major parties and the central government were forced to reckon. In Wales the main impetus for nationalism was the demand to revive the Welsh language. But in Scotland, where the burden of the complaint was economic, nationalist sentiment pointed to the North Sea oil, lying in latitudes parallel to the Scottish coast, which the Scots would control if independent of the English. In the general election of October 1974, the Scottish Nationalists gained 31 percent of the votes cast in Scotland. After that, however, their current slackened. When Parliament enacted a measure of devolution,[14] and separate referenda on this issue were held in 1979 in Scotland and Wales, too few voted affirmatively for an Assembly to be set up in Edinburgh or Cardiff.

After mid-1979, however, not only did the Conservatives regain control of Parliament, but Margaret Thatcher's reactionary policies became ascendant within the Conservative Party. Political hostility soon developed into open warfare between the central government and the governments of London and the six metropolitan counties which had Labour majorities. Thatcher responded by demonstrating unequivocally where power lies within the British system—to wit, at the center. Always preferring the private sector to the public, and being therefore as opposed in principle to local government functions as she was to those at the center, she used against the local authorities one of her two strongest weapons: the control of finance. First, she imposed an upper limit on the amount of revenue which they could raise by local taxes (or rates, as they were called). Later, she sought to shift the base of these local revenues from the rental value of people's homes to their wage or salary. Her other big gun, the legislative supremacy of Parliament, was then deployed against the six metropolitan counties and the Greater London Council, all in Labour hands. She simply abolished them, and then redistributed their functions to units of more limited jurisdiction which the central departments could more easily control.

---

[14]Under this proposal, there were to be Assemblies for Scotland and/or Wales, elected by the voters of those regions, with powers to legislate in certain spheres and administer services financed annually by appropriations from the central Parliament.

Let no one be under any illusions about the *realpolitik* of the British constitution. Whatever may be rhetorically proclaimed about noble traditions of local liberties, power in the United Kingdom resides in Westminster and Whitehall.

American Federalism, The Start of an Invention

More decentralized in form and fact is the government of the United States. In this respect, as in separating the three branches, the framers of the Constitution clearly expressed their preference for a dispersion of powers. Their accomplishment was the novel and ingenious one of federal union, undoubtedly the most distinctive, enduring, and influential contribution of America to the art of government. In what did the novelty consist? Prior to 1776 the 13 colonies were bound to Britain, severally and separately. In no way were they linked together. But to declare independence, to win a war, and build a new nation, required union. The first framework designed for this purpose by the Continental Congress was experimental, and its construction was imperfect. Under the Articles of Confederation a government was organized for the United States, but the problems of postwar development exposed its powerlessness. The Congress resembled not so much a legislature as a conference of ambassadors, acting under the instructions of the state governments. Its most important decisions required a majority of at least nine states; and the Articles themselves could not be amended without unanimity. The central authority was weak in its executive arm and altogether devoid of a judicial branch. For revenues and for troops it depended on what the states contributed.

A few years of experience with that system soon exposed its inadequacies. The Congress lacked the authority to weld the states into a unity, to mitigate their commercial rivalries, to establish a sound currency, to remove the causes of domestic disorders,[15] and to foster American interests abroad. The delegates to the Philadelphia Convention of 1787 were sent for the purpose of revising the Confederation. Fortunately they exceeded their instructions and drafted the Constitution of a federal union. As Hamilton saw it, the flaw in the Articles was that the parts predominated over the whole. The principal weakness, in his diagnosis, was the dependence of the government at the center on the states which served as intermediaries between it and the individual.[16] It was this defect which the Constitution removed, thereby inaugurating a more perfect union. The new central government was equipped with a Congress which could legislate and tax; an executive, with its own agencies of enforcement; and a

[15]Such as Shays's Rebellion in 1786.
[16]*The Federalist*, no. 15.

judiciary, with authority to preserve an equilibrium between the whole and the parts and to uphold the supremacy of the Constitution. Above all, the federal government now derived its mandate directly from the people as voters and carried its services directly to them as individuals.

When George Washington became president, with him was inaugurated the principle of a new type of federal union, the like of which was unknown earlier and was unfamiliar to the generation which created it. Leagues were no novelty, nor were confederations. But all of them, and the Articles of Confederation, were alike in the essential feature that power lay with the parts, while the central institutions provided machinery for cooperation, not for government. What distinguishes a federal union from leagues, confederations, and unitary states is that everyone in it is subject to and is served by three levels of government, because every parcel of land in the United States falls under three jurisdictions—federal, state, and local.[17] What further distinguishes a federal union is that its constitution makes it impossible for the federal government to abolish the member states or for them to eliminate the federal government. The governments at both higher levels are derived directly from the people, and the constitution not only creates a national authority, but guarantees to the states their permanent position within the union. Thus, after the Civil War, Chief Justice Chase described the American system as "an indestructible union composed of indestructible states."[18] This meant that the states could not break up the federal union or the authority that unifies it, nor could the latter destroy the states and substitute a unitary system.

Centralization in American Government

The virtue of federalism is its flexibility in extending a single jurisdiction to a larger area and to more people, while permitting diversity and decentralization. But federalism, like any enduring system, does not remain the same. In the United States, for example, it had to adapt to the expanding numbers and power of the American nation; to industrialization and its social aftereffects; to the migration of millions from Europe; to participation in two world wars; to the growth of national sentiment and the exercise of international leadership. Such events led to changes which were called in the 1930s "the new centralization" and "the new federalism." The immediate cause of modifications in the federal structure was the assumption by governments of new functions at all three levels.[19] However, the rate and degree of growth have differed from one level to another, so that the

---

[17]Except for the District of Columbia, which comes solely under federal jurisdiction.
[18]*Texas* v. *White*, 7 Wallas 725 (1868).
[19]See chapter 7, section on "Emergence of Big Government."

former equilibrium among the three has altered. Until 1932, more than half of the government in the United States was local, in the sense that local revenues and expenditures exceeded those of the federal and all the state governments combined.[20] What happened thereafter was a spectacular extension of federal activity in response to the depression of the early 1930s and the resulting demands for unemployment relief and social security. In the traditional mode of distributing powers under the federal system, on the local governments fell the first responsibility for finding remedies. Their fiscal resources, however, were insufficient for their legal and political obligations. Consequently, the cities and counties turned elsewhere for aid—first, to their state legislatures, which gave what help they could, but in most cases were themselves too weak financially to underwrite the whole bill. Eventually it was the federal government under Roosevelt's New Deal which mobilized the resources of a nation to alleviate a catastrophe of national scope.

Six years (1932–1938) of legislative debate, electoral decision, and judicial review brought a federal commitment to such policies as the regulation of agricultural prices along with subsidies, unemployment relief and public works, social security, the public generation and sale of hydroelectric power, fixed maximum hours and minimum wages in industry, control of the securities market, insurance of bank deposits, and more. For some of these programs, limited precedents had been established earlier. In other instances federal intervention was entirely new. In every case, however, the scale of these federal undertakings was unprecedented. Nor during Roosevelt's presidency was any amendment made in the text of the Constitution, save the one which, ironically, reduced federal authority by restoring the control of the liquor industry to the states.[21] Central jurisdiction was extended by elastic interpretations of the interstate commerce and general welfare clauses and by the liberal use of the doctrine of "implied powers."[22]

Equally important for the working of federalism were some techniques adopted more systematically than before. The New Deal inaugurated a new era of intergovernmental relations. The older federal system has been compared to a three-layer cake with icing thinly spread around the horizontal layers. Most of the work of government was conducted at one level with little or no reference to the others. The states, it is true, exercised some controls over the localities within their midst. But federal-state relations were few and loose, while federal-local relations were nonexistent. After the New Deal, everything changed. Federal-state relations

[20]Consult on this point the figures in table 3.

[21]The Twenty-First Amendment, repealing the Eighteenth.

[22]Formulated in the opinion of the Court in *McCulloch* v. *Maryland*, 4 Wheat. 316 (1819).

TABLE 3. Public Finances and Public Employees in the American Federal System, 1902–1985

	GOVERNMENT REVENUES (000,000'S OMITTED)			GOVERNMENT EXPENDITURES (000,000'S OMITTED)			GOVERNMENT EMPLOYEES— CIVILIAN (000'S OMITTED)		
	FEDERAL	STATE	LOCAL	FEDERAL	STATE	LOCAL	FEDERAL	STATE	LOCAL
1902	653	183	858	565	136	959	—	—	—
1913	962	360	1,658	958	297	1,960	—	—	—
1932	2,634	2,274	5,381	4,034	2,028	6,375	—	—	—
1938	7,226	4,612	5,646	7,687	3,082	6,906	—	—	—
1944	51,399	6,714	6,665	99,448	3,319	7,180	3,365	—	—
1950	43,527	11,480	11,673	42,429	10,864	17,041	2,117	1,057	3,228
1956	81,294	18,903	19,453	72,644	15,148	28,004	2,410	1,268	4,007
1962	106,441	30,115	31,506	105,693	25,495	45,053	2,539	1,680	5,169
1968	153,676	68,460	70,171	178,862	66,254	72,357	2,984	2,495	6,884
1972	223,378	112,309	113,162	242,186	109,243	116,913	2,795	2,937	7,872
1980	564,000	213,000	156,000	526,000	173,000	259,000	2,988	3,753	9,562
1984	752,000	316,000	240,000	829,000	243,000	356,000	3,021[1]	3,924[1]	9,685[1]

[1] 1985 figures.

SOURCES: Historical Statistics on Government Finances and Employment: Census of Governments, 1962; U.S. Statistical Abstracts; and data from Bureau of the Census. Blanks indicate that the data are not available for these years. Grants from one level to another are included, as expenditures, at the level that spends the money; and, as revenue, at the level that collects it. Trust fund data are also included. On this general subject the reader should consult Frederick C. Mosher and Orville F. Poland, *The Costs of American Government* (New York: Dodd, Mead & Co., 1964), to whom I am indebted for advice in preparing this table.

became closer. Federal-local relations were established. Federal-state-local cooperation was frequent. Much of this was done by expanding a device employed sparingly before the 1930s—the conditional grant-in-aid. For running the new model federal machine the fuel and lubricant were the financial grants which a government of wider jurisdiction and broader taxing powers allocated—on conditions—to smaller units. Thus, the modern three-layer cake is cut and consumed in vertical slices. Various functions (for example, social security or the regulation of agriculture) are performed nowadays by the governments of all three levels acting in unison.

The cause of these readjustments is clear. When government is decentralized, functions must be assigned to the levels where they are appropriately conducted. How do we determine "appropriateness"? The problem is to find a working conformance between people, areas, resources, and services. Theoretically, each unit of government should give service to an area whose people need it and have the money to pay for it. In practice, that would result in gross inequalities between areas. Most of the modern changes in federalism were caused by social needs for which the political boundaries drawn in a preindustrial society were inadequate. When business corporations and trade unions are organized nationwide, producing goods which move across state lines, labor relations can no longer be confined to the states' jurisdiction. When a metropolis requires a daily supply of fresh milk of certified quality to be sold at a price which remunerates producers, processors, and distributors, agreement is needed among the authorities of the city and counties, of the states whose farms supply the milk, and of the federal government which supervises interstate compacts and regulates farm production. When factories and automobiles pollute the air, when industrial waste or domestic sewage contaminates a river, lake, or ocean, the remedies require strong government and the reciprocal efforts of separate jurisdictions. When welfare recipients move from an impoverished to a prosperous region, becoming a charge on the latter's budget, their assistance, retraining, and employment are partly a national problem, not wholly state or local. When a river valley in a backward area suffers from floods and erosion, only an authority wider and wealthier than the affected states and localities can raise them nearer to the national average. In today's world, people are more mobile. New industries choose the most advantageous among a variety of sites. Cities attract people by the work they offer, but many of the well-to-do commute from the suburbs. The economy and its human material are flexible, but political boundaries are rigid. A jurisdictional line, once drawn, is hard to erase. To eliminate a city or county is all but impossible; to abolish a state is unthinkable. The structure retains its decentralized form. In theory, powers continue to be distributed as constitutional law ordains. But the transformation of our society and the pressures on modern government have remolded their relationships.

The National Enforcement of Equality

The effect of these pressures can be observed in two major policy developments since the 1950s. One of these has concerned our social relationships at home; the other, our relations with other governments. One is primarily a moral question; the other is military. Both have had a centralizing effect.

The domestic issue has been the controversy about school integration. The problem of winning acceptance for the principle that children of different races may be educated together is especially relevant to the issue now under discussion. Both aspects of the choice between concentration and dispersion of powers have come to the fore in the conflicts that erupted in so many areas. Through the tortuous episodes of this struggle to enforce equality under law, all three branches of government at all three levels were compelled to participate and did so. The record illustrates what can happen when the political process uses government as a catalyst to speed a social revolution. Under a system where powers are dispersed, built-in structural cleavages facilitate the tactics of obstruction. Significantly enough, the leadership came, and had to come, from the center. There, it was the Supreme Court that took the initiative, affirming the principle of equality and instructing the federal district courts to apply it in local areas. Congress originally gave the Court no help, being paralyzed by the capacity of southerners to filibuster in the Senate and by their control of key committee chairmanships through seniority. Eventually, however, the national pressure of majority opinion squeezed out of Congress the two Civil Rights Acts of 1957 and 1964. Successive presidents grappled with the problem of enforcement, although neither Eisenhower nor Kennedy seemed to relish what he had to do. At the local level and in the capitals of the states concerned—more particularly Arkansas, Alabama, Mississippi, Louisiana, and Virginia—opinions were divided. Moderates believed that some integration had to be accepted and argued in favor of obeying the law, however distasteful its terms. But generally the extremists prevailed, and they pushed the legislators and governors into impossible defiance of the United States— witness the postures of Governors Faubus of Arkansas, Barnett of Mississippi, and Wallace of Alabama.

As far as these events concern the issue of concentration or dispersion, two conclusions emerge. One is that a system of divided jurisdictions permits the passing of ticklish responsibilities from one agency to another. By default of the other branches, the judiciary exercised leadership and, by interpreting the law, was in reality helping both to make and enforce it. The other result has been to strengthen central power. Even the Eisenhower administration, which by policy and conviction favored less government in general and less central government in particular, was impelled politically to impose the authority of the nation on the affairs of a school board. The long-accepted principle that school education was strictly a local, or at most a state, concern gave way before the greater principle that fundamental human rights (for example, the dignity of the individual that flows from equal treatment) form a national obligation. Local discrimination had to be abolished in this case by central authority.[23]

The Military Impact on Federalism

Besides these domestic developments, the tendency to centralize was reinforced by what happened on the international front. The two world wars of this century were such that no major power could remain outside the struggle. On a federal government the effects of participating in a conflict for survival are drastic. War is always a centralizer. It increases the control of the state over society, since protection and security become a people's paramount concern and these are preeminently the responsibility of the state. In addition it concentrates in the capital city the authority to plan, decide, and execute in order to promote a speedy and unified direction of military operations. Evidence for this is contained in the nation's budget. In 1916 the expenditures of the federal government amounted to $734,000,000. By 1919 the figure had risen to $18,515,000,000. With the "return to normalcy" under Harding that amount was cut back by 1922 to $3,373,000,000. The same story was repeated in World War II. In 1940 federal expenditures stood at $8,998,000,000. The effort to defeat Germany and Japan cost the United States, in 1945 alone, the unprecedented sum of $100,405,000,000, of which over $80,000,000,000 represented appropriations for the war and navy departments. Victory over the Fascist powers was again reflected in a reduction of expenditures, especially for the military services. Thus in 1948 federal outlays were under $34,000,000,000. After that year, however, the strained relations with the Soviet Union and Communist aggression in Korea in 1950 sent the federal budget soaring once more to the higher altitudes of public finance. In 1952 federal outlays approximated $80,000,000,000, of which some four-fifths was directly attributable to the obligations incurred in past wars, the cost of operations in Korea, aid to friendly foreign governments, and military preparedness as insurance against another world war. In 1968 federal expenditures reached a total of $178,862,000,000. Of this amount, as much as $79,000,000,000 was spent by the Department of Defense alone—in addition to war-related expenditures of other agencies—and $30,000,000,000 of that sum (that is, $3,500,000 in every single hour) was the immediate price of the involvement in Vietnam, the subsequent cost being the inflation of the 1970s which that war set in motion.

But even those amounts were dwarfed by the size of the military

---

[23]In 1979 the federal government brought suit against the Chicago schools on this issue. See also chapter 5, section on "Educational Equality."

expenditures from 1982 onward under the Reagan Administration. Federal agencies which served domestic needs were placed on a slimming diet, amounting in some cases to starvation, while the Pentagon waxed fat.[24] This was the more curious because it revealed an inherent contradiction in the professed aims of the right-wing. Hostile to government in general, and therefore most hostile to its strongest level, the Right was bent on cutting down the federal agencies and transferring many of their functions to the states. But the amount available to the latter was consolidated into block grants totaling less than the separate grants previously given for specific programs.[25] The aim of restoring to the federal system an equilibrium which it had lost had much to commend it. The attempt in this instance, however, was flawed by the huge escalation of the military budget and by the conservative dislike for the social services.

When a modern state is preoccupied with military tasks, irrespective of whether the political system be democratic or autocratic, the framework of its institutions will be skewed to the performance of this primary function and the mobilization of the requisite power. Because of the military need for coordinated planning, unified command, continuous vigilance, and speedy action, a system concentrated on its own defense is unlikely to maintain either checks and balances between branches of government or the powers of state governments vis-à-vis the nation. Separation and dispersion are difficult policies to practice in a world scarred by the wars of the past and scared about those of the future.

Theme and Variations: Canada, Australia, and India

The example of American federalism has set a precedent for others. The Swiss Confederation was convulsed in 1847 when seven Catholic cantons sought to secede, but were defeated by the Protestant majority in a short civil war. Next year, the victors rewrote their constitution and created a federal union patterned closely on the United States. For the first[26] time since 1291, when the cantons of Uri, Schwyz, and Unterwalden launched the confederation with a mutual defense pact, the Swiss organized a genuine central government which has lasted for 14 decades.

One may speculate whether the Swiss would have followed the Ameri-

---

[24]See chapter 7, section on "Emergence of Big Government."

[25]The figures tell their own story. In 1953 federal aid amounted to a little over 10 percent of state and local expenditures. That had risen to 18 percent by 1968, and to 26 percent in 1978. In 1984 it had dropped to 19.5 percent.

[26]A partial exception is the unitary state Napoleon imposed on the Swiss. This was accepted, however, only under foreign duress and proved so unworkable that Napoleon himself aided the Swiss in restoring confederation.

can model if the Civil War had already broken out in the United States. A possible clue is provided by what happened in Canada in the 1860s. There, a federal union was formed for three reasons. Economic depression had struck the maritime settlements of Nova Scotia, New Brunswick, and Prince Edward Island, and recovery was sought within a wider framework. A unitary government had proved unworkable for the French and English inhabitants of Quebec and Ontario. Cool relations with the United States[27] and a determination to hold the West for Canada enforced the argument for a national authority. Federal union seemed the obvious solution, since it would permit the incorporation of the Atlantic seaboard with the upper St. Lawrence region, the separation of Quebec from Ontario, and the eventual inclusion of western territories when adequately peopled. But the recent experience of the near-dissolution of the American union in the Civil War convinced the British and Canadian statesmen that the central government of Canada must possess more powers than belonged to its counterpart in the United States. Thus, whereas the federal government of the United States was organized on the principle that its powers are delegated to it by the Constitution while the states retain the residue, the Canadians reversed this by delegating powers to the provinces and reserving the rest for the Dominion.[28] In Canada, moreover, the national government (in effect, the cabinet) has authority to veto provincial legislation, an ultimate weapon clearly intended to bolster national supremacy.

With or without this last power, however, the Canadian case demonstrated another important discovery; it was possible to fuse the American and British patterns by combining federalism with the cabinet system. Concentration of powers, or integration, at the center along with dispersion of powers, or decentralization, in the field of Dominion-provincial relations— that is the Canadian compromise. This solution is also workable elsewhere, in the South Pacific as well as in North America. When the Australian states federated to form their present Commonwealth in 1900, the same pattern was followed in the sense that federal-state relations were modeled on those of the United States while the British preference for a fusion of legislative and executive powers was continued in the cabinet.

More remarkably, what was done in Canada and Australia has also been tried in India. To provide a workable structure of self-government for a people of over 700 million is no small task, especially when they comprise a medley of ethnic, religious, and linguistic diversities and the

[27]These were due to the British government's unfriendliness to the North during the Civil War, and to intimations of possible expansion by the United States in the north and northwest.

[28]On this point compare the Tenth Amendment to the U.S. Constitution with the British North America Act, 1867, Sec. 91–93. The Swiss copied the American pattern in their federal Constitution, Article 3, as did the Australians later. Commonwealth of Australia Constitution Act, Secs. 51, 52, 107.

wealth is distributed with appalling inequality. The constitution which the Indians adopted on becoming independent owes much to the experience of Britain and America. From one, they took the cabinet; from the other, federalism. Both institutions have survived thus far, but with major departures from the norms which are acceptable in the West. More than once, "President's rule" (i.e., direct control from the center) has been invoked with dictatorial effect. Nehru ousted the freely elected government of a state, which was communist, and imposed one to his liking. His successors have followed this example in other states whose governments opposed the center, but were not communist. His daughter, Indira Gandhi, suspended civil rights from 1975 to 1977, jailed her opponents, intimidated the courts, and muzzled the press. The electorate retaliated by voting her out of office, but later, disillusioned by the alternative, voted her back in. But the authoritarian side of her personality, revealed in her resentment of those who would not bow to her will, impelled her into a course of action toward the Sikhs in the Punjab which recoiled on her own head, ending with the tragedy of her assassination. The Congress Party then chose her son, Rajiv Gandhi, to succeed his mother as Prime Minister. What kind of democracy is this where in almost all of four decades of independence, a dynasty of three members of one family has monopolized power over so huge a population? As for Indian federalism, Rajiv Gandhi, too, after first adopting a conciliatory policy toward the Sikhs, in 1986 decreed "presidential rule" (i.e., control from Delhi) over the Punjab.

Federalism under Strain: Brazil, for Example

The difficulty in applying the federal principle under the pressures of the twentieth century has been an experience common to many countries. The depression of the early 1930s produced untold strain in federal systems, some of whose component units became, in fact, insolvent. Zurich, Ontario, and New South Wales could afford what Graubunden, Nova Scotia, and Western Australia could not. It made no sense for a constitution to assign functions to a level of government, but to withhold the fiscal means of supporting them. If this was true in countries whose economies were relatively developed, *a fortiori* the imbalance was compounded among peoples still burdened by a colonial past. This general truth can be illustrated by the case of Brazil.

Since becoming a republic in 1889, the Brazilians have experimented three times with constitutionalism, a federal regime, and a limited democracy. The constitution of 1891 was modeled after the United States and attempted a dispersion and separation of powers. Indeed, there were grounds for hoping that the balance between unity and diversity required by federalism was adaptable to the Brazilian reality. In the huge area of the

Estados Unidos de Brazil—much of it in Amazonas, Mato Grosso, and Pará, still uncharted and unoccupied—the contrasts will satisfy the most meticulous devotee of a pluralist society. The history, folklore, and contemporary attitudes of Brazil abound with the distinctive traits of cities, provinces, and styles of life. This is not a country of uniformity but of a diversified social base, and its politics reflect that character. For some time the two largest states, São Paulo and Minas Gerais, shared the lead and alternated in occupying the presidency.

But that equilibrium was too precariously poised to withstand the centralizing forces which transformed society and politics in the first half of the twentieth century. When the worldwide depression struck Brazil in 1930, the political system collapsed along with the economy. Getulio Vargas then emerged as the man who discarded the constitution, and imported from Italy a new regime (*Estado Novo*) of fascist style. His power lasted until the end of World War II when, like most dictators, he fell. Accordingly in 1946 the Brazilians redrafted their constitution and resumed their interrupted experiment in federalism, constitutionalism, and the beginnings of democracy. That second attempt lasted almost two decades, but broke down in 1964. What happened, and why?

The essence of the answer can be summarized in three points. First, the principles of a federal system appeared as an alien import and were never fully incorporated with the inherited tradition. In adapting itself to modernity, Brazil suffered the disadvantage that its Portuguese past could not help it in the present. Therefore, Brazilians had to search outside for other models to emulate. But whatever they introduce—be it American federalism, the British parliamentary system, Italian fascism, or communism in either the Russian or Chinese variety—is vulnerable on the ground that it is foreign. Second, although federalism accords properly with the size of Brazil and its social diversity, the component units, or states, are too unequal. The majority are still so backward and lacking in financial resources that they are unable to support the services a modern government must provide. The states that do possess the wherewithal are São Paulo, Guanabara (the city of Rio), Minas Gerais, and Rio Grande do Sul. But of these, the one state of São Paulo, embracing the city of the same name, exceeds the rest in population, capacity, and power. With 18 percent of the country's populace, in the early 1960s the state of São Paulo alone accounted for one-third of the national income, supplied 45 percent of the revenues collected by the union, and produced 55 percent of the industrial wealth. Its government collected 46 percent of the total revenue of all states combined, and its local authorities took in 47 percent of all local revenues in the country. Under these conditions, the balance between the center and the parts which federalism presupposes was utterly lacking, and the great majority of the states depended on grants from the union.

Finally, this centralizing tendency was reinforced by the requirements and results of a rapid industrial development. All society was convulsed by the changes that industrialization set in motion. But the other needed revolutions—agrarian, social, and political—did not keep pace with the industrial. In fact, they were deliberately postponed by the prevailing oligarchy which did not wish to lose its privileges and share them with a larger number. Poorly managed by successive presidents and congresses, the Brazilian economy floundered in a chronic position of internal inflation and external insolvency. Matters came to a head in 1964 when President Goulart advocated economic and political changes which the Left supported. That was the signal for the Right to mobilize. A grouping of property holders, governors of leading states, and army commanders ousted the president, installing a retired marshal in his place. The latter governed by decree, postponed elections, and deprived opponents (including two ex-presidents) of their civil rights.

After the *golpe*, the military secured their grip on the Brazilian people, five successive presidents being army generals. In the first decade their rule was repressive in the extreme. They banned political parties, censored the press, tortured prisoners, and governed with police-state terror. In the economy they drove ahead with a rapid industrial expansion which was reckless of human and social cost. Profits, production, and exports soared, as the rich became ever richer. The gap continued to widen between them and the poor; and the physical environment, urban and natural, along with the Indians of the Amazon, were crushed under the juggernaut of "Order and Progress." Resistance to this inhumanity was led by the Church, which underwent a revolution from below and abandoned its earlier stance of buttressing the power structure. Civilian opposition increased in the late 1970s as society began to pay the price for its headlong economic development and mounting disparities. Realizing at last that a majority of the public had had enough of being stamped on by military heels, the soldiers after two decades returned to their barracks. Elections were then held in which the candidate favored by the military was defeated. In 1985 the first civilian in 21 years was installed as president. Not long after, the Brazilians set to work once again to write a new constitution.

The Individual in Revolt

When the dominant influences of this century in politics, economics, and technology are considered in unison, ours would appear an era of integration and centralization. Many of the driving forces in modern society combine in this direction—the demand for human rights and greater equality of conditions, the extension of the market and standardization of its products, the quest for social security and economic stability, the continuous reiteration of identical messages in the press, radio, and television. True enough—and the evidence is all around us in whatever direction we turn.

But in politics a trend in any one direction always produces a countertrend toward the opposite. Hence in the sixties a contrary tendency began to manifest itself. It consisted in resistance to our contemporary society, to its professed values, as well as to the structure and style of its operation. Since the political system is enmeshed in the social order, those who reject the leading characteristics of society have attacked the leaders of its government, seeing in them the personification of the power that sustains the structure. This swelling chorus of protest, taking on the dimensions of a political force, is not simple in its origins or singleminded in aim. Its assault has been levied on certain traditional elements as well as on others of recent date. Most significant of all, it is worldwide in scope and is not confined to any one species of political system or culture. Its effects have already been felt in communities as varied as the USA and the USSR, Great Britain and France, Yugoslavia and Czechoslovakia, West Germany and Canada, Mexico and Japan.

The nature of this movement can be deciphered by noting the objects of its attack. Certain targets are broad conditions or trends—for example, depersonalization, materialism, established authority, centralization, "the system." Others are more specific—the war in Vietnam, racial or cultural discrimination in housing, education, or employment; authoritarianism in universities and schools, and in organized religion.

That today's urban-industrial environment breeds anger and anxiety should surprise nobody. Such feelings stem from the conviction that our social structure has grown too cumbrous and that its organization and procedures are too complex. Countless individuals have a sense of incomprehension and therefore of helplessness. People feel lost—caught within the toils of a social mechanism which, in their experience, becomes ever more distant, impersonal, and routinized. Our lives are controlled by huge, distant systems, public and private, which are faceless and unresponsive. If you have a complaint and pick up the telephone, to whom do you speak? You write them a letter and receive the standard answer from the computer. Those social scientists and behavioral psychologists, who obscure the obvious with fancy jargon (of Greek or Latin derivation), label the results "alienation" or "anomie," or they say that institutions are "dysfunctional." Translated, this means that things are working badly and people are fed up.

The topic of this chapter—the relationship between central and local authorities and the distribution of powers between them—supplies abundant examples to fortify that feeling. Most modern states have been conspicuously less successful in local government than at the center. The transformation of the physical environment alone has created new conditions affecting individual lives and extending over areas for which traditional boundaries are obsolete. We are endangered by the damage to our habitat—the poisoning of air and water and the rape of the land. Millions are victims of social disorganization, especially apparent in the largest metropolitan centers whose streets are choked with traffic, fumes, and crowds, which reverberate with noise, and which resemble jungles of concrete and glass. When, in addition, these monsters become insolvent, as happened to New York City and Cleveland, they cannot even be justified as purveyors of needed services. Hence, the resentment against centralization and bigness in general is now expressed as a new search for the small community.

Beyond these general conditions from which we all suffer, there are the special grievances of those situated on the outer fringe of a community or at the base of its society—the poor, the young, and any minorities identified by race, religion, or language. Together, these react against what they designate collectively as "the system." Frustration turns to rage and rage to violence when remedies come with glacial slowness or not at all; the resort to violence is then triggered by the instant communication supplied by the mass media. The television screen in particular brings to the eyes of the underprivileged the daily images of an affluence they do not share, at the same time as it reports with contagious effect the explosive outbursts from any corner of the world. Hence, although the occasion, dimensions, and immediate protest may vary, the same thread connects Watts and Londonderry, Mexico City and Tokyo, Columbia University and the Sorbonne; hence, too, the reassertion of cultural identities which differentiate a person from the majority or redefine one's remoteness from the centers of power. This takes the form of the nationalism, particularism, or separatism of Scots, Welsh, and Bretons; of French-speaking Canadians; of Croats and Slovaks; of Tartars, Kurds, and Sikhs.

When injustices are ignored or condoned by those who have the power to change them, an emotional revulsion arises which ends with an ethical challenge. Established authority is then endangered by the repudiation of its moral claim. As people question its legitimacy, the process begins in which authority will be stripped down to power, and power degenerates to brute force.[29]

All of this is involved in the issue discussed in this chapter, the ever-oscillating relations between the small community and the great society. To which unit do we owe our primary allegiance? If citizenship requires participation, at what level do we participate the most? With what unit do we feel identified? Those questions bring us to the fifth issue.

---

[29]See chapter 3, section on "Abuse of Force."

12

The Size of States and the Relations between Them

Territorial Basis of the State

We come to the final threshold—the effect on government of the size of the area it controls. This is the fifth of the classic issues which give the state its character and politics its content.

Many questions are wrapped up in this issue. What is the most desirable and practicable unit of government? Can a state be too small or too big to function effectively? What is the community which the state organizes? What loyalty inspires the people inside the same political boundaries to feel they belong together? Must a state have a piece of territory to guard as its own? Is there any other basis, besides the territorial, for organizing a state? When many states coexist, what should be the relations between them? What is the meaning of international politics, international law, and international organization, and is there anything that can be called international government?

It is now a universal rule that for a state to exist and be recognized as such by others there must be an area within defined boundaries over which it exercises jurisdiction. Some modern examples will illustrate the point. Until 1860 the papacy ruled a belt of land in the center of Italy running from the west coast to the east. When Italy was unified in 1860–1861, the new kingdom absorbed the Papal States. The pope retained only the city of Rome, and this too he lost in 1870. In that year the papacy ceased to be a state, although it did not cease to have political influence. Half a century later, Mussolini and the pope reached an agreement (the Lateran Treaty of 1929) about church-state relations. Under its terms a Vatican State was constituted, covering 109 acres in the heart of Rome, which has received ambassadors from foreign powers and has sent nuncios to their capitals. Because of its temporal jurisdiction over this pocket handkerchief of territory, the papacy was again recognized as a state.[1] Another case in point is the history of Poland. That kingdom, formerly a great power in Eastern Europe, was partitioned in 1772, 1793, and 1795 and obliterated by the joint action of Russia, Prussia, and Austria. No Polish state existed until one was reestablished in 1919. That lasted two decades, but again disappeared in 1939 by partition between Nazi Germany and Stalin's Russia. With the German defeat in 1945 the state of Poland arose once more from the ashes. A third example is that of Israel. Although Jews were dispersed in other lands and persecuted for centuries, their religion and culture survived. There was no Jewish state, however, until 1949 when the United Nations sanctioned the partition of Palestine and granted Israel recognition, which the new state assured for itself by success in combat.[2]

What matters, then, is that a state must have some territory to call its own. How much is immaterial. At present, the largest in territorial extent is the Soviet Union, occupying one-sixth of the earth's land surface. In population, China outstrips the rest with numbers exceeding one billion. And at the other extreme, for a *reductio ad absurdissimum*, there is Nauru whose 7000 persons occupy eight square miles.[3]

Kinship: The Earlier Basis

The fact that a modern state must own some land invites the question whether this has always been so. Can government be erected on another foundation than area? The answer is "yes." In an earlier stage of social development government was generally based on kinship rather than territory. A political relationship between people was derived from the physical bond of common heredity. Authority was thus a by-product of ancestry. Frequently the unit of political organization has been created by the collection of families into larger groupings of tribes or clans. Historical

---

[1] A new treaty was signed in 1985. Italy still recognizes the Vatican as an independent state where the Pope exercises temporal rule. The major innovation is that Roman Catholicism no longer has the status of Italy's official religion.

[2] By the end of the 1980s, however, only Egypt among Israel's neighbors had accorded it official recognition.

[3] Fortunately for the rest of us, they do not yet have an atomic bomb.

research on this point is confirmed by linguistic evidence. The vocabulary of politics, ancient and modern, contains many terms whose roots come from words that connote human procreation and birth. The Greek *phule*, meaning "tribe," derives from the verb *phuein* (to "bring forth" or "beget") and has the same etymology as *physique*. The subdivision of the *phule* called the *phratria* (that is, fraternity or brotherhood) was a clan composed of kinsmen and was used in Athens for political as well as religious functions. Likewise the *genos*, or "clan," is formed from a root that means "to be born," as is the identical Latin word *gens*, which has yielded the terms *genocide* and *gentile*.[4] *Nation*, in Latin *natio*, is taken from the verb *nasci*, "to be born," which has also given us *nature* and *nativity*.

Two conditions could make kinship a possible or appropriate basis for governmental organization. First, the group must not be too large. The bigger it becomes, the remoter the physical connection must be, until eventually a belief in a common ancestry is more fiction than fact.[5] The state has often resembled the family writ larger. But there are certain inherent limits to the elasticity of the family concept. To enlarge it indefinitely is to cease to take it seriously. Second, besides its relevance to a small group, kinship was appropriate for a community that was nomadic. If military or economic reasons compelled people to move, on what better principle could they unite? For working or warring[6] together the kin group was a convenient, ready-made association.

When these conditions no longer applied, political organization had to seek an alternative foundation. Those who gave up the life of the nomad for that of the peasant found in territory a substitute for kinship. The state was then organized around the fact that people were neighbors rather than kinsfolk. The land under them became more relevant politically than the genes inside them. The transition from one principle to the other is familiar in the early history of many peoples.[7] In some instances even the exact events and time of the substitution are known.[8] Few political changes have

---

[4]Also *gentle* and *gentleman*—though any resemblance between these and politics is purely coincidental.

[5]The political mythology of the Greeks, whose name for themselves was Hellenes, contained the belief that they were all descended from one ancestor, Hellen, just as the ancient Hebrews assumed a common descent from Abraham.

[6]Shakespeare gives a reverse twist to this ancient principle when he has Henry V say to his army in the eve-of-Agincourt speech:
We few, we happy few, we band of brothers;
For he to-day that sheds his blood with me
Shall be my brother; be he ne'er so vile
This day shall gentle his condition.

Henry V, IV. 3. 60–63

[7]Thus the Romans, whose original popular assembly was the *comitia curiata* (based on the *curia*, a kin group), set up alongside of it the later *comitia tributa*, an assembly based on a territorial unit, the *tribus*.

[8]For example, in Athens the constitutional reforms of Cleisthenes in 510 B.C. replaced the *genos* (a kin group) by the *deme* (a local subdivision) as a unit for governmental purposes.

wrought so revolutionary a transformation as this. Previously, when the state was an extension of the kin group, there was an immediate link between person and person through kinship. When territory took the place of kin, people were linked by their common relation to land which served as their intermediary. Thus was a new factor introduced into the political equation, raising a host of derivative problems. When land became the foundation of government, its ownership, distribution, and use had political effects. Your status depended on whether you were an owner, tenant, or serf. Control of the land meant control of those on it. Wealth, rank, property, and power found here their common denominator.

The Optimum Area for the State

Thence arose the perplexing problem of the shape and size of the land area over which the jurisdiction of the state could extend. The kin group, for obvious reasons, did not admit indefinite extension. If a political association based on kinship sought to incorporate persons of different stock, some formula or fiction, such as "adoption," had to be invented. A state set up on a territorial basis confronted no such difficulties. Conceivably it might expand by accumulating more segments of land and thus acquiring control over those who resided thereon. But certain obstacles prevented an indefinite enlargement of terrain. If the area exceeded a certain limit, could its military defense be ensured? Could it be administered from one center? Would its inhabitants feel a sense of union? What would be its relations with other states similarly organized? Whether these relations would be friendly, hostile, or indifferent would be determined by size as well as propinquity, by community of interests or conflict. Of necessity, the pygmy must tolerate the giant. The latter could also be tolerant, if so minded—but only by grace. A small or medium state, placed between two larger ones, could serve as a buffer, keeping them apart. Its survival would depend on balancing one side against the other, on being correctly polite to both but intimate with neither (witness Uruguay or Switzerland).

Since a state, like an individual, can never be "an *iland,* intire of it selfe,"[9] its destiny is always involved with that of others. In their external affairs all states seek two permanent objectives. These are safety, in the physical or military sense, and prosperity, in the material or economic sense. Governments must insure themselves against attack in order to survive. They attempt to raise their living standards by exports and imports. These aims do not alter, but the means of attaining them do. In one era safety and prosperity will be best promoted by methods and techniques that would be unsuitable at a later age. The unit of government in vogue at any time is that which seems, under the conditions prevailing, the most

[9]See chapter 2, p. 30.

tolerably adequate for the two goals. But when it becomes so intolerably inadequate that people no longer feel safe or prosperous under its aegis, they turn to some other unit which holds out a new hope.

In this way one can analyze the various units of government that have been employed successively. It is these twin permanent objectives of foreign policy that give meaning to the continuing debate over the optimum unit of government and the appropriate size of the state. During three millennia the Western world has experimented with three solutions to this problem and is currently groping for a fourth. In chronological order these have been the city-state, empire-state, and nation-state. The fourth may be the region-state. Ultimately, the possibility exists of a world-state. But that ideal is still remote from today's practicalities. What light is thrown on the nature of government by these attempts and aspirations?

The Greek *Polis*

The city-state (or *polis*) was the characteristic unit of political organization in the Mediterranean region from the tenth to the third century B.C. Typically it consisted of an urban nucleus and an adjacent rural area. Food production in the one supplemented defense, commerce, government, and the arts in the other. Its population, like its area, was small—anything over 100,000 being abnormal. The reasons for a state on this scale are explicable by geography, scarcity of agricultural land, and difficulties of communication. Practically everywhere in Greece, in central and south Italy, in Sicily, along the coastline of Turkey, and in the islands of the Aegean, the interior was rugged, broken, and mountainous. Land forms created barriers, rather than a passage, and offered opportunities for roadblocks and ambush. But the sea was an open highway, as long as piracy was suppressed. Most settlements, therefore, were located on the coast, wherever there was a usable harbor, or at some defensible strong point, slightly inland but connected with a nearby port (for example, Athens and Peiraeus, Rome and Ostia).[10] These conditions imposed limits on the size of the state, the primary considerations being that its inhabitants must receive physical protection and should not exceed their food supply.

But it was impossible to preserve a stable equilibrium. That was precluded when population grew because of a high birth rate—though partially offset by a high death rate. When the state could no longer contain its numbers, what outlets were available? One was for a section of the citizen body to depart and found a new settlement, a colony or "home away from home" (*apoikia*) as the Greeks called it. A second was to indulge in wide-

---

[10]From this standpoint Sparta and Thebes were exceptional, since they were inland cities that succeeded in making history.

spread commerce and search for distant markets and sources of food. Athens and Corinth did both, and became commercial and colonizing powers. This policy, if successful, might bring prosperity, power, and even luxury. But it involved far-off commitments with long sea lanes to guard and the risk of starvation if they were cut. The third possibility was to expand by warfare and appropriate the resources of another community. To this practice, states were led by population pressure[11] and commercial rivalries, and also by political ambitions.

Anarchy and Imperialism in Classical Greece

The combination of military insecurity and inadequate economic resources impelled the city-states to experiment with wider unions. Various methods of enlarging the scope of political organization were accordingly tried. One was to establish a league of states, which could ostensibly cluster around a common shrine, as the Amphictyonic League joined in the worship of Apollo. Or it could be frankly constituted for defense with some powerful member for its nucleus, like the Boeotian League over which Thebes presided. In these leagues lay the rudiments of federalism. But the structures never developed sufficient firmness and were weakened or destroyed by rivalries within or blows from without. Another way of broadening the unit of government was for some unusually powerful state to carve an empire for itself, signing up as allies the smaller fry who accepted protection and imposing its domination on whoever resisted. All the big states tried in turn to achieve this leadership (the Greeks called it *hegemony*), as opportunity seemed for the moment to smile in their direction. First it was Sparta, then Athens, then Sparta again, then Thebes, and finally Athens once more. None of these efforts succeeded because even the mightiest could not forever prevent their unwilling subjects from trying to throw off the yoke, and because the aggrandizement of one superstate conjured up a coalition of rivals. Thus it was Athens that led the opposition to Sparta. Then, when Athenian leadership menaced others, a powerful alliance of Sparta, Corinth, and Thebes was arrayed against her and Greece was torn asunder in the agony of the Peloponnesian War (431–404 B.C.). With Sparta again predominant, Athens and Thebes joined to restrain her; but when their success was followed by Theban supremacy, Sparta and Athens sided together. The balance of power, practiced in modern times by giants, was no mystery to those Lilliputians.

The worst of this situation was that their jealousies and divisions left the Greeks a tempting prey to the powers on their periphery. Their tradi-

---

[11]Plato ascribed the cause of war to the need of a growing population for more land to supply the necessary food. *Republic*, ii. 373.

tional foes were the Persians. The Greeks came in conflict with them when the Persian empire, which Cyrus founded, sought in its westward expansion to engulf the Greek settlements along the coast of Asia Minor and these settlements were reinforced by the Greeks farther west (for example, by Sparta). The Persians thereupon decided to strike at the heart of the Hellenic world. The expedition they launched in 490 B.C. was repulsed by the Athenians at Marathon. A decade later came the major invasion by strong sea and land forces commanded in person by Xerxes. His offensive power was broken in the series of encounters that made immortal the names of Thermopylae, Salamis, and Plataea. On this occasion the city-states, led jointly by Sparta and Athens, reached their high point of unity. But as the danger receded, their solidarity melted and Persian diplomacy and military power were able again to take advantage of Greek discord. A century and a half later, the same tactics were employed by the astute Macedonian king, Philip the Great. By the alternate use of strength and cajolery he insinuated himself into the chaotic politics of the Greek world, systematically extending his influence until, when Athens was finally bestirred by the oratory of Demosthenes (that is, the "Philippics") to rally a coalition against him, the hour was too late. The autonomy of the *polis* was extinguished in the battle of Chaeronea (338 B.C.). When Alexander took over his father's legacy, he confirmed the position of the Greek states as a dependency of Macedonian power.

Considering that the Greeks lost their liberties because of an inability to combine in a larger union, it is astonishing that the political philosophies of the two most eminent Greek thinkers are scaled to fit the small dimensions of the *polis*. Though familiar with larger formations (for example, the kingdoms of Persia, Egypt, and Macedon), Plato and Aristotle wrote a theory of government that took the size of the *polis* as ideal.[12] Aware of the economic and military reasons for its limited territory and population, they also provided a philosophical justification. Unity, they argued, is the greatest political good. A people will feel united only if they have a sense of belonging together. This they will lack if they are too many, for they will then lose the spirit of a single community. What is too large cannot be understood, since it passes the limits of comprehension and is no longer orderly or rational. A community, moreover. must be self-sufficient. If too small to maintain itself (for example, a family or a village), it must be absorbed into a greater whole. But if too large, its interests become involved in the well-being and goodwill of others so that it ceases to be strictly autonomous. Hence the Aristotelian conclusion that the upper limit in size is a citizen body of adult males who can be assembled in one spot at one time and hear one speaker.

---

[12]In Aristotle's case this is still more extraordinary in view of his connection with Macedon. His father had served as physician to Philip and he himself was tutor to Alexander.

The most interesting aspect of this theory is its deviation from so much of Greek history and its impracticality for the times when it was written. If the Platonic-Aristotelian doctrine was formulated on the right lines, then most of the city-state politics known to us proceeded on wrong lines. Nor could the philosophers plead that their speculations were dated to an early stage in the development of the *polis*, for Plato flourished in the first half of the fourth century B.C. and Aristotle in the second half. Indeed, when Aristotle wrote the *Politics*, the conquests of his pupil, Alexander, had destroyed the independence of the unit of government about which the master continued to theorize. What is evaluated in the *Politics* is an institution, the *polis*, which was already receding into history because it could no longer ensure either physical security or material prosperity. In this instance at least, philosophy's function was to write the postscript to the end of an epoch, thereby for once exemplifying Hegel's remark that "the owl of Minerva takes its flight only when the shades of night are gathering."[13]

The Roman Peace

But in the movement of history, the night that closes one era is followed by the dawn of another. The inability of Alexander's successors to hold his conquests intact and the rivalries of the kingdoms into which his empire was subdivided made the central and eastern Mediterranean a scene for conflict. It was left to the West therefore to produce a power that could accomplish what all others had failed to do—the military subjugation and political consolidation of the Mediterranean world. Such in fact was the achievement of Rome. The means employed by this doyen of empire builders deserve a scrutiny, not merely for antiquarian interest, but because their effects are still felt today.

The Romans had one method for founding an empire, another for governing it. New possessions, or provinces, they acquired by a blend of military might and judicious bribery. Their soldiering became renowned for its qualities of sturdy courage and dogged tenacity, and the legions, when commanded by a Scipio, Sulla, or Caesar, were invincible. In their initial engagements they were likely as not to suffer defeat. But once they had reorganized and found a competent general, they revealed their knack of always winning the last battle. To their subjects the conquerors presented the gift on which they prided themselves most, the Roman peace (*pax Romana*). But this "peace," though eventually it brought order, security, and the reign of law, could be a brutal experience whenever its victim was a formidable opponent or a rebellious former subject. The Roman was a

---

[13]This is the closing sentence in the last paragraph but one of the preface to his *Philosophy of Right* (1820).

pitiless foe when he played for the high stakes of empire, Nearby rivals like Alba, Veii, and Capua were crushed or destroyed. Carthage was razed to the ground. Corinth was sacked and blotted off the map. Even the famed clemency of Caesar did not spare from death the brave leader of the Gallic uprising, Vercingetorix. The majestic formulas of the Roman law were grounded in a politics of frightfulness (*Schrecklichkeit*) which even a Nazi could admire.

To govern their empire, however, the Romans used other techniques.[14] Once they had cowed a people into submission, they proceeded to raise them to partnership within the empire. The process was slow. For, whether they constructed a road or an aqueduct, a legal code or a civilization, the Romans built for eternity and were not disposed to hurry. Adroitly they would win over the potential leaders of a conquered community (those, that is, who had not been sold into slavery or massacred) by conferring favors on men of wealth and the heads of influential families. These then became the clients (*clientes*) of Rome. In return for their privileges, instead of becoming the instigators of local revolt, they cooperated with the imperial authority.[15] Thus with the grant of citizenship, the Latins, the Italians, and eventually the inhabitants of the provinces found themselves sharing in the benefits of empire. Why then rebel when the Roman masters had abandoned their exclusiveness and from every province the roads of opportunity could lead to the city on the Tiber?

Besides peace, law, and citizenship, the Romans scattered the seeds of their civilization among the peoples within their jurisdiction. Throughout the provinces they planted centers from which their culture might spread. For this purpose, the chosen medium was the city—whether this were of ancient foundation and incorporated by Rome as a municipality, or some new colony of Roman émigrés, or an army camp on the frontier where the legions kept vigil against the "unpacified" and "uncivilized" peoples beyond. Here one might find the schools that taught provincial children the Latin tongue; the central-heated villas of the Roman administrators; their baths; yes, and their circuses. Rich dividends were yielded by this policy of Romanization. Not only did people far afield become assimilated in their thoughts and ways to the pattern of Rome (witness the Latin culture shared in common to this day by France, Italy, Portugal, and Spain), but talented individuals from the provinces were drawn to the capital or applied their abilities in her service.

But the process of cultural assimilation, remarkable though it was,

---

[14]Two of these, the development of the *jus gentium* and the gradual extension of the imperial citizenship, were described in chapter 5, section on "The Classical Roots of the Doctrine of Equality."

[15]This is similar to the policy successfully followed for many decades by the British in India.

succeeded only in the western portion of Rome's dominions. Latin could dominate France, Spain, Italy, and North Africa. But it could not oust the Greek tongue from its ascendancy in the eastern Mediterranean. Politically and militarily one, the empire was cut culturally in twain, with the Adriatic as the geographical boundary. It was understandable, therefore, that the structure of government would eventually conform to the social division. The Emperor Diocletian accordingly sliced the empire into two halves (in A.D. 286), assigning the administration of one half to a colleague. Unity was later restored by Constantine, who also moved the capital from Rome to the city of Byzantium, which he renamed for himself (A.D. 330). But the empire once more fell apart at the seams and was partitioned between the sons of Theodosius, after their father's death in A.D. 395.

Limits of the Roman Empire

After the third century A.D. the sprawling mass of the Roman Empire could be ruled from one center only with the greatest difficulty and by an exceptional man. This was due to a mixture of changes taking place both inside the boundaries of the empire and beyond. As Rome added to her possessions and laboriously cemented the political mosaic of the Mediterranean world, the question was inevitably posed: Where should expansion stop? With every new acquisition Rome lengthened the frontier she had to defend and the lines of communication from the capital to the perimeter. A permanent military establishment was required, as legions must be stationed at the chief danger points, and their loyalty and that of their commanders created anxiety for no few emperors. Besides, the incorporation of more peoples with alien ways imposed further strain on the absorptive capacity of the Graeco-Roman civilization. Where would the Roman Eagle find the limit of its cruising radius?

The limits were set at the two extreme points where the force which Rome could exert was at last matched by the defensive strength of another people with a resistant culture. One place was in Germany. With the conquest of Gaul (that is, France) completed, the Romans fanned out across the Rhine, hoping to make the Elbe their frontier. But the hostility of German tribes, aided by the thick cover of their forests, was climaxed in A.D. 9 when they ambushed and decimated an army of three legions. The emperor, Augustus, accepted this verdict and drew back his frontier to the Rhine. The other point at which distance weakened the striking power of Rome was in the East where the civilization of Greece confronted that of Asia. For centuries the control of the interior highlands of Turkey, of the Arabian desert and the river valleys of the Tigris and Euphrates, was hotly contested by oriental monarchies and occidental invaders. Here in this embattled region, the cockpit then as now of East-West relations, the Romans retrod the paths and refought the issues of the Trojan War, the Graeco-Persian Wars, and the campaigns of Alexander. But the legionary, superb infantryman though he was, could not so readily dominate a terrain whose aridity forced men to be mobile and placed a premium on the camel or the horse. When the army of Crassus was cut to shreds by the Parthians[16] at Carrhae (53 B.C.), it was cavalry that won the day. Sometimes with success, but more often not, the emperors sought to plant the Eagle on the Euphrates, making it the Rhine of the East. Even when the limit was attained, however, the Romans were never able to recreate that union of occident and orient of which for a brief moment Alexander the Great had seen and left a vision. Albeit a titanic achievement, the empire of Rome was not universal. Before the opposition of Germans and Parthians its expansion halted.

Then came the time when the power that Rome could direct outward was exceeded by the pressures upon her from north and east. The reasons for her decline and fall have long been a topic of speculation among historians, searching for a single root cause in the general complex of disintegration. To Christian theologians the humbling of Rome was a sign of the wrath of God for the sins of the city. To Gibbon Christianity itself appeared responsible, for by glorifying meekness and pacifism it was supposed to have weakened the martial nerve of the population. Economists have noted the evidence of economic decay—the decreasing fertility of the soil, especially in Italy; the impoverishment of the citizen farmers and the chronic shortage of precious metals and ensuing monetary crises, the huge corps of imperial civil servants and the fiscal difficulties of the exchequer. Add for good measure the turmoil created by the ambitions of rival generals, who competed for the succession to the emperorship, and the insecurity and loss of life and treasure when the control of an empire hung periodically on the decision of civil war. So far had internal dry rot proceeded that when the empire's outer shell was finally cracked in the West (A.D. 410), the soft substance inside crumbled before the blows of Goth and Visigoth and Vandal. Like the city-state of the fourth century B.C., Rome could no longer provide for its citizens those two essentials of government—security and prosperity. Therefore it fell.

The Medieval Dream of Universal Order

Politics is often molded by the survival of a memory. Few examples of this truth are as striking as the spell that the name of Rome has never ceased to

---

[16]The "Parthian shot" was their celebrated trick of feigning retreat and, when the enemy gave chase, turning around on horseback and firing a last murderous volley into their pursuers.

shed. Long after it collapsed in the West, the empire continued to influence politics because of the remembered fact that it had once existed. The feat of uniting the Mediterranean world, of which Rome proved itself capable, inspired a series of would-be imitators; and autocratic rulers entitled czar or kaiser have proudly taken the name of Caesar.

The first attempt was by Charlemagne in A.D. 800. Two circumstances had occurred in the three preceding centuries to make his venture feasible. First, the "barbarians" from the north, falling heir to the legacy of Graeco-Roman civilization, slowly imbibed its characteristics. As the Romans before them were educated by the Greeks they conquered, so the victorious Franks, Goths, and Lombards became Christianized and partly Romanized, and such cultural assimilation made easier politically the revival of a single empire. A second factor was the stimulus of a new pressure from outside. This was the growth of the militant power of Islam, which rose out of the Arabian desert and turned the flank of Europe by its lightning spread across North Africa. As André Maurois has written:

> Mahomet died in 632; by 635, the Moslem armies were at Damascus, in 641 at Alexandria, in 713 at Toledo. In 725 the Arabs pushed up the Rhone Valley as far as Autun. These new conquerors could not be assimilated as the Germans had been. The Franks had admired Rome and adopted Christianity; the Moslems remained faithful to their own ways and religion. At the beginning of the eighth century, they were virtually masters of the Mediterranean. They occupied the whole of Spain, and a portion of southern France.[17]

The popes of the eighth century were preoccupied with fear that the Crescent might supplant the Cross. No less concerned were the kings of the Franks, whose dominions were menaced by the advance of the Saracens. An additional reason impelled the popes to bid for French support. From their north Italian base in the Po Valley the Lombards were spreading south and threatening Rome. The Franks, in the rear of the Lombards, were natural allies for the papacy. First to Charles the Hammer, then to Charlemagne, the pope appealed for protection. When Charlemagne by the close of the eighth century had established his supremacy in Western Europe, he struck a mutually advantageous bargain with the pope. Using his temporal power to bolster the church, in St. Peter's on Christmas day, A.D. 800, he received from Pope Leo III the title "Emperor of the Romans."

But words and ceremonies, though in politics they have symbolic value, cannot alone perpetuate the realities of empire. His successors were unable to maintain the unity of the territories that Charlemagne had knit together. In 843 his three grandsons divided their patrimony. One obtained the eastern section, comprising portions of Germany. A second

---

[17]*Histoire de la France*, vol. 1 (New York: Editions de la Maison Française, 1947), p. 41 (my translation).

received in the west a large slice of France. To the third, Lothair, was given a middle kingdom, following the direction of the Rhine and extending from north Italy to the North Sea. Much of the subsequent history of Europe relates to that division: the separate political development of the French to the west of the Rhine and the Germans to the east, and the struggle between them for control of the middle kingdom. Once again, however, the idea of a single empire outlived the disappearance of the fact. This time it moved east, cropping up among the Germans, whose efficient ruler Otto the Great was crowned emperor by the pope in 962. Henceforth, for what it was worth, the title of emperor and the claim to universal empire remained with the Germans. Thus was the stage set for the medieval politics of conflict between a German-based empire and an Italian-based papacy.

To the problems of the size of the state, the Middle Ages contributed an ambitious dream imperfectly realized. The governing concept of the period was that of a universal society permeated with the Christian spirit. Lacking, however, were the means to make the dream come true. The medieval structure was a dual one, with church and state organized to take care of human spiritual and bodily needs respectively.[18] On the temporal side, the universal society was a pretentious fiction to which the facts bore no resemblance. Because of the feudal system, localism was the order of the day.[19] Kingdoms were mostly patchwork quilts, where much depended on the personality of the reigning king. Central authority was frequently defied, with difficulty imposed. The Holy Roman Empire embraced a group of German principalities. But its writ did not run in France or Spain, in England or Lombardy. After the fall of Rome and the turmoil of the Teutonic invasions, the state had suffered fragmentation, and its essential functions were as often as not decentralized. Rather than be without shelter amid the perils of a world in flux, people rebuilt security and prosperity in small oases of local order.

On the ecclesiastical side, the dream came nearer to fulfillment. The Roman Church had a centralized authority, a single canon law, a common ritual and theology. As a citizen of Rome in any province could formerly appeal his case to Caesar, so in matters pertaining to salvation—and they were many—a Christian could appeal to the pontiff, who jealously guarded the principle of uniformity. Stern punishment was meted out to heretics. The Albigenses in the southwest of France and the Waldenses in the southeast, who deviated from the Latin rite and challenged Roman authority in the late twelfth and early thirteenth centuries, were fiercely attacked and all but exterminated.[20] Nor was the church loath to invoke for this purpose

---

[18]See chapter 6, section on "The Christian Revolution: Church-State Dualism."

[19]See chapter 10, section on "The Medieval Dispersion of Powers."

[20]It was at this time and in this connection that the papacy inaugurated the Inquisition which was responsible for infamous cruelties in the name of religious orthodoxy.

the military forces of the temporal sword. Whoever indeed paid more attention to realities than forms could argue that the imperial mantle had fallen on the shoulders of the pope, not on those of the Holy Roman emperor.[21] Certainly many a clergyman, in order to associate his church with the symbols of Roman power, talked as if the most important place in the Christian world were not Jerusalem or Bethlehem, but Rome.

The Cracks in Medieval Unity

Yet there precisely was the rub! One reason for such talk was that Rome lay in the West, whereas the Holy Land belonged to the East. The split of the Roman Empire into two halves, divided by language and having separate administrative capitals in Rome and Constantinople, outlived the social and military breakdown of the western half. In the East a Byzantine empire based in Constantinople continued in existence. Associated with it was the eastern church employing a Greek rite, and further differing from the western church in being a department, rather than an independent partner, of the state. Situated closer than Rome to Islam, the eastern church and empire was harder pressed by the upsurge of oriental power. In 637 Jerusalem passed into the hands of the Moslems, though Christian pilgrims were still admitted to the holy places. But in 1071 the Turks of the Seljuk dynasty captured the city from their Islamic rivals and forbade entry to Christians, and the Byzantine Empire was too enfeebled to challenge them.

Then was initiated that series of dramatic events which, more than anything else, reveals in its true perspective the medieval assumption of a universal society. These were the Crusades. No less than seven were launched in the period between 1096 and 1270. The Turkish policy of sealing off Jerusalem provided a pretext and an occasion. To drive the infidel from the Holy City and recapture it for Christendom was the mission preached by Peter the Hermit, evangelist of the First Crusade (1096– 1100). But the motives and objectives were as mixed as the participants. The various French kings who blessed the enterprise saw an opportunity to extend their influence in the East and there found a Latin kingdom. North Italian merchants welcomed a chance of creating or reviving a trade with the Levant to which Turks and Saracens offered so serious an obstruction. A motley assortment of religious zealots, adventurers, fortune seekers, footloose knights, and romantics were lured by the glittering prospect of excitement, mystery, and plunder. The papacy itself was influenced by three-sided calculations. Under the banner of the Cross, raised by the Church Militant, the unity of Western Europe could be consolidated. A

---

[21]In a later century such a hostile critic as Thomas Hobbes wrote in the *Leviathan:* "And if a man consider the originall of this great Ecclesiasticall Dominion, he will easily perceive, that the Papacy, is no other, than the *Ghost* of the deceased *Romane Empire*, sitting crowned upon the grave thereof." Part 4, chapter 47 (Everyman's Library), p. 381. Italics in original.

display of occidental strength on the continent of Asia would check the onrush of Islam by penetrating its own domain. Furthermore, the superiority of Rome over Constantinople, of the Latin rite over the Greek, would be triumphantly asserted if the Christians of the West accomplished what those of the East could not. That this thought was by no means last or least among papal hopes seems clear. Certain of the Crusades were as evidently directed against the Byzantine power as against that of the Seljuks, and the fourth in the series (1202–1204) actually resulted in the temporary establishment of a Latin kingdom in Constantinople!

Perhaps the most remarkable aspect of these expeditions is that so many were sent and that they were prolonged for nearly two centuries. This can prove only one thing—that those who launched and led the Crusades were convinced of their political value. Despite the difficulties of transporting an army from Western Europe to Palestine and supplying it at such a distance, despite reverses and failures,[22] the organization of Crusades developed into a medieval habit. They must, therefore, have produced a profit which nowhere appears on the military balance sheet of gain and loss. Nor is that profit hard to discover. It was the kind of gamble expressed in the maxim that a divided community should prosecute a vigorous foreign policy. The Western Europe of that time was hardly a happy band of brothers, and the unity to which the papacy aspired had to be created through subjective loyalties as well as structured institutions. The papacy hoped this inner consolidation could be achieved by attacking an outer enemy; by hostility, not only to Islam, but also to the eastern church; by a policy of clenching both fists and brandishing both swords, not of turning the other cheek. The medieval Christian society, in short, was not fully unified and was never universal. Christendom itself was split, and against it was arrayed the militancy of a rival faith and culture.

Even a series of Crusades, however, could not cement the cracks in the West's foundation walls or prevent new fissures from opening up. The structure of the feudal economy and church-state dualism began to sag in the fourteenth century and broke in the fifteenth. The theories of Thomas Aquinas were predicated upon an ideal of universality and a social hierarchy reinforced by rural conservatism. But between Thomist doctrine and political and economic actualities the gap grew even wider, until one bore as little relation to the other as the Aristotelian *polis* did to the results of Macedonian statecraft. The same fundamental causes that had brought first the city-state and then the Roman Empire to its downfall were operating again in the fourteenth and fifteenth centuries. The unit of government, contrived earlier to yield the necessary minimum of security and

---

[22]For instance, the First Crusade did succeed in taking Jerusalem (1100). But in 1187 the city once more fell into Moslem hands. Recovered in the Fifth Crusade (1228–1229), it passed again to the Turks in 1239.

prosperity, was no longer adequate. Because of conflicts among the feudal nobility, the rise of urban centers desiring a wider extension of commerce, and the schism and corruption in the papacy followed by the Protestant Reformation, a new territorial unit had to be organized wherein people could once more feel themselves safe and could work to be prosperous. Nor should one overlook the effects of the invention of gunpowder. Applied to war, it blew the knight in armor to bits, thus lowering the status associated with his military importance. Shakespeare refers to this when he describes "a certain lord, neat, and trimly dress'd," who enraged the battle-weary Hotspur with his foppish manner and elegant chitchat.

> And that it was great pity, so it was
> This villanous saltpetre should be digg'd
> Out of the bowels of the harmless earth,
> Which many a good tall fellow had destroy'd
> So cowardly; and but for these vile guns,
> He would himself have been a soldier.[23]

Similarly the vanished world of the medieval knight-errant and his illusions form the subject of Cervantes's satire in *Don Quixote*. The windmills at which the superannuated knight tilted were cannons and commerce. Under such sponsors Western Europe started its third experiment in the search for the state of ideal magnitude.

Birth of the Nation-State

This third attempt, the nation-state, marked a new departure in two ways. Because the medieval system combined an ideal of universalism with the realities of localism, its successor differentiated itself by rejecting both. The result was a focus on the nation. This spelled a reaction against both the universal order and the local. Since the new unit was to be the nation, the new unity must be national. The nation would now impose itself on the localities, while simultaneously defying the larger outside orders of papacy and empire. Consequently, the nation-state differed from its predecessors—city-state and empire-state—by reason of its intermediate size. Its area was larger than the city-state, but smaller than the empire-state of the Roman and medieval pattern. Thus did its architects hope to avoid the extremes of a unit which was too little or too large. The new arrangement had the appearance of a compromise. Perhaps this time Europe would strike the happy medium. Here at least was one angle from which the nation-state could be seen and judged.

---

[23]*I Henry IV*, 1. 3. 59–64.

But something as complex as the nation state presents many angles. Viewed in time, the nation-state flourished as the dominant unit of government for almost four and a half centuries. I would place its birthdate in the later decades of the fifteenth century. In 1469, the year of Machiavelli's birth, a marriage between Ferdinand of Aragon and Isabella of Castile sealed the union and inaugurated the sixteenth-century greatness of Spain. Martin Luther was born in 1483, and with him a generation that was to commit the irrevocable acts of the Reformation. Two years later, after his victory at Bosworth Field, Henry VII ascended the throne of England. Himself a Lancastrian, he married Elizabeth of York in 1486, thereby founding the Tudor dynasty and healing the feud between rival aristocratic clans which had brought upon England the Wars of the Roses.[24] And when did the death throes of the nation-state commence? Probably in 1914,[25] though death cannot yet be officially certified.

Viewed in space, the nation-state illustrates a singular combination of politics with geography. Those that were organized earliest and rose to prominence in the sixteenth and seventeenth centuries—Spain, Portugal, England, France, and the Netherlands—were situated on the coast with direct access to the Atlantic. However, the initial reasons for the influence of the seaboard states of the West lay in the East. In 1453 the Turks succeeded in a centuries-old dream by the capture of Constantinople and extinction of the Byzantine Empire. Thereupon, with complete strategic command of the Mediterranean's Asiatic fringe, they consummated the policy already applied in Jerusalem and elsewhere. Europeans were denied access to the region under Turkish-Arabian control. The caravan routes which for over a millennium had given the West its most direct approach to the trade of the East were cut. A crippling economic blow was dealt to such commercial states as Venice, of whom Wordsworth later wrote:

> Once did she hold the gorgeous East in fee;
> And was the safeguard of the West.

Between Europe and India, Islam had stretched its crescent of steel and cordon of sand.

To this challenge the Europeans replied with a search for alternative routes to the rear of the obstructive Moslems. The Portuguese prince, Henry the Navigator, sent out a series of expeditions to chart a course round Africa. Financed by Isabella in 1492 the Genoese captain Columbus sailed west and found what he thought were the Indies.[26] Thus was a New

---

[24]See chapter 9, section on "The Struggle between Kings and Nobles."

[25]See chapter 13, section on "Anarchy among Nations."

[26]Besides Columbus, the leading men who pioneered the ways to the future were Vasco da Gama, discoverer of the route around the Cape of Good Hope; Pedro Alvares Cabral, who found South America and landed in Brazil; Amerigo Vespucci, who gave his name to America; and Fernao de Magalhaes, after whom the Straits of Magellan are called.

World opened up to compensate for the loss of the Old, so that soon the spoils of Mexico and Peru were replacing the treasure of the East. The effect of this geographical reorientation was to give to the English Channel and the Straits of Gibraltar the significance formerly possessed by the Dardanelles and the Isthmus of Suez. The routes linking Europe to the rest of the world no longer pointed east, but south and west. The great inland sea, the Mediterranean, ceased to be the main artery for traffic. It became instead a side road, for the Oceanic Age had begun. Through centuries past, the calculations of political and military strength were primarily computed in terms of land power, since the landlocked Mediterranean could be commanded by armies—as the Romans, who were no sailors, had demonstrated. Now, however, the sea figured with equal, or in some cases greater, prominence. The peoples who bordered on the Atlantic saw the coast as their front door and, when it was opened, the corridors of a stale diplomacy were freshened with briny breezes. Upon the wave of sea power the nation-state floated to its destiny. What started, though, as an Atlantic phenomenon did not remain a preserve of the western seaboard. Not the least remarkable aspect of the nation-state has been its capacity to spread. The city-states were never able to extend over much more than the coastal fringe and islands of the Mediterranean. Even the empire-state and medieval Christendom were stopped in their advance. But the nation-state has left no portion of the world uncovered. All of Asia, Africa, and South America has now been subdivided into nation-states. No previous unit of government achieved so extensive a coverage.

There are three explanations for this. The chief characteristic of sea power is its mobility, which facilitated the spread of Western European influence. Second, the Europeans, when coming into contact with non-Europeans, possessed a superior technology in many fields—hence the urge for non-Europeans to borrow from Europe not only its techniques but also its political system. The third reason is more subtle. The nation-state seems to operate with a contagious magic on those beyond its borders. The pressure that one people organized around the principle of nationality exerts upon another has often stimulated a growth of rival feelings. Thus the attempts of English kings to extend their grip on France and secure its throne assisted the birth of French nationhood, of which Joan of Arc in the years 1429–1431 supplied a flaming symbol. The might of Spain in the sixteenth century was challenged by English seamen in duels which ranged across the Atlantic and the Caribbean and into the Pacific. When the Spanish Armada was defeated in 1588, Elizabeth's England experienced that outburst of national *élan* to which Shakespeare's histories are testimony. The protracted hostilities of Poland and Russia developed in both an ardent patriotism. Napoleonic conquest set spurs to Prussian reorganization and speeded the pan-German aspirations on which Bismarck later rode to power. Austrian resistance to Italian unification boomeranged against the Hapsburgs by giving Mazzini and Cavour a target to attack. British rule in

India eventually provoked an Indian national sentiment. The action of the United States in forcing Japan to open itself to contact with the world (1853–1854) aroused a rapid reaction in the overthrow of the shogunate, industrialization of the economy, and the aggressive nationalism that reached its climax in 1941. Likewise Japan's own endeavor to subjugate the mainland, coming on top of successive encroachments by European powers, added motive and momentum to China's revolution.

Components of Nationality

These facts require explaining. What is there about the nation-state that has made it an article for export and encouraged the domestic manufacture of a competing product? What makes a community a nation? What makes a nation organize a state? Above all, what is a nation?

Any unit of government will reflect and inspire certain feelings among its citizens. If the state is adequate in providing security and prosperity, that feeling will be one of positive loyalty. This is the subjective side of government because it includes the emotions and attitudes, the hopes and hates and sympathies, for which people find fulfillment in their politics. Every kind of state, in order to survive, must breed an appropriate patriotism as the counterpart to its institutions. The city-state glorified its own achievements, so that a person took pride in being Athenian or Spartan. The empire-state inculcated a loyalty to Rome, while the medieval society sought to unify mankind through acceptance of the Christian creed. The same has been true of nation-states. In this case the subjective element is a feeling of nationality, which stimulates in a group the sense of belonging together. When people unite around a national symbol, they think, live, and act—and, if necessary, die in warfare—not as Athenians, Romans, or Christians, but as Americans, Russians, or Germans.

Building the American Nation

How do such sentiments arise? What are the conditions of nationhood? If a nation must have a sense of belonging together, anything shared may help to weld people into a nation. Conversely, whatever divides them weakens their union. Hence the foundations of nationality are embedded in the structure of society. Any of the associations, through which we combine or compete in our economic, religious, cultural, and other activities, can become politically significant if it affects national unity or division. Consider some examples. The slavery issue precipitated a crisis that almost destroyed the American nation. "A house divided against itself cannot stand," said Lincoln quoting the Scriptures. "I believe this government," he went on, "cannot endure permanently, half slave and half free. I do not expect the

Union to be dissolved,—I do not expect the house to fall; but I do expect it will cease to be divided. It will become all one thing, or all the other."[27] In that instance a social cleavage culminated in civil war because of the interests and feelings arrayed on the two sides, and their near-equality of strength.

Another American case can be cited, however, which also involved the fundamentals of the social system, but was settled differently because a huge majority confronted a small minority. In 1846 the Mormons trekked to the western wilderness to found their own community under the dictates of their church. Yet their Promised Land could not escape the pursuit of the society they had left. When the hour arrived for Utah to be organized as a state, Congress would not confer statehood until the Mormon church abandoned polygamy. That raises an interesting point. The Constitution gives Congress exclusive authority in admitting new states. But on the question of the family and its place in the social order, the document is silent. Nevertheless, Congress felt that the Constitution assumes, though it does not specify, that one man may not have several wives simultaneously. This government could not endure permanently, part monogamous and part polygamous; it had to become all one thing, or all the other!

Among the bonds that make for national unity, it is customary to include a common language, common race, and common religion. Those who speak the same tongue, worship in the same faith, and belong physically to the same branch of mankind, possess similarities and escape potential misunderstandings. The United States has absorbed millions of immigrants from many lands and molded their children and grandchildren to a new design. Out of the "melting pot" has flowed the material of an American nationality. What made this possible? Much of the credit belongs to provisions of the Constitution which tolerate the practice of any religion, guarantee to individuals the same fundamental rights, and allow for the naturalization and enfranchisement of aliens. These principles were reinforced by the opportunities of an expanding economy and the conformist tendencies of the public schools which taught one language and imparted the same basic beliefs to the younger generation.

That is not to say that such a phenomenon as the creation of a new nationality for 240 million people could be accomplished without friction and end in complete assimilation. When Catholics arrived from Ireland in great numbers during the 1840s, some Protestants voiced and organized an opposition. When Italian and Slavic immigration increased in the decades between the Civil War and World War I, qualms were felt by anxious Anglo-Saxons.[28] Divided by religion, Americans have been united by the

[27]From the speech at Springfield, Illinois, on his nomination to the United States Senate, 17 June 1858.

[28]This problem forms a central theme in André Siegfried's *America Comes of Age* (London and Toronto: Jonathan Cape, 1927). Second edition, reprinted 1974 by Da Capo Press.

English language, which for reasons of economic and social convenience became the common medium of expression. Since the 1960s, however, the increasing numbers of Hispanic immigrants, both legal and illegal, from Central and South America and the Caribbean have challenged the monopoly of English. Consequently in the states along the southern border, from California to Florida, bilingualism was officially endorsed in many school districts, especially in the lower grades. Voting ballots have also been printed by some states in the two languages, although this practice was rejected in 1986 by a referendum in California.[29]

Most difficult of all, however, has been the absorption of America's oldest minority, the blacks,[30] who have been the victims of more persistent discrimination than any other group. In their case the racial difference has outweighed all of the human and cultural similarities—including the fact that they are English-speaking Christians. If American blacks are to overcome in the 1990s the inequalities which most of them still experience, the principal lever for progress must be to improve their economic opportunities, which can only happen if they are better educated.

The Problem in Europe

1. The Effects of Cultural Division

Among the nation-states of Europe the problems of race relations are relatively minor. But language and religion have cut the continental jigsaw puzzle into most irregular shapes. Europe contains three principal cultures—Latin, Germanic, and Slavic. Except for Switzerland and Belgium (the latter a less successful union than the former), no nation-state has been compounded of Latin and Germanic elements. Similarly, in east-central Europe no nationality has ever been formed out of a Latin-Slavic blend, save in the case of Poland and possibly Yugoslavia. For, though the Poles are Slavs, their church retained its link with Rome; and in Yugoslavia the Croats are Latinized and Catholic, while the Serbs are Slavs and follow the Greek rite. A fusion of Germanic and Slavic people into one nation has been even harder to accomplish. The only state which had both the chance and motive to do this—Austria—was unequal to its opportunity. The Austrians organized their government on the principle of German ascendancy, and, in contrast with the Roman policy, admitted none but the Hungarian Magyars

---

[29]Asian immigrants have also added to the linguistic complexities of primary education in California. But their mastery of English in high schools and the universities has been repeatedly demonstrated by the honors they have won.

[30]See Gunnar Myrdal, *The American Dilemma*, rev. ed. (New York: Harper & Row, 1962).

to the charmed circles of influence. Slavs were not welcomed as partners in the citadels of power.[31]

The Austrian case throws a glaring light on the nation-state in Europe. The Hapsburg Empire originated and continued because it kept the Ottoman Empire at bay. The Slavs were the subject of a squeeze and, to the extent that they could act for themselves, might choose a Hapsburg emperor or a Turkish sultan. Both left much to be desired. The odds were by no means always in the favor of Austria, whose crassness was a match for Turkish cruelties. Indeed the Balkan Christians of the Eastern Orthodox Church were at times more tolerantly treated by the caliphate than by the papacy. But to those who thought in terms of contrasting Europe and Asia, Austria could at least claim to be Europe's champion. Even so, the appeal of Vienna to the Slavs fluctuated in inverse ratio with Turkish strength. When Ottoman power was expanding, Vienna might seem the lesser evil. But when the Turks declined in the nineteenth century, the Austrian empire lost its *raison d' être*. Then came the opportunity that Austria missed. To avoid a series of wars of independence, she had to unite her multinational empire around a comprehensive loyalty and, as Rome had done, turn subjects into partners. This would involve either decentralization from Vienna and the grant of more power to Hungarians, Czechs, and others, or a sharing of authority at the center. The former solution was applied only to Hungary. The latter, which meant a representative legislature and abandonment of autocracy, implied also the sacrifice of German leadership. To Metternich and his successors, these consequences were unthinkable. Hence, amid the babel of national aspirations which its domination provoked, the Austrian autocracy waltzed to its own destruction.

The dilemma of the Austrians, caught between their desire for German superiority and the demands of a multinational population for equality, is connected to the national consolidation of two neighbors, Germany and Italy. At first glance it is puzzling that these countries were not unified until four centuries later than Spain, France, and England, and that their unification, when it finally came, occurred in the same decade (1860–1871). The reasons can be discovered, however, in the policies of Austria and the papacy and in the relationship between them, the roots of which reach back to the Middle Ages. The attempt to organize Western Christendom under the Holy Roman Empire and the papacy was formulated in terms of a universal society. In fact, however, the papacy was based on Italy, a portion of which the popes governed as temporal sovereigns, while the empire acquired a German base. Even when pope and emperor cooperated, it was not in either's interest to permit the other to consolidate his

---

[31]Hitler expressed in the opening chapters of *Mein Kampf* the antipathies of a German-speaking Austrian, from a lower social class, toward the Slavic subjects of the Hapsburg Empire.

jurisdiction over Germany or Italy respectively. If Italy remained divided, the pope's position was more precarious and he was less able to dominate the emperor. If the empire was a loose and tenuous union, the emperor was less likely to control the pope. Each must therefore support a balance of power in the other's terrain to prevent a concentration of power by his rival.

As the Reformation sapped the foundations of Catholicism by breaking the unity of western Christendom, so the emerging nation-state challenged the empire by negating its claims to universalism. Not until the end of the Thirty Years' War (1648) were the division of western Christendom and the system of nation-states accepted as irrevocable features of Europe's political order. In the eighteenth century both papacy and empire steered against the prevailing wind and current with enough power to keep at a standstill. But in the century that followed, the dominant forces were industrialism, laissez-faire economics, liberal democracy, and a latterday nationalism which, because belated, was all the more intense. Against these, empire and papacy set themselves in opposition; and, being on the defensive and compelled to retreat, found themselves allies in a futile resistance.

Neither Germany nor Italy could be unified except by defying both the Hapsburgs and the pope. Metternich had condemned the union of all Germans in a single state as "an infamous object." Those who thought in pan-German terms hoped to include Austria in a German state, but wanted to exclude her non-German subjects. For her part, Austria refused to pay for admission into an all-German state the price of losing her empire; and until the middle of the nineteenth century, while unwilling to unify Germany herself, she was strong enough to prevent anybody else from doing so. A similar situation existed in Italy, of which Austria controlled the northeast. To unify Italy meant the defeat and expulsion of the Austrians. Metternich had declared that Italy was only a geographical expression and he intended to keep it so. The other obvious loser in any Italian unification was the papacy, which would have to surrender its temporal rule over the center of the peninsula. Consequently, when the Kingdom of Italy was established in 1860, and when Bismarck's Prussia (Protestant-led) organized the German Reich in 1871, nationalism triumphed in both cases over a multinational empire and a supranational church.

2. The Religious Cleavage

If it was difficult to create a nationality in Europe out of mixed cultures, it was no less difficult to mix religions. The most successful nation-states have been those containing a large majority of either Protestants or Catholics. The oldest nation-states are witnesses to this truth. In Britain the Protestant Reformation triumphed—and though England could amalgamate with Wales and Scotland, she never absorbed the Catholic portion of Ireland. In France and Spain the Catholic Counter-Reformation triumphed. Thus in all three countries early nationalism was associated with religious intolerance. Only in exceptional cases has a nation been formed with a blend of Protestants and Catholics in relatively equal strength. On this point the example of Switzerland is instructive. Because of the work of Zwingli in Zurich and Calvin in Geneva, portions of Switzerland became Protestant strongholds. But its geographical proximity to France, Austria, south Germany, and north Italy made the Swiss strategically important to the papacy, and the Jesuit order attempted to recapture their allegiance. In 1847 a minority of Catholic cantons seceded—without success; hence in 1848 the Protestant majority wrote the new federal constitution—which banned the Jesuits from Switzerland.[32] But though religion has split the Swiss, and though language divides them into French, German, and Italian sections, their union is helped by the fact that the religious and linguistic divisions cut across each other. While Geneva is French-speaking and Calvinist, Neuchatel and Fribourg are French-speaking and Catholic. Whereas Bern and Zurich are German-speaking and Protestant, Luzern and Schwyz are German-speaking and Catholic.

Even this, however, would not account for the miracle of Swiss nationhood if there were not an additional reason. Instead of incorporation into France, Germany, Austria, or Italy, the Swiss have chosen to become Swiss because of their reaction to the pressures of surrounding big powers and because geography made defense and independence practicable. Furthermore, the survival of their state has been guaranteed by their consistent policy of permanent neutrality. The Swiss, therefore, illustrate the point that nationality is often a response to a pressure exerted from without. But they illustrate something else. When analyzing the nation-state one should ask whether the nation helps create the state or the state the nation. In fact, examples occur of both, which proves that, while a nation may be molded out of social factors, it can also originate in politics. Switzerland is an example of a state being organized first, and a national sentiment developing second. So is the United States, where the foundation of a federal government in large part preceded and then promoted the ripening of an American nationality. In other words, to live under the same system of government and the tradition it acquires with the lapse of time stimulates a popular sense of belonging together. Thus it is not only the English language, the monogamous family, and the abolition of slavery which have contributed to an American nation, but also the attachment to the Declaration of Independence and the Constitution and to such names as Franklin, Washington, Jefferson, and Lincoln.

Conversely, a group that already feels a national unity because of a common language, literature, and religion may eventually develop such cohesive force as to found a state. Witness the modern instances of Poland

---

[32]*Constitution of the Swiss Confederation,* Article 51.

and Israel. This is especially likely to happen to a minority group governed by a repressive majority of different language or religion. Where an intolerant majority monopolizes the government, the minority, unable to take part in politics on an equal basis, clings to other associations than the state, seeking thereby a medium for its own representation. Often this role has been assumed by religion, which supplied a structure and a voice for a group that felt itself suppressed. Thus the Catholic church traditionally assisted the nationalism of the Poles and their resistance to czarist Russification. The same church provided the Irish with a vehicle of opposition to the British and has been the mainstay of the French-Canadians. Jewish synagogues, transmitting the *Torah* from one generation to the next, kept a Hebraic culture alive among a sorely persecuted people. On Cyprus the Greek church led the agitation against British rule; and in Burma the Buddhist priesthood, also at odds with Britain, lent its support to the independence movement. Similarly on the South African veld the Dutch Reformed church fostered the fierce nationalism of the Afrikaner extremists.

Nationalism and the Arts

As a substitute for religion, or to supplement it, an emergent nationalism, excluded from the government of the state, may find an outlet in the arts (especially music and literature) and in higher education. Thus nationalistic Poles have sung their folk songs and played their Chopin. The Czech renaissance was expressed musically by Smetana and Dvorak. The "blood and iron" of Bismarck's Reich was rendered into appropriate music by the pompous Wagner, who was understandably a favorite of Hitler. The significance to nationalism of the arts lies in their appeal to the intelligentsia, who have been the prime movers in many national uprisings. This further explains the interest of nationalists in education, in fostering their own language, and in organizing institutions of higher learning—hence the importance of Charles University in Prague to the Czechs, of the Hebrew University to the Zionists, of the University of Cairo to the Egyptians; hence the well-known phenomenon of an ardent nationalism and political activity on its behalf among the university students of so many lands; hence the insistence of nation builders on reviving their ancestral tongue, as Hebrew again became a living language in Israel, and as the government of Eire officially adopted Erse even though Irish literati like Shaw, Joyce, O'Faolain, and Yeats were writing in matchless English!

The interaction between national feeling and cultural achievement is significant. The foundations of the state may be embedded in the material needs of safety and prosperity. But while these are essential needs to satisfy, they alone do not complete the development of the human being. Political organization, which serves our creature comforts and safeguards life itself, can also minister to the spirit. When a governmental system imbues a people collectively with self-respect and strength, the most gifted individuals in the group may be stimulated by the surrounding *élan* to creative production in literature, philosophy, the sciences, and the arts. Thus it is that great luminaries have shone with intellectual and aesthetic brilliance in the very century when a people attained politically "their finest hour." It was hardly an accident that the most glorious period of Athenian culture coincided with the peak of Athenian power after the combat against the Persians; that the golden age in Roman literature coincided with the establishment of the Augustan peace; that the thirteenth century, which witnessed a flowering of medieval genius, saw the papacy at the height of its ascendancy under Innocent III and his successors; that intellect and the arts flourished so brilliantly in seventeenth-century Holland, when the Dutch nation, self-liberated from Spanish rule, was riding the crest of financial and maritime leadership; and that the reigns of Elizabeth I and Victoria, which mark two high points of Britains's political influence, presided over some of the most notable of her achievements of the mind. With each unit of government, therefore—city-state, empire-state, and nation-state—examples can be found of a correlation between political success and cultural greatness.[33]

That the love of one's country has provided an inspirational focus for rare creative work is evidence of the capacity of the nation-state to serve humanity well. Countless are the poets, writers, musicians, painters, scientists, and scholars who have been stirred by national pride to activity of intellectual or imaginative eminence. Such an emotion has offered to many a sensitive spirit an attraction not to be equated with the crudities of jingoism. On that positive note, before the analysis turns to the pathology of nationalism and the decline of nation-states, let this chapter end.

---

[33]The two are not always correlated, however; for example, the Italian Renaissance, despite Machiavelli's pleadings, did not produce a political record that matched the artistic output.

13

Nation-States vs. International Order

The Crisis of the Nation-State

No unit of government has attained enduring peace and prosperity. The Greek system, by emphasizing the autonomy of each urban-rural cluster, prevented wider unions. Efforts to achieve these by combining freely did not last long. and attempts to enforce unification, though tried repeatedly, provoked opposition and war. Rome, beginning like the rest as a city-state, was the only one to achieve a lasting success in the imperial role, thereby eliminating the independent city-state and imposing the new unit of empire. But even Rome could not command the world,[1] and the peace and unity to which she aspired reached their bounds in the north and east. The same was true of the Middle Ages when popes and emperors sought the holy grail of universal order. In neither sphere, however, did practice arrive at universality. Each of those experiments groped for a structure within which people could obtain welfare in safety. Each lasted only as long as it fulfilled the need; each collapsed when it could do so no longer.

The change from one unit to another, whether smaller or larger, is revolutionary, and it is a revolution of a deeper kind than those upheavals

---

[1]The concept of expansion from a city to the world (*ab urbe ad orbem*) was a rhetorical flourish, never a political reality.

to which we ordinarily apply the term. To alter fundamentally the size and scale of one's unit of government is a more radical transformation than to substitute one ruling group for another or to introduce a new style of constitution. That is why this kind of revolution is so rare. Indeed, as was observed in chapter 12, in the Western world it has occurred only twice since the institution of the *polis*.

Our age in history, however, in my judgment is the third instance of this revolution. For the nation-state is now retracing the history of its predecessors. It emerged at a time when it was more capable than the medieval system of supplying humanity with security and well-being. But this unit of government, like the rest, is failing to meet these objectives. Consequently, it is now obsolescent and will become obsolete. Our contemporary world shows many signs of being in transition from the outmoded nation-state to some new unit. Seen in historical perspective, the age in which we live is comparable to the readjustment that occurred between the breakdown of the *polis* and the rise of the Roman Empire or between the collapse of the medieval order and the founding of the nation-state. Once more, an experiment is under way to discover the territorial unit best adapted to ensure prosperity and security in the twenty-first century. Since modern internationalism, however, is a reaction to the declining adequacy of nationalism, the discussion must continue where the last chapter ended. What failings has the nation-state revealed? Is some more workable alternative in sight?

Despite the strivings of states to build nations and of nations to organize states, few perfect correspondences exist between nationality and statehood. The world still exhibits instances of peoples united by a common culture, language, and religion who aspire to a national consciousness and seek to formalize it in a state of their own.[2] Conversely, there are states which include in their jurisdiction a subject people who are unincorporated in the national body politic. In some countries those subjects are a minority; in others—South Africa, for example—they are the majority. Also there are numerous states, some of them very new, which contain inhabitants, but do not constitute a nation. These facts require explanation. Since the nation-state has been in vogue for over four centuries, why so imperfect a correlation between statehood and nationality?

Imperialism and Sea Power

The answer must be sought in historical timing and in a set of economic and military factors all combining in a political result. When the nation-state was born, with it appeared its twin—sea-powered imperialism. How inseparably these were connected is plain to read in the annals of Spain,

---

[2]E.g., the Kurds, who are partitioned among Iraq, Iran, and Turkey.

Portugal, England, France, and the Netherlands. Of course, the practice of imperialism, which consists in the forcible subjection of a community to alien rule, was no novelty. Nor was the employment of sea power, as the Athenians, Phoenicians, Norsemen, and Venetians may bear witness. What was new, however. was political expansion on an oceanic scale. The discovery that the earth was round and could be circumnavigated was quickly put to a use that challenged comparison with Rome. The peoples of Western Europe first mapped the world; then with guns and galleons they partitioned it.

The result was a succession of struggles for maritime supremacy, colonial acquisition, and the wealth to be gained thereby. The first pair of competitors were Spain and Portugal. Between their claims Pope Alexander VI arbitrated in 1493. By his award and the Treaty of Tordesillas in 1494 the non-European world was divided. To Spain was assigned the exclusive possession of all that lay more than 1110 miles to the west of Cape Verde; to Portugal, all that lay east. Such an award was no more acceptable to Catholic France than to Protestant England, both of which had ambitions of their own. When Spain was humbled by the English victory over the Armada and the Dutch had fought successfully for independence, the Atlantic seaways were open to new contestants. Neither France nor England could take full advantage of its opportunity until internal disunion was overcome. This was achieved in the seventeenth century by the triumph of Catholicism and absolute monarchy in one country, of Protestantism and Parliament in the other. Then the two powers were ready to inaugurate their second Hundred Years' War over wider battlefields on sea and land. The epoch that opened with Britain's resistance under Marlborough[3] to the aims of Louis XIV closed with Napoleon's downfall at Waterloo. In between occurred the colonial rivalry, extending long and far, wherein France during the Seven Years' War (1756–1763) bowed to the British in India and North America, but revenged itself by aiding the United States in the War of Independence. To the latter setback Britain responded by speeding up the technological revolution of her industries in the struggle against Napoleon, and later by reorganizing her empire on the principle of self-government for the component parts as they matured.[4] Thus, with her nearest military rivals worsted or enfeebled, Britain preempted the nineteenth century.

Secure in the assets of a factory system whose productivity then led the world, and of a navy and merchant marine predominant in every ocean, the people of a small island off the coast of Europe constructed and

---

[3]John Churchill, first Duke of Marlborough, victor of the battles of Blenheim (1704) and Ramillies (1706), was an ancestor of Winston Churchill.

[4]This principle was first officially recommended for Canada in Lord Durham's Report (1839) and applied in that country in 1846–1847.

commanded an empire which by 1914 covered one-fourth of the land surface of the globe and contained one-fourth of its population. In this climactic episode, sea power, the progenitor of the nation-state, had reached the ultimate. To make it possible, the varied talents of an ebullient age contributed their quotas—Victoria, the queenly symbol; Palmerston, the swashbuckling spirit; Disraeli, the imagination and brains; the City of London, the financial sinews; Kipling, the ballads; and Gladstone, the outraged liberal conscience in self-rebuke for sins it did not prevent.

Contradictions of Sovereignty

The success of imperialism, however, and its duration for four centuries, involved the nation-state in a fundamental inconsistency. Depending on the angle of view, this unit of government can be considered the opposite of either localism or internationalism. Both of those were characteristic of the medieval period, one receiving theoretical[5] lip service and the other reflecting more accurately the realities of social organization. Since the nation-state rejected the system immediately preceding, neither local autonomy nor international control was tolerable to its architects. The centralizing tendency of the nation-state, drawing powers and functions from the localities to the capital, was described earlier.[6] Now is the place to discuss the external relations of nationalism.

As in other respects, the doctrine that was the maid-of-all-work for the nation-state—the theory of sovereignty—here, too, was enlisted into service. Sovereignty was construed to mean that the government of the nation-state, supreme within its own jurisdiction over local bodies and churches, acknowledged no political or legal superior beyond its territorial boundaries. "My dogs," as Queen Elizabeth I of England once phrased it, "shall wear no collars but mine own." Authority, allegiance, and law were to be the exclusive monopoly of the nation-state, and as such, were not articles for import across national frontiers. Were they, however, articles for export? There lay the inconsistency. Whatever its professions, the nation-state acted on a double standard. Both in external and internal affairs it claimed to be a law unto itself. Limitations on its freedom of action diminished its sovereignty and consequently were inadmissible. But, though unwilling to submit to control from outside, it professed to see no wrong in subjecting others to do its own will. Imperialism violated the principle of sovereignty by denying to others the very freedom on which the nationalist insisted. In effect, throughout the entire era of the nation-state, the politi-

---

[5]Except in the ecclesiastical sphere, where the international power of the church was more than theoretical.

[6]See chapter 10, section on "Sovereignty and Absolutism in the Nation-State."

cal ordering of humanity never conformed consistently to the ideal of having a number of separate units of government, each self-contained. Imperialism meant dividing humanity into elite peoples who ruled, and whose nationality could find outlets for expression; and subject peoples whose national aspirations were suppressed. Hence imperialism negated the first premise from which the nation-state proceeded. It is no accident that the twins, which were born together and have lived in perennial incompatibility, in this century are dying together.

This combination of nationalism with imperialism and the ensuing dilemma produced an economic counterpart. From the sixteenth century to the eighteenth, or before laissez-faire policies became prevalent, prosperity was sought by applying political concepts to economics. The politics of nationalism was matched by the economics of nationalism, that being the essence of the mercantile system.[7] Correspondingly, political imperialism was yoked to economic imperialism. Colonies, considered as the "possessions" of the imperial power, were organized to supply it with raw materials and precious metals, as they were also to import its manufactures and carry their commerce in its ships. This is not to deny that additional motives influenced the settlement or acquisition of colonies. The desire of dissident minorities to emigrate; the strategic quest for bases, ports of call, and defensible frontiers; the missionaries who preached the Christian gospel—many a magnet, besides trade, attracted nations to plant their flag on distant shores. But that the single most important factor in empire building was the economic can hardly be denied. Through imperialism the nation-state could grow more prosperous—or so it was hoped.

From the standpoint of security an empire was as much a liability as an asset. True, the treasure yielded by some colonies could be used to build more warships and pay more troops in order to defend the mother country and keep subjects more surely in subjection. But colonies situated across oceans were remote and exposed. They might prove hard to defend against an invader or to hold against a rebellion. Furthermore, when the imperial power was itself in danger of attack on its home terrain, less force could be spared for garrisons abroad. By spreading its resources thin, the imperial nation-state exposed many hostages to fortune. It was therefore vulnerable to amputation at the extremities or attack at the heart. The latter risk was the primary concern of nation-statesmen, since colonies were of no avail if the motherland was insecure. Hence in every case the organization of the nation-state passed through a phase of expansion and consolidation wherein the purpose was to arrive, if possible, at a defensible frontier. Let us observe what happened and the consequences.

The United Kingdom, as Great Britain is officially called, was created by absorptions and additions. England, itself a fusion of smaller and pre-

---

[7]See chapter 7, section on "Medievalism and Mercantilism."

viously separate kingdoms, provided the nucleus for a larger union. Amalgamation with Wales was achieved by conquest in 1284. Scotland and Ireland, both larger than Wales and less accessible, presented more formidable problems. But their independence posed a threat to England since a continental enemy like France could form an alliance with the Scots or Irish and threaten England from the flank or rear. An island has an obvious frontier in its coastline. The union of England and Scotland, facilitated by the triumph of Protestantism both north and south of the border, was formally effected in 1707. "John Bull's other island,"[8] whose proximity made it strategically vital, could be conquered, but largely because of religious differences could not be absorbed. All that remained thereafter was for Britain to control the seas around her coasts and prevent any one power from dominating the European mainland. If this was done, her security was assured. The same problem confronted the continental nation-states, but with an important difference. They had a land as well as a sea frontier to defend. Besides navies, therefore, they had to maintain standing armies, which affected their internal politics, tending to reinforce the authoritarian structure of their government. Armies, more easily than navies, could reach the heart of an enemy state. Napoleon could cross the Pyrenees but not the Channel, and Frenchmen and Germans have marched in and out of each other's territories for centuries.

The military conditions imposed by geography go far toward explaining why it was Britain, and not any of her rivals, that emerged as the strongest power in the nineteenth century. But in that century new factors intervened which in the short run enhanced the might of Britain, yet in the long run contributed both to her decline and to that of the nation-state system. The intruding element was the technology of industrialism and the economic potentialities thus unleashed. Its immediate effect was to create a productive capacity exceeding the needs and resources of the nation-state. Britain had always engaged in foreign trade. But now in volume and extent this trade grew to unprecedented proportions.[9] The terrain that the nation occupied did not yield all the raw materials that manufacturers required. Nor did its population offer a market sufficient to consume their output. More than before, the prosperity of peoples became interdependent.[10] If somewhere in the world production was curtailed or purchasing power declined, if the price of a basic commodity fell or it was replaced by a substitute, other economies were intimately affected thousands of miles away.

---

[8] The title of a play set in Ireland by G. B. Shaw.

[9] A century and a half ago, half of the trade of the entire world passed through the port of Liverpool.

[10] The British adoption of free trade in the 1840s was a frank recognition of this fact.

Anarchy among Nations

The nation-state was now hopelessly caught in a tangle of contradictions. As if it were not already difficult enough to make the boundaries of state and nation coextensive, it became evident that the territorial unit chosen for military purposes was at variance with the area appropriate to economics. Protection was organized to run along national lines; prosperity, across them. The task of organizing a unit wherein the needs of nationality, security, and prosperity would coincide harmoniously was well-nigh impossible, and the situation was rendered more chaotic by the competition between states for the same objectives. An area which a state considered strategically necessary for its own protection might be inhabited by people whom a neighbor regarded as belonging to its own nationality. Valuable resources in the borderland between two states would be sought by both. Thus Alsace-Lorraine, the Low Countries, the Brenner Pass and the Trentino, Bohemia, the Polish Corridor, Suez, and Panama were scenes of international rivalry and conflict.

Under such circumstances, the nation-state became less and less capable of providing the minimal needs of protection and order. At its best, it maintained order within its own territory and minimized, without eliminating, the possibility of civil war; but it could not guarantee that international relations would be peacefully conducted. The doctrine of sovereignty combined internal stability with external anarchy. In essentials, therefore, the history of the nation-state repeated (with a change of scale, because the unit was larger) the earlier experience of the city-state. International relations were like inter-*polis* relations, and the old drama was reenacted in modern dress. Like city-states before them, nation-states were small, medium-sized, or big. If small, their only chance of survival was to accept protection from the biggest power nearby, or if they lay between rival powers, to announce their neutrality and hope it would be respected. Medium-sized states could also serve as buffers to keep their larger neighbors from one another's throats. They might, however, be induced to enter into systems of alliances, since their support or opposition could have some effect on the balance of power. Their riskiest policy, of course, was to be afflicted with delusions of grandeur and dress in big-power costume without having the measurements to fill it.

The major states picked up the script which Athens, Corinth, Sparta, and Thebes had written. Each in turn strove for leadership. Each was destined to strut and fret its hour upon the stage—Spain, Austria, France, Britain, and Germany. All had their periods of ascendancy. None could perpetuate its domination, because new challengers arose against every champion. The result was that throughout more than four centuries the nation-state system was incapable of securing a lasting peace. Major convulsions recurred with frightening regularity—the Thirty Years' War (1618–

1648), the War of the League of Augsburg (1688–1697), the War of the Spanish Succession (1701–1713), the Wars of the French Revolution (1793–1815), World War I (1914–1918), and World War II (1939–1945). These were interspersed with more limited conflicts, so that scarcely a decade went by without an outbreak of hostilities somewhere. The history of most countries contains testimony to prove that establishing a nation-state does not guarantee a continuous peace. The United States, for example, has engaged in four major wars (1776–1783, 1861–1865, 1917–1918, 1941–1945) and five minor ones[11] (1812–1815, 1846–1848, 1898, 1950–1953, 1965–1973) so that, on the average, the peace has been broken in every third decade.

The Consolidation of Land Masses

The perennial anarchy of nation-states and the discordance between national politics and international economics were not the only reasons for the ending of an era. Another was the declining effectiveness of sea power. When this century opened, the peoples of the Atlantic seaboard were losing the advantages which had so long been theirs. Fresh opportunities for expansion were being discovered to the east and west. The new goal was to consolidate the continental land masses under the jurisdiction of a single state. Three attempts of this kind were made. The first was by Germany. The marriage of the Prussian army with the industries of the Ruhr and Rhineland created a formidable power in the north-center of Europe. From this base, with a strategy formulated in terms of land domination, the efficient and ruthless German *Reich* set out to unify the continent. Twice its leaders tried this in wars they instigated. Twice they were beaten, but at a dreadful cost. Since Germany with its central position enjoyed the advantage of interior lines, she could be defeated only by encirclement. Thus, the Atlantic nations perforce were allied with Russia in World War I and again in World War II. Even the western front could not be maintained by Britain and France alone, who in both wars, and particularly in the second, needed American participation to defeat the common foe. Europe's loss of power after 1945 was the price paid by an entire continent for the necessity of curbing German ambitions.

The other two attempts have had different results. From the Atlantic seaboard American democracy expanded westward to the Pacific. Simultaneously, czarist Russia fanned out eastward along northern Asia, incorporating Siberia in its dominion and crossing the Bering Strait into Alaska.

---

[11]This distinction means that victory in a major war requires the mobilization of a people's entire resources in order to survive, while a minor war requires only a limited effort and does not involve a danger to survival.

The phenomenon of states which spanned continents was noted by Tocqueville, who in 1835 made this prophetic comment:

> There are, at the present time, two great nations in the world which seem to tend toward the same end, although they started from different points: I allude to the Russians and the Americans. Both of them have grown up unnoticed; and while the attention of mankind was directed elsewhere, they have suddenly assumed a most prominent place among the nations; and the world learned their existence and their greatness at almost the same time. All other nations seem to have nearly reached their natural limits, and only to be charged with the maintenance of their power; but these are still in the act of growth; all the others are stopped, or continue to advance with extreme difficulty; these are proceeding with ease and with celerity along a path to which the human eye can assign no term. . . . Their starting point is different, and their courses are not the same; yet each of them seems to be marked out by the will of Heaven to sway the destinies of half the globe.[12]

By the time the United States and Russia had attained a size which dwarfed the nation-states of Western Europe, the same technology which had already outmoded the economics of nationalism shattered its military defenses. If the nation-state floated into history on the wave of sea power, it sank under assault from the air. Blériot flew across the English Channel in 1909; in 1919 Alcock and Brown flew the Atlantic. Applied on only a limited scale in World War I, air power was decisive in the strategy of World War II. When the Nazis in 1941 defied the British control of the sea and captured Crete from the air, they rang down the curtain on an epoch. Four years later, when the Japanese surrendered their islands after being the victims of two atomic bombs, they acknowledged realistically that the old politics must conform to the new physics. The foundations of the state have been relocated above in the stratosphere and in outer space.

Collective Insecurity

Abundant evidence confirms that the nation-state can no longer provide protection and prosperity within its own borders. In the first half of this century two wars occurred whose theater of operations was the world. Together they demonstrated that the anarchy of the nation-state system breeds contagious insecurity and allows few to isolate themselves from its effects. The fears, suspicions, and distrust of nation for nation cause each to maintain whatever armaments it can afford, and their costliness is a drain on economies that otherwise could progress in the arts of peace. For other than military reasons, these same economies have become interdependent, rendering them vulnerable to worldwide movements over which no single nation has control. To this truth the depression of the early 1930s

---

[12]Alexis de Tocqueville, *Democracy in America*, part 1, trans. Henry Reeve (New York: J. & H. G. Langley, 1841), chap. 18, pp. 470–71.

bore witness. As a plague sweeps across political frontiers, the same malady struck at one country after another, producing the same symptoms: falling prices, lowered purchasing power, rising unemployment, reduced revenues from taxation, unbalanced budgets, bankruptcies, and default on debts. Prosperity, as well as peace, had become indivisible.

This worldwide succession of events in a 30-year period—war, depression, and war again—offered the clearest proof that an international society was emerging for which the nation-state was an unsuitable unit of government. Not only in trade and commerce, but in cultural contacts and the movement of ideas communication between peoples had become easier and more rapid. As in the fifteenth and sixteenth centuries a national order could not predominate unless the localism of the medieval system was abandoned, so in the twentieth century an international order could not prevail if politics were conducted through national channels. Paradoxically the determination to build security within the borders of the nation-state contributed to everybody's insecurity. States behaved severally like individuals who place their reliance on self-protection and carry weapons on their person instead of resorting to public agencies such as police and courts. That system, whether imagined by Hobbes or practiced under frontier conditions, produces only disorder which is what has happened in a world of nation-states. The efforts of each to build protection nationally has failed to protect us internationally. What is more, the particularism of nation-states has obstructed a development from the protection of each to an order embracing all. International politics had reached an impasse— and it illustrates the general problem of human association discussed in chapter 2. The relations between states were characterized by too much competition and too little cooperation. All suffered from the harmful effects of pursuing their aims in self-centered isolation. They were insufficiently aware that the objectives which all had sought separately could be better achieved if all cooperated collectively. Some method had to be devised of securing protection through order and of infusing the latter with a concept of justice. In short, the need to reorder the relations between states was similar in principle to that of harmonizing associations within the state. The jurisdiction of government had to become more nearly coextensive with the ambit of society.

The Search for Remedies

Because the problems are manifold, the search for remedies has ranged the gamut from legal to military, from economic to political. Historically, the first attempt to mitigate the ferocity of the strong was the formulation of a body of international law.[13] Its rules were designed to regulate the

---

[13]Grotius, the Latinized name of the Dutchman de Groot, published the foundation work in this field in 1625.

competitive self-interest which governments practiced in their mutual dealings. But independent means of enforcement were lacking. Only the threat of retaliation might serve to restrain an aggressor, and it seldom stopped the bigger bullies. Another method was to provide machinery for arbitration, so that disputes between governments could be resolved or compromised by a tribunal that both parties accepted. Arbitration was notably extended in the later nineteenth century, especially in Anglo-American relations. But it depended on a prior willingness to submit to the machinery and to accept its outcome.

At the end of World War I, more ambitious experiments were launched. The International Labor Organization—composed of representatives of governments, employers, and workers—was created to negotiate agreements for bringing industrial conditions to a common standard. The Permanent Court of International Justice provided a bench of jurists representing the principal legal systems of the world. They gave advisory opinions, when requested, or tried cases which governments asked them to adjudicate. Third in this trio was the League of Nations, whose central function was to preserve peace. This it sought by political means, establishing a forum for diplomacy and negotiation. When all else failed and war erupted, the League could evoke sanctions against the government that was declared the aggressor. But their application depended on the voluntary cooperation of the member states. Economic sanctions were attempted once, against Fascist Italy in 1935–1936 when Mussolini invaded Ethiopia. They failed because too many states refused to participate.

In all such experiments, a central problem emerged with stark clarity: the organization of power in the international arena. Each of the institutions or procedures mentioned above was an exploratory device to govern an evolving international society. But the agencies employed to run the machinery were still, at this stage, the very nation-states which needed to be restrained. If these perceived enough of a common interest, they could agree to cooperate. But if their competing interests appeared paramount, how was a wider sphere of order to be maintained? No means were found to stop Japan's aggression against China, or Italy's against Ethiopia, or Germany's against Austria, Czechoslovakia, Poland, and France. World War II was the price paid for the shortcomings of the Versailles Treaty and the inadequacies of the League of Nations.

The United Nations

At the end of World War II humanity received its second chance within a generation. The problem confronting the victors in 1945 was even more urgent than in 1918 because prosperity and security were more seriously jeopardized. Not only were the economies of many countries shattered, but the long-range bomber loaded with an atomic cargo and flying at jet-propelled speeds constituted a greater menace to life than any previous destructive weapon. To organize a general economic recovery and police the world against future acts of aggression would require global solutions. So during the years 1944–1946, a number of new international bodies were established. All but one of these are specialized agencies in the sense that their work is limited to a particular function or service whose programs are often technical in content.[14] The exception is the United Nations, which, as the successor to the League, took over the general responsibility of promoting cooperation between states and keeping them at peace.

A comparison of the League Covenant with the United Nations Charter shows that the latter was intended not to repeat its predecessor but to remedy its defects. Though it embraces a wide range of international problems from declarations of human rights to control of atomic weapons, the United Nations organization was influenced from the start by more realism and fewer illusions than its predecessor. The League did not measure up to the ordeals of the 1930s because it lacked bullets to enforce compliance with its ballots. Consequently, when the Charter was drafted, provisions for enforcement were included, and the Security Council became the cutting edge of the new organization.

Its strength was quickly put to the test. Almost from birth, and before the bone structure had hardened, the United Nations was forced to take arms against a sea of troubles. Several assumptions which had run current in 1945 were found wanting. First, the expectation that the Kuomintang would rule China was not fulfilled. Their overthrow by Mao's forces brought one-quarter of the human race under Communist control at one stroke, changing the balance of power in Asia with profound consequences for relations between East and West. Next, the belief that Western states, after defeating Japan, could maintain their former empires over nonwhite peoples was unrealistic. The Dutch lost the East Indies, which became the state of Indonesia. The French, defeated at Dien Bien Phu, were forced out of Indochina, which was then subdivided into a trio of new states. In Africa they granted independence to their colonies and to Tunis, and eventually, after a long struggle, left Algeria to the Algerians—that is, to the Muslim majority. The Belgians, who did little to prepare the Congo for self-government, suddenly reversed their intention to hold on and abandoned the region to its own devices. As for Britain, a nation which had still accounted in 1938 for one-fifth of the world's trade was too impoverished to shoulder its former commitments. The liquidation of empire proceeded inexorably. Beginning in 1948 with the independence of India, the cere-

---

[14]Examples are the International Monetary Fund; the International Bank for Reconstruction and Development; the Food and Agriculture Organization; the World Health Organization (WHO); and the United Nations Educational, Scientific, and Cultural Organization (UNESCO).

monies of withdrawal were reenacted throughout Asia and Africa. By 1985 the areas remining under London's control were a scattering of small possessions, mainly economic and military liabilities, and of a few ports and islands strung out along the routes to vanished glories.[15]

Elsewhere too, the sometime dominance of occidental peoples has evoked a reaction of angry outburst and violent challenge. Mossadegh led the way in Iran by taking over the properties of the Anglo-Iranian Oil Company. Nasser repeated this coup in Egypt by nationalizing the Suez Canal, after which he set about fomenting movements throughout the Arab world to expel Western influences. Indeed on every continent, the opposition to colonialism has become one of the most active political forces of our time. The words and deeds of 1776 have been much imitated and oft repeated—sometimes with a sound that rings true, sometimes with a false note—in Accra, Cairo, Djakarta, Delhi, and other capitals. Nor can their influence be successfully resisted. In the final decades of the twentieth century, uneasy sways the head that sways an empire.[16]

As the old-style empires disappear from the map, the cumulative results of the transformation are visible in the expanding membership of the United Nations. What began in 1945 as an organization of 51 states has grown in less than half a century to more than three times that number. When the government of China was finally seated in the early seventies, the United Nations came closer to the universality which is its ultimate goal.

Keeping the Peace

For a decade and a half after 1946, world politics, as practiced both in the United Nations and outside, was primarily influenced by the opposition between the Communist governments and the Western democracies. The United Nations had been predicated on the belief that the coalition of states which won the war against fascism would continue to act in substantial harmony. Nor could one otherwise justify the veto power of the five principal states in the Security Council, since, if they failed to cooperate,

---

[15]Hong Kong, the most significant of these, will revert to China in 1997. Spain wants Gibraltar back, but the Gibraltarians prefer their link with Britain. The Falklanders, all 1800 of them, are still under the Union Jack as a result of the British victory over the Argentines in 1982, an anachronistic conflict reminiscent of the nineteenth century. But the islands, besides being a drain on the British Treasury, remain vulnerable to invasion.

[16]The second edition of this book, published in 1960, contained this prediction (p. 394): "Indeed, if one projects into the future the trends of the last 12 years, it seems certain that the French cannot maintain their hold on Algeria, that a handful of British planters cannot monopolize the Kenya highlands, and that the Afrikaner Nationalists cannot perpetuate the privileges of Europeans in South Africa." Two of those predictions have come true. The third will take longer.

the United Nations would be doomed to deadlock. But as long as Stalin lived, not only cooperation, but even a tolerable coexistence, was out of the question. For at least a decade the major activities of the United Nations— diplomatic, technical, and peacekeeping—were hampered by the formation of two potent and antagonistic blocs: one led by the United States, the other by the Soviet Union. In June 1950, when North Korea attacked South Korea, it proved possible for the Security Council to authorize collective aid to the South only for the reason that the Soviet delegate had walked out[17] six months earlier and the Russian seat was empty at that moment.

In 1956, at the time of the Suez affair,[18] the United Nations emerged as the effective agent for ending hostilities in Egypt, inducing Britain, France, and Israel to withdraw their armies, and subsequently policing the Gaza Strip and the Gulf of Akaba. The political reasons for this achievement invite reflection. In the first place, the majority opinion throughout the world sided with Egypt. Although Britain, France, and Israel had the military means to make their will prevail, a political fact—the concerted pressure of international opinion—compelled them to pull their armies back. The second, and conclusive, fact was the concurrence of the United States and the Soviet Union, both of whose governments at that time were unwilling to court the displeasure of the Arabs. But simultaneously with the events at Suez, the Soviet Union sent the Red Army into action in the streets of Budapest in order to reinstall the Communist government which had fallen from power through a popular uprising. Action by the United Nations against the Soviet Union, however, was not possible because of the widespread fear of initiating measures that could lead directly to a third world war between the superpowers.

Since then there have been other occasions when the United Nations has been charged with peacekeeping responsibilities—which means that various countries contributed contingents to serve under its flag and maintain order in areas where there was danger of war. This necessary, but unwelcome, service was performed in both the Congo and Cyprus, despite the objections of the Soviet Union and France, which refused to pay a share of the expenses. Indeed, the United Nations undertook those particular functions on the basis of votes in the General Assembly, where, unlike the Security Council, the veto of the five principal members does not apply. However, it was shown in May 1967 that the opposition of the government of the country in which the United Nations places its forces can constitute a veto of its own. When Nasser demanded that the United Nations withdraw its peacekeeping units from the Gaza Strip and from Sharm-el-Sheik at the

[17]Over the issue of the Council's refusal to place a representative of Beijing in China's seat.

[18]In October 1956, Israel sent its army to occupy the Gaza Strip from which Egypt was mounting commando raids against Israeli settlements. The British and French sent in their forces to retake the Suez Canal, which Nasser had nationalized earlier.

entrance to the Red Sea, the Secretary-General complied. The consequences were immediate. Egypt began closing the Gulf of Akaba to Israeli shipping. Then the six-day war erupted in which Israel crushed the combined forces of Egypt, Jordan, and Syria. Not until 1974, after the fourth bout of hostilities between Egypt and Syria on the one side and Israel on the other, was the flag of the United Nations brought back to the center of this battlefield to police the cease-fire along the Suez Canal and the Golan Heights. And necessarily so. No other agency existed, national or international, in which the belligerents, as well as the United States and the Soviet Union, could acquiesce.

Subsequently, however, in that very same region the ineffectiveness of the United Nations as a peacekeeper was glaringly exposed. After the Palestine Liberation Organization was driven from Jordan, it moved into Lebanon, taking control of much of its territory and upsetting the ever-delicate balance between the Christian and Muslim communities. Soon, Lebanon disintegrated into civil war. Syria then marched in and occupied the north, while the Israelis backed a Christian militia in the south as a buffer between their northern frontier and the PLO. The United Nations dispatched a peacekeeping force to keep the hostile groups apart, but to no avail. Bent on destroying the PLO, the Israelis drove to Beirut in 1982, and, when they later withdrew south, the UN contingents were caught in the cross fires of warring Lebanese militias. Since the United Nations does not have overwhelming force at its disposal, it can only function where the belligerents are ready for a truce and can be induced to observe it.

In terms of the loss of life, however, and general devastation, the most murderous conflicts since 1960 originated as civil wars in which other governments involved themselves. Such were the attempt of Biafra to secede from Nigeria, which failed; the split between East and West Pakistan, where the former became the independent state of Bangladesh; and Vietnam, where, contrary to the Geneva Agreement of 1954, the United States backed a separate regime in Saigon to oppose the one in Hanoi. In none of these cases was the United Nations effective in mitigating or ending the hostilities. What did have a decisive effect was the amount of aid or direct military intervention from outside. Thus, Great Britain helped Nigeria; India sided with Bangladesh; while the United States struggled in vain to prop up a rickety regime for South Vietnam. Relations between the United States and the United Nations were at their lowest point during the Johnson and Nixon administrations, when American forces were fighting in or over Vietnam, Laos, and Cambodia, while the Secretary-General of the United Nations, U Thant, was Burmese and Buddhist. In that same area, after America's involvement ended, Cambodia was the stage for one of the most horrifying tragedies of this century. Civil war was compounded by the rival ambitions of China and a Soviet-supported Vietnam to control this hapless peasant society—one-third of whose people are believed to have perished.

International Relations in a Double-Standard World

Although the rivalry of major powers is common enough, the raw materials for conflict are everywhere at hand in the inequality of conditions that divide vast sections of the human race. Throughout Asia, Africa, and South and Central America, most human beings are illiterate, undernourished, squalidly housed, and meanly clad. Poverty, disease, and ignorance dog their brief lives.[19] Probably the great majority of people have always fared this way—or at least have so fared throughout the few millenia over which historical records extend. It is manifestly impossible for a double-standard world to be a contented one, and inequality, as Aristotle noted, has ever been a fertile source of revolution. But, though social upheavals have not been wanting in the past, their effects were formerly less widespread and less interconnected than those that characterize our epoch. Until a few centuries ago, large segments of humanity and entire civilizations endured in isolation from one another. A change of dynasty in China stirred not a ripple in Europe. The death of a Russian autocrat caused little concern beyond the borders of Muscovy. Discussions or decisions on the banks of the Potomac, the Thames, or the Seine did not make the whole welkin ring. The supply and control of oil, iron ore, and uranium were not matters of global life or death.

All that has changed. For our woe or weal, we have made of all the world a single stage where the drama of human fate is enacted in scenes that shift rapidly from place to place but form part of one plot. What distinguishes our age from those that have gone before, and complicates the solution of its problems, are the extension of the community of interests to an area as wide as the world, the greater volume of information and speed in communicating it, and the deeper awareness by millions of their common lot. The huddled masses of humanity—"the wretched of the earth," as Fanon described them—not only yearn to breathe free; they also crave a share in things they have never enjoyed. The demand for economic development, to be achieved rapidly, has become the item of first priority for governments of countries with a backward technology and a traditional social system. Such circumstances make a spawning ground for political

---

[19]In 1978, 800 million (one-fifth of the human race) were "trapped in . . . absolute poverty; a condition of life so characterized by malnutrition, illiteracy, disease, squalid surroundings, high infant mortality, and low life expectancy as to be beneath any reasonable definition of human decency." Robert S. McNamara, president of the World Bank, in a foreword to *World Development Report, 1978.* In the same year, the UN Fund for Population Activities broke down the total as follows: 500 million malnourished, 100 million lacking clean water, 800 million illiterates, 350 million unemployed or earning less than $50 a year, 250 million living in slums, 1.6 billion without basic health care. (Estimates from a report on *The State of World Population.*) The report analyst, Peter Adamson, stated that "less than 30 percent of the world's people have more than 70 percent of the world's resources. The third world . . . may have 70 percent of the world's people and 80 percent of the world's population growth, but it only has 7 percent of the world's industry and 10 percent of the world's wealth."

movements of many kinds. People who resent their underprivileged status, but who are politically unsophisticated, will readily listen to promises and follow a prophet. If lucky, they discover wise counselors whose government has their interests at heart, a Nehru or a Nyerere. But they are just as likely to find that their prophet is a fraud and the promises were bogus. Or, they may encounter obstruction by those who reject the claims of the masses to more equal treatment. Out of this milieu come regimes which may be fascist, communist, nationalist, racist, militarist, theocratic, or democratic. Once the top is off the bottle and the genie is out, there is no telling what shape it will assume.

When the Charter of the United Nations was written, many recognized that colonial aspirations for independence and the general desire of people in underdeveloped areas for higher living standards are a constant source of friction and hence a possible cause of war. For this reason the structure included among its principal organs both a Trusteeship Council and an Economic and Social Council. The former was intended to safeguard the interests of weaker peoples, whose government the United Nations entrusts to another state. The goal of the Economic and Social Council is to lessen the gap between the technologically advanced communities and the backward. Despite inadequate budgets, significant aid has been rendered to underdeveloped countries by the United Nations through its Technical Assistance Administration and specialized agencies. Besides the granting of loans, this help consists in gathering and publishing information, disseminating scientific knowledge, and recruiting teams of experts and individual technicians who go to work in countries which request assistance. Their programs for the most part are practical and specialized: a loan to build a steel mill or a dock, eradication of malaria, development of fisheries or reforestation, control of narcotics, reduction of illiteracy, the installation of a tax system, and so on.

Problems of International Cooperation

However constructive, such activities do not lack their quota of difficulties. The budgets of international agencies are grossly inadequate. Their poorer members, which need the help, have nothing to give. The wealthy, which must contribute most of the total, may be self-centered or may feel that they are already paying enough.[20] They may then oppose a budgetary

---

[20]In fact, they do not give nearly enough. The Organization for Economic Cooperation and Development, whose members consist of the advanced industrial economies, has recommended that each country give at least 0.7 percent of its GNP to help the less developed. In the 1980s, only Sweden, Norway, and the Netherlands exceeded that. The United States continues to be the single biggest donor, in absolute figures. But US aid has steadily dropped as a percentage of the GNP. In the early 1960s it stood at 0.75 percent, but it fell to under 0.25 percent in the 1980s. Moreover, in the years of the Reagan presidency, the bulk of the aid given was military, not economic.

increase, since they are the donors, not the recipients, of aid. Competent personnel are hard to recruit, because many persons see better opportunities in their own national civil service or because governments are sometimes disinclined to offer their best staff to an international agency. Because of political obstruction, some of it unrelated to the issue at hand, it may be impossible for the delegates at a conference to pick the best program from the alternatives available. The Arab governments, supported by the Communist regimes, will use the occasion to reprimand Israel, while Black African states are making white-dominated South Africa their target. Will the FAO always adopt policies which run counter to the profits of agribusiness and giant food-processing corporations? Can WHO sponsor programs for contraception or abortion in areas of poverty and overpopulation when these are denounced by the celibate male clerics of the Catholic Church? Similarly in the ILO, which treads the thorny path of employer-employee relations, or at UNESCO, which seeks to combat ignorance and enrich humanity with the treasures of mind and spirit, the conflict between competing interests or opposed philosophies is a hindrance to positive action.

What accentuates these problems is the touchiness of national governments whenever an issue is raised that they deem vital. Where a great power is involved, other states are reluctant to outvote, and cannot coerce it. But small states too produce governments and leaders who can be particularly stubborn and self-willed in what seems to them their special interest. In particular, the rulers of countries that emerged recently from a dependent or colonial status are torn two ways. Without aid from outside—loans, investment, goods, and technicians—they cannot develop their economies and raise their living standards to the level they desire. But aid will normally be accompanied by some list of conditions, some attachment of strings, which then is interpreted in the guise of "foreign control"—especially when the aid is received from one government instead of from an international source. Those who were recently subject to another power will chafe at new restraints, even when their source is an international agency. Furthermore, those who in opposition consistently proclaim fine-sounding principles can be seen making concessions to expediency when in office.

The crux of the problem can be simply stated: All over the world there are people who are dependent in their economics and technology but have strong feelings about their political independence. That paradox is explicable by the time lag in the spread of the nation-state. This unit of government, as we saw, originated in Western Europe in the fifteenth and sixteenth centuries. Its full force was not felt in Eastern Europe until the nineteenth. Among colonial peoples the first effective blow for national independence was struck in North America in 1776, with Latin America following suit five decades later. In the closing decades of the nineteenth century the force of nationalism began to explode in Asia, and the results have been manifest in recent history. Last came Africa, where much writing is already visible on the wall—and more will be written.

Contrary to my theme, however, some will maintain that today's world expresses the final triumph of the nation-state which has at last covered the globe. Now that the old colonial empires have virtually disappeared and the membership of the United Nations has trebled, is this not evidence of the vitality of nation-states? And is it not true that national sentiment continues to be a powerful force in many countries?

The facts are not in dispute, but I interpret them differently. The strength of national feelings is a familiar example of the normal time lag between a change in reality and the perception of it. In the history of politics and the evolution of society, sentiments which have been attached to an institution will remain strong for several generations after its potency has been eroding away. Today's nationalism often exists in inverse relation to the realities that could support and justify it. In addition, I would contend that the contemporary proliferation of new states, supposedly sovereign and independent, signifies not so much the success of the system as its *reductio ad absurdum*. Just as the splitting and subdivision of the *polis* produced eventual chaos around the Mediterranean in the fifth and fourth centuries B.C., so has the liquidation of empires and the grant of self-government to former colonies multiplied the areas of disorder in the second half of the twentieth century.

To construct an international order out of today's disparate elements is truly a formidable task. The mansion of peace and prosperity must be built with bricks of different materials and varying shapes and sizes. The edifice includes once-mighty states like Britain and France; states which now stand in the forefront, like the USA and the USSR; those with huge populations, like China and India, which nurtured ancient civilizations and will again be mighty when their potentialities are unleashed; states which give few thanks to the past, but consider themselves, as does Brazil, "lands of the future"; those that made their bid for imperial hegemony and failed, but have recovered economic strength and are regaining political influence, such as Germany and Japan; medium-sized states, some developing peaceably, others aggressively in wish or deed; others again of which little need be said except that they exist; and then an odd assortment of small fry—buffer states such as Belgium, Austria, or Uruguay; a few neutrals of the Swiss or Swedish model; the client-states like Bulgaria, Liberia, Cuba, or the Philippines; the Phoenix-style creations of Poland or Israel; and the anomalies of Iceland, Luxembourg, Botswana, two Koreas, and Tuvalu. Among recent additions to the list are many which are states by fiction, governments by courtesy, and nations only in the imagination. Nevertheless, all are clothed in the panoply of juridical attributes which other states accord to each new member of the club. Yet, looking at them, one cannot fail to see—as the boy said of the emperor in the fairy tale—that they are naked. If statesmanship be an art, as some aver, what artist ever worked in so intractable a medium?

Whatever one's political viewpoint, nobody can deny that, as we enter the final decade of the second millennium A.D., the world is characterized by much tension, conflict, and outright hostility between states, and that most human beings on every continent exist in an atmosphere of insecurity. Many factors contribute to this, but in a political analysis, which concerns itself with the activities of states, the root-cause can be simply diagnosed. We are beset with a fundamental contradiction between the old political divisions of humanity into a multiplicity of nation-states and the newer realities of an emerging world society. The latter are particularly evident in the economic sphere and in matters technological and military. In today's world, there is but one economy and it is global. Within this, all countries are interdependent, and within it there operate at will the huge multinational corporations which transcend national boundaries. Assets counted in the billions can nowadays be transferred from market to market, or continent to continent, in the time it takes to place a telephone call. Plants which employ thousands, on which a whole locality may depend for its livelihood, are constructed, closed, or reorganized, as a result of decisions in a corporate office on another continent.

Add to this the complications which the newest technologies inject. Sometimes a boon to humanity, they can also be a curse. Think of the aftereffects and all the international ramifications of the disasters at Union Carbide's factory in Bhopal, India, and the nuclear power plant at Chernobyl in the Ukraine. The pollution caused by acid rain is a continuous source of friction between the United States and Canada, between Norway, Germany, and Great Britain. Everybody, it has been said, is upstream or downstream from somebody else. The sources of many of today's difficulties are located within national jurisdictions, but the fall-out is international.

Added to that is the military dimension, itself a product of the newest technology. A strategic missile launched nowadays from either the United States or the USSR would reach its target, with a trajectory over Canada, in 20 minutes or less. In 1945, only three atomic bombs existed, all in the hands of the United States. By the 1980s, there were estimated to be over 50,000 nuclear warheads in the stockpiles of five governments: namely, the United States and the Soviet Union, which together possess the vast majority, plus China, France, and Great Britain.[21] Yet new weapons are added every year, and smaller governments, including some which are thoroughly disreputable, are encouraged to buy conventional weapons of increased sophistication and destructiveness. Add up the military expendi-

---

[21]India, which has conducted an atomic explosion, and several other governments reportedly have the capacity to assemble a nuclear bomb at short notice.

tures of all governments on our planet, and you find that the world spends two millions of dollars for this purpose every single minute. More is consumed annually by the military than by health and education combined. Indeed, the world spends for war in one day as much as the peace-keeping agency, the United Nations, spends in an entire year for peace. These figures amount to a collective insanity—and the agency primarily responsible is the nation-state which divides human beings from one another and therefore engenders distrust and rivalry.

Though it has acted constructively in several disputes, all too frequently the United Nations is powerless to do more than debate, declare, and deplore. On most major issues it has been so rent by internal hostilities that it lacks the capacity to decide and enforce. Speakers in the Security Council and the General Assembly often talk to their home audiences with scant prospect of influencing their principal antagonists. Nevertheless, even in its restricted role, this institution performs an indispensable function. It is the only association that houses the divided fragments of humanity. It is the closest we have yet come to a common deliberative forum for the conscience of mankind. Its freedom of debate impels all governments to reply in public to the worst criticisms that foes can hurl, whether merited or false. Its survival for half a century marks a step toward the ultimate goal of "the Parliament of Man, the Federation of the world."[22]

Region-States in the Making?

But the realization that politically the world is not yet one in heart and spirit has persuaded some that prosperity and security may perhaps be organized through institutions intermediate between the nation-state, which is outmoded, and a global state, which humanity is still too divided to operate. There are signs that a new unit of government is already evolving. The peoples who live around the coasts of the Atlantic have begun experimenting with a variety of novel unions. On the mainland of Western Europe there are the European Community and the Council of Europe. Linking the two sides of the ocean are the Organization for Economic Cooperation and Development and the diplomatic and military agreements of the North Atlantic Treaty Organization. These schemes enlarge the area for military, political, technical, and economic cooperation among peoples who mainly[23] share the same civilization. Indeed, when one reflects on the divisions which have marked the history of Europe or the differences of attitude between the New World and the Old, what was accomplished in one generation was truly remarkable.

[22]Tennyson's words from the poem "Locksley Hall."
[23]I add this qualification because Turkey is a member of NATO, and Japan of OECD.

Among the positive gains are the postwar recovery of the Western European economies; their steps toward integration in such essential matters as coal and steel, atomic energy for peaceful uses, and tariff policies; the coordination of peacetime planning for military defense; the regular consultations and informal discussions between their heads of government, foreign secretaries, and leaders of opposition parties; and finally, the growing realization that their interests are intertwined. Most importantly, the United States and Canada jointly helped to underwrite and stimulate the union, declaring a common interest with Western Europe in the vital concerns of safety and prosperity. If these relationships continue, an ocean will become, not a barrier that separates, but a highway that unites. As was the Mediterranean to the *pax Romana,* so may the Atlantic prove to be the "inland sea" of the Western civilization. Nothing in this, however, is certain. Whereas the decade of the 1950s witnessed an acceleration in the regional integration of nation-states, during the sixties that movement slowed down. In some spheres it was even halted by a resurgent nationalism, which was most evident in France and was stimulated by de Gaulle—although this phenomenon was by no means confined to him or restricted to his country. After the presidency of France changed hands, however, the European Community was able to add three new members and, later on, another trio, bringing its total to twelve.

Nor is this pattern evolving in the Atlantic region the only instance of its kind. Something similar in general aim, though different in principles and method, has been established in Eastern Europe by the Soviet Union. There, the military relationships were formalized by the Warsaw Pact (1955), as were economic relations in the Council for Mutual Economic Assistance (1959). Both resemble their Western prototypes in embracing a greater range of territory and population within a common system. The economic organization in this case has been guided by concepts of centralized state planning. The military arrangements are largely inspired by past memories and fears of future German invasion. Underlying the forms, however, the stark reality has consisted in Soviet power imposed to further Soviet interests. On various occasions (Hungary in 1956 and Czechoslovakia in 1968) the Soviet Union employed its military power to install persons amenable to its wishes in charge of governments which it plainly envisaged as satellites.[24] Nor can there be any doubt that, directly or indirectly, its presence in the background was a leading factor in the decision of the Polish military to seize power in 1981 and then suppress the independent trade union "Solidarity."

Elsewhere in the world—in Asia, Africa, and Latin America—regional entities have been drafted on the European model. So far, these exist mainly on paper without conspicuous success in practice. When the mem-

---

[24]As it also did in another region, when it invaded Afghanistan in 1980.

ber states themselves are unstable and their governments ill organized, their addition into a larger unit means compounding the same weaknesses. It is nevertheless true that in various subregions of these continents, some of the same reasons and occasions for ultimate integration already exist as may be found in Western Europe—that is, the need to encourage economic growth by diversification in wider markets, the advantage of geographical contiguity, the memory of a shared past, and elements of a common culture in the present. But such potentialities cannot be realized until traditional customs and institutions have been radically changed and a political will to unite becomes paramount.

If we extrapolate the developments of the last three decades and do not fly too far ahead of the facts, we can discern the possibility of a new and wider unit of government. To distinguish this from the nation-state or a world-state, could we not call it the "region-state"? Through the nascent region-state, some portions of humanity may perhaps construct their political defenses against economic blizzard and nuclear annihilation. How urgent is the need can be gauged by projecting into the future two contemporary facts. One is the worldwide rise in population, increasing now so rapidly that its implications have been termed "explosive" by demographic experts. The reduction of the death rate, improvement of health, and material gains from industrialism will do for Asia, Africa, and Latin America what they did for Western Europe and North America. There will be millions more to feed in each coming decade—to feed, let alone to be prosperous. If the "Malthusian checks" of poverty and war are no longer acceptable, wider political unions and more enlightened policies will be required to augment the supply of food and industrial goods. The second inescapable fact is the technology which enables us to place satellites in orbit around the earth or propel them beyond the gravity of our planet. Already human beings have walked on the moon and satellites have reached the planets of the solar system. Now that we have voyaged into outer space, air power is being superseded by a more formidable weapon. Where will our endangered species locate our military defense tomorrow? Humanity arrived on the moon long before peace was constructed on earth. Is it not self-evident that the nation-state, a unit which evolved under the special conditions of the sixteenth and seventeenth centuries, is inadequate to govern us under the conditions of the twentieth? The new population and the new pollution, the new technology and the new weapons, point ultimately to a new unit of government.

Contours and Contents of Region-States

Yet a word of caution is necessary, lest hopes be raised too high and then be cruelly dashed. A region-state will present problems of organization fully as complex as its predecessors. If it was difficult to delimit the boundaries of the nation, will it be easier to define those of the region? An example is the North Atlantic Treaty Organization, which already reaches as far east as Greece and Turkey. Some states, moreover, have interests in more than one region. Thus the United States belongs to the North Atlantic Treaty Organization as well as to the Organization of American States and we have a major stake in the affairs of the Pacific with contractual commitments to Australia, the Philippines, and Japan. Nor should one assume that wars between region-states are impossible. The region-state can justify itself only if it provides a broader framework for enhancing the economic well-being of all its members, and if each presents such a picture of strength to a possible antagonist that nobody will run the risk of initiating a third general war from which none can emerge unscathed. Some of the same factors that impede the task of international organization can also be obstacles to the formation of region-states. To create the latter, a union may be required between a superpower and a group of medium-sized and smaller countries. But nationalism or differences of living standards may provoke a rift in that relationship, and the superpower may even aggravate the difficulties of leadership by demonstrating that might is not always correlated with wisdom. This can be illustrated from the experiences of both the United States and the Soviet Union.

Since 1947, the United States has been the nucleus of a large and loosely structured coalition which includes virtually all of the world's most advanced communities and many that are backward. Out of their rich resources, financial strength, and great productive capacity, the American people rendered economic and military assistance to numerous governments in the hope that such aid would increase their means of resistance to armed aggression from without and political upheaval from within. The results of this program have been as varied as the characters of the recipients. Where the government is honest and the people in general are hardworking and self-disciplined, the American contribution was successful. In some instances, however, corrupt cliques and incompetent governments misused or squandered much of the aid that was granted. Thereafter, the donors feel disposed to attach conditions that the recipients must fulfill. But when that happens, the nationalistic pride of the latter is outraged and they will voice angry protests that their "sovereignty" is being invaded. The American public sees a portion of its tax dollar appropriated to finance the foreign aid programs which, while they help other countries, are thought to promote simultaneously the interests of the United States. That such efforts sometimes provoke resentment rather than thanks may surprise those who provide the money. But it is not normal in the relations between groups, any more than in the relations of individuals, for the stronger, wealthier, and luckier to meet with gratitude and affection, or for the dependent to like their position. Moreover, in numerous instances those dependent on the United States happen to be privileged oligarchies, which have no intention of sharing power and its perquisites with their own have-nots. Consequently, the weapons which the United States has placed at the disposal of such oligarchies have been employed in internal contests for power—with the obvious result of fostering anti-Americanism among the victims.

The hand of a great power usually rests heavily on the smaller states close by, which it considers as lying within its sphere of influence. In this respect, the record of successive American governments in the Caribbean and Central America has repeated the unsavory pattern of other dominant states throughout the history of Europe and Asia. For almost a century, the United States has infiltrated, intervened, and invaded, installing governments to its liking wherever possible. The history of our relations with Cuba, the Dominican Republic, Grenada, Haiti, Mexico, El Salvador, Panama, and Nicaragua has been that of an imperial power toward its dependencies. At the moment when I write this, the Reagan administration is actively assisting a centrist regime in El Salvador against its opposition of left-wing guerrillas. In Nicaragua, it is helping right-wingers, who include supporters of the ex-dictator, Somoza, in their military effort to overthrow the Marxist Sandinista regime. What meanings do we attach to the fictions of "independence" or "sovereignty" under these conditions?

Divisions within East and West

Meanwhile, in another part of the international jungle another superpower has flexed its muscles to control the course of events. Almost without exception,[25] the countries under Communist rule are underdeveloped socially, economically, and politically. During Stalin's lifetime, the relations of the Soviet Union with other "dictatorships of the proletariat" were far from harmonious. The imposition of Moscow-directed programs, the requirements of orthodoxy in word and deed, and the doctrinaire application of uniform principles to diverse situations generated much discontent even within parties as strongly disciplined as the Communists are wont to construct. For a decade after 1945 a spectacle frequently witnessed in one Eastern European country after another was the "discovery" of treasonable plots within the party hierarchy, and the vilification, imprisonment, or execution of persons formerly idolized as Communist heroes. Much of this was due to the subordination of other people's interests to that of the Russians and to the understandable reaction of various Communist leaders in satellite states who gave priority to the feelings of their fellow citizens. In Yugoslavia, the man who was master of his domestic situation dared to

[25]From the standpoint of living standards and general development, the two most advanced areas under Communist rule, at the time when they were sucked into the Soviet orbit, were the Bohemian portion of Czechoslovakia and East Germany.

flout the Kremlin by placing his own country first. Similarly, after Stalin's death, the suppressed resentment of other peoples in Eastern Europe came to the surface, as manifested by riots in East Germany, defiance in Poland, and an outright revolt in Hungary which the Russians crushed with force. Subsequently, the Russians gave proof that the concept of their sphere of influence was being applied to central Asia. This time, they intervened with great strength in Afghanistan, replacing one Communist leader with another, and then becoming bogged down in their attempt to subdue the fiercely independent tribes of the mountainous region. The underlying reason for this Soviet action is significant in what it portends for their future policy toward the Islamic population of the Asian republics of the USSR. The Khomeini revolution in Iran provoked in Moscow the fear that a similar fundamentalist reaction might attract supporters in the neighboring state of Afghanistan and then seep northward. In a way, they were trying to construct a *cordon sanitaire* against religious contagion.

Nor has the other Communist superpower been slow in letting its neighbors feel its might. The Chinese placed their grip on the mountain fastnesses of Tibet, then encountered a full-scale rebellion which they crushed. Likewise in 1987 when Buddhist monks organized demonstrations in Lhasa to protest against rule from Beijing, the Chinese had to use the troops to reimpose their authority. Not only that, but they also took military action in the Himalayas in the border region where India and China meet and have since occupied and held an area which the Indians claim as theirs. Also, to the south, the age-old pressure of China upon Vietnam has been maintained with border skirmishes. It is not without interest that the two Marxist superpowers of Europe and Asia, which have always denounced western imperialism, have been reestablishing an *imperium Sovieticum* and an *imperium Sinicum*, respectively. New gospels do not necessarily eradicate old sins.

The reference to these as two superpowers, not one, suggests a further reflection on trends that were increasingly apparent in the 1960s. In the preceding decade the mutual hostility of two powerful blocs dominated the course of world politics. Since then, however, significant changes have occurred. Relations between Americans and Russians became less antagonistic after Stalin died, so that limited agreements became possible on selected issues (such as cultural exchanges and the ban on nuclear explosions in the atmosphere). The confrontations in 1961 over the construction of the Berlin Wall, and in 1962 over the Soviet missiles in Cuba, were settled by diplomacy without a shot fired—although the tanks and bombs were ready. Simultaneously, cracks appeared inside each bloc, which, though small at first, widened with the years. The Atlantic alliance had come into being because Western Europe depended on the United States for economic aid and for military protection against the Soviet Union. But after their economies recovered and a milder climate thawed the "cold war" ice, European leaders began to proclaim their own declarations of independence. Such notions were not loudly voiced in West Germany, whose people, divided from the East and devoid of nuclear bombs, needed American help. But in France, the union of Gallic pride and Gaullist personality resulted in a new nationalism expressing itself in European as distinct from Atlantic terms. Thus, in all the crucial spheres—economic, military, and political—the question posed to the peoples of the West was: Shall our civilization sustain two power blocs or one? Shall the Atlantic Ocean be our inland sea or a frontier between us?

Simultaneously, across Asia the Communist monolith was cracking into two. China's break with the Soviet Union offered to Marxist regimes an alternative gravitational field. Many of the Communist parties divided into factions, pro-Moscow or pro-Beijing. Hence the bipolar politics of the 1950s evolved into the triangular relationships of the sixties. Whereas earlier the United States had helped Yugoslavia to remain independent of the Soviet Union, and the latter reciprocated by aiding Cuba, when tiny Albania extricated itself from Soviet hegemony, Maoist China gave it support. There was thus a greater flexibility both within the blocs and in the relations between them. This indicates how fluid is the process of making region-states and how limited is the control of the superpowerful. In 1979 China could barely punish Vietnam, and Khomeini's Iran was flouting the United States. In seven years the Soviet Union had not completed the subjugation of Afghanistan. Are not the forces of politics more potent than those of the nuclear bomb?

Like any established system, nationalism dies hard. Old sentiments and old ideas continue to have their force in the present, sometimes most fiercely among those to whom they have come late, for no nationalism is as prickly and sensitive as a new one. Although the old empires are liquidated, the fragmentation is occurring faster than the reverse process of merging. Region-states may be in the making. They could help in organizing the larger areas in which we may find our safety and prosperity. But in any case, region-states alone will not be enough. They, too, have to learn to live together within one world, for which a truly global organization is required. Such problems as the population explosion (with all its implications of a death explosion as well), the gulf between haves and have-nots, and the control of nuclear weapons are of universal concern. Hence, the region-states, too, if indeed they do succeed in becoming organized, will need ultimately to realize that to live means also to let live. Otherwise they are certain to start in motion a train of rivalry that could lead to the destruction of the human species.

The conclusion is self-evident. Political inventiveness must find a way to substitute cooperation for competition and simultaneously consolidate both the world and its regions.

14

The Dynamics of Political Change

The Unity of the Political Process

A surgeon who operates on the human body must sew the patient together and see that the severed tissues reunite. A psychiatrist, after unraveling the tangles of the unconscious mind, is supposed to reknit the threads of personality to a changed design. The same obligation befalls the political scientist who analyzes the social order. Dissection of a whole into its parts contributes to clearer understanding. But unless the parts are reassembled, all that one obtains is an understanding of isolated fragments, not of the related pieces of a unity. The purpose of this chapter, therefore, is to stitch the seams and observe the larger pattern.

The discussion to this point can be summarized thus: Politics is the process in which a community confronts a series of great issues and chooses between opposing values. Almost universally the institution through which this is done is the state, though on occasion the same role has been performed by religious, economic, or kinship groupings. Government consists of the machinery, personnel, and methods used by the state to carry out its functions. In every political situation, in every type of state, and under all forms of government, the same basic issues are always present and they must all receive a solution. Since each issue admits of more than one choice, states and their governments differ in the choices they embody and in the manner of combining them.

This way of understanding politics offers insights into some of its characteristics whose significance would otherwise be missed. Too many political analyses reduce the subject to terms and categories that are primarily static. That is an unfortunate by-product of an attempt that is laudable in itself—the effort at logical exposition. Logic aims at concepts and propositions which are, as far as possible, unambiguous and mutually exclusive. But the actualities of politics—as distinct from theories about them—are fluid and mobile. Hence it is difficult, and can be inaccurate, to impose a rigid framework on shifting materials. A political philosophy, which satisfies the conceptual tests of a logical system, often fails at the no less rigorous task of explaining political phenomena as they have been, as they now are, and as they may be. To be successful, a political analysis must meet two criteria. It should designate the underlying problems that are the invariable constants and indicate the variable modes of resolving them.

The reasons for these requirements, and for the necessity of both, are implicit in the treatment attempted in this book. To argue that the political process is composed of constant factors is to recognize the similarity between situations separated in time and place. If one speaks of politics, state, and government in Greece of the fifth century B.C., Rome of the first century A.D., the age of Thomas Aquinas, the revolutionary century from 1688 to 1789, or the world of Roosevelt, Churchill, Stalin, and Hitler, there must be some unifying threads which, despite the manifold differences, persist unbroken. Presumably the problems confronting Pericles or Augustus, Louis IX or Louis XIV, Lincoln or Nehru, were similar, and may appropriately be grouped as incidents in our constant striving to control the present and shape the future. To conceive of the Connecticut Yankee at King Arthur's Court was a stroke of fancy. But a Pericles in the White House would have found himself as much in his element as a Roosevelt in the Athenian Assembly. The issues that both statesmen faced and the skills they practiced were sufficiently alike for their abilities to be transferable. Likewise a Clodius with his gang fights in the streets of Rome could have changed places readily with a Capone in Chicago. As a stream of history flows uninterruptedly from prehistoric times to the present without regard for our divisions into periods, so does a stream of politics rise at a source concealed in our primeval past and follow its single course down to the rapids and whirlpools of our century.

Permanent Problems, Changing Solutions

But, though its flow be continuous, a stream will change direction. Its main channel can shift. Its current may be fast for a while or sluggish. Similar is the action of politics. For its continuity represents the unity of energy, not of mass. It is a unity of flux and movement. It extends over time, not over space. Throughout its process runs a rhythm that is ever changing because it is patterned from issues whose solutions change. In the opportunity for choice conferred by each issue lie the springs of political dynamics.

How are such changes manifested? Many examples have been noted in this work of the human tendency to tack and turn like sailors taking advantage of the wind. The history of politics reveals an expanse of creative activity which allows wide room for inventiveness and resource. After making what progress they can in one direction, people veer around and strain toward another point. Thus the monistic city-state of Greece and Rome was replaced by the Christian experiment in church-state dualism. This in turn gave way to the monism of nation-state sovereignty, which was later followed by the attempt to separate the economic order from politics. The unit of government has likewise passed through a succession of forms. City-state, empire-state, and nation-state have all been tried and tested. Each yielded what benefits it could and then succumbed to conditions for which it ceased to be appropriate. So too with the other great issues. Humanity perennially explores new ways of meeting old problems, as the United States in 1787 pioneered with the structure of federalism; or we revive under different circumstances a system used centuries before, just as the American Republic designed its institutions with a separation of powers similar to what the Roman Republic once employed.

Interaction between the Great Issues

There is, however, another aspect of the process of political change whose operation is more intricate than what has so far been described. If politics forms a single compound which can then be analyzed into five basic elements, it would follow that when one component undergoes a major alteration, the remainder are likely to be affected. This probability raises a fundamental question: When people turn to a different solution of any issue, are there consequent changes which that decision tends to produce among the rest? Does the evidence of history suggest that specific solutions of the respective issues ordinarily accompany each other in pairs or groups? If so, one could indicate which alternatives are mutually compatible and which are not—and that would constitute a valuable guide for interpreting the past and predicting the future. On the other hand, one may find that no relation—positive or negative—can be traced between some pairs of issues, in which case a choice among one set of alternatives would be unconnected with, and thus irrelevant to, a choice among another set. There is only one way to discover whether this is the case. Every issue must be discussed in relation to every other, in order to detect any possible pattern in which their solutions tend to combine.

1. The Relations of Privilege or Equality to Other Choices

Take first the choice between regimes of privilege and equality. What correlation is there between either of these and the manner in which other issues are solved? Does a swing from privilege to equality, or vice versa, lead to corresponding reversals in the treatment of other issues? Wherever a few privileged persons are in a position of superiority over a much larger number, the dominant oligarchy will use all means to enable them to stay on the top of the heap. Necessarily, the favored few must possess political power and therewith must control the state—or they will eventually be ousted from influence by those who do. Does this mean, however, that when an elite monopolizes the government, the entire society is subordinated to the state in monistic fashion? Or is it possible for privilege to be associated with pluralism, in which case, though politics would be reserved for the few, the functions of the state vis-à-vis other associations would somewhere be limited?

The historical answer is that the principle of oligarchy, as such, does not necessitate either a pluralist or monistic policy by the state toward society. Oligarchies have in fact been associated with one or the other. Thus in the medieval period, when the state was controlled by an oligarchy of nobles and the church by an oligarchy of priests, the prevalent theory of politics was steadfastly opposed to monism. Where a conquering people has taken over the government of the conquered, the victors have sometimes been content to restrict their authority to a few essentials (for example, finance, police, and military affairs), leaving their subjects otherwise free from state control. Such, in general, was the character of British rule in India. By contrast the czarist autocracy in Russia during the eighteenth and nineteenth centuries contrived a complete subordination of society to the state. Similar in spirit have been the modern one-party dictatorships—whether Fascist, Nazi, or Communist—whose efforts to make the functions of the state coextensive with social activity have become a byword.

What happens when a regime of privilege is replaced by one of equalitarianism? Does the latter have a closer affinity with monism or pluralism? The evidence indicates that a sizable extension of the citizen body is likely to be accompanied by an extension of the functions of the state, though there may be a time lag before the latter takes full effect. The period that can throw most light on this problem is the century from 1840 to 1940. During that time the spread of democracy culminated in many states with the achievement of universal suffrage, and with this was associated a tremendous increase in the functions of their governments. Was this combination of events a coincidence or a case of cause and effect? Without doubt, the latter. Generally, the impetus behind the movement to extend the franchise came from a desire to remedy specific ills by political action. Some of these ills were due to differentiations of humanity into classes which determined the breadth of opportunity available to their members. Other ills were of economic origin and stemmed from the union of industrialism with urbanism. Political equality, signalized by the ballot, was desired as a means to social and economic betterment, and the state was then employed as the instrument of equalization. Hence as new voters were enrolled, political parties formulated programs to represent their interests, and these were eventually translated into legislative and administrative form. Being composed of people who were poorer and underprivileged, the recently enfranchised were disposed to invoke the powers of the state, since other social institutions treated them as inferiors.

The choice between privilege and equality can be precisely correlated with the next pair of alternatives: authoritarian or controllable government. A system dedicated to the exaltation of a privileged few dares not submit to any procedure of genuine control by the governed. The texture of privilege is stained with the dye of authoritarianism, for in no other way can a minority obtain and enforce the submission of the majority. No less true is the converse. Wherever equalitarianism is substituted for privilege, the governed seek institutional means to keep the power of their officials within bounds. Equalitarianism is no more compatible with authoritarianism than is privilege with accountability.

Turning, however, to the choice between unity or dispersion of power, one finds no definite correlation with either oligarchical or majority government. A few examples will make this plain. In the Middle Ages, when politics was certainly reserved for the few, the structure of authority was loose-knit, while powers were highly dispersed. The church struggled with the state. The localities resisted the center. The nobility defied the king. On the other hand, various modern oligarchies, especially those of Nazi Germany and Fascist Italy, have been totally centralized and integrated. The same contrasts may be observed among equalitarian systems. Whereas government in the United States was constructed according to the principles of federal decentralization and the separation of branches, the British system evolved with the predominance of central over local authority and of the cabinet over the other institutions at the center.

The same can be said concerning the size of the state and its possible effect on the enlargement or contraction of citizenship. A comparison of ancient city-states with modern nations demonstrates that either oligarchy or its opposite can flourish indifferently in states of Lilliputian or mammoth size. This conclusion is further reinforced if the suggestion offered in chapter 13 should prove correct, namely that a new governmental unit— the region-state—is now emerging. Here again, within units of comparable scale, the same contrast may be observed of a privileged Communist party hierarchy in the Eastern bloc and ballot-box equalitarianism in the Atlantic community. The size of the political unit, therefore, has no direct bearing on the internal distribution of rights and influence.

2. The Accompaniments to Monism and Pluralism

Let us apply the same method to the second of the great issues. The preference for a state of limited or comprehensive functions has been discussed in relation to the alternatives of privilege or equality. How are the other choices affected by the adoption of either pluralism or monism? Suppose we look at some contrasted examples. Medieval society was emphatically pluralist, alike in principle and practice. The same society exhibited a government both in church and state that was not responsible to the governed. Pluralism by itself, therefore, is no certain guarantor of freedom. On the other hand, as nineteenth-century America proves, pluralism and freedom can be mixed in one compound. The same can be told of experiments in monism. There are classic instances of a monistic state combined with a controllable government. Such was the Athenian *polis* in its heyday. Such is contemporary Britain, where a parliamentary majority may legally do anything, but is ordinarily circumspect in using its theoretical powers. Similarly, in New Zealand, the state is all-powerful within society, yet the government is emphatically subject to popular control. But monism can also be harmonious with dictatorship. Indeed, the most notorious dictatorships of this century make state and society indistinguishable. One could hazard the hypothesis that, because the modern dictatorship arises for nationalistic or economic reasons, or from a desire to accomplish a cultural revolution rapidly (Kemalist Turkey, for example), authoritarian regimes today are less likely to tolerate social pluralism than in the past. Beyond the line where the boundaries of state action are drawn, opposition may develop against those in power.

The other aspect of power, its unity or dispersion, has a more obvious connection with monism and pluralism. There is an understandable tendency for a monistic state to construct authority on a centralized and integrated plan. Where a state assumes the responsibility for overseeing other associations and their activities, it is less practicable to have a governmental structure in which the branches are too independent and the localities too autonomous. Traditionally, therefore, a monistic state like Britain has had its powers both centralized and integrated. In a pluralist state, on the other hand, both separation of branches and devolution from the center are suited to the prevailing character of a government whose functions are limited. Where the activities to be conducted are fewer, there are fewer chances of overlap, duplication, or conflict between agencies and their programs. Hence there is less demand for a unified focus of power. Moreover, as American experience in the twentieth century testifies, a government of restricted scope, if impelled by economic or military necessity to expand its activities, must simultaneously modify its previously accepted canons of separate branches and federal-state dualism. The United States today contains more evidence than 50 years ago of unification among branches and levels of government, because more is done by every branch of government at every level and these additional activities would collide unless they were somehow coordinated.

Whether the size of the state influences the functions it undertakes is more difficult to determine. On this point, history suggests some tentative hypotheses but no conclusive verdict. The classic case of a state whose expansion covered a huge area and population is the Roman Empire. Rome successfully organized an administrative apparatus, legal code, and military machine to unify its diverse and scattered provinces. It was much less successful, however, in uniting the peoples of its empire with a common loyalty. Deliberate efforts were made to employ religion for this purpose. But when little headway was made with the official ritual of the Olympian deities, or the worship of Mithra, or the deification of emperors, Constantine turned to the Christian faith to inspire a unity of sentiment that was otherwise lacking. The effect of his action, however, was to substitute dualism for monism, and thereby to reduce the scope of state activity. Hence the problem of extending the size of the state outward was solved only by diminishing the sphere where the state could operate inward.

Similar in a sense has been the experience of the United States. The process of peopling a continent from the Atlantic to the Pacific, from the forty-ninth parallel to the Rio Grande, was accompanied by the organization of society along pluralist lines. The circumstances under which the state expanded its territory and population in North America were ill suited to a monistic view of the role of government in society. Elsewhere, however, there have been instances to the contrary. The growth of European Russia was associated with the establishment of a powerful state that embraced and absorbed the entire social order. Later, when czarist power spread across central Asia to the Pacific, the same all-pervasive state controlled and directed the expansion. The change in scale never resulted in modifying the monism of the Russian *vlast*.[1] However, in drawing this contrast between the United States and Russia, one should remember that the expansion of the United States, though it encountered opposition, did not face a hostile neighbor of equal force on the same continent. The consolidation of the Muscovite state, on the other hand, was achieved in the teeth of prolonged and repeated warfare against nearby powers (Poland, Sweden, Prussia, Turkey, the Tartars, and so forth), and the military stamp left an ineradicable imprint on Russian government in the form of complete state domination of society, which the Communists have continued with more pervasive methods.

If large states then can be either monistic or pluralist, what about small ones? There is some evidence to indicate that, as the size of the unit of

---

[1] A word, not precisely translatable into English, meaning governmental power viewed in its totality. It corresponds fairly closely with the Roman concept of the *imperium*.

government decreases, the number of functions performed by the state in society increases. At any rate, the smallest territorial unit in the history of the West, the Greek *polis*, was characterized by comprehensive state control. So little was that control questioned that Plato and Aristotle do not even include in their political theory a discussion of the possible or desirable limits of state activity. Nor is it hard to understand why monism should bring advantages to smaller units. Where a state is composed of a small population in a small area, it is simple, effective, and inexpensive to organize the activities of society under one institution only. In such a community many, if not most, of the inhabitants can have direct face-to-face contact. If separate institutions are created for governmental, religious, economic, and other purposes, their members are likely to be the same persons reassembled in different guises. In a little state, pluralism would seem superfluous; only in larger units does it make sense.

3. How the Remaining Issues Combine

The third issue—the choice between dictatorial or responsible government—was considered above in its relation to the extensiveness of citizenship and of governmental functions. But how do the rival conceptions of the source that validates authority affect the problem of whether powers are better unified or dispersed? Between these pairs of alternatives there seems no positive correlation. The United States and Britain are countries in whose political systems the authority of officials is derived from the will of the governed. Yet the structure of power is highly dispersed on the American side of the Atlantic and highly unified on the British. Apparently, then, it is not directly relevant to the politics of freedom to inquire whether the mechanics of government conform to the one design or the other. The same alternatives may be found in regimes of authoritarianism. In the medieval period the mass of the populace was expected to obey the established authorities. Nevertheless, those authorities were subdivided into numerous fragments. In the modern dictatorship unswerving obedience to officialdom is the duty of the masses. But authority in this case (except for Yugoslavia) is solidly compacted together, and the colossus that doth bestride the state reveals on its surface no seams or fissures.

Whether the size of the state has any connection with authoritarianism or its opposite is the next question. At first glance, size appears immaterial, since governments of small, medium, and huge states have belonged to either variety, some being controllable and others irresponsible. Sparta, Spain, Germany, and the Soviet Union are examples of one kind. Athens, Switzerland, Britain, and the United States illustrate the opposite. Mere size, however, is not the only factor. In a world of many states, size is relative. A state may be safe or insecure according to the kind of neighbors it has and their friendliness or hostility. Irrespective of size, any state that feels threatened[2] or that harbors aggressive intentions will emphasize the need for military organization, which influences the character of the government in an authoritarian direction. The so-called "garrison state,"[3] applying to government the discipline of a barracks, can often[4] be explained in terms of relations between states and not as the phenomenon of a single state standing in isolation.

Finally, to complete the circle of correlations, two issues remain whose effects on each other must be discussed. Can any connection be traced between the size of a state and a preference for a dispersed or unified structure of power? To answer this, one must recall[5] that relations between levels of government are not the same as those between branches functioning at the same level. The problem of centralization is not identical with that of integration, and the size of the state bears more immediately on the former than on the latter. It needs little elaboration to show that, the smaller the state, the less the likelihood of decentralization.[6] Indeed, in the city-state virtually all government is conducted at one center. Conversely, as population and territory increase, the sheer growth in size creates complexities and adds to the difficulty of communications. Regional diversities are likely to become pronounced. Differences of soil, climate, and resources will lead to divergent economic interests. Expansion may be accompanied by the absorption of mixed cultures with hankerings for autonomy. Separatist tendencies will be a by-product of bigness—witness the attitudes of the Old South to the United States, of the Ukraine to Russia, of Western Australia to the Australian Commonwealth, of Manchuria to China. No matter what the internal character of its government may be in other respects, any large state must permit a measure of decentralization. Neither Washington nor Moscow,[7] neither Brasilia, Delhi, nor Ottawa, can undertake the entire government of the sprawling territories under its jurisdiction. Understandably, therefore, federalism is found in some of the world's largest states.

As contrasted with the problem of centralization, the choice between integrating and dispersing the structure of governmental power is not so

[2]The small state of Israel is one of the most highly militarized in the world today.

[3]A phrase of Harold D. Lasswell.

[4]Not always, of course. Some garrison states are such because a conquering elite is holding down a larger subject population, for example, Sparta.

[5]See chapter 10, section on "Centralism or Localism, Separation of Powers or Integration?"

[6]The exceptional case of Switzerland is due to the mountainous geography and cultural dissimilarities.

[7]The genuineness of federalism in the Soviet Union is vitiated by the power monopoly of the Communist party, which insists on political centralism. Administrative decentralization, however, is necessitated by the physical extensiveness of the Soviet Union.

obviously linked with size. States with tightly integrated institutions have run the gamut of size, from diminutive to huge. It is questionable, however, whether the same can be said about the separation of branches and its application to states of different magnitude. Two famous instances of governments embodying the principle of separation are the republics of Rome and the United States. But it was the tragedy of the Roman Republic, and also a fundamental reason why the century from 133 B.C. to 31 B.C. suffered from prolonged constitutional crisis and spasmodic civil war, that the checks and balances between the branches of the Roman government were unsuited to the territorial expansion of Rome's imperial power. When the Senate clashed with the consuls, and the home authorities conflicted with a proconsul in an outlying province, civil turmoil and military weakness resulted. Hence, in order that an empire might be governed, the emperorship arose to integrate the powers at the center.

How does this apply to the United States? Has the expansion of the American Republic imposed any strain on the traditional separation of government into three branches? Undoubtedly it has. The adjustments required by the depression of the early 1930s certainly evoked the need for closer cooperation between presidency, Congress, and Supreme Court. Still more acute have been the tensions arising in the aftermath of World War II. The assumption by the United States of a position of international leadership made it necessary to pursue long-range policies and shoulder long-term commitments in conjunction with other governments. For this purpose not only harmony between the president and the Congress, but also agreement between the major parties, was required. The results were substantially good until the bipartisan foreign policy foundered in 1949 and 1950 on the issues of China and Korea. Simultaneously a new problem was precipitated to the forefront of American politics. The dissension between President Truman and General MacArthur, climaxed by the latter's dismissal, involved more than the supremacy of civil over military authority. For the first time the American Republic faced the same question as Rome confronted in the case of Sulla or Caesar, and Britain in the case of Clive or Hastings in India: How does the home government control a strong-willed commander in a distant theater? To solve this problem, the Republic of Rome gave way to an empire, the balance between royal prerogative and parliamentary power in Britain was superseded by the rise of an all-powerful cabinet. Whether some comparable change will occur in the structure of American government remains to be seen.

At the end of the 1980s, it is ominously clear that the rise of the invisible government and the accompanying expansion of presidential power are a direct threat to the balance between branches which the Constitution established and to the rule of law on which the entire system is based. No democracy in the past ever succeeded in reconciling the exercise of massive strength abroad with the maintenance of restraints at home. It is that contradiction which at this moment is straining the U.S. Constitution to its limits.

Not only is it reasonable to expect some major structural changes, but desirable to have them. The government of a democracy rests on the assumption that those who represent the majority should hold office but should be continuously and publicly confronted by their critics. This has the merit of focusing responsibility for action on one side, for dissent on the other. However, while it is essential in democratic politics always to have two or more organized parties, it is of dubious wisdom to divide between them simultaneously the authority for actually taking decisions. Because of the different electoral procedures and length of terms of the president and the two Houses of Congress, it is possible for one party to run the executive branch while the other controls the legislature, as occurred during Eisenhower's second term, throughout Nixon's occupancy, and in Reagan's final two years. Such a division, which can aggravate conflict of policy and divergence of outlook, may cause harm in domestic matters because it is likely to lead to either inaction or unsatisfactory compromise. In foreign affairs, too, the consequences can sometimes be injurious to the national interest.[8]

For it is incorrect to say, as a fact or as a wish, that politics ends at the water's edge. It does not, and in certain cases it should not. Many crucial problems of our time, such as a respect for human rights, overleap national boundaries. Some of the issues on whose future solution our civilization depends cannot be settled within the confines of the present-day nation. They require negotiation between the governments of many states. On these matters there is frequently as much room for legitimate disagreement between equally loyal and dedicated citizens as there is on problems strictly internal in scope. In countries with vast commitments in the world beyond their borders, the political parties, to the extent that they differ in philosophy, may appropriately stand opposed on both the strategy and tactics of foreign relations. For that reason, the machinery of government can be seriously clogged, if political rivals control its different branches. A strong case exists for unity of decision and fusion of responsibility between the legislative and the executive, especially in the conduct of diplomacy. But equally strong is the need for vigilant and constructive criticism by an informed opposition, which has a continuous incentive and responsibility to expose the majority's mistakes.

---

[8]On the other hand, it must be remembered that when President Johnson plunged the country into war in Vietnam, the most outspoken opposition came from members of his own party—notably led by Senator Fulbright.

The Great Issues Applied to Democracy, Totalitarianism, Fascism, and Communism

This analysis may suggest some ways of applying the techniques used in this book. In the introductory chapter, I suggested that the political process can be more clearly understood if its complexities are unraveled in terms of its component issues. Politics has been presented as an arena of controversy about permanent problems which permit alternative solutions. This conception allows for various applications, which can now be discussed. Thus, the great issues can be the framework for comparing the political characteristics of broad historical periods, for comprehending the rival systems of the modern world, and for explaining the distinctive features of contemporary politics. Let me review these themes.

In the political conflicts of our century, the rival systems have been described as democracy, totalitarianism, fascism, and communism. Each of these connotes both concepts and institutions. Each is necessarily all-inclusive, since it comprises the whole political system. For that reason each is difficult, if not impossible, to define briefly. In lieu of definition, however, they can be identified and compared by reference to their solutions of the great issues.

Take democracy first.[9] There are two issues which permit only one solution if a state is to be democratic. In regard to citizenship, a democracy must be equalitarian, allowing a fair opportunity for all to participate in the conduct or control of their government. To the extent that they are denied this right, the state falls short of democracy's ideal. Further, in such a state the source of authority must lie in the governed, who need effective means for bringing their representatives or officials to account. This is another way of saying that the essentials of democracy are equality and liberty. Fused together, these form the bedrock on which the foundations of democracy must always rest. With regard to other issues, democracy is neutral. It has been associated with either pluralism or monism, with a concentration or dispersion of power, and with any size of territory or population.

Totalitarianism is indifferent to the size of the state, but on the other four issues its requirements are specific. It results from combining privilege, monism, authoritarianism, and unity of power. When these are compounded, the sum represents the most complete (that is, total) domination of society by the state and of the state itself by a few.

Fascism and communism are not easy to define or compare. For one thing, fascism did not take the same form in Italy under Mussolini as in

[9]On this subject, see my book *The Democratic Civilization* (New York: Oxford University Press, 1964).

Germany under Hitler or in Spain under Franco. For another, the realities of communism deviate so much from the principles of Marx that one must be careful to state whether the theory or the practice is being discussed. On the issue of citizenship, a fascist state proclaims that, because of human inequalities, participation in government is reserved for the few.[10] Marxist theory is equalitarian, but communist practice, as initiated by Lenin and developed by Stalin, has been oligarchical and has reestablished a society with sharp differentiations of rank and reward. The functions of the state know no limits in fascist theory, since it is the state that to Mussolini embodied the supremacy of the nation and to Hitler the supremacy of the "Aryan race." In practice, however, both regimes encountered opposition from the religious quarter and had to live with a church they could not crush. Monism is more complete in the communist state, where private ownership of the means of production is virtually eliminated,[11] which is not the case under fascism, and where the church (except in Poland) is subservient. Paradoxically, however, it was Marxism, from whose doctrines has emerged the most powerful state of all, which proclaimed that the state would wither away when socialism was achieved! Both communist and fascist systems, when they come to the problem of the source of power, are similarly authoritarian in theory and in practice. Each has aped the other in establishing the dictatorship of a single disciplined party ruling the masses by a mixture of propaganda and coercion. Likewise, the concentration of power has been pushed to the same extreme point by all these regimes. As to the size of the state, however, fascism and communism are different. The former is inherently nationalist. Communism in principle and by preference is international, since its fundamental concept of the proletariat leaps across national boundaries. Yet, as Tito's Yugoslavia first demonstrated, and as other communist governments have since manifested in varying degrees, communism too can be as permeated with nationalism as other systems.

Historical Perspective on the Great Issues

The analysis of states in terms of the five great issues may serve another purpose. It can be applied to the successive broad periods in the political history of the West: the Graeco-Roman city-state, the Roman Empire, the Middle Ages, the nation-state. Which solutions of the great issues were prevalent in each period?

---

[10]Hitler went much further than Mussolini in his racial doctrines and his exclusion of women from public life.

[11]In practice, however, a certain degree of private enterprise was reintroduced by some communist regimes in the 1980s. The results were quite significant in Hungary and China.

1. The Graeco-Roman City-State

Citizenship at that time was severely restricted in the oligarchies but was considerably extended in democracies like Athens. Nowhere, however, was it perfectly equalitarian, since slaves and women were relegated to an inferior status. The functions of the state were everywhere considered coextensive with society. Examples occurred of authoritarian and of responsible government, of the unity and of the dispersion of power. Typically and ideally, the size of the state was the simple *polis*, but the largest cities were atypical and tried to found empires.

2. The Roman Empire

This state moved steadily from privilege toward juridical equality, though the latter was never granted to women or slaves. Initially, the functions of the state were unlimited, but limits were accepted when Christianity was adopted. Under the Republic, an unsuccessful attempt was made to locate authority in the governed. Later, power was placed in the emperor through his command of the army. Powers were centralized when the state was small; decentralized, when it expanded. At the center, powers were dispersed under the Republic, but were integrated into one power in the empire. In size, Rome was the giant of antiquity, forming an antithesis to the *polis*.

3. The Middle Ages

In the eyes of God, all were equal. In earthly practice gross inequalities prevailed and politics was an arena for the privileged. The functions of the state were drastically curtailed by its copartnership with the church. Government was authoritarian in fact, though theories to the contrary persisted. Power was decentralized and dispersed to the maximum degree. The unit of government was as large as Christendom in the ecclesiastical sphere, but was localized on the temporal side.

4. The Nation-State

This period commenced everywhere with the rule of privilege, but many states have been moving toward a broader equalitarianism. The early nation-state was allied with monism in the guise of sovereignty. In the nineteenth century, however, the challenge of economic change led to doctrines of dualism and pluralism. Nation-states have been either unified or dispersed. They have varied in size because of the difficulty of making nation and state coterminous, and several have contradicted their own principles by building empires.

The Uniqueness of Twentieth-Century Politics

How has our own age sought to solve these issues, and what solutions can be expected in the twenty-first century? A world depression, two world wars, and the revolutionary ferment of the last 40 years are evidence that this century is one of crisis. When the nature of the crisis is clarified in terms of the great issues, our age appears to possess a unique character unparalleled earlier. The modern world is undergoing three major transformations simultaneously—in the relations of person to person, of state to society, and of state to state. In each of these spheres a drastic change of scale is occurring. The drive toward equalitarianism involves more people as political participants. Pluralism has been yielding to increased state activity. Meanwhile, under the stress of technological innovation, with its economic and military by-products, new units of government are being sought as replacements for the nation-state. It is this threefold expansion— the fact of new government, both bigger and smaller, doing more for more people—that makes contemporary politics distinctive and gives our problems a complexity without precedent. Any one of these changes would be hard to undertake with success. But when all three occur together, and when each impinges on the other two, the task of finding a solution is much more formidable. Never before have we confronted simultaneously the triple need to establish more equality and more functions of government in states of new magnitudes. What is more, this is not occurring in one corner of the globe, or even on one continent. Tomorrow's solutions, if they are to work, have to be projected on a scale as wide as the earth itself. Eventually they must embrace all humanity. To produce the ideas, the institutions, and the inspiration that will encompass such changes presents a political challenge to match the physical revolutions of electronics, nuclear power, and space rockets. Nor is there anything predetermined about the character of the solutions or the methods that will be used in reaching them. Any prediction of future trends, therefore, is hazardous. Nevertheless, the alternatives can be reviewed and their implications spelled out.

Equalitarianism Today

The age-old choice between privilege and equality has assumed a new form in the twentieth century. The social consequences of industrialism, which brought more people into closer contact in crowded cities and required literacy and further education; the invention of improved and speedier communications; the spread of the printed word by the press and magazines; and the extended range of eye and ear through radio, motion pictures, and television have ushered in an era of mass politics, so that the power that drives the wheels of government depends on what beliefs millions accept and what facts they have been told and happen to remember. The masses of mankind are much less the passive subjects of politics than in the past. Instead, they are becoming active participants. Their participation, however, can be organized in alternate ways. Tremendous though it be, the change of scale has not removed the choice between privilege and equalitarianism. What it has done is to augment the difficulty of achieving either solution. The competition between democracy and communism is a struggle between rival systems for the same objective—the allegiance of the mass of humanity.

The promise of communism is to pulverize the existing order and eliminate whatever social and economic inequalities it contains. But the result, because of the monopoly of power by one party, is to reestablish a new type of privilege to which political power provides the entrée. The chief concession that communism makes to equalitarianism, and a major difference between the Russia of today and that of the czars, is that communism recruits its privileged oligarchy from a much wider segment of society. The promise of democracy, on the other hand, is to cut the ties between political power and privilege by offering the masses alternative leaders and programs through two or more parties, thus preventing the formation of a permanent caste. The impact of the numerical increase in participants produces a different response in the two systems. The one-party state attempts to organize its millions by demanding conformity and discouraging dissent. Outwardly this method gives an appearance of power by its display of solidarity. Inwardly, however, the intolerance to new ideas puts the brakes on progress. The democratic state organizes its inhabitants by tolerating multiformity and leaving scope for political competition. This is a source of strength, because new thoughts may be freely expressed and discontents can receive an airing. But there are some attendant risks. Conflict between groups may delay and even prevent discussion; private interests, uncontrolled, may capture public power; or two large organizations (for example, Democrats and Republicans, or a corporation and a trade union) may cease to function as rivals and, instead, by monopolizing power together, may exclude a genuine alternative.

If millions are organized politically and are to stay loyal to the system, performance means more than promise. For communism, a major difficulty is the discrepancy between what it professes—liberation and equality—and what it practices—intolerance and privilege.[12] The rigidities of the one-party system with its power monopoly make it difficult for the underprivileged to challenge their masters. The latter, in order to explain

---

[12]George Orwell, *Animal Farm* (New York: Harcourt, Brace & World, 1946) satirizes this inconsistency in the slogan: "All animals are equal. But some animals are more equal than others."

the contrast between their sayings and their doings, and justify perpetuation of their dictatorship, propagate the view that they face a hostile world which seeks to destroy them. This exemplifies the dictum that "Politics as a practice, whatever its professions, had always been the systematic organization of hatreds."[13]

Democracies, too, depart at times from their own professed principles, and permit substantial discrimination against women and against racial, religious, ethnic, or economic groups in their midst. Serious difficulties arise when a democracy fails to apply in other sectors of society the equalitarianism it insists on in politics. Thus, in Britain during the nineteenth century the equalitarian tendencies expressed in broadening the franchise ran counter to the privileged status of the aristocracy and the general stratification of people into upper, middle, and lower classes. Similar were the consequences produced by industrialism, allied with laissez-faire notions, in the United States and Britain. By the time World War I broke out, gross inequalities prevailed in the distribution of property and income. Indeed, the contrast then existing between the political power of the many and the economic power of the few supplied a repetition of Aristotle's view that democracy is a struggle of the poor against the rich. During this century, therefore, democracy has tackled and continues to confront a pair of associated problems: how to transfer the fundamentals of equalitarianism from politics to the rest of the social order, and while leveling up, avoid an excess of leveling down which would destroy incentive and deny recognition to talent. Suffice it to say that the democratic state has accomplished much in the last hundred years, but has plenty left to do.

The same verdict—that gains have been made, but much remains undone—can be rendered in the sphere of race relations. This problem constitutes an aspect of equalitarianism fully as crucial as the economic or social aspects. Indeed, in many communities the ordering of relations between different races is the central problem on which everything else hinges. It is the attitude toward race that governs economic development and molds the ethos of society in Hawaii and Brazil, in South Africa and South Carolina. In both domestic and international politics the spokesmen for racial exclusiveness are doomed to be the faction leaders of a losing minority. They can never be the representatives of a majority. This holds true alike within the United States and the United Nations.

A further form of discrimination which has yet to be eradicated is as old as the dawn of history. This is the discrimination against one-half of the human race. It has been practiced persistently by the male sex at the expense of the female in virtually every culture. Today, throughout most of the world, these traditional modes of inequality continue with but little change. In certain societies, it is true, women have received equality in legal

[13]Henry Adams, *The Education of Henry Adams*, chapter 1.

status and in the right to vote and to hold office. Even in these respects, however—and certainly in most matters pertaining to employment and careers, to social freedom and education—either inequalities persist, or such equality as has been conceded turns out to be more formal than real. Seldom does a woman of equal, or even superior, abilities stand the same chance in life as a man. The double standard is with us still.

The Twilight of Pluralism

It is no accident that the age of "the common man" and woman has witnessed everywhere an expansion of the functions of government, and that the politics of equality has provided an impetus toward monism. In the nineteenth century the nations that were foremost practitioners of laissez-faire in the relation of politics to economics, and of pluralism in the relation of the state to society, were of two kinds. Britain then led the field in industrialization; the United States had a vast territory to people and develop, and such was the distribution of property that private associations could finance an economic transformation with substantial independence of the state. In this century, however, circumstances have fundamentally altered. Intensified competition for foreign trade among industrialized states; the vanishing of the frontier in the not so New World; domestic political pressures for aid to the underprivileged; the need for regulation of overmighty private groups; and finally the mobilization of entire peoples for victory in war and readjustment afterward have aggrandized the state and made the twentieth a century of monism.

Because a society in rapid flux requires a central focus for organization, the latter-day advocates of pluralism have been placed on the defensive and forced into retreat. Some, like G. D. H. Cole, who was a pluralist when he argued for guild socialism, or Harold J. Laski who wrote as a pluralist until the depression of the 1930s, reversed their positions and accepted the logic of monism. Others maintained their original view, but with increasing difficulty. Robert M. MacIver, for instance, admitted the need for society to be unified, but refused to acquiesce in the state as its unifier. Instead—as a Greek playwright whose plot had become too tangled used to bring in a deity to extricate his characters in the last scene, or as Adam Smith relied on unseen hands to bring harmony out of competition[14]—he introduced his ideal of "community." This is a sense of belonging together which people are supposed to feel in sufficient force to prevent a plurality of associations from flying asunder. But how community is realized and made articulate is unclear, especially since MacIver did

---

[14]See chapter 2, section on "Self-Development and Selfishness."

not concede that it should be organized and expressed through any association with power to override the rest—which would be monism.

Other pluralists modify their basic theory and make such concessions to the state that, after denying admission to monism at the front door, they let it creep in at the back. Thus Friedrich A. Hayek, who denounces socialism and planned intervention by the state in economic matters, advocates planning *for* freedom and insists that powerful private monopolies and combines must not be allowed to stifle genuine competition.[15] Inevitably, however, this ideal, to be enforced, requires a stronger state and more governmental regulation of the economy than fits Hayek's premises. Other pluralists distinguish between the internal structure and the external activities of private associations. They agree that the state should have the power to intervene in external conflicts (for example a strike or lockout in a major industry) that disturb the peace and prosperity of the whole society. Then they perceive that the policies pursued externally by a big business firm or a big union may be connected with the character of its internal structure. Oligarchical tendencies, whether in corporate management or in trade union control, may sometimes lead a business executive or union boss on the path of aggression so that he or she may maintain dominance within the organization by winning victories over opponents outside. Consequently, the pluralist may admit that there is a case for the state to prescribe the conditions that the government of a private association must satisfy. But all these expedients lead to the same conclusion. Any pluralist who holds that society is or should be a unity, or who recognizes the need to mitigate public clashes between private groups, must eventually admit the fundamental point of monism that society requires a coordinator, and must then face the political corollary that the state qualifies for that task more appropriately than any alternative organization. The most genuine pluralist is the anarchist, who wants to be rid of government altogether. But that philosophy has never found a workable formula for its ideal of spontaneous, voluntary cooperation.

Problems of the Monistic State

A state which embraces monism avoids the weaknesses by which pluralism is beset, but confronts other problems. Monism may assume one of several guises. In its extreme form, as envisaged by Plato, the state settles the difficulty of rival associations by eliminating them and absorbing their functions. But the notion that a single institution could serve all the needs of twentieth-century society, though a logical possibility, is no more prac-

15*The Road to Serfdom* (Chicago: The University of Chicago Press, 1944).

ticable, in view of the scale and complexity of the requisite organization, than the opposite extreme of anarchism. Of workable monism there are two alternatives. One is for the state to enforce its control over other groups by permitting no more than one association to serve each major need and interest. Thus organized, society would possess a single system of public education permeated by only one philosophy, a single state-established church intolerant of heterodoxy, a single state-directed economic structure professedly abolishing struggles between occupations and classes, and so on. Monism of this sort, unlike the Platonic variety, is not confined to the realm of speculation, since it is the goal to which the modern totalitarian regimes aspire.

The third kind of monism tolerates a variety of associations for each human need. Thus, if people are free to worship as their consciences dictate, society will contain numerous religious faiths with different creeds. If opportunities exist for a person to learn various skills and move from job to job, or to own property and invest in a choice of enterprises, divergent economic interests will arise which reinforce themselves by establishing alternative associations—corporations, trade unions, cooperatives, and the like. Under such circumstances, the principle of toleration or, in its wider sense, freedom has the result of dividing society into competitive groups. People who are pulled apart, however, by economic institutions, by organized religion, or by cultural traditions, can be reunited through citizenship. In that case, as the monist sees its functions, the state serves to bind society together. It then becomes irrelevant whether one is agnostic or Catholic, Jew or Protestant, black or white, male or female, manufacturer or employee, farmer or teacher, provided that all are equal citizens who share the same basic rights and duties, and owe the same allegiance. Thus on the political plane, by sharing citizenship, human rights, and governmental services in common, individuals can acquire a sense of belonging together and may achieve the unifying focus they otherwise lack.

To attain this goal through the politics of monism depends on avoiding certain pitfalls. For one thing, the possibility of unifying society by the state is qualified by the size of area and population to which the jurisdiction of a single government extends. When continents and people are parceled out among nation-states, the solidarity that each state achieves within its borders stops abruptly at international frontiers. The nation-state system unites the nationals of a state, but its existence separates them from nationals of other states. Pluralists point out, however, and with truth, that social relationships, though most numerous among persons of the same state, reach further afield. Religion is a bond between the citizens of many countries. Trade relations create a common interest between the producers of one nation and the consumers of another. Scientific, professional, and cultural bodies draw their membership from the practitioners of different lands. The present boundaries of society are wider, therefore, than the boundaries of politics.

States in Space

We have seen that the state emerged historically[16] to organize some basic services in response to universal needs. To give protection, maintain order, administer justice—for such functions as these are states created and governments instituted. It follows then that, wherever such activities are organized, the political process is *ipso facto* at work and the seeds of the state are being sown. In this present age every eye can see that the same tendencies which ushered in the nation-state are again operating to create its successor. For ensuring security and prosperity, we have found our present units too small to be effective. Therefore, we turn for salvation not to national power alone but to international arrangements; not to sovereignty but to alliances, federations and mutual commitments; not to the exclusive interest of a single state but to a wider community of interests. In the liquidation of the older imperialism, we observe the disappearance of colonial systems, the recognition of new and often unsteady governments, and a need to reunite political clusters which have split into fragments. Some of our urgent problems are soluble only on a scale of territory and population larger than even the greatest of nation-states now contains.

Another crop of problems has sprouted from a fertile field of political controversy. Some of these are age-old conditions which only now are beginning to receive proper attention; others are unprecedented in human experience. The former include those continuing examples of social injustice, of human inhumanity, to which I referred earlier—racial prejudice, religious bigotry, discrimination against women, and the gulf between haves and have-nots. Certain of these stigmata on our civilization—for example, the contrast between affluence and poverty—are even becoming more acute. But, the significant new feature is the attitude now prevailing toward such conditions. Too many people either ignored them in the past, or if they were aware of them, felt apathetic. This is no longer the case. Today there is not only awareness, but also concern—although admittedly the feelings of the concerned run the gamut from empathy with the underprivileged to hostility and fear.

Some novel problems, however, have risen recently to beset us, which contain potentialities for eventual disaster. First is the population explosion, which threatens to engulf the planet with a tide of humanity and, if unchecked, will surely lead to mounting misery and recurrent wars. Cou-

---

[16]See chapter 3, section on "The Primary Function of the State."

pled with this is the ever-present possibility of nuclear annihilation, since weapons that could exterminate our species are now lodged in human hands. Third is the increasing burden of expenditures for armaments, which become more complicated and more costly and yet have made nobody safer. Next is the continuing pillage of our physical environment: the poisoning of air, land, and water, the reckless and wanton destruction of our habitat. Finally, we are afflicted by the onrush of technological innovation—the revolution which more and more subordinates us to the imperatives of our machines and has the social effect of enmeshing us in huge, impersonal bureaucratic systems which deaden and dehumanize the spirit.

The cumulative result is more than merely to transform our society. Whether we like it or not, we are undergoing a social revolution. Once again, the human race is adrift from our wonted moorings. We feel ourselves floating on the ocean of an uncertain fate. We know not into what vortex its currents may plunge us. Is it any wonder then that this century thus far has been the most violent in all history? From rage or ignorance or despair, people react with passionate brutality—hoping either to unleash or to block the process of change.

And what implications does this have for government? One point at least can be affirmed with certainty. No social revolution of these depths and dimensions can occur without a consequential revolution in our government system. Since the changes sketched above are global in scope and universal in character, no state and no species of politics will remain unaffected. Is it possible to discern the outline and direction of this revolution? And how is it related to the great issues that form the subject of this book?

Doubtless, the political responses will vary along the lines mentioned in the opening chapter.[17] Some will abandon the effort to understand or control. They will resign themselves to submitting to the dictate of events. In that case, as Emerson warned, "things [will] be in the saddle and ride mankind." Others, however, will seek to apply their reason and their faith to assist us in becoming the masters of our fate. It is to these that I address myself.

One aspect of the contemporary revolution in society is the basic alteration in the scale and size of the problems we confront. Just as conditions that had once been local became national, so now have many of the latter passed into the international domain. But another, seemingly contradictory process is at work. Conditions long assumed to be national are now being redefined as subregional or even local. Let us explore these twin tendencies more closely, for their elucidation may offer clues to the solutions we seek.

For many centuries the community to which people belonged in fact

---

[17]See chapter 1, section on "The Ant's-Eye View of Society," and following sections.

and to which they felt attached was their immediate locality, bounded by the short radius of day-to-day contacts. This was true for practically everybody during the history of the *polis* and of the empire-state. The advent of the nation-state, however, broadened the boundaries of political identification as it also enlarged the frontiers of human transactions. Centralized governments emerged. They wielded powers that strongly affected life and well-being, and they supplied services and performed functions on which more individuals came to depend. In a sense that was by no means rhetorical, community and nation became increasingly coextensive.

The revolution now taking shape under our eyes has precisely the effect of breaking that connection. It is dissolving the links of the old-style community while it creates new relationships whose boundaries are as vague as they are varied. Because of such relationships, communities are emerging in fact (objectively, that is) before the subjective attitudes and loyalties have been readjusted. Hence the stresses and tensions, the dissent and demonstrations, the alienation and ambivalence, by which humanity, both young and old, is racked asunder.

We can visualize what is happening as a set of concentric circles. Quite a few circles would be needed at this time in history; and two of them, comprising both old and new relationships, would appear considerably more problem-ridden, and therefore more important, than in the past—the local community and the community that cuts across national frontiers. Both these aspects of our contemporary society were mentioned earlier, albeit separately. Now let us observe their connection. At the international level, problems have emerged (the supply, control, and price of oil, for instance) which can no longer be resolved by a single government acting alone, but only by agreements among a group. Obvious examples of this occur in the military and economic spheres, where, to put it bluntly, national solutions are *no* solutions. When the range and extent of a problem is international, international policies are required—and, with them, their ultimate corollary: supranational institutions.

Simultaneously, however, at the local level—traditionally much despised and generally ignored—people find that life itself is now affected or afflicted by dangers which also are ungovernable by present means. Social injustices give rise to protests and then to civil commotions; these disturb the local peace and may threaten life and limb. At the same time, our cars and factories pollute the air we breathe, while domestic sewage and industrial waste poison the water of our rivers and oceans. Then, too, millions live in swarms which are ever more congested. Cities have expanded into metropolitan complexes embracing suburban clusters and a sprawl of satellite towns. Residents of these towns may travel over 50 miles to work—plagued, more often than not, by substandard commuter railroads and congested highways.

How can we cope with such situations rationally and intelligently?

Obviously not through the governmental machinery that has been traditional for the last hundred years or more. It cannot be asserted too emphatically or too often that this social revolution has doomed the sovereign, centralized, independent nation-state. That has become outmoded and obsolete because it is now too small for some of the problems humanity must solve and too large for others. Not only are its foundations eroding, but its roof is caving in. Many of its powers must be redistributed by delegation, both above and below. The world cannot handle its emergencies of overpopulation, underdevelopment, and poverty, except through supranational agencies. Nor can it remedy the ills of congestion, pollution, inadequate transportation, and urban ghettos without recreating the community of the local region. Because of the social problems which require ordering by government, I predict an eventual backlash against the taxpayers' revolt of recent decades. The total volume of governmental functions is likely to increase, not decrease. What will change will be the allocation of functions at the various levels.

For the future, therefore, if we are to survive as a species—and nothing less is at stake—we must devise unprecedented institutions for these unprecedented conditions. We should be willing to experiment with new layers and levels of government simultaneously; our concepts of citizenship must be readapted both to the smaller and more intimate and to the larger and more extensive. The individual will henceforth be a member of several communities, ranging from local to global, and our machinery of government—state boundaries included—must follow the geography of the problems. Unless it does, solutions will never be forthcoming. Expressed in terms of the great issues, all this signifies a change in the solutions to the fourth and fifth issues preferred during the last hundred years. We may expect in the future to see a flight from centralism along with the evolution of supranationalism.

The Methods of Political Change

Contemporary trends are unmistakably leading toward more equality, more governmental functions, and larger states. But what happens to the remaining issues when changes of this magnitude are occurring? The answer can be expressed in terms of the distinction between political ends and governmental means.[18] Of the five great issues, three are the prime movers in relation to the processes of change because they provide the goals for action. Analyze the revolutionary crises of history and you find that the items in dispute have always included one or more of the following: the extensiveness of citizenship, of state functions, and of the size of the state.

[18]See chapter 3, section on "The Use and Monopoly of Force," and following sections.

A major increase or contraction in any of these is likely to set off a chain reaction of consequent changes. The two issues concerning authority—the question of its source and its unity or dispersion—are not themselves the independent originators of political change. They resemble rather what statisticians call "dependent variables." Constitutions, institutions, and the distribution of power, to the extent that these are concerned with structure and procedure, are undeniably important, but their importance is most immediately felt by politicians and officials—that is, by the practitioners who operate the system. The mass of the people are most directly interested in the concrete results that government brings in their daily lives and lifetime dreams. They can understand the need for redistributing powers and redesigning institutions when there are substantial goals to be attained for which established methods are unsuitable. Anyone who doubts this should recall the worldwide effects of the economic depression of 1929–1934 upon political systems. A change from dictatorial to responsible government, from unity of power to dispersion of powers—or vice versa—is likely to follow, and not precede, a shift of preference between equality or privilege, pluralism or monism, and a big or small area. Those directing the transition from any of these alternatives to its opposite have often employed authoritarian means, plus a concentration of power, to obtain their results. Especially does this happen when those who were influential under the older regime offer fierce resistance to change or when speed seems to the innovators a condition of their success. Contrariwise, the test of a mature and basically united people is their ability to absorb major changes without resort to dictatorship or loss of liberty.

The Nature of Revolution

In this capacity to absorb great changes, and in the manner of accomplishing them, a significant distinction may be noted among political systems. The role of government in the evolution of society is profoundly affected by the timing of changes as well as by their content. No social order is ever completely static. Most societies generally undergo continuous change which is imperceptibly absorbed. But there are occasions when the rate of change is sharply accelerated, and adjustments are attempted or accomplished with rapidity and urgency. Any kind of change imposes a strain since it involves a departure from settled practices and a dislocation of established institutions. Excessive speed may make the strain intolerable and lead a society to the breaking point.

Changes can differ in depth as well as speed. Some modifications of an existing order may be only surface deep. Others may reach far down and shake the foundations of society. When a party defeats its rival at a free election peacefully conducted, and a new administration and legislative majority replace their predecessors, the top personnel and some of the programs of government will alter. But the civil service, the judiciary, and most of the policies already in force continue to operate without change. This method of assimilating innovations gradually, and on the whole harmoniously, has become standard practice in democratic states. A deeper change is one that alters not merely the government. but also the constitutional system under which it is organized. The Philadelphia Convention of 1787, for instance, had to reach decisions on more fundamental matters than are ordinarily settled in periodic elections. But the most profound changes of all, inducing the greatest disturbance and most intense controversy, are those that refashion the foundations on which society reposes. The substitution of one form of property for another and basic modifications in ownership and distribution, a major religious upheaval, a sharp challenge to long-cherished cultural values—such movements impinge on entrenched interests and arouse the strongest emotions. It is impossible to consummate changes of this sort without producing political repercussions.

The most extreme changes are revolutions. In the light of the preceding discussion, what does this term mean? When one group takes over power from another within the framework of the same constitutional system and by a procedure constitutionally defined and mutually accepted, that is no revolution. But when the constitution as well as the government is reconstructed, then a revolution occurs. If, besides constitutional renovation, society is transformed root and branch, the character of the revolution becomes still more thoroughgoing and the most turbulent disorders usually ensue. Finally, when changes of government, constitution, and social order are simultaneously attempted at breakneck speed, state and society suffer agony and convulsion under the momentum of the driving force. In this way it is possible to distinguish between the major revolutions that have taken place in the last 300 years. The American Revolution from 1775 to 1789 involved a change in government and constitution, but conserved most of the social fabric—its economic system included—in much the same design as before. The English Revolution between 1640 and 1688 altered both constitution and government, settled the issues of Protestant-Catholic and church-state relations, and confirmed the prominence of a new urban commercial class. The French Revolution, which began in 1789, went much further than the English in the ferment—economic, philosophic, and cultural—that it evoked throughout society as a whole.[19] The Communist Revolutions, which took control of Russia in 1917 and of China 30 years later, probed the deepest of the four and have been responsible for the most penetrating and intensive overhauls of a social order of which history has record.

[19]This explains why Edmund Burke, who approved the principles, methods, and results of England's seventeenth-century revolution, was aghast at the French Revolution and reacted to it conservatively.

All these revolutions, it may be noted, were accompanied by warfare, which in the English case took the form of civil war only, and in the other four cases involved conflict with foreign powers as well. While the constitutions that emerged from the English and American Revolutions successfully provided a peaceful method of governmental change for the future, violence was initially required to lay that groundwork of constitutionalism. The four revolutions whose effects were not confined to the state but spread to society, namely the English, French, Russian, and Chinese, produced the phenomenon of dictatorship with extraordinary powers concentrated in the hands of one man or a tiny clique. Significantly, the American Revolution, which was content to limit itself to a political change without transforming the social order, did not succumb to dictatorship; and while other countries had to resort to Cromwell, to Robespierre and Napoleon, to Lenin, Trotsky, Stalin, and Mao, the needs of the United States were adequately served by Washington and Jefferson.

Dictatorship in a Time of Change

Besides the cases just cited, there are many recent instances of peoples who spawn a dictatorship while undergoing drastic change. Witness the power acquired for a while by Hitler or Mussolini, by Ataturk or Nasser, by Castro or Perón, by Mao or Tito. The frequency of this occurrence suggests some further reflections on the subject of change. Undeniably a community in convulsions is prone to yield to a Directory, a Politburo, a military junta, or the dynamism of a "strong man" whose personality thrusts itself above the leading clique. The reason is to be found in the practical demands and the psychology of crisis conditions. A society deciding major issues faces momentous, and perhaps irrevocable, choices. Collectively its members share the élan, the heightened tension, the sense of adventurousness, and with these the fears and anxieties concerning the outcome, which any period of rapid flux calls forth. It is always more difficult politically to chart a course for change than for conservatism. The former opens many avenues of choice. The latter prescribes one route—continuation, as far as possible, of the status quo.

To minimize the risks and uncertainties of change, and to offset the weakness that division produces, a society in crisis will be urged to submit to a pattern of discipline and thus reassert its unity and solidarity. Authoritarianism will be represented as a source of strength, because it is supposedly efficient, single-minded, and fast moving. In our century many circumstances have appeared to set a premium on such factors. People who seek in warfare an outlet for their aggressions, or who smart under the humiliations of a defeat, have often acquiesced in dictatorship. A long-lasting and widespread economic depression brings loss of savings, unemployment, or bankruptcy to individuals who then lend a willing ear to the advocates of desperate remedies. Or again, a technologically backward community, proud of its ancient memories, faces the challenge of a different culture equipped with superior machines and scientific knowledge. Forced to adapt themselves to alien novelties, yet wishing to preserve enough of their traditional ways so that their identity may not be lost, millions of people attempt to combine the seemingly contradictory policies of heavy borrowing from abroad with a positive reaffirmation of their own cultural distinctiveness. The psychological result in this last case is a state of ambivalence. The dependent group admires and respects those whose techniques it copies, but also fears and resents them. The political result, not infrequently, is like a state of siege.

This helps to throw some light on one of the most interesting political problems of our century: the common association of dictatorship with nationalism. The building of a nation-state does not, in and by itself, necessitate either dictatorship or democracy. There are, however, two sides to nationalism, which face in different directions. So far as its internal aspect is concerned, nationalism unites people with a common loyalty to their political association. It imparts a sense not only of belonging together, but of belonging together as equals, because nationality does not admit of degrees. In this way nationalism and democracy are compatible, and it is therefore understandable that many political leaders with perfect consistency have been both nationalists and democrats—for example, Lincoln, Mazzini, Masaryk. Viewed externally, however, nationalism asserts the individuality of the group and its separateness from others. When this emphasis on uniqueness happens to be linked with the uncertainties of a time of troubles—due to military or economic reasons or cultural readjustment or a combination of these—the aggressions and frustrations within the group are siphoned into the channels of dictatorship. That has occurred not only in European states which yielded to the embrace of fascism or communism, but also in Latin American and Asian countries, which wanted to catch up with Western technology and at the same time rid themselves of colonialism.

From Protection to Perfection

Thus, for all its enlargement of scale, the search for solutions to humanity's political problems will require, both now and in the future, a continuing selection among the same perennial choices and an elaboration of the same basic patterns in presumably more intricate forms. As politics encompasses a wider embrace, the horizons of the state expand and governments assume more duties. It is a far reach from the fortification of a hilltop to walking on the moon, from control of a river valley or a city to the ordering of a planet, from participation by a few to equalized liberties for all. The mode and means may vary, but the principles at stake do not. Humanity still must choose, or allow a fraction of its number to make the choices for the rest. The risk is serious, since the penalties for bad government have increased in the same proportion as the potentialities for good. Hitler outdid Attila, as a future tyrant could outdo him.

The state originated in our need for protection, which required the organization of force. A government amasses force initially, and monopolizes it finally, in order to repel any threats, internal or external, to life and limb. But the history of the functions of the state consists in advancing from protection and order to justice and the good life. This does not mean that the state abandons or surrenders its duty of protecting its members. Far from it. The state that ceases to protect ceases to be a state. But, after ensuring the conditions that make life possible, the state must proceed toward the goal of a good life. It is precisely this changeover that presents a supreme challenge to the architects of government. For how does force or power fit in with welfare? The concept of welfare is broad. It embraces economic prosperity, moral well-being, and the whole system of values composing a civilization. Such considerations transfer the issues of politics from the starting point of physical safety to the terminus of an ethical ideal. The creation of the state resembles the construction of a dwelling to shelter the life of society. A house has foundations to stand on, just as a state is built on our fundamental need for protection. But people do not lead their daily lives in the basement of their homes. The living room is raised some feet above ground level, and here the members of the household develop the relations that can give to life a quality of love, nobility, and taste. And it is, or can be, the same with politics. The function of the foundations is to support the upper framework which houses the political life of humanity and makes us civilized.

That actual states do not always reach the ideal, and at times depart from it by deliberate choice, is obvious enough. There have been, and continue to be, many governments that build no higher than the basement and force their subjects to stay there. Also, when the warlike politics of an anarchic world compel all states, even those concerned with welfare, to reemphasize the priority of physical protection, humanity rushes to the refuge of the bomb shelter. The state may fail, then, to subordinate the force it must employ to the ethical ideal for which we grope. What was the servant may emerge the master. The power that founded a government can become the means whereby the will of the governing group is forcibly imposed throughout society. In that case, their regime is a tyranny, and when linked with monism, the product is totalitarian. Hence, the crucial test of the would-be monistic state is to keep its stock of power within bounds and sublimate power in the service of the good. Unless this is done, there is no superior merit in monism as against the pluralist alternative. For why flee from anarchy into the embrace of despotism?

The first problem, then, is to organize power, yet keep it under control and legitimize it as authority; to unify society through the state, but avoid the authoritarian means and the regimented end. That is the third of the great issues, which offers the choice between freedom and dictatorship. There is no certain way of guaranteeing freedom. It is possible, though difficult, to establish and operate a politically free society. It is not too difficult to suppress freedom entirely by a perversion of power. All that can be prescribed is a set of conditions which, if adhered to, tends to encourage the attainment of freedom and discourage its opposite. These conditions depend on planning a constitutional system that builds the right of criticism and opposition into the central structure of government. Applied in detail, this principle spells itself out into universal suffrage, periodic elections, the coexistence of two or more parties, and opportunities to form new political combinations. Where such requirements are met, liberty is better guaranteed than by the pluralist reliance on mutual conflict between private associations and their general rivalry with the state.

Politics and the Good Life

But the institutional checks just mentioned, while basic to the politics of freedom, do not ensure the good life. Though liberty may be assisted by procedural arrangements, the purpose of the latter is also to reach decisions about policies. The contents of such decisions, as well as the ways of reaching them, must be encompassed in the philosophy of the state, since the ends accomplished are more significant than the means employed. Hence, the state seeking to integrate society must embody an ethical ideal. Otherwise, instead of the good life taking priority over power, power will steal the priority from welfare—in which case no reply can be given to Augustine's question: What else is the state but a great robber band if it lacks justice? But as it happens, two of the great issues, the first and second, have a direct bearing on the contents of policy. Whenever the state administers a program, a service is supplied for some or all of its citizens. This evokes controversies over the appropriateness of the service and the designation or selection of recipients. Should the state, for instance, pay and provide for large-scale schemes of low-cost housing? If so, to whom should houses be assigned? Should it embark on programs of social security, covering all the major hazards, economic and physical, that flesh is heir to between birth and death? If so, who should be eligible for benefits, and how should the financing be apportioned?

Questions like these have other implications for society than that of freedom. They suggest that the state accept some responsibility for influencing the distribution of material goods; that it provide at least a minimum below which no person be allowed to sink, while encouraging all to raise their status above the minimum by their own efforts. To say this is to recognize that social and economic privilege—expressed in a grossly unequal distribution of property, income, security, and living standards—is no more desirable than the political privilege of a limited class or caste. That, in other words, is an affirmation of the principle of equality. How can the state, which assumes the direction of society, organize the race of life so as to mix equality with liberty? It is possible to do this if the state ensures equality for all at the starting tape; if it provides fulfillment to the more talented; and if it guarantees some minimum to each contestant. These criteria satisfy the test of welfare. More than that, by blending the rights and duties of the individual with those of society, they point the way to a conception of social justice. It is only when this is achieved that power, besides being rendered safe by the politics of freedom, also acquires a moral legitimacy. The degree of approximation to this standard is some measure of the level of civilization that a people has attained. Conversely, a subordination of welfare to power and the disregard of social justice is an index of inhumanism.

Finally, it is through this concept that the difficulty stated in the beginning of this book may be resolved. Human beings, as was observed, associate in groups under the contrary impulses of cooperation and competition. But to reconcile the two has always posed a problem. Perhaps the answer is found when liberty and equality are synthesized under the higher concept of the good life. It is in our concern for the human condition that we express our altruism, cooperativeness, and sense of solidarity. It is in the personal achievement of creative growth that each of us displays individuality. To maintain both principles in equilibrium and use them constructively in the solution of the great issues, to unite the good person with the good society, is the wisdom of statesmanship. When the power of government is directed in the service of that ideal, the good life emerges into the realm of the possible, and the art of politics becomes a voyage of ethical discovery.

Bibliography

In one form or another, the great issues are discussed in these classics of political thought: Plato, *Republic;* Aristotle, *Politics;* Machiavelli, *Prince* and *Discourses;* Hobbes, *Leviathan;* Locke, (second) *Treatise of Civil Government;* Montesquieu, *Spirit of the Laws;* Rousseau, *Social Contract;* Burke, *Reflections on the French Revolution;* Hegel, *Philosophy of Right;* the *Federalist Papers,* by Hamilton, Madison, and Jay; Marx, *Communist Manifesto;* Mill, *Essay on Liberty* and *Considerations on Representative Government.*

Insight into how governments work is contained in de Tocqueville, *Democracy in America* and *The Old Regime;* Wilson, *Congressional Government;* Bryce, *The American Commonwealth* and *Modern Democracies;* Bagehot, *The English Constitution.*

Among the significant books written in this century are: Laski, *Grammar of Politics;* MacIver, *The Modern State* and *The Web of Government;* Lasswell, *Politics: Who Gets What, When, How;* Freidrich, *Constitutional Government and Democracy;* Lindsay, *The Modern Democratic State;* Schumpeter, *Capitalism, Socialism, and Democracy;* Easton, *The Political System.*

Index